Repairs: tenants' rig

Stephen Knafler is a practising barrister specialising in public law. He is the General Editor of the *Community Care Law Reports*, the author of *Remedies for Disrepair and Other Building Defects* (Sweet & Maxwell, 1997) and a contributor to De Smith, Woolf and Jowell's *Judicial Review of Administrative Action* (Sweet & Maxwell, 1995).

Jan Luba is a practising barrister specialising in housing law. He writes regular articles (with Nic Madge) for *Legal Action* on recent developments in housing law and is co-author of *Defending Possession Proceedings* (LAG, 1997).

Repairs: tenants' rights

THIRD EDITION

Jan Luba and Stephen Knafler

Legal Action Group
1999

Third edition published in Great Britain 1999
by LAG Education and Service Trust Limited
242 Pentonville Road, London N1 9UN

First edition by Jan Luba 1985, second edition by Jan Luba 1991

© Stephen Knafler and Jan Luba 1999

Figures 1 to 33 are reproduced with the permission of the Chartered Institute
of Housing from *House Construction: a basic guide* by Woodhead (1984,
Institute of Housing).

Figures 34 to 39 are reproduced with the permission of Butterworth
Heinemann, a division of Reed Educational & Professional Publishing, from
Dampness in Buildings (2nd edn) by Oxley and Gilbert (Butterworth
Heinemann).

The extracts in appendix I from BS 5250: 1989 *Control of Condensation in
Buildings* are reproduced with the permission of BSI under licence number
PD\1999 0861. Complete copies of the standard can be obtained by post from
BSI Customer Services, 389 Chiswick High Road, London W4 4AL.

The article 'Damp housing, mould growth, and symptomatic health state' by
Platt, Martin, Hunt and Lewis, published in (1989) 298 *British Medical
Journal* 1673, is reproduced with the permission of the British Medical
Journal.

The table of most common building defects at p29 is reproduced with the
permission of Macmillan Press from *Building Surveys, Report and
Dilapidations* by Seeley (1985, Macmillan Press).

The Legal Aid Board guidance in appendix H is reproduced with the
permission of the Legal Aid Board.

British Library Cataloguing in Publication Data

A CIP catalogue record for this book is available from the British Library

ISBN 0 905099 49 4

Typeset by Regent Typesetting

Printed in Great Britain by Bell & Bain Ltd, Glasgow

Contents

Table of cases

Table of statutes

Table of statutory instruments and rules

Lists of figures and tables

Figures 1–33 are reproduced from Woodhead *House Construction: a basic guide*
Institute of Housing, 1984.
Figures 34–39 are reproduced from Oxley and Gobert *Dampness in Buildings*
2nd edn, Butterworth-Heinemann Ltd, 1994.

Table 1 is reproduced from Seeley *Building Surveys, Report and Dilapidations*
Macmillan, 1985.
Tables 2 and 3 are reproduced from Oxley and Gobert *Dampness in Buildings*
2nd edn, Butterworth-Heinemann Ltd, 1994.
Table 4 is reproduced from Landlord and Tenant Act 1985 s8 (see appendix D).

Preface

The origins of this book lie in a series of articles commissioned and published by *Legal Action* magazine almost 20 years ago (see 'Tenants Rights to Housing Repairs' February 1982 *Legal Action* 13). They were designed to provide raw legal material for the small cohort of lawyers and legal advisers, many based in law centres, who were at that time taking up the cases of tenants living in far from satisfactory housing conditions.

That the book has reached a third edition is no cause for celebration. It reflects only the continuing needs of tenants with disrepair problems, which in turn stem from the lack of maintenance and improvement that has been taking place in the stock of rented housing. For the largest providers of rented housing – local authorities and other social landlords – the past two decades have witnessed unprecedented constraints on their ability to fund the building and refurbishment of rented homes. At the other end of the market, in the private rented sector, the decline in already poor conditions has continued largely unchecked. The need for advice about housing disrepair is greater than ever. On the brighter side, there are now many more advisers and lawyers specialising in housing law than perhaps would have been imagined 20 years ago.

After initial publication in 1985, a second edition of the book appeared, after too long a delay, in 1991. At least that gap was no longer than the one between the government's own national *House Condition Surveys*, describing the parlous state of the rented housing stock. But this third edition has been much longer (too long!) in coming. Thankfully, advisers waiting for it were able to turn to Stephen Knafler's *Remedies for Disrepair and other Housing Defects* (Sweet & Maxwell, 1997) for some of the updating material needed.

It seemed obvious therefore, as my own efforts to revise the work became bogged down in the demands of a busy legal aid practice, for LAG to invite Stephen to pick up the challenge and complete the task of revising this work. Notwithstanding the distractions of his own ever more successful practice at the Bar, Stephen has more than satisfied his commission.

Readers will find useful contents summaries at the beginning of each chapter. Previous users of the book will find that much has changed. The opening chapter on housing conditions has been transformed from descriptive narrative into highly practical introductions to the construction and inspection of housing (chapter 1) and of common defects (chapter 2). The previous chapters on landlord liability in contract and tort have been blended into a consolidated description of tenants' civil rights (chapter 3). The remaining chapters are more familiar but all have been thoroughly revised, updated and re-written. The appendices of useful primary materials have been substantially extended.

What the reader will not find is any mention of the long overdue reform of both statutory and common law rights so much needed to improve the lot of tenants in the worst housing conditions. Expectations of a changed climate for those tenants may have been raised by the election of a new government in May 1997. It had legislation ready for immediate use in the form of a draft Bill attached to the Law Commission's report on *Responsibility for State and Condition of Property* (March 1996). Frustratingly, in February 1998 consideration of implementation was deferred until after conclusions were reached on the reform of the housing fitness standard – a process that has itself taken more than a year.

For their part, the judiciary, while busy (as this third edition demonstrates) deciding a torrent of new cases arising from disputes over housing disrepair, have not been responsible for any new departures in the development of the common law or the interpretation of housing statutes. The shadow of *Cavalier v Pope* (which decided that a landlord owed no duty of care when letting property) hangs over us still from 1906 and the legal fiction of caveat lessee (which assumes that the incoming tenant had a free choice to inspect and then take or decline a rented home) had an unwelcome resurrection earlier this year.

What is desperately needed is a radical overhaul of the basic law governing housing disrepair. Lord Woolf recommended as much his final report on the *Review of Civil Justice*. Let us all hope that it will not be too long before a fourth edition of this work will be able to reflect such reform.

Jan Luba
June 1999

Introduction

It is probably fair to say that the first two editions of Jan's book (published in 1985 and 1991) enlightened a generation of legal advisers and encouraged them to get repairs carried out on behalf of tenants and compensation paid. I hope that this edition does not have the reverse effect.

Thanks are owed to Jan for writing the book in the first place and keeping a friendly eye on proceedings this time round, to my patient and tolerant editors at LAG and to everyone who has allowed their material to be reproduced. I hope that the book will be useful.

The law is up to date as at 1 June 1999.

Stephen Knafler
June 1999

House and flat construction

Different types of construction

1.1   Housing stock can be approximately dated and broadly categorised as old traditional (late 19th century to 1940), prefabricated (1945–1955), traditional (1940–1970), industrialised (1960s) or rationalised traditional (1970 onwards).

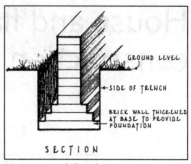

Figure 1: Brick foundation

1.2   Some of the typical construction features of each category of housing are described in this chapter in order to assist the legal adviser in interpreting the technical language of survey reports and in understanding the broader construction context in which housing defects arise.

Old traditional: late 19th century to 1940

1.3   **Foundations** Foundations usually consisted of a few additional courses of bricks laid on compressed ground or broken stone. The purpose of these additional courses was to extend the width of the base of the wall and thereby spread the building load (see figure 1). Cavity walls (see below) were normally built on concrete strip foundations (see figure 2). It is the concrete strip in concrete strip foundations which spreads the building load.

1.4   **External walls** External walls were solid and made of locally produced brick. They were usually 9″ thick (see figure 3). Cement rendering to the external face of walls (to prevent water penetration) was common. Damp-proof courses became increasingly common as the 19th century progressed. They originally consisted of a course of overburned bricks, of slate, of tiles or of engineering (strong, water resistant) bricks. At the very end of the 19th century builders started to

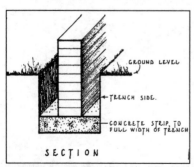

Figure 2: Concrete foundation

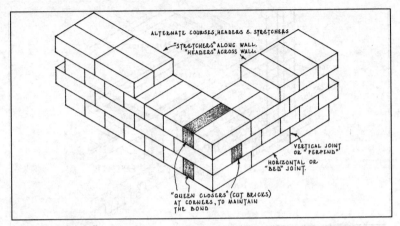

Figure 3: Solid wall

use bituminous compounds, asphalt, metals and plastics (see figures 4 and 5).

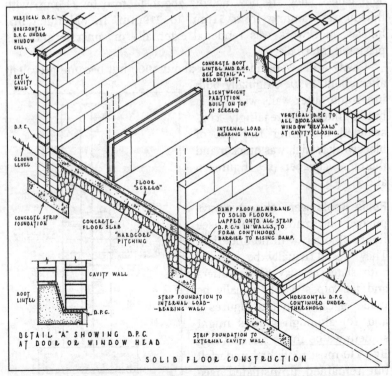

Figure 4: Damp-proof course – solid floor construction

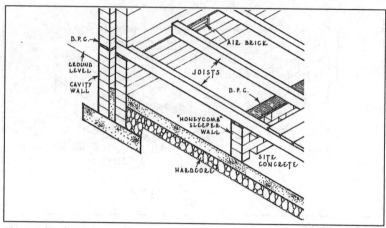

Figure 5: Traditional suspended floor

From about 1919, builders started to use blockwork to increase the speed of construction. Blocks were made from cement and other aggregates. They are now usually about 448mm by 215mm with thicknesses ranging from 51mm to 219mm. In old traditional houses, blockwork was rendered externally in concrete and was plastered internally.

Cavity walls were found from about 1900 but became prevalent after about 1930. Originally both inner and outer walls were brick, but builders increasingly constructed the inner leaf out of blockwork, which was quicker and therefore cheaper (see figures 6 and 7).

1.5 **Roofs** Roofs were almost always pitched and made of timber (see figure 8), often with no underfelt. They would usually be covered with slates or clay tiles. Gutters and fall pipes would usually be made of cast iron (see figures 9 and 10) although gutters might sometimes be made out of wood. By 1930 most roofs had underfelt but remained uninsulated (see figure 11).

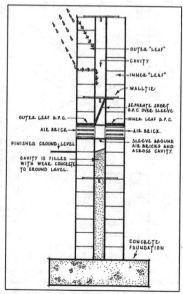

Figure 6: Cavity wall – section

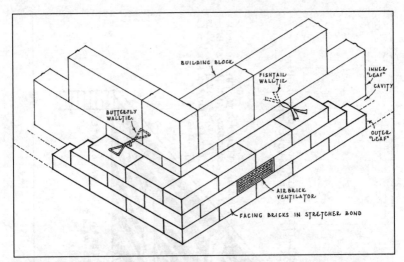

Figure 7: Cavity wall – general arrangement

1.6 **Floors** Floors were almost always solid in the kitchen and store areas. After about 1919 builders supplied a primitive form of damp-proof course to solid concrete floors by coating the upper surface with a bituminous adhesive and adding thermoplastic tiles. In the rest of the house both the ground and upper floors would be suspended timber floors (see figure 12 for a modern suspended timber floor).

1.7 **Internal walls/ceilings** Until about 1930, the internal walls of the kitchen and store areas were often left unplastered. Ceilings were made of lath and plaster. In some of the older houses, walls too would be made of lath and plaster.

1.8 **Joinery** Windows were wooden, vertical sliding sash windows. Timber or steel (commonly referred to by the trade name Crittal) casement windows were introduced in about 1930 (see figures 13–15 for window frame terminology and different types of window). Doors were wood panelled or boarded.

1.9 **Plumbing** Plumbing was lead, until about 1930, by which time iron or galvanised steel became prevalent (see figures 16 and 17).

1.10 **Heating** There were open fireplaces in most rooms. There might be a cauldron for boiling water in the kitchen.

1.11 **Other** Bathrooms were normally off the kitchen at ground-floor level. The kitchen would contain few if any cupboards (food would

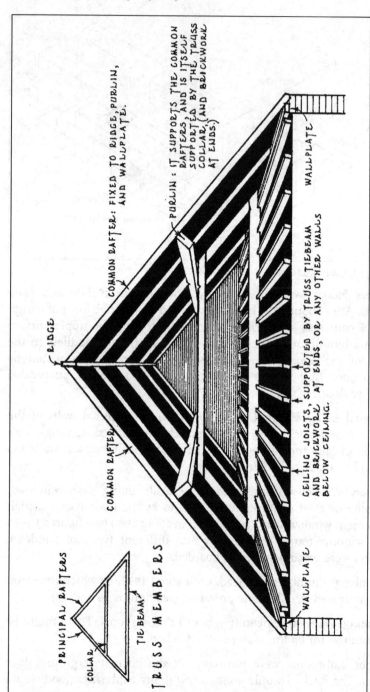

Figure 8: Old traditional roof

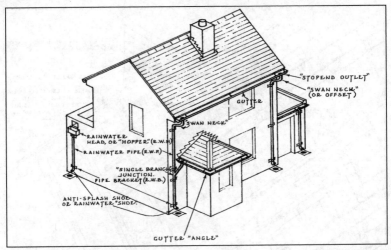

Figure 9: Roof drainage

be stored in a separate larder, which would contain a cold slab). The free-standing sink would often have no drainer. There was minimal provision of electric power.

Traditional: 1940–1970

1.12 In the immediate aftermath of the second world war, most new houses were prefabricated (see below). As skilled labour and traditional materials became more readily available in the 1950s, the use of relatively traditional building techniques resumed.

1.13 **Foundations** As with old traditional.

1.14 **External walls** Improvements in transport led to less reliance on local brick and greater use of a variety of facing bricks of different textures and colour. Coke breeze blocks became readily available for

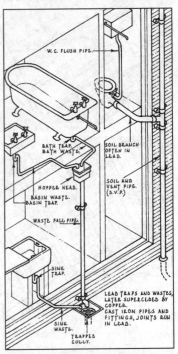

Figure 10: Waste and soil drainage – old two-pipe system

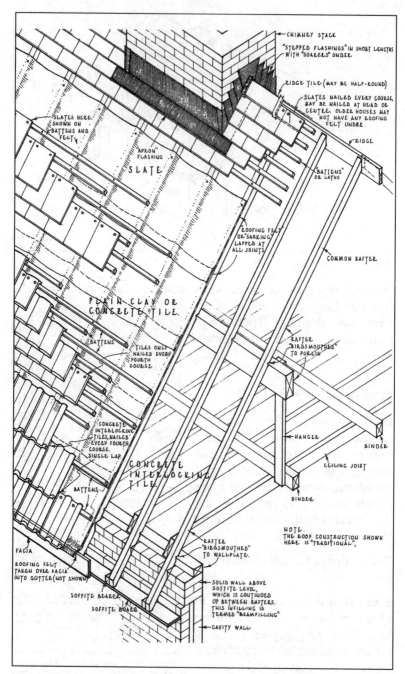

Figure 11: Pitched roof coverings

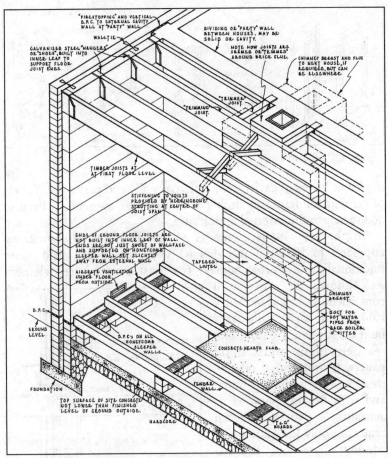

Figure 12: Modern suspended timber floors

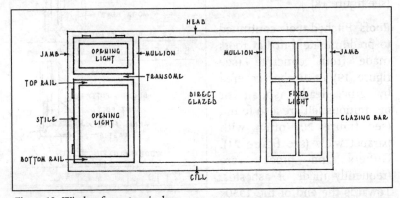

Figure 13: Window frame terminology

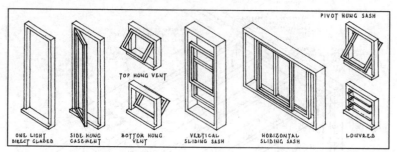

Figure 14: Types of window

the inner leaves of cavity walls, internal walls and partitions. Panels of cement rendering or timber boarding were sometimes used to add variety to the external appearance.

In the late 1950s elements of the modular, prefabricated approach to building (see below) were introduced into more traditionally constructed houses. The most common new element was known as cross wall construction: brick or block gables and party walls were built on site but the front and rear elevations were in-fill panels, manufactured off-site, usually with a timber frame and with timber, plywood or asbestos panels, often requiring only the addition of window glass and external door hanging after installation (see figure 18).

1.15   **Roofs** Pitched roofs continued to predominate, but flat roofs made from concrete (see figure 19) or timber covered by zinc, lead, asphalt or bituminous felt are also found (see figure 20) often with parapet walls (see figure 21). Gutters and pipes were frequently made of asbestos. Towards the end of the 1950s

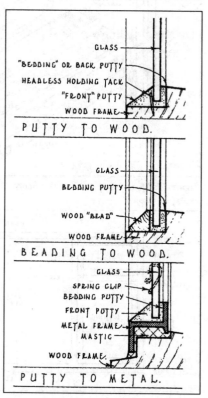

Figure 15: Window glazing

plastic gutters and pipes were introduced and gradually became dominant.

1.16 **Floors** As with old traditional, although solid floors were now usually thermoplastic-tiled or asphalt-covered.

1.17 **Internal walls/ceilings** Builders generally used coke breeze blocks or stud partitions (see figure 22) for internal walls. Before about 1930 almost all internal walls (even if load bearing) were stud partitions. Brick or block then became most common (particularly for load bearing internal walls). All walls would now be plastered. Ceilings were still lath and plaster.

1.18 **Joinery** Normally, windows were casement but could be made of wood or metal. Pivot windows and glass panelled external doors were introduced.

1.19 **Plumbing** Copper pipework and wastes were introduced. Plastic piping was used from the late 1950s.

1.20 **Heating** Background heating including central heating was occasionally included, at least to the ground floor. By the late 1960s almost all new houses were built with central heating, following the publication of the Parker Morris Report on Standards in 1961, which became mandatory in 1969 (see figure 23).

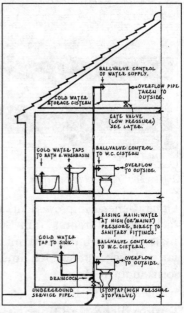

Figure 16: 'Direct' cold water supply

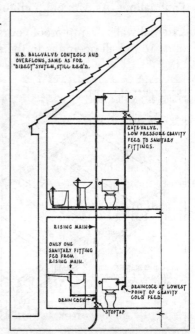

Figure 17: 'Indirect' cold water supply

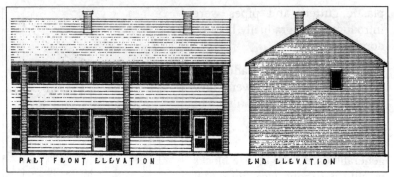

Figure 18: Cross wall construction

1.21   **Other** General improvements took place in kitchen and bathroom facilities. Bathrooms came to be located upstairs. Insulation materials were introduced: initially merely fibreboard around water tanks, hessian or soft felt around pipes and thin quilting over the joists in the roof space.

Rationalised traditional: post-1970

1.22   **Foundations** As with old traditional.

1.23   **External walls** Damp-proof courses are found at ground-floor level and around all openings in the structure (eg, doors and windows).

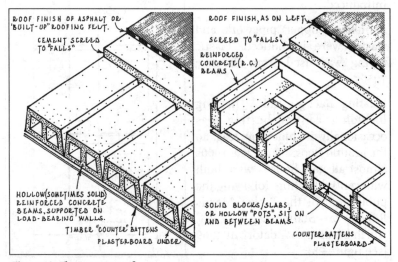

Figure 19: Flat concrete roofs

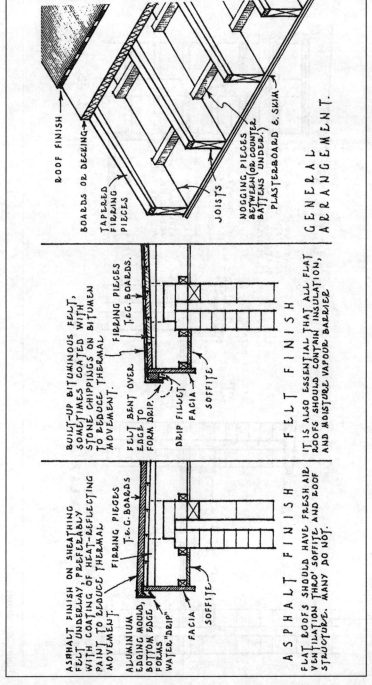

ROOF FINISH

BOARDS OR DECKING

TAPERED FIRRING PIECES

JOISTS

NOGGING PIECES BETWEEN (OR COUNTER BATTENS UNDER.)

PLASTERBOARD & SKIM

GENERAL ARRANGEMENT.

BUILT-UP BITUMINOUS FELT, SOMETIMES COATED WITH STONE CHIPPINGS ON BITUMEN TO REDUCE THERMAL MOVEMENT.

FIRRING PIECES

T.&.G. BOARDS.

FELT BENT OVER EDGE TO FORM DRIP.

DRIP FILLET

FACIA

SOFFITE

FELT FINISH

IT IS ALSO ESSENTIAL THAT ALL FLAT ROOFS SHOULD CONTAIN INSULATION, AND MOISTURE VAPOUR BARRIER.

ASPHALT FINISH ON SHEATHING FELT UNDERLAY, PREFERABLY WITH COATING OF HEAT-REFLECTING PAINT TO REDUCE THERMAL MOVEMENT.

FIRRING PIECES

T.&.G. BOARDS

ALUMINIUM EDGING MOULD, BOTTOM EDGE FORMS WATER "DRIP"

FACIA

SOFFITE

ASPHALT FINISH

FLAT ROOFS SHOULD HAVE FRESH AIR VENTILATION THRO' SOFFITE AND ROOF STRUCTURE. MANY DO NOT.

Figure 20: Flat timber roofs

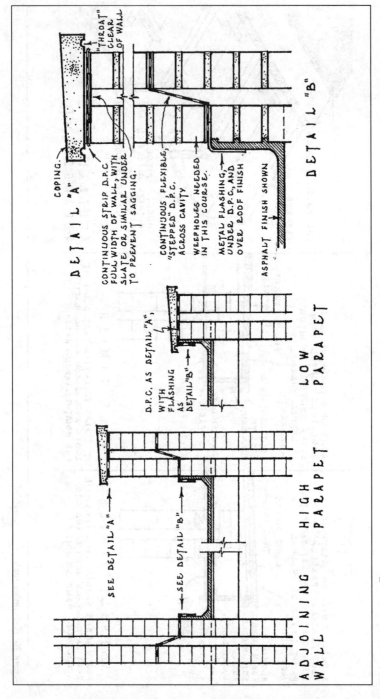

Figure 21: Parapet walls

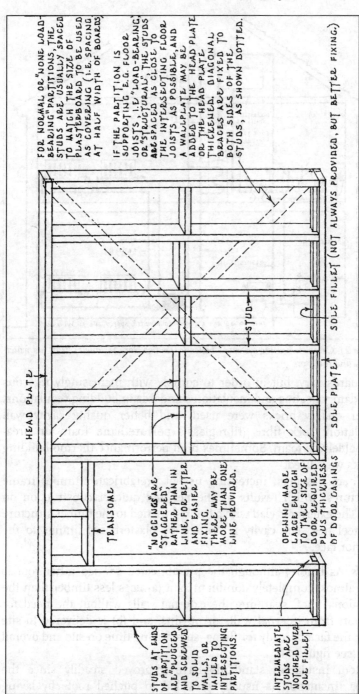

FOR NORMAL OR "NONE LOAD-BEARING" PARTITIONS, THE STUDS ARE USUALLY SPACED TO MATCH THE SIZE OF PLASTERBOARD TO BE USED AS COVERING (I.E. SPACING AT HALF WIDTH OF BOARDS).

IF THE PARTITION IS SUPPORTING, E.G. FLOOR JOISTS, I.E. "LOAD-BEARING" OR "STRUCTURAL" THE STUDS ARE SPACED AS CLOSE TO THE INTERSECTING FLOOR JOISTS AS POSSIBLE, AND A WALLPLATE MAY BE ADDED TO THE HEAD PLATE OR THE HEAD PLATE THICKENED. DIAGONAL BRACES ARE FIXED TO BOTH SIDES OF THE STUDS, AS SHOWN DOTTED.

HEAD PLATE

←STUD→

SOLE PLATE

SOLE FILLET (NOT ALWAYS PROVIDED, BUT BETTER FIXING.)

TRANSOME

"NOGGINGS" ARE "STAGGERED", RATHER THAN IN LINE, FOR BETTER AND EASIER FIXING. THERE MAY BE MORE THAN ONE LINE PROVIDED.

OPENING MADE LARGE ENOUGH TO TAKE SIZE OF DOOR REQUIRED PLUS THICKNESS OF DOOR CASINGS.

STUDS AT ENDS OF PARTITION ARE "PLUGGED AND SCREWED" TO SOLID WALLS, OR NAILED TO INTERSECTING PARTITIONS.

INTERMEDIATE STUDS ARE NOTCHED OVER SOLE FILLET.

Figure 22: Stud partition wall

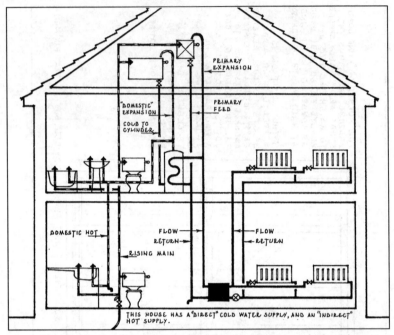

Figure 23: Complete heating system – boiler (shown as black rectangle) heats hot water supply and radiators

Standards vary, but in order to comply with increasingly rigorous mandatory heating and insulation standards in building regulations, better quality bricks were used, and better quality cavity wall insulation: rock fibre (fibreglass), polyurethane foam or urea-formaldehyde foam. Sometimes high performance thermo-building blocks were used.

There has been increasing use of prefabricated timber frame structures, which results in cheaper and quicker construction on site. The exterior is clad with a brick skin, tied to the timber structure by steel ties. The cavity is created by plasterboard linings to the interior face.

1.24   **Roofs** As before, although the prefabricated trussed rafter roof is now almost completely dominant as it (a) uses less timber than the traditional roof, spanning the external walls without the need for support from internal walls or purlins, and (b) is delivered to site from the factory ready for fixing, so reducing time on site and overall cost (see figure 24).

Roof insulation standards have improved steadily since the 1970s. Insulation is usually provided to pitched roofs by laying

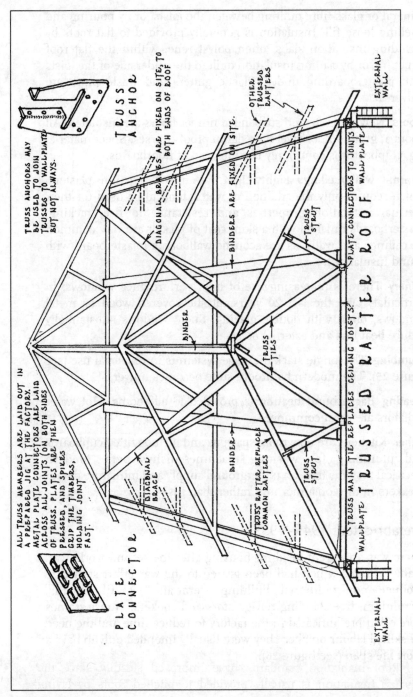

TRUSS ANCHORS MAY BE USED TO JOIN TRUSSES TO WALLPLATE BUT NOT ALWAYS.

TRUSS ANCHOR

EXTERNAL WALL

OTHER TRUSSED RAFTERS

DIAGONAL BRACES ARE FIXED ON SITE TO BOTH ENDS OF ROOF

BINDERS ARE FIXED ON SITE.

TRUSS STRUT

PLATE CONNECTORS TO JOINTS

WALL PLATE

BINDER

TRUSS TIES

TRUSS STRUT

TRUSS MAIN TIE REPLACES CEILING JOISTS.

TRUSSED RAFTER ROOF

WALLPLATE

TRUSS RAFTER REPLACES COMMON RAFTERS

BINDER

DIAGONAL BRACE

ALL TRUSS MEMBERS ARE LAID OUT IN A PREPARED JIG AT THE FACTORY. METAL PLATE CONNECTORS ARE LAID ACROSS ALL JOINTS (ON BOTH SIDES OF TRUSS. PLATES ARE THEN PRESSED, AND SPIKES GRIP THE TIMBERS, HOLDING JOINT FAST.

PLATE CONNECTOR

EXTERNAL WALL

Figure 24: Trussed rafter roof

mineral or glass-fibre quilting between the joists, or by pouring and levelling loose fill. Insulation is generally provided to flat roofs by including insulation slabs, often polystyrene, within the flat roof structure, or by nailing insulation quilt to the underside of the joists with plasterboarding under. Plastic gutters and waste pipes are universal.

1.25   **Floors** New concrete and suspended timber floors are insulated. All floors at ground floor level have damp proof courses. Sheet material (eg, chipboard) is commonly used instead of floorboards.

1.26   **Internal walls/ceilings** Lightweight, pre-mixed gypsum plasters, which require only the addition of water, tend to be used for their thermal insulation properties and resistance to fire/cracking. Plasterboards finished with a skim coat of plaster are very common on ceilings and walls, as are acoustic wallboards (plasterboard with sound insulation).

1.27   **Joinery** There is increasing use of high performance windows; in particular, over the last 20 years, plastic covered wood or metal windows, often with double glazing. Such windows substantially reduce heat loss and external noise.

1.28   **Plumbing** The single stack drainage system is in universal use (see figure 25). The modern bathroom suite becomes universal.

1.29   **Heating** Background heating is provided to all rooms. Hot water radiators are most common.

1.30   **Other** Kitchens are now more spacious and include fitted cupboards and plumbing for washing machines/dishwashers. Modern electrical systems have an underground supply and miniature circuit breakers in the consumer unit rather than fuses.

Prefabricated: 1945–1955

1.31   There was an urgent need for housing after the second world war. Many factories which had been geared to the war effort started to produce non-traditional building elements, eg, fibreboards, aluminium, free-standing refrigerators and cookers. House frames were often prefabricated in the factory to reduce time and the need for skilled labour on site. They were usually intended only to have a short life span (see figure 26).

1.32 **Foundations** As with old traditional.

1.33 **External walls** A wide variety of construction materials were developed. Steel or reinforced concrete frames were common, with panels made from asbestos, steel, aluminium, timber or concrete, although an external skin of traditional bricks was often provided.

1.34 **Roofs** Roofs were generally trussed but had a very low pitch. They were usually covered with metal or asbestos (a lightweight covering was needed because the structure was lightweight). Builders often installed flat concrete roofs in this period (see figure 19).

1.35 **Floors** As with old traditional, although they could often be concrete rather than suspended timber.

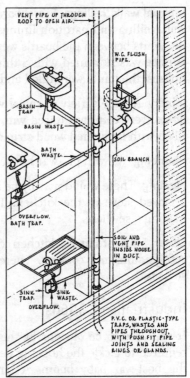

Figure 25: Waste and soil drainage – single stack system

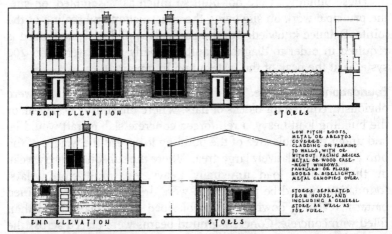

Figure 26: Prefabricated houses

1.36   **Internal walls/ceilings** Fibreboards and plasterboards were used for wall, ceiling and partition linings. In the better-constructed houses the joints between the boards were covered with scrim cloth and the surface was skimmed with a thin coat of plaster. In poorer quality houses, the joints were filled and lining paper applied.

1.37   **Joinery** A wide variety of metal windows were used. Cheaper flush doors were common (faced with plywood, melamine or hardwood, filled with laminated wood strip or compressed paper).

1.38   **Plumbing** As with pre-war houses.

1.39   **Heating** There would usually be an open fire in the living room and a closed stove in the kitchen. There might be some background heating elsewhere.

1.40   **Other** Mass-produced kitchen cupboards became common, also refrigerators and cookers. There was greater provision of electric sockets.

Industrialised: 1960s

1.41   It appeared to be obvious by the 1950s that drastic measures were required to tackle the housing deficit caused by slum clearance and the post-war baby boom. A large number of modular building systems were developed, based on factory-produced structural frames of timber, steel or concrete, usually with factory-produced infill panels, often of concrete.

These buildings were not built so much as 'assembled' on site, the principal work on site being the construction and sealing of the joints. Detailed knowledge of the particular building system used is required in order to diagnose faults properly (there were over 200 systems at the peak of the system building period).

1.42   **Foundations** As before, for houses. Stronger foundations were obviously required for blocks of flats. Where the subsoil was weak or the building load heavy, a reinforced concrete slab or raft would be laid under the whole area of the building to spread the weight of the building over a relatively large area. Where the subsoil was very weak or the building load unusually heavy, eg, multi-storey flats, foundations would be piled: holes were drilled to a predetermined pattern, reaching down to a suitable load bearing layer, and then filled with concrete. Concrete ground beams were placed across the top of the piles and the building sat on top of these (see figure 27).

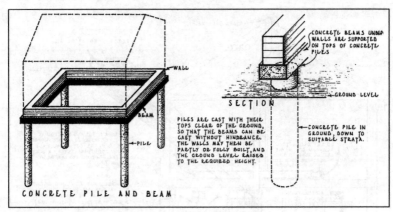

Figure 27: Concrete pile and beam foundation

1.43 **External walls** Prefabricated panels of 'no fines' (see para 1.52) concrete mixed on site were added to reinforced concrete or steel frames made in the factory and delivered to the site. Large panel systems were designed to be erected on site rather like a building 'kit'.

1.44 **Roofs** Roofs, again, were factory made and simply added to the building. They were usually flat because flat roofs are cheaper and quicker to build.

1.45 **Floors** Depended on the type of system but all floors to flats in blocks would be made of solid concrete.

1.46 **Internal walls/ceilings** The building material used depended on the type of system, but concrete walls and ceilings would be common in blocks of flats.

1.47 **Joinery** The type of joinery used depended on the type of system.

1.48 **Plumbing** Single stack drainage.

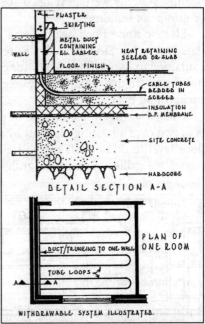

Figure 28: Electric under floor heating

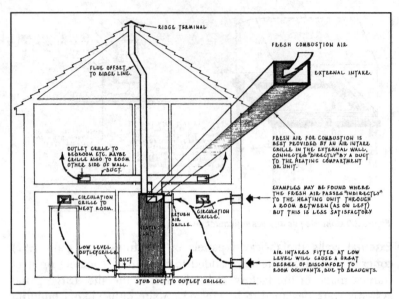

Figure 29: Ducted warm air heating

1.49   **Heating** This again depended on the type of system. A number of heating systems were developed specifically for large blocks of flats or groups of buildings.

Electric underfloor heating was inserted into the solid floors of flats in blocks. Electric cables were embedded in the floor slab or contained in metal tubes. Their function was to heat up the floor slab itself (see figure 28). The system provided an even degree of background heat.

Ducted warm air heating can be gas, electric or oil fired. Fresh air is drawn over a heating element by a fan then passed along ducts at floor level to other parts of the building, into which the warm air passes via grilles. Return air grilles mix returning cooler air with

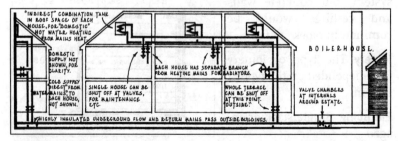

Figure 30: District heating system

fresh combustion air for filtering, heating and circulation (see figure 29).

Hot water for taps and radiators was often supplied by a district heating system (see figure 30).

Building materials

1.50 **Brick** Bricks are almost always made of clay baked in a kiln. They

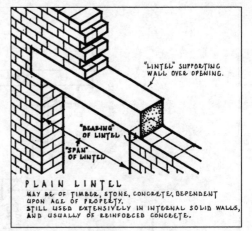

Figure 31: Exposed lintel

range in size from 215mm × 102 × 65 to 290mm × 90 × 90. The main type of bricks are: commons (internal bricks or bricks to be covered by render); facings (more attractive looking external bricks); and engineering (very strong bricks with a high resistance to water absorption so used for basements, retaining walls or as a damp-proof course).

1.51 **Blocks** Blocks are made from cement and other aggregates, eg, clinker (breeze), sand, shale and, more recently, pulverised fuel ash (PFA) which is very light. Blocks now often contain a core of insulating material such as polystyrene. They can be load bearing or non-load bearing and are 448mm × 215mm with thicknesses ranging from 51mm to 219mm.

1.52 **Concrete** Concrete is a mixture of cement, sand and aggregates, eg, gravel, crushed limestone or granite. Clean water is added. The mixture sets to provide hard structural material.

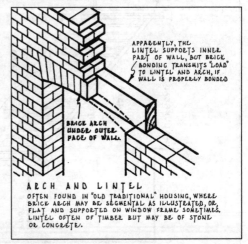

Figure 32: Concealed lintel

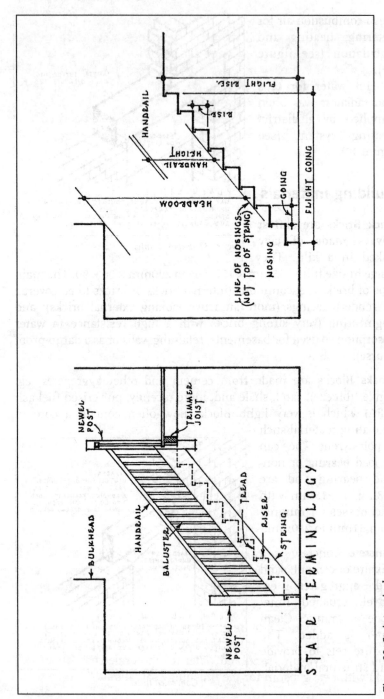

Figure 33: Stair terminology

The proportion, by volume, of cement, sand and aggregate determines the strength. Concrete can be reinforced by the addition of steel bars or mesh. Foundations and slabs are usually laid in situ and reinforced. Beams or lintels are usually precast and reinforced at the factory for fixing on site. From the 1950s on, 'no fines' concrete was used for housing, that is, concrete without 'fines' (sand or fine aggregate). No fines concrete has better thermal insulation and is fast setting, leading to greater construction speed. The outer face of concrete walls is usually rendered.

1.53 **Damp-proof courses** A horizontal DPC is provided to internal and external walls in the form of a waterproof strip at least 150mm above ground level to minimise the risk of bridging. Pre-war DPCs might be a layer of slate, two courses of engineering bricks or a layer of bitumen-based material. Modern DPCs in walls are plastic. DPCs in ground-floor solid floors are a continuous membrane or sheet of plastic lapped at all joints within the area of the floor and at the junction with the horizontal DPC to external walls to ensure continuity (see figure 4). Pre-war dwellings frequently had no DPC in solid ground-floor areas, while immediately after the war a DPC was often provided by applying bitumen and thermoplastic tiles to the upper surface of the concrete. Where cavity walls are bridged, eg, by windows, both horizontal (to the head and sill) and vertical (to the jambs) DPCs are provided. DPCs are provided to parapet walls and chimneys, where metal flashings are also used (see figure 21).

1.54 **Lintels** Openings in brickwork for doors or windows are spanned by lintels, beams which support the load above the opening, ie, part of the weight of the wall above the opening including the weight of any floor or ceiling transmitted to the wall. Lintels in external walls require DPCs. Lintels may be exposed or concealed (see figures 31 and 32).

1.55 **Mortar** Mortar glues bricks together. It is made from a mixture of cement, lime or other plasticiser and sand, to which water is added. Different types of mix are used for different types of brick/site conditions.

1.56 **Plaster** Up to about 1920, lime plaster was used, made from lime, water and sand mixtures. It has been superseded by gypsum plaster: a mixture of gypsum, sand and water for the undercoat (about $5/8''$ thick) with neat gypsum for the finishing coat (about $1/16''$ thick).

Plasterboard is usually $^3/8''$ to $^1/2''$ thick and gypsum based. There is either a standard grey finish, or one side might be faced with insulating aluminium foil (often for use on ceilings) or cream paper designed not to need decoration. Joints are covered with scrim cloth and the surface is skimmed with a coat of finishing plaster; alternatively, joints may be filled and lining paper applied.

Old buildings have lath and plaster ceilings and sometimes even lath and plaster walls. Narrow timber laths are laid across ceiling joists (or timber uprights to the wall) with a small gap between each lath. Cow hair is added to the plaster mix as a binding agent. The ceiling is then plastered with the plaster pushed between and over the laths and finished with a thin finishing coat of plaster.

1.57   **Staircases** See figure 33 for stair terminology. Staircases in houses are always made of timber and are usually made off site. Staircases in flats are sometimes made of concrete.

Common building defects

For complete chapter contents, see overleaf

Introduction

2.1 The purpose of this chapter is not, of course, to train legal advisers to diagnose building defects or to become barrack room surveyors. Its purpose is to enable the legal adviser to understand the basics of expert evidence.

2.2 In 1975 the Building Research Establishment (BRE) carried out a survey[1] which indicated that the most common defects are those shown in table 1.

Table 1: Most common building defects

Building type	Defects (per cent)				
	condensation	rain penetration	cracking	floors	roofs
Council houses	59	13			
Council flats	38	33			
Private houses	18	33	20		
Private flats		64			
Factories		29	29		
Offices		28	19	28	23
Schools				32	39
Hospitals				35	26

Note: Shops, churches and universities showed no clear pattern.

[Source: Seeley *Building Surveys, Report and Dilapidations* Macmillan, 1985]

2.3 According to Oxley and Gobert[2] about one-third of dampness problems in houses are rising damp related while about two-thirds are condensation damp related. This estimate is based on a survey carried out by the BRE Scottish Laboratory between November 1979 and March 1980[3] and on the Protimeter Laboratories' own analyses of wallpaper and plaster sent for chemical analysis.

1 *Current Paper 30/75: Building failure patterns and their implications*, by I L Freeman, HMSO, April 1975.
2 *Dampness in Buildings*, 2nd edn, Butterworth-Heinemann Ltd, 1994.
3 *Dampness: one week's complaints in five local authorities in England and Wales* by CH Sanders and JP Cornish, HMSO, 1982.

Foundations

2.4   The purpose of foundations is to transmit the weight of the building over a sufficient area of soil so that the building structure has a stable base. For different types of foundations see chapter 1, figures 1, 2 and 27.

2.5   Unstable foundations can be the result of deterioration to the foundation materials, eg, a sulphate attack on concrete. There is rarely sufficient sulphate or acid in the ground to successfully attack foundation components, but aggressive chemical components of fill material can disintegrate slabs and brickwork (especially burnt colliery shale).

2.6   Most unstable foundations are caused by movement in the surrounding ground.

2.7   Clay soil is a major cause of foundation movement.[4] The reason is that clay swells and shrinks according to its moisture content much more than other types of soil. Foundations in open ground less than 1m deep but in clay soil are likely to be subject to seasonal movement resulting in small, unsightly cracks which can however be easily masked.

2.8   Foundations can be undermined by the removal of ground support, mining operations, severe and prolonged rainfall, leaking drains or services or plant roots, particularly tree roots, extracting moisture from the soil and causing it to shrink. If tree roots are the cause, it is important to determine whether the tree is mature or still growing. If the tree is mature, its removal may do more harm than good by permitting unusually large amounts of water to remain in the soil, thereby causing the clay to swell and pressurise the foundations. Pruning is usually the safest course with mature trees. If, however, the tree is still growing and has already caused foundation movement, then this movement is likely to become more serious over time. Therefore, felling or severe pruning is the usually the only safe course.

2.9   Differential movement can occur when bays, rear additions or internal partitions are built on shallower foundations than the main house.

---

4   *BRE Digest 251: Assessment of damage in low rise buildings* HMSO, July 1981.

External walls

2.10   As Seeley observes,[5] external walls suffer in particular from: (a) inability to support imposed loads resulting in distortion and/or cracking, (b) inability to keep out the weather, (c) inability to insulate from cold with resultant condensation and (d) deterioration of cladding materials.

Structural cracking

2.11   Cracked brickwork may or may not result in structural instability, depending on the type of brick, the extent of the cracking, the nature of the load, whether there is bulging or other movement and the type of wall ties used.

2.12   BRE investigations into prefabricated reinforced concrete houses[6] show that most reinforced concrete components are deteriorating. The cause is mostly carbonation of the concrete, but in some cases corrosion of the steel frame by chloride in the concrete is causing the concrete to crack.

Poor joints in prefabricated dwellings

2.13   Loose or even unstable joints are a major problem in prefabricated and industrial systems. Large panels of concrete walling are connected on site to other such panels and to the prefabricated structure. The joints between panels and the prefabricated structure are often poorly designed and/or executed resulting in water and wind penetration or even structural instability. This is a particular problem in high rise buildings which are considerably more exposed to wind and rain.

Wind and rain

2.14   Exposure to rain can trigger a chemical reaction between the sulphate contained in bricks, particularly older bricks, and the tricalcium aluminate found in cement, resulting in the expansion and in extreme cases the disintegration of brickwork joints.

5   Ivor H Seeley, *Building Surveys, Reports and Dilapidations*, Macmillan, 1985.
6   *Information Paper 1P 16/83: The structural condition of some reinforced concrete houses of Boot, Cornish unit, Unity, Wates and Woolaway construction*, HMSO, October 1983.

2.15   Frost action can spall bricks and disintegrate mortar, particularly in free-standing or parapet walls. Water expands when frozen, often enlarging the crack in which the water lay prior to freezing. Once that crack becomes larger, it can receive more water, which will consequently expand more when frozen, enlarging the crack still further (and so on).

2.16   Frost action, or the process of wetting and drying, can crack render or cause it to detach from the wall. A major contributory cause is poor design or workmanship in the application of render.

2.17   In timber framed houses, the structural timbers are at risk of decay if exposed to severe or persistent moisture, eg, by being exposed to rain during storage before use, by the use of inadequate wood preservative or as the result of puncture/poor fixing of vapour barriers. Vapour barriers and insulation are fitted to the exterior face of structural timber so that the temperature of the timber is kept as closely as possible in equilibrium with the temperature inside the dwelling. That reduces the risk of condensation and rot to the timbers caused by moisture.

2.18   Penetration of damp through brickwork can occur as the result of porous bricks, defective pointing, hairline cracks in rendering, vegetation on the external face of the wall or a lack of adequate weathering detail to external projections. Driving rain can easily penetrate one-brick solid walls, particularly in the wetter parts of the country (south-west, western and north-west England) and to the south and south-westerly elevations of buildings (ie, walls facing the prevailing winds and rain).

2.19   There should be no water penetration through the inner skin of a properly constructed cavity wall but it can occur as the result of the cavity being bridged by mortar droppings in the cavity on wall ties, on DPC trays or at the base of the wall, by ineffective DPCs at window and door openings or by leaking rainwater goods.

Rising damp

2.20   Rising damp can be a major problem, particularly with older properties. Water in the soil is naturally drawn up through brickwork and concrete, which are porous, by capillary action. The ground water rises through the foundations and into the walls, appearing as damp patches on the internal surfaces of walls. Old buildings may not have a DPC or it may have deteriorated. Newer buildings may have a DPC but it might become bridged by soil

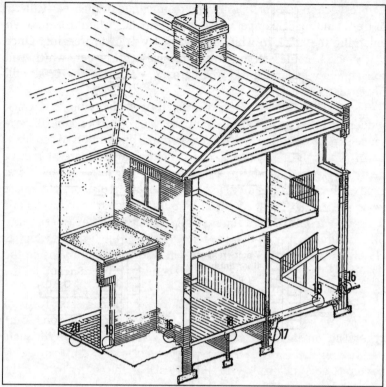

Figure 34: Possible sources of rising damp. **16**, *Earth or path bridging damp-proof course;* **17**, *earth retaining wall not tanked (ie, no vertical damp-proof membrane) leading to a wet wall and a very high humidity in the cellar. No air brick or other ventilation to the cellar;* **18**, *missing damp-proof course under joists resting on sleeper wall;* **19**, *missing damp-proof course under floor and door frame,* **20**, *when a solid floor is persistently very wet, this may be due to a faulty or missing damp-proof course.*

placed against the wall at a higher level than the DPC, by the construction of porches, sun lounges and the like or by provision of external rendering right down to ground level below the DPC.

2.21   Diagnosis of rising damp is initially by way of moisture meter but can be confirmed by a simple laboratory salt analysis. See figures 34 and 35 for illustrations of rising damp and bridging.

2.22   Skirtings often have to be replaced because rising damp has caused them to rot. Plaster nearly always needs to be replaced because even if it has not perished, the soil salts left behind by rising damp are hygroscopic, that is, water-attracting; so even when rising damp has been stopped by the provision of an effective DPC the plaster will saturate itself unless replaced because the hygroscopic salts will attract moisture from the atmosphere of the house. Most

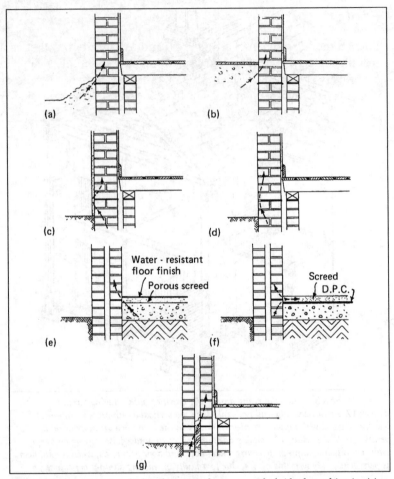

Figure 35: Seven ways in which a damp-proof course may be bridged, resulting in rising damp. **(a)** Bridging by earth; **(b)** bridging by path; **(c)** bridging by rendering; **(d)** bridging by mortar pointing; **(e)** and **(f)** bridging by floor screed; **(g)** bridging by mortar dropping in cavity

replastering is carried out straight after the insertion of the new DPC and before the bricks have completely dried out. This can cause problems as, in the course of drying out, the bricks will continue to extrude hygroscopic salts into the plaster. Therefore, new plaster laid shortly after the provision of a DPC is usually of a type which is water and salt resistant. Replastering is always carried out up to 400mm above the highest recorded incidence of damp to make allowances for earlier high tides of rising damp which may have left deposits of hygroscopic salts in the plaster.

Roofs

2.23 Pitched roofs (see chapter 1, figures 8 and 11) admit rainwater as a result of defective flashings, shrunk or broken cement fillets, slipped or broken slates or tiles, choked or defective gutters, absent or defective DPCs to parapet walls or life expired slates (poorer quality

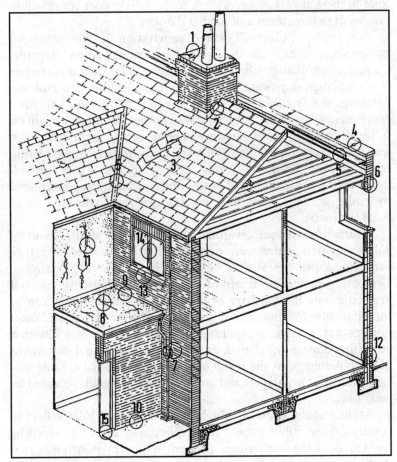

Figure 36: Rainwater ingress. **1**, *poorly capped chimney;* **2**, *faulty rainwater protection (cement flaunching) where chimney stack passes through the roof (lead or zinc would be better);* **3**, *displaced roof tiles;* **4**, *faulty coping stone, without damp-proof course;* **5**, *defective parapet and valley gutter lining;* **6**, *lack of cavity tray over window head;* **7**, *defective rainwater pipe and hopper;* **8**, *cracked felt on flat roof and incorrect fall to flat roof;* **9**, *missing lead soaker adjacent to flat roof;* **10**, *rain splashback over damp-proof course;* **11**, *defective render;* **12**, *mortar droppings on ties between the two leaves of a cavity wall, transmitting penetrating rain to the inner wall;* **13**, *defective window sill admits water;* **14**, *poorly painted window frame;* **15**, *no threshold to prevent driving rain*

slates have an approximate life expectancy of up to 70 years) or tiles (poorer quality tiles have an approximate life expectancy of up to 40 years). See figure 36.

2.24   Water penetration or condensation can cause the roof timbers to rot. Where loft insulation has been installed, the roof needs to be ventilated to reduce the risk of condensation damage to roof timbers. Roof timbers are also vulnerable to insect attack. Poor construction can result in movement and further damage.

2.25   Flat roofs can permit water penetration if the structural components decay as the result of condensation damage. Condensation damage often occurs if there is no vapour barrier or roof ventilation to prevent warm air from the inside of the building entering the roof structure and condensing on structural components. Flat roofs also permit water penetration as the result of: (a) inadequate or deteriorated weathering details around copings, upstands, parapets or gutters; (b) tears, splits or rucks in the roofing material over structural beams; and (c) punctures or general deterioration of the surface of the roofing material, often exacerbated by inadequate falls permitting ponding (particularly in the case of older flat roofs).

2.26   Bitumen-based roof coverings will deteriorate as the result of solar radiation which can cause oxidisation and temperature variation across the surface resulting in differential expansion. Temporary protection is afforded by bedding reflective mineral aggregate onto the top layer of bitumen but the chippings can in time puncture the bitumen. Bitumen is extremely friable and most failures are caused by splitting as the result of the bitumen stretching during installation, as the result of structural movement of the building, or as the result of areas of differential expansion – eg, at skirtings to parapets and other weathering details – caused by solar heat.

2.27   Asphalt roofs again should be protected by a solar reflective covering. Most failures result from splitting or cracking caused by movement of the substratum, differential movement between roof deck and parapet wall or other projection, or from interstitial condensation.

2.28   Water penetration is commonly caused by blockages to rainwater downpipes at low level. This results in water backing up and penetration occurring at a higher level. There may be insufficient gutters, gutters which have an insufficient fall or damaged gutters, eg, gutters which are holed.

Floors

Chemical attack

2.29   The concrete slab of solid floors may deteriorate as the result of chemical attack by soluble salts in the soil or hardcore below.

Damp solid floors

2.30   Old solid floors will probably not have a damp-proof membrane and so obviously will be damp. Concrete, brick or stone floors can remain damp indefinitely without deterioration (the bricks and concrete used in foundations, for example, are permanently saturated). Concrete, terrazzo or clay tiles will transmit this damp without loss of adhesion or material damage. Other floor coverings, however, will lose adhesion and/or shape and in extreme situations disintegrate. Skirtings and other timber in contact with the floor can be expected to rot. If the plaster has been taken down to floor level it absorbs the damp and soil salts in the damp solid floor by capillary action, bridging any DPC in the wall. The result is rising damp in the interior of the house and this can lead to perishing plaster, rotting skirting boards and damaged decorations.

2.31   Newer solid floors will contain a damp-proof membrane: usually a layer of bitumen, asphalt or, more latterly, plastic laid under the floor screed. Rising damp can then only affect plaster taken down to floor level if the joint with the horizontal DPC to the wall is not properly lapped.

2.32   If the floor covering is substantially waterproof, some dampness will inevitably occur under it. This is the result of small amounts of damp from the soil (DP membranes are never perfect and will allow small amounts of moisture through), or from the drying out of concrete screed, becoming trapped between the DP membrane in the solid floor and the floor covering. Unless very high moisture readings are obtained, this type of damp can be ignored. If left uncovered, or covered with a permeable floor covering such as carpet, the moisture will readily evaporate.

2.33   Moisture is a troublesome enemy of ground-floor suspended timber floors because it can lead to decay and, in severe, cases dry rot. It is essential that timber used for suspended ground floors has been properly seasoned and preserved, that sleeper walls supporting joists contain effective DPCs and are honeycombed to permit air to flow, that internal walls contain ventilation holes and that air bricks are provided at all walls to avoid stagnant corners. Ideally, adjacent solid floors should contain air ducts.

2.34   Common faults are sagging or springing, resulting from overloading; inadequately sized, supported or fixed joists; lack of strutting; or poorly fixed or worn floorboards.

Internal walls/ceilings

2.35   Plaster can be damaged by rising, penetrating, traumatic or condensation damp.

2.36   In addition, plaster can perish and fall down as the result of laths in lath and plaster ceilings or walls decaying, slipping or having been placed too far apart for the plaster to bond.

2.37   Poor workmanship during installation, old age and natural deterioration are all common causes of plaster cracking or losing its adhesion.

2.38   Poor plaster can be readily identified because it emits a hollow sound when tapped. If wallpaper is removed such defective plaster may fall off the wall in chunks.

Joinery

2.39   Moisture causes most problems associated with wood joinery: swelling, distortion, deterioration of finish and destruction by fungi. Wood should be properly seasoned and preserved before use in buildings. Some types of cheap timber actually resist preservative treatment and are therefore susceptible to rapid decay.

2.40   Unprimed glazing beads and rebates lead to decay as do inadequately sealed joints between members. The design of some cheap windows actually promotes the entry and retention of water. Symptoms are putty failure, discoloration of paint near joints, swelling and jamming of opening lights, soft wood beneath defective paint.

2.41   The results can include cracks and draughts; rainwater penetration through cracks; moisture penetration by capillary action through saturated wood; excessive condensation.

2.42   Poor quality joinery is a particular problem in high rise buildings, which are appreciably more exposed to wind and rain.

2.43   Joints between members of doors can shrink, permitting water penetration and decay. If there is no weather boarding at the bottom of the door, water can penetrate internally and will cause rot to occur to the door. Again, incompetent painting allows water penetration to take place. Poorly fitted doors, or doors which, as a result of age, are pulling on their hinges can be unpleasantly draughty.

2.44   External decoration is often applied too quickly with the result that paint does not protect external timber in the way that it should: timber is not primed, insufficient coats of paint are applied, paint is not allowed to harden inbetween coats, or paints are thinned on site to facilitate speedy application (but the resultant film of paint is too thin and not durable).

Plumbing

2.45   Taps leak when the washers wear or the metal seatings become eroded. The result is wasted water, irritation and staining to sinks or baths. Ball valves may fail to close because of a perforated float, a worn seating, a defective washer or grit/limestone deposits with the result that the cistern or tank continues to fill, causing water to discharge from the overflow pipe with possible resultant damage to brickwork, particularly if the overflow is not well drained or is set too close to the house. Severe leaks can occur in winter as the result of water freezing, expanding and bursting the pipes which contain it, unless vulnerable pipes are lagged, pipes are run in safe places wherever possible and there is background heating.

2.46   Galvanised iron water storage tanks can fail as the result of contact with copper feeder pipes or as the result of water dissolving minute particles of copper piping and carrying them into the tank. The copper particles engage in electrolytic (galvanic) action with the zinc coating of the tank. The resultant corrosion can be avoided by suspending a sacrificial magnesium anode in the tank. Unprotected steel can rust, leading to leaks.

2.47   Single stack drainage systems need to be carefully designed and constructed if they are to work effectively, with proper falls and traps. Particular care is required with high rise buildings, both as to design and construction but also as to maintenance and inspection because blockages of the system can exert massive pressure on pipework, with explosive results.

2.48   With use, wash hand basins, sinks and baths work away from the wall with the result that water runs behind, sometimes causing the wooden floor below to rot, or additional pressure is put on the pipes carrying water, which are therefore more likely to leak.

2.49   The pipe joints and sometimes even the pipes of drains can crack as the result of pressure from the foundations, vehicles, tree roots, movements of ground below the drains. The rigid cement mortar joints formerly used with clay pipes are particularly vulnerable. Drains can be blocked by silt or household waste, particularly if laid to an insufficient fall.

Other

2.50   Electric systems should be checked at least once every five years, in accordance with the regulations of the Institution of Electrical Engineers. Wiring usually lasts about 30 years. Pre-1950 circuits can be identified by their round pin plugs and rubber sheath wiring. Sockets and switches on damp walls should be checked regularly for rust or perishing of the sheath wiring.

2.51   Gas installations also require regular checking to ensure that the products of combustion are being safely discharged into the open air through suitable flues: see Gas Safety (Installation and Use) Regulations 1998,[7] which require yearly inspections by qualified personnel. Pipes and fittings can corrode or become loose, resulting in leaks.

2.52   Apart from boiler failure, heating systems can fail or operate poorly as the result of air locks, furring or corrosion of pipes or simply poor design, eg, boiler, too small, excessive lengths of flow and return pipes, poor quality fuel, insufficient lagging of pipes.

Condensation

Basic condensation

2.53   This most pernicious defect is sadly also the most common. It is particularly prevalent in council flats and houses. A BRE report of 1982 estimated that over 3.5 million dwellings were affected: over 1.5 million seriously so.[8]

---

7   SI No 2451, see appendix G.
8   *BRE Report: Dampness: one week's complaints in five local authorities in England and Wales* by CH Sanders and JP Cornish, HMSO, 1982.

2.54   Warm air can hold more moisture than cold air. When warm air meets a cold surface the warm air cools and releases some of its moisture as condensation.

2.55   Moisture in air contributes to the total atmospheric pressure of that air. This contribution is called the vapour pressure of air and is nowadays measured in millibars. Air which contains relatively high amounts of moisture has a higher vapour pressure than air which contains lower amounts of moisture. As a result, moist air disperses towards dry air. That is why moist air from kitchens and bathrooms disperses throughout a dwelling. Moist air at relatively high vapour pressure within a dwelling seeks to disperse by all available routes (including through the structure) to the outside.

2.56   Condensation can occur (a) when the inner surface of the structure of the dwelling is cooler than room air (surface condensation), or (b) when vapour pressure pushes moist air through the porous inner leaf of a dwelling and that air condenses in the colder conditions which pertain between inner and outer structural leaves (interstitial condensation).

2.57   The term relative humidity (RH) expresses as a percentage the actual vapour pressure of an air sample relative to the total vapour pressure it could sustain at the same temperature, eg, air which has a relative humidity of 70% at 20 degrees centigrade contains about 70% of the moisture which it is capable of containing at that temperature. If the temperature increases then the air can contain more moisture and its relative humidity goes down. If the temperature decreases then the air is able to contain less moisture and its relative humidity increases.

2.58   If moist air is cooled, a point is reached at which it becomes saturated, ie, it can no longer hold all of its moisture. That point, the point at which condensation occurs, is known as the dew point.

2.59   The relationship between humidity, dew point and air temperature can be looked up in psychrometric charts published inter alia in British Standard 5250: 1989 (see figure 37). The wet bulb temperatures (the sloping straight lines) can be ignored. The vertical straight lines show room temperatures. The horizontal straight lines refer to amounts of moisture in the air in terms of vapour pressure (dotted horizontal straight lines) and in terms of grams of moisture per kilogram of dry air (straight horizontal unbroken lines). The curved lines show the relative humidity which air will have given the combination of (a) a temperature and (b) a moisture content. For example, point C demonstrates that air which is at 20 degrees centigrade and has a moisture content of 17 millibars vapour pressure has a relative humidity of 70%. Point D demonstrates what happens when air with that same vapour pressure of 17 millibars is cooled to a temperature of about 14.5 degrees centigrade: the relative humidity increases to 100%, ie, saturation (very severe condensation). This is what can often happen when air made moist by normal living activity in a reasonably warm dwelling where the room air temperatures are 20 degrees centigrade disperses towards the outside and meets a colder structural wall which is at about 14.5 degrees centigrade.

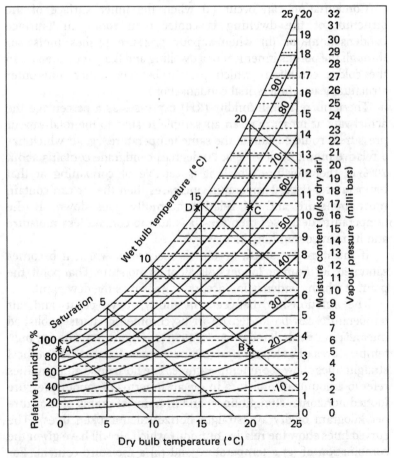

Figure 37: A psychrometric chart showing the interrelationship between moisture contents and temperature (BS 5250: 1975)

Understanding what dampness is

2.60　It is impossible to understand condensation dampness without understanding dampness itself: what is it and when does it become a danger to the building and its occupiers?

2.61　The atmosphere of a normal living environment has a relative humidity of between 30% (typically found in a well heated and ventilated modern office) and 70% (typically found in a classroom full of children).

2.62　Building material is properly described as damp if it is wetter than building material which is as dry or damp as the atmosphere in a normal range of living environments.

2.63　Most construction materials in a modern building (for example timber, plaster, paper and brick) both contain moisture and absorb moisture. Construction materials are likely to absorb moisture if the dwelling has a high relative humidity but are likely to release moisture into the dwelling if the dwelling has a low relative humidity. At all relative humidities the construction materials in the building will eventually reach a state in which they are in equilibrium with the air, ie, they have emitted or absorbed all the moisture they are capable of emitting or absorbing.

2.64　Wood is the key to the whole question because although there are variations between hardwood and softwood and between different species of each type of wood, all wood when tested demonstrates remarkably similar behaviour in relation to vapour pressure. When the relative humidity of air is 80% for example, virtually all wood will absorb sufficient moisture as to have a moisture content itself of about 19% (eg, if weighed, dried and weighed again in laboratory conditions its weight would be shown to have been 19% comprised of moisture: moisture content equals the wet weight of material minus the dry weight of material divided by the dry weight and multiplied by 100). See figure 38 for a chart demonstrating the approximate relationship between relative humidity and the moisture content of wood.

2.65　Charts of this type can be made for other types of building material but they would be of no value: different types of plaster, different types of brick, or even different bricks of the same type all have such different relationships with relative humidity that it is not possible to produce an average or standard chart showing, for example, that at 80% relative humidity all bricks will have a moisture content of, say, 5%. What is known, however, is that different

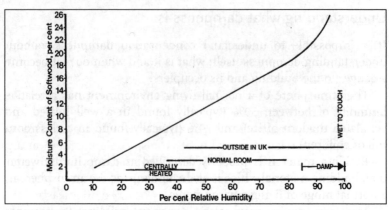

Figure 38: Wood moisture content and air relative humidity

materials are damp when certain levels of moisture content are reached. See table 2 for some examples.

Table 2: Moisture in various building materials

Material	Moisture content %	Interpretation
Wood	4	Extremely dry
Some mortar	4	Dry
Some bricks	4	Damp
Other mortar	4	Damp
Other bricks	4	Wet
Plaster	4	Very wet
Wood	12	Air-dry
Brick	12	Saturated
Plaster	12	Not possible

[Source: Oxley and Gobert *Dampness in Buildings*, see note 2]

2.66   If relative humidity in the building exceeds 85% (in those circumstances wood has a moisture content exceeding 20%) then moulds, wood decay, fungi and mites will develop rapidly. This is so, even though at such levels there will be no visible dampness. Wood, for example, does not feel or look damp until it has a moisture content of about 30% (ie, the relative humidity is about 97% or 98%). If the relative humidity in the building is between 75% and 85% (wood moisture content equivalent 19% to 20%) such adverse consequences follow, but more slowly.

Measurement of dampness

2.67   The effects of condensation can often be seen: stained or mouldy decorations are a notorious example. These defects can be seen even when condensation is no longer occurring.

2.68   Measuring dampness in the atmosphere or in construction materials is more difficult.

2.69   There are a number of instruments which are capable of measuring the relative humidity of atmosphere in a room at any given time or over a period of time: hygrometers and thermo-hygrometers are the most usual but there are a number of others.

2.70   Alternatively, a moisture meter can be used to measure the dampness in building materials. The moisture which is normally present in a building material such as brick is, in chemical terms, 'bound', ie chemically combined and permanently part of the structure of the material. It is not really water at all any more. What a moisture meter measures is 'free water', eg, water which is free or available to take part in new chemical reactions or support mould and fungi. The technical description of what moisture meters measure is water activity (Aw). Water activity is precisely analogous to relative humidity: if the relative humidity is 85% then the Aw will be 0.85, eg, the wood will rot because it is in equilibrium with a relative humidity of 85%, and therefore has an excess of moisture beyond the moisture content it would have in a normal atmosphere, expressed as a water activity of 0.85%. If the building material were wood, we would know that its moisture content was about 20% (see figure 38).

2.71   Water activity or Aw is measured in different ways, but the conductance type of moisture meter does it by inserting two electrodes into the building material to be tested. Building materials when dry do not conduct electricity but are 'insulators'. Free water, however, dissolves minute amounts of soluble material found in building materials. Many of the constituents of the material once dissolved are ionizable, that is, once dissolved each molecule splits into a particle with a positive charge and a particle with a negative charge. When the electrodes are inserted into the building material the positive particles travel to the negative electrode and the negative particles travel to the positive electrode. Once the particles reach the electrodes they give up their charges. The moisture meter measures the small amount of electric charge produced. In measuring that charge the moisture meter is in effect measuring the amount of free water, or water activity, in the given material. The dampness spectrum on a protimeter shows how the readings are made: see figure 39.

Why condensation is now so prevalent

Ventilation type problems

2.72   Condensation was rare before the second world war because in older houses water vapour used to escape out of the house before condensing.

2.73   When open fires were prevalent most of the moisture vapour in dwellings went up the chimney flue and was never seen again. Nowadays most old chimneys and their flues have been closed off. Modern houses do not generally contain open flues.

2.74   Windows and doors are now designed to better standards and are less draughty and better insulators for noise and heat. But they also permit less water vapour to escape the dwelling. Indeed, double glazed windows (unless properly ventilated) considerably increase the risk of condensation because (a) they are tight fitting and prevent escape of moisture vapour, and (b) the air space between glazing and

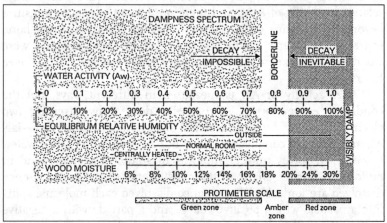

Figure 39: A 'dampness spectrum'. The relations between several different ways of expressing the significance of water in material are illustrated in the diagram which can be called a 'dampness spectrum'. It is drawn on a regular scale of relative humidity (RH) from zero to 100 per cent and exactly corresponding to this is a scale of 'water activity' (Aw) from zero to unity which is a very useful measure of wetness and dryness much used in industry. Wood moisture content (average soft wood) is shown and the correspondence between the moisture content and relative humidity is easily seen. The 'visibly damp' indication is very approximate.

the usual thermal breaks on the metal frames prevents condensation occurring on the window itself (single glazed windows tend to condense so much water vapour they act almost like dehumidifiers). Increased use of roof insulation can also prevent moisture escaping upwards.

2.75 Modern life creates more vapour: we bathe more, boil more kettles, cook more, wash and dry more clothes – such activities being carried out in the house itself rather than in a separate wash-house or isolated scullery.

2.76 It is more common for homes to be left unoccupied and unheated in the day, so that the outside walls lose heat, with the result that moisture producing activities tend to be carried out more intensively over shorter periods of time. See table 3 for a table demonstrating typical daily moisture emission in a five person household.

Table 3: Typical moisture production within a five person dwelling

Regular daily emission sources	Moisture emission per day/kg or litre
Five persons asleep for 8 h	1.5
Two persons active for 16 h	1.7
Cooking	3.0
Bathing, dish washing, etc	1.0
Total, regular sources	7.2
Additional sources	
Washing clothes	0.5
Drying clothes	5.0
Paraffin heater (if used)	1.7
Total, additional sources	7.2
Combined total	14.4

Note 1: The table does not include moisture introduced or removed by ventilation.
Note 2: The high moisture input from clothes drying shows the importance of designing for its control.
Note 3: The considerable emission during cooking, which is of short duration, indicates a need for local control.
Note 4: The water vapour emitted by flueless oil stoves significantly increases condensation risk. (Flueless gas appliances also produce a considerable quantity of water vapour.)

[Taken from BS 5250: 1975]
[Source: Oxley and Gobert *Dampness in Buildings*, see note 2]

2.77   Substantial rising or penetrating damp can significantly exacerbate condensation problems, particularly in warm rooms, by adding moisture to the air.

Insulation type problems

2.78   Another cause of condensation is cold bridging. Cold bridging occurs when structural elements of the building which are highly conductive of cold, eg, concrete lintels, or columns of ring beams which have not been thermally insulated, produce cold spots on otherwise relatively warm walls.

2.79   Similarly, the reinforced concrete panel systems used in prefabricated and industrial housing tend to produce cold walls and little circulation of air. Accordingly, insulation again is a prime consideration when remedying condensation.

Heating type problems

2.80   The blocking up of open fires and the failure to provide appropriate background heating systems in cheaper, new houses results in many dwellings which are simply not adequately heated. The result is that external walls are very much colder than the warm moist air produced by cooking, washing and general living.

Remedial measures

2.81   Improvements have to be made to ventilation, insulation or heating: or to a combination of these. Fungicidal washes can clean and sterilise affected walls, which can be redecorated with fungicidal paint but these are only adjuncts to long-term remedies and should rarely be used in isolation.

2.82   The document known as BS 5250: 1989 *Control of condensation in buildings,* published by the British Standards Institution, contains an authoritative standard code of practice for the control of condensation. Some of the most important statements are set out in appendix I.

Diagnosing condensation or rising damp

2.83   Rising damp is soil in solution. The solution contains chlorides and nitrates. If a surface scraping is taken from wallpaper or plaster, for example, simple laboratory analysis will prove whether or not the damp contains such salts and is therefore rising damp. Condensed water is pure and contains no salts.

2.84   Moulds and fungi need pure, for example condensed, water as food. Therefore they are associated with condensation damp. Soil salts usually kill mould and fungi, which accordingly are not usually seen where the damp is rising damp.

2.85   With rising damp, moisture moves up through the wall and from the inside of the wall towards its outer surfaces. A test with a deep wall electrode will show that the interior of the wall is wetter than the exterior. On the other hand, condensation starts on the outside of the wall and works inwards: and indeed will not penetrate any building material which is covered with a vapour check such as vinyl wallpaper or a few coats of gloss paint.

2.86   Rising damp tends to wet skirting boards and ultimately to rot them. Condensation itself rarely moistens wood, although the dripping of condensation water can have the same effect.

2.87   Both rising damp and condensation tend to affect the lower part of the wall: but rising damp rarely rises higher than about a metre above ground level (unless the walls contain a vapour check preventing evaporation and forcing the damp to rise further in order to evaporate).

2.88   The upper edge of rising damp demonstrates a sharp change from wet to dry. Areas of damp caused by condensation tend to be indistinct and merge into dry areas.

2.89   Condensation is associated with areas which are colder than the rest of the house, eg, behind paintings and furniture, or in cupboards placed next to external walls, in bedrooms and hallways, where there are cold bridging beams.

2.90   Condensation is an intermittent phenomenon and, when surveyed, the affected area may not actually be damp, even though it may remain visibly mouldy.

CHAPTER 3

Civil rights

For complete chapter contents, see overleaf

Introduction

3.1   Fraud apart, there is no law against letting a tumble-down house, and the tenant's remedy is upon his contract, if any.[1]

Although this broad declaration must now be read subject to much statutory and judicial development, the terms of the tenancy remain the foundation of most tenants' claims.

The contract of letting

3.2   A tenant occupies premises under the terms of a contract of letting. This contract may be made orally or in writing or may even be inferred from the circumstances (for example, where a person occupies premises and the landlord accepts money as rent[2]).

3.3   The terms of the contract or 'tenancy agreement' may be:

1) expressly incorporated into the agreement either orally or in writing; or

2) implied into the tenancy agreement either by statute or by the operation of common law.

Whether express or implied, these terms may impose an obligation on the landlord to carry out repairs, which s/he is then contractually bound to perform.

3.4   The terms of a tenancy can be varied by agreement. Secure tenancy agreements can be varied unilaterally by the landlord pursuant to Housing Act (HA) 1985 s102.[3] The adviser should therefore ascertain whether the original terms as to repair have been varied.

Express terms

3.5   If the tenancy agreement contains an express term imposing a repairing obligation on the landlord, the adviser should consider whether this covers the disrepair in question. This involves asking

---

1   *Robbins v Jones* (1863) 15 CB (NS) 221 at 240.

2   *Street v Mountford* [1985] AC 809; *AG Securities Limited v Vaughan* [1990] 1 AC 417; *Brikom Investments v Seaford* [1981] 1 WLR 863.

3   *Palmer v Sandwell MBC* (1987) 20 HLR 74; *R v Brent LBC ex p Blatt* (1991) 24 HLR 319.

(a) what activity has the landlord contracted to perform? (b) on which parts of the dwelling has the landlord contracted to perform this activity?

3.6   It is common for landlords to (a) contract to carry out repairs (but not to carry out improvements, to keep the premises in as good a state as when let, or to ensure that the dwelling remains suitable for human habitation); and (b) contract to repair only the structural or external parts of the dwelling (not the internal, non-structural parts such as internal doors, kitchen fittings, decorations and so forth).

3.7   The adviser must however carefully check whether the tenancy agreement contains repairing obligations which are more extensive. For example, in *Johnson v Sheffield CC*,[4] the tenancy agreement provided that the landlord would keep the dwelling 'fit to live in'. The landlord was therefore liable in civil proceedings for severe condensation and mould growth not involving structural or external disrepair. Other landlords may have contracted to keep parts of the interior in repair, or to keep fittings in repair and working order.

Meaning of 'repair' and 'disrepair'

3.8   Repair is the converse of disrepair. There must be disrepair before the landlord is liable to repair. Disrepair occurs when there is deterioration, ie, when part of the building is in a worse condition than it was at some earlier time.[5]

Inherent defects

3.9   It follows that the landlord is not liable under a repairing obligation simply because part of the dwelling was designed or constructed badly. If the dwelling has always had the defect in question there has been no deterioration. In *Stent v Monmouth DC*[6] the front door did not have weatherboarding and permitted rainwater to penetrate into the dwelling but the landlord was not at that point liable because the door had always been defective in that respect. In *Post Office Properties Ltd v Aquarius Properties Ltd*[7] a defective kicker joint

---

4   (1994) August *Legal Action* 16.

5   *Post Office v Aquarius Properties* [1987] 1 All ER 1055; *Quick v Taff-Ely BC* [1986] QB 809; *Anstruther-Gough-Calthorpe v McOscar* [1924] 1 KB 716.

6   (1987) 19 HLR 269.

7   [1987] 1 All ER 1055.

allowed ground water to penetrate laterally into a basement but the landlord was not at that point liable because the joint had always been defective in this way.

3.10   It would however be going much too far to say that landlords are never liable to put right building defects which are 'inherent', ie, which have been present since construction. In *Stent v Monmouth DC*[8] the rainwater penetration eventually caused the door itself to rot, ie, deteriorate. Because the landlord was obliged under the terms of the tenancy agreement to keep the door in repair it was required to repair the door. It was not relevant that the deterioration had been caused by an inherent defect. Further, the court ordered the landlord to repair the door in such a way that future rainwater penetration and future disrepair to the door would not occur: by installing a proper, weatherproof door. In effect, the court ordered the landlord to rectify an inherent defect in order to remedy current disrepair and prevent future disrepair.

3.11   If the inherent defect causes disrepair to other parts of the building for which the landlord is responsible under the terms of the tenancy agreement, the court will normally require the landlord to remedy that damage.[9] If it would be practical and sensible to remedy the underlying defect, to prevent it from causing the same disrepair over and over again, then the courts will order the landlord to remedy the inherent defect.[10] The only exception occurs when the work involved is disproportionately extensive and/or costly.

Disproportionately extensive or costly work

3.12   It is always a question of degree whether that which the landlord is being asked to do can properly be described as a repair, or whether on the contrary it would involve giving back to the landlord a wholly different thing from that which he demised.[11] Examples of work which has been held to be too extensive or costly to be a 'repair' are: the complete replacement of foundations;[12] the complete

8 (1987) 19 HLR 269.

9 *Staves and Staves v Leeds CC* (1991) 23 HLR 107.

10 *Ravenseft Properties v Davstone (Holdings) Ltd* [1980] QB 12; *Halliard Property Co Ltd v Nicholas Clarke Investments Ltd* [1984] 1 EGLR 45; *Quick v Taff-Ely BC* [1986] QB 809; *Elmcroft Developments Ltd v Tankersley-Sawyer* (1984) 15 HLR 63.

11 *Stent v Monmouth DC* (1987) 19 HLR 269.

12 *Lister v Lane* [1983] 2 QB 212.

replacement of cladding to high rise building;[13] and the replacement of whole of steel frame.[14] Whether or not the work required is too extensive or costly in any given case will depend on exactly what work is required, what it is likely to cost, how long it will prolong the life of the dwelling and what the terms of the tenancy agreement are.[15] Denning LJ has given guidance as to the test to be applied:

> If the work which is done is the provision of something new for the benefit of the occupier, that is, properly speaking an improvement; but if it is only the replacement of something already there which has become dilapidated or worn out, then, albeit that it is a replacement by its modern equivalent, it comes within the category of repairs not improvements.[16]

More recently, Sachs LJ has said that the correct approach is to

> ... look at the particular building, look at the state which it is in at the date of the lease, look at the precise terms of the lease, and then come to a conclusion whether, on a fair interpretation of those terms in relation to that state, the requisite work can fairly be called repair.[17]

The most recent guidance is in *McDougall v Easington DC*,[18] where Mustill LJ said:

> It is sufficient to say that in my opinion three different tests may be discerned, which may be applied separately or concurrently as the circumstances of the individual's case may demand, but all to be approached in the light of the nature and age of the premises, their condition when the tenant went into occupation, and the other express terms of the tenancy:
> (i)   whether the alternations went to the whole or substantially the whole of the structure or only to a subsidiary part;
> (ii) whether the effect of the alterations was to produce a building of a wholly different character than that which had been let;
> (iii) what was the cost of the works in relation to the previous value of the building, and what was their effect on the value and lifespan of the building.

13 *Holding & Management Ltd v Property Holding & Investment Trust Ltd* (1989) 21 HLR 596.

14 *Plough Investments Ltd v Manchester CC* [1989] 1 EGLR 244.

15 *Holding & Management Ltd v Property Holding & Investment Trust Ltd* (1989) 21 HLR 596.

16 *Morcom v Campbell-Johnson* [1956] 1 QB 106.

17 *Brew Bros Ltd v Snax* [1970] 1 QB 612.

18 (1989) 21 HLR 310.

Small defects

3.13   Conversely, small defects such as nail holes and minor cracking to the plaster or rendering are in many cases not considered to be sufficiently serious as to amount to disrepair.

3.14   The reason is that the courts have qualified the meaning of disrepair. It does not mean any degree of deterioration, but deterioration which as a matter of fact and degree is unacceptable after taking into account and making allowances for the age of the premises, their character, the local area and the type of tenants likely to want to rent them.[19]

Repair and decoration

3.15   An obligation to repair includes an obligation to carry out decoration required to preserve whatever is to be repaired.[20] It should also be noted that the requirement to 'repair' carries with it an obligation upon the landlord to make good or redecorate on completion of works.[21]

Prevention of future damage

3.16   An obligation to repair can include an obligation to prevent future damage.[22]

Patch repairs or complete renewal

3.17   The obligation to repair can sometimes require the landlord to completely renew or replace part of a dwelling as a way of carrying out a repair.

3.18   In *Elmcroft Developments Ltd v Tankersley-Sawyer*,[23] for example, the landlords conceded that their obligation to repair the structure required them to hack off and replace damp wall plaster but denied

---

19   *Anstruther-Gough-Calthorpe v McOscar* [1924] 1 KB 716; *Stanley v Towgood* (1836) 3 Bing NC 4; *Perry v Chotzner* (1893) TLR 477; *Plough Investments Ltd v Manchester CC* [1989] 1 EGLR 244.

20   *Irvine v Moran* [1991] 24 HLR 1.

21   *McGreal v Wake* (1984) 13 HLR 107; *Bradley v Chorley BC* (1985) 17 HLR 305.

22   *Holding & Management Ltd v Property Holding & Investment Trust Ltd* (1989) 21 HLR 596; *McDougall v Easington DC* (1989) 21 HLR 310.

23   (1984) 25 HLR 63; (1984) 270 EG 140.

that it required them to tackle the source of the dampness (rising damp) by installing a DPC. Ackner LJ said:

> The patching work would have to go on and on, because as the plaster absorbed (as it would) the rising damp, it would have to be renewed and the cost to the [landlords] in constantly being involved in this sort of work, one would have thought, would have outweighed easily the cost in doing the job properly. I have no hesitation in rejecting the submission that the appellant's obligation was repetitively to carry out futile work instead of doing the job properly once and for all.

3.19   The notion that patch repairing was sufficient to discharge the duty was similarly rejected in *Stent v Monmouth DC*.[24] In that case there had been a problem for over 30 years of rot to a wooden front door and frame. The landlords had repeatedly cut out and repaired parts of the door and frame and from time to time replaced the rotten wooden door with another wooden door which then rotted. The Court of Appeal had no hesitation in holding that on the facts the obligation to 'repair' was not discharged by these patch repairs. The council 'had the obligation to make good the design defect which caused the collection of water which occasioned the rotting'. This was achieved by installing a self-sealing aluminium door.

3.20   In summary, the test of whether patch repairs will suffice is whether tackling the root cause would be a 'mode of repair which a sensible person would have adopted; and the same reasoning applies if for the word "sensible" there is substituted some such word as "practicable" or "necessary"'.[25] The burden is on the tenant to lead the evidence which shows that further patch repairs will not suffice and that a more radical repair or replacement is necessary.[26]

Blocked conduits

3.21   Gutters and flues which are blocked are in disrepair.[27]

24 (1987) 19 HLR 269.
25 Per Stocker LJ in *Stent v Monmouth DC* (1987) 19 HLR 269, at 284–285.
26 *Murray v Birmingham CC* (1988) 20 HLR 39.
27 *Bishop v Consolidated London Properties Ltd* (1933) 102 LJKB 257; *Greg v Planque* [1936] 1 KB 669; *Passley v Wandsworth LBC* (1996) 30 HLR 165.

Remedy

3.22 The remedy for a breach of an express covenant is an action in contract for damages and specific performance of the covenant: see chapter 4. The tenant will be required to show that the landlord had notice of the defect: see below.

Common law terms and duties

3.23 At common law the landlord has no duty to repair or to ensure that the dwelling is habitable.[28] Neither is the landlord under a duty of care to take reasonable steps to ensure that any occupier of the premises let does not suffer personal injury or damage to his/her property as the result of defects to the premises.[29] That is the historic reason why the express terms of the contract are of such importance.

3.24 The common law does, however, imply some repairing obligations into tenancy agreements. Occasionally, common law duties, eg, in nuisance or negligence, apply to the landlord and tenant relationship.

Lettings of furnished dwellings

3.25 Where the landlord lets a furnished dwelling for immediate occupation it will be an implied term of the contract that the premises are fit for human habitation at the start of the tenancy.[30]

3.26 The term does not apply to lettings of unfurnished dwellings.[31] Furthermore, the obligation is strictly an initial one, ie, that the premises are fit when let.[32] However, the term will be broken if the dwelling is initially unfit but the lack of fitness becomes obvious only at a later stage of the tenancy.[33]

3.27 The courts have held that dwelling houses are unfit for human habitation at common law if they are infested by bugs,[34] have a

---

28 *Cavalier v Pope* [1906] AC 428; *Robbins v Jones* (1863) 15 CB(NS) 221; *Boldack v East Lindsey DC* (1998) 31 HLR 41.
29 *McNerny v Lambeth LBC* (1989) 21 HLR 188.
30 *Smith v Marrable* (1843) 11 M & W 5; *Hart v Windsor* (1844) 12 M & W 68.
31 *McNerny v Lambeth LBC* (1989) 21 HLR 188.
32 *Sarson v Roberts* [1895] 2 QB 395.
33 *Harrison v Malet* (1886) 3 TLR 58.
34 *Smith v Marrable* (1843) 11 M & W5.

defective drainage[35] and sewerage system,[36] or carry an infection,[37] or if there is a lack of safety,[38] or an insufficiency of water supply.[39] Note, however, that the obligation is confined to fitness for habitation and that the implied term does not require the landlord to ensure that the premises are in structural repair when let, eg, cracked ceiling plaster will not be covered.[40] Today, the courts may be willing to look at the statutory definition of unfitness; which is somewhat broader, see chapter 7, in considering whether premises are unfit at common law.

Dwelling-houses held under a licence

3.28   Where there is a licence and not a tenancy then a term may be implied requiring the licensor to take reasonable care to ensure that the condition of the dwelling does not cause personal injury to any of the occupiers or damage their property.[41]

Means of access and communal facilities

3.29   The landlord is impliedly obliged to take reasonable care to keep means of access and communal facilities (such as shared rubbish chutes, or lifts) in repair and proper working order.[42]

Ancillary property owned by landlord

3.30   The courts will generally imply a term imposing a duty on the landlord to take reasonable care to ensure that the condition of ancillary property retained in his/her ownership (for example, the roof, common hall, water tanks, heating plant or drains) does not

35   *Wilson v Finch-Hatton* (1887) 2 Ex D336.
36   *Harrison v Malet* (1886) 3 TLR 58.
37   *Bird v Greville* (1884) C & E 317; *Collins v Hopkins* [1923] 2 KB 617.
38   *Edwards v Etherington* (1825) Ry & M 268.
39   *Chester v Powell* (1885) 52 LT 722.
40   *Maclean v Currie* (1884) Cab & E1 361.
41   *Greene v Chelsea BC* [1954] 2 QB 127. See also *Smith v Nottinghamshire CC* (1981) *Times* 13 November; *Wettern Electric Ltd v Welsh Development Agency* [1983] 1 QB 796 and *Morris-Thomas v Petticoat Lane Rentals* [1986] 53 P&CR 238.
42   *Miller v Emcer Products* [1956] Ch 304; *Liverpool CC v Irwin* [1977] AC 239 and *King v South Northamptonshire DC* [1992] 1 EGLR 53; *cf Duke of Westminster v Guild* [1985] QB 688.

deteriorate so as to cause personal injury to tenants or damage to
their property.[43]

3.31   The landlord will also be liable for any common law nuisance
arising on ancillary property owned by him/her and impinging upon
the tenant's dwelling-house.[44]

Correlative obligations

3.32   If the tenancy agreement requires the tenant to pay for certain works
or services it will usually be implied that the landlord will actually
perform those works or services.[45]

3.33   Other tenant's obligations can also result in implied terms
binding on the landlord. In *Barrett v Lounova (1982) Ltd*,[46] the tenant
was contractually bound to decorate internally. There were no
express repairing obligations binding on the landlord and Landlord
and Tenant Act 1985 s11 (see paras 3.57–3.82) did not apply as the
tenancy began before 24 October 1961. The dwelling was in a poor
state of repair, suffering from severe rainwater penetration as the
result of roof defects. The Court of Appeal held that it was an implied
term of the agreement that the landlord would keep the structure
and exterior of the dwelling in repair:

> It is obvious, as shown by this case itself, that sooner or later the
> covenant imposed on the tenant in respect of the inside can no
> longer be complied with unless the outside has been kept in
> repair ... In my view it is therefore necessary, as a matter of
> business efficacy, to make this agreement workable, that an
> obligation to keep the outside in repair must be imposed on
> someone.

3.34   The extent to which correlative obligations such as this may be
imposed remains unclear.[47]

---

43 *Dunster v Hollis*, [1918] 2 KB 795; *Cockburn v Smith* [1924] 2 KB 119; *Gordon v
    Selico Co* [1985] 2 EGLR 79, and *Duke of Westminster v Guild* [1985] QB 688.

44 *Sampson v Hodson-Pressinger* [1981] 3 All ER 710 (noise) cf *Baxter v Camden
    LBC* [1999] 2 WLR 49; *Gordon v Selico Co Ltd* [1986] 1 EGLR 71 (water
    penetration) and *Sharpe v Manchester CC* (1977) 5 HLR 71 (cockroach
    infestation).

45 *Edmonton Corporation v Knowles* [1962] 60 LGR 125.

46 [1990] 1 QB 348.

47 *Demetriou v Poolaction Ltd* [1991] 25 EG 113; *Adami v Lincoln Grange
    Management Ltd* (1997) 30 HLR 982.

Quiet enjoyment/derogation from grant

3.35   A landlord either expressly or by necessary implication contracts to give the tenant 'quiet enjoyment' of the premises for the duration of the letting. This may be breached in circumstances of disrepair, for example by a landlord failing to keep watertight the building containing the tenant's flat, thereby allowing the flat to be penetrated by rainwater or dampness,[48] or carrying out work on other parts of the building causing noise and nuisance to the tenants.[49]

3.36   The covenant does not create new repairing obligations, but if the landlord fails to perform his/her obligations or carries out those obligations so as to interfere unreasonably with the tenant's occupation there will be a breach of the covenant of quiet enjoyment in addition to other causes of action.[50]

3.37   A landlord shall not 'derogate from his grant' of a tenancy to the tenant. This implied term may be breached in relation to disrepair if a landlord allows premises retained in his/her ownership or occupation to be in such a state as to interfere with the tenant's tenancy. However, the act or omission of the landlord must be shown to stem from the landlord's own deliberate or voluntary behaviour in failing to carry out a repairing obligation or in performing some other activity which makes it impossible for the tenant to inhabit the dwelling house.[51] The principle of derogation from grant cannot be used to create new repairing obligations.[52]

The landlord builder

3.38   If the landlord designed or built the dwelling s/he owes subsequent tenants the same duty of care in negligence as is owed by builders who do not subsequently become the landlord of the dwelling, that is, a duty to take reasonable care to ensure that the dwelling does not contain any latent defects which cause personal injury or property damage.[53]

---

48   *Booth v Thomas* [1926] Ch 397; *Gordon v Selico Co Ltd* (1986) 18 HLR 219.
49   *Mira v Aylmer Square Investments Ltd* (1989) 21 HLR 284; *Sampson v Wilson* (1994) 26 HLR 486.
50   *Duke of Westminster v Guild* [1985] 1 QB 688; *Southwark LBC v Mills* [1998] 3 WLR 49 (subject to appeal to the House of Lords).
51   *Chevron Petroleum (UK) Ltd v Post Office* (1987) SLT 588.
52   *Duke of Westminster v Guild* [1985] 1 QB 688 and *Hafton Properties v Camp* [1994] 1 EGLR 67.
53   *Rimmer v Liverpool CC* [1985] QB 1; *Murphy v Brentwood DC* [1991] AC 398; *Target v Torfaen BC* (1991) 24 HLR 164.

3.39   Defective Premises Act 1972 (DPA) s1 imposes a duty on all
those, including landlords, who undertake work for or in connection
with the provision of a dwelling to do the work in a professional or
workmanlike manner and use proper materials, so as to ensure that
the dwelling is fit for human habitation when completed. See
appendix A for the full text of DPA s1.

3.40   The duty is owed by builders as well as architects, surveyors,
specialist sub-contractors and so forth. It is also owed by the
employer, eg, the local authority or property development company
which engages the builder to do the work: DPA s1(4). The duty is
owed to the person for whom the dwelling is initially provided and
to all persons subsequently acquiring a legal or equitable interest in
it. The duty is not extinguished by any disposal of the reversion: DPA
s3. The duty is owed in respect of work commenced after 1 January
1974.

3.41   Being tortious, the duty will extend only to personal injury or
property damage, not to pure economic loss or defects to the
dwelling itself which might make occupation uncomfortable or
distressing.[54] The duty applies to omissions.[55] The dwelling must be
unfit and not merely defective.[56]

3.42   The scope of DPA s1 is restricted by DPA s2 which excludes all
dwellings covered by the NHBC scheme (which covers nearly all new
private sector development). DPA s1 is accordingly likely to apply
only to new public sector building and both public and private sector
conversions or alterations.

3.43   The cause of action is treated as accruing when the work (or any
post-completion remedial work) is completed.[57] The limitation
period will probably be six years by virtue of Limitation Act 1980 (LA)
s2, since liability appears to be strict. It is however arguable that
liability is conditional on negligence being proven, in which case LA
s14(A) will extend the limitation period to three years from date of
knowledge if later than the accrual of the cause of action, subject to
a 15-year long-stop. If the claim includes a claim for personal
injuries, LA s11 will apply (limitation period of three years from
accrual of cause of action or date of knowledge if later).

---

54 *Murphy v Brentwood DC* [1991] AC 398; *D&F Estates v Church Commissioners*
    [1989] AC 177 and *Department of Environment v Thomas Bates & Son* [1990] 2
    All ER 908.
55 *Andrews v Schooling* [1991] 1 WLR 783.
56 *Thompson v Clive Alexander* (1992) 59 BLR 77.
57 *Alexander v Mercouris* [1979] 3 All ER 305.

3.44   The landlord who carries out work after the tenancy begins will probably be held to owe his/her tenant the same duty of care that any contractor would owe the occupier, that is a duty to take reasonable care to ensure that defective workmanship or materials do not cause personal injury or property damage.[58]

Statutory implied terms for the benefit of tenants

3.45   As seen above, the basic rule at common law is that the landlord is not liable for housing defects except in so far as provided in the tenancy agreement. The common law exceptions to this rule, as set out above, are piecemeal and limited in scope. As a result, parliament legislated to imply limited and basic repairing obligations into certain types of tenancy.

Landlord and Tenant Act 1985 s8

3.46   The Landlord and Tenant Act 1985 (LTA 1985) s8 implies into lettings at a low rent, for example, certain periodic tenancies, two separate contractual terms which are absolute and non-excludable:

1) that the premises are fit for human habitation on the date of letting; and
2) that the premises will be kept fit for habitation, by the landlord, throughout the duration of the tenancy.

See appendix D for the full text of s8.

3.47   Both terms apply to lettings of whole houses or parts of houses LTA 1985 s8(6). The apparently wide scope of s8 is, however, limited by the narrow range of lettings to which it applies. In order to have the benefit of these implied terms the annual rent[59] (irrespective of who pays the rates[60]) must be less than the maximum amounts shown in table 4.

---

58 *Ball v London CC* [1949] 2 KB 159 and *Billings (AC) & Sons v Riden* [1957] 3 All ER 1.
59 *Whitcombe v Pollock* [1956] 106 LJ 554; cf *Kirkpatrick v Watson* [1943] Ir Jur Rep 4.
60 *Rousou v Photi* [1940] 2 KB 379.

Table 4: Maximum rents of lettings to which LTA 1985 s8 applies

Date of letting	*Maximum rent*
Before 31 July 1923	£40 London; £26 in boroughs or districts with over 5,000 people; £16 elsewhere
On or after 31 July 1923 and before 6 July 1957	£40 in London; £26 elsewhere
On or after 6 July 1957 and before 1 April 1965	£80 in London; £52 elsewhere
On or after 1 April 1965	£80 in inner London; £52 in outer London and elsewhere

3.48 If the letting was originally at a rent not greater than the maximum figure shown above, the tenant has the benefit of the implied terms. The current rent is irrelevant. As will be apparent, very few periodic tenancies remain which can benefit from s8. The failure to uprate the rent levels to give protection to more recent tenants has attracted judicial comment in the Court of Appeal.[61] The government has declined to increase the rent levels, as in its view the s8 provisions are 'effectively out of date', having been overtaken by the more modern provisions of s11.[62] A Department of the Environment LTA 1985 consultation paper[63] invited comment on the continuing usefulness of s8. The Law Commission has reported[64] that, subject to certain exceptions, legislation should impose a term in the case of leases of dwellings for less than seven years that the landlord will keep the dwelling fit for human habitation, applying the criteria contained in Housing Act 1985 s604 (see para 7.7). The Law Commission's proposals have yet to be acted on.

3.49 Section 8 is not applicable to a letting for a fixed term of three years or more where it is expressly agreed that the tenant will put the premises into a condition reasonably fit for habitation (s8(5)). If the letting contains no such term, the benefit of s8 extends to any long lease which fulfills the low rent condition, in addition to periodic tenancies.

61 *Quick v Taff-Ely BC* [1985] 3 All ER 321.
62 Lord Skelmersdale, HL Debs col 370, 22 October 1986.
63 *Repairing obligations under the Landlord and Tenant Act 1985* June 1989.
64 Law Com 238.

3.50   The section gives the landlord an express power to enter and inspect premises after giving the tenant or occupier 24 hours' notice in writing of his/her intention to do so (s8(2)).

3.51   In determining whether a house is fit for human habitation, regard is to be had to its condition in respect of: repair, stability, freedom from damp, internal arrangement, natural lighting, ventilation, water supply, drainage/sanitary conveniences, facilities for the preparation and cooking of food, and facilities for the disposal of waste water (not the new 'unfitness' standard described in chapter 7). The house is deemed to be unfit for human habitation if, and only if, it is so far defective in one or more of these respects that it is not reasonably suitable for occupation in that condition (LTA 1985 s10).

3.52   Breaches of the terms implied by s8 have been successfully established in a wide range of cases, for example, a small house in which the sole window in a main room could not be safely opened,[65] premises where plaster had fallen from the ceiling,[66] the complete collapse of a ceiling,[67] and accommodation in which a sanitary convenience was defective and serious dampness had accrued from defective guttering.[68]

3.53   It should be noted that liability arises only in relation to the defects within the premises let to the tenant, so that for example defective common staircases[69] and incursions of vermin from elsewhere,[70] will be outside the scope of the terms implied by s8.

3.54   A 'rule of thumb' guide to the standards required by s8 was set out by Atkin LJ in 1926:

> If the state of repair of a house is such that by ordinary use damage may naturally be caused to the occupier, either in respect of personal injury to life or limb or injury to health, then the house is not in all respects reasonably fit for human habitation.[71]

3.55   The courts have, however, developed a serious limitation to the usefulness of s8 by confining its application to premises which can be made fit by the landlord at reasonable expense.[72] This controversial decision rests on a concession made in argument and

65   *Summers v Salford Corporation* [1943] AC 283.
66   *Walker v Hobbs & Co* (1889) 23 QBD 458.
67   *Fisher v Walters* [1926] 2 KB 315.
68   *Horrex v Pidwell* [1958] CLY 1461.
69   *Dunster v Hollis* [1918] 2 KB 795.
70   *Stanton v Southwick* [1920] 2 KB 642.
71   *Morgan v Liverpool Corporation* [1927] 2 KB 131.
72   *Buswell v Goodwin* [1971] 1 WLR 92.

has no foundation within s8 itself but it has stood unchallenged for over two decades.

3.56   Advisers already using s8 should note the exemption of lettings of temporary accommodation owned by local authorities in clearance areas or as individual unfit properties, which is now to be found in HA 1985 s302.

Landlord and Tenant Act 1985 s11

3.57   LTA 1985 s11 implies into tenancy agreements an obligation on landlords to effect basic repairs which is both absolute and non-excludable. (Section 11 replaced HA 1961 s32. For the full text of LTA 1985 ss11–17 see appendix D.)

3.58   The obligation is as follows (as amended by HA 1988 in respect of tenancies entered into on or after 15 January 1989):

11(1) In a lease to which this section applies ... there is implied a covenant by the lessor –
  (a) to keep in repair the structure and exterior of the dwelling-house (including drains, gutters and external pipes),
  (b) to keep in repair and proper working order the installations in the dwelling-house for the supply of water, gas and electricity and for sanitation (including basins, sinks, baths and sanitary conveniences but not other fixtures, fittings and appliances for making use of the supply of water, gas or electricity), and
  (c) to keep in repair and proper working order the installations in the dwelling-house for space heating and heating water.

(1A) If a lease to which this section applies is a lease of a dwelling-house which forms part only of a building, then subject to subsection (1B), the covenant implied by sub-section (1) shall have effect as if –
  (a) the reference in paragraph (a) of that subsection to the dwelling-house included a reference to any part of the building in which the lessor has an estate or interest; and
  (b) any references in paragraphs (b) and (c) of that subsection to an installation in the dwelling-house included a reference to an installation which, directly or indirectly, serves the dwelling-house and which either –
    (i) forms part of any part of a building in which the lessor has an estate or interest;
    (ii) is owned by the lessor or under his control.

(1B) Nothing in subsection (1A) shall be construed as requiring the lessor to carry out any works or repairs unless the disrepair (or failure to maintain in working order) is such as to affect the lessee's enjoyment of the dwelling-house or of any common parts, as defined in section 60(1) of the Landlord and Tenant Act 1987, which the lessee, as such, is entitled to use.

3.59   The landlord cannot exclude the obligation imposed by s11 by the use of express contractual terms. Any term purporting to exclude liability (s12(1)(a)) or transfer it to the tenant (s11(4)) is void.[73]

3.60   The landlord or the landlord's agent is given a statutory right to enter premises for the purpose of viewing the condition and state of repair on giving the tenant 24 hours' notice in writing: s11(6).

Interpreting s11

3.61   Owing to the breadth of the implied terms contained in s11, the component parts have been subject to close scrutiny.

3.62   **'keep in repair'** The covenant to keep in repair is a continuing obligation to keep up the standard of repair in the dwelling throughout the duration of the tenancy. Moreover, it also requires the landlord to put the premises into repair if they were not in good repair at the outset of the tenancy.[74]

3.63   For the scope of works covered by the term 'repair' see paragraphs 3.8 to 3.21 above.

3.64   **'the structure and exterior'** For s11(1)(a) or s 11(1A)(a) to apply it must be shown that there is some part of the structure or exterior which is in a state of disrepair and therefore requires 'repair', ie 'the covenant will only come into operation where there has been damage to the structure and exterior which requires to be made good'.[75] Evidence of damage to decorations, clothing, bedding, curtains etc is all to no avail unless some part of the structure or exterior can be shown to require repair.

3.65   The structure is less than the whole dwelling but more than just the load bearing elements. It is usually taken to refer to:

> those elements of the overall dwelling house which give it its essential appearance, stability and shape. The expression does not extend to the many and various ways in which the dwelling house will be fitted out, equipped, decorated and generally made to be habitable ... in order to be part of the structure of the dwelling house a particular element must be a material or significant element in the overall construction.[76]

73 *Irvine v Moran* (1991) 24 HLR 1.
74 *Proudfoot v Hart* (1890) 25 QBD 42.
75 *Quick v Taff-Ely BC* [1986] QB 809; [1985] 2 All ER 321.
76 *Irvine v Moran* (1991) 24 HLR 1. See also *Pearlman v Governors of Harrow School* [1979] QB 56.

3.66 It is the opinion of the Law Commission that internal plaster should be treated as part of the structure for the purposes of LTA 1985 s11 (Law Com 238 at 69) and there are a number of cases in which concessions have been made to that effect or the court has assumed that plaster was part of the structure.[77] The only binding authority directly on the point however is that plaster is not part of the structure for the purposes of LTA 1985 s11.[78]

3.67 The exterior is the outside or external part of the dwelling-house. Liability under the covenant extends to all outside parts of the demised dwelling.

3.68 The interpretation of the words 'structure' and 'exterior' may be illustrated as follows:

1) a partition wall between the dwelling and another house or flat is part of the structure or exterior;[79]

2) in relation to a house, the path and steps which are the immediate and ordinary means of access are within 'exterior'[80] but the paving of the backyard is not;[81]

3) the roof[82] (if any) is part of the structure of a house as is any skylight it contains (see below for roofs of flats);[83]

4) the walls are part of the structure, together with any cement rendering;[84]

5) external joinery will usually be part of the structure, and failure to paint it so as to protect it from rot will be a failure to repair;[85]

6) windows will be part of the structure if they are a substantial and integral part of the wall.[86] On the other hand, the ordinary windows in a house or flat are part of the exterior of the dwelling.[87]

---

77 *Quick v Taff-Ely BC* [1986] QB 809; *Staves v Leeds CC* (1991) 23 HLR 107; *Palmer v Sandwell MBC* (1978) 20 HLR 74.

78 *Irvine v Moran* (1991) 24 HLR 1, cf the county court case (decided by Sedley LJ as he now is) *Hussein v Mehlman* [1992] 2 EGLR 87.

79 *Green v Eales* (1841) 2 QB 225.

80 *Brown v Liverpool Corporation* [1969] 3 All ER 1345.

81 *Hopwood v Cannock Chase DC* [1975] 1 WLR 373.

82 *Commissioner of Customs & Excise v Sutton Housing Trust* [1983] STC 399; [1984] STC 352.

83 *Taylor v Webb* [1937] 2 KB 283.

84 *Granada Theatres v Freehold Investment (Leytonstone) Ltd* [1955] 1 WLR 70.

85 *Crawford v Newton* (1886) 2 TLR 877.

86 *Boswell v Crucible Steel Co of America* [1925] 1 KB 119; *Holiday Fellowship v Hereford* [1959] 1 WLR 211.

87 *Ball v Plummer* (1879) *Times* 17 June.

3.69   Where the dwelling house is a flat, 'structure and exterior' has been held to extend to: the outside wall(s) of the flat, the outside of the inner party wall of the flat, the outer sides of the horizontal divisions between the flat and the flats above and below, and ceilings and walls of the flat.[88] Where the ceiling and roof of a top-floor flat form an inseparable structural unit, the roof will be within the structure or exterior of the flat. In the case of other flats, whether a common roof is within the covenant will be a question of fact according to the particular circumstances.[89]

3.70   **'the dwelling-house'** Means the building or part of a building which is let to the tenant wholly or mainly as a private residence: LTA 1985 s16(b).

3.71   The 'structure and exterior' with which s11(1)(a) is concerned, then, is the 'structure and exterior of the dwelling-house' let to the tenant, ie, the tenant's own house or flat. Usually, therefore, the provision could not be used by the tenants of the lower of two flats to get the roof over the upper flat repaired, even if the disrepair was causing damage to the lower flat, since on any view the roof would not be part of the structure or exterior of their own flat. The position is now different for tenancies commencing on or after 15 January 1989. In these more recent tenancies, the term implied by s11 is extended to include not only the structure and exterior of the demised premises but also the remaining parts of the building in which the landlord retains an estate or interest (s11(1A)), providing the disrepair is in fact 'affecting the lessee's enjoyment' of his/her own dwelling-house or the common parts.

3.72   **'keep in ... proper working order'** These words necessarily presuppose that at the start of the tenancy the relevant installations were in proper working order, so that, if by reason of disrepair or design fault an installation has never been in proper working order, a landlord with knowledge of the defect will be in continuing breach of the implied term.[90]

---

88 *Campden Hill Towers v Gardner* [1977] QB 823.
89 *Douglas-Scott v Scorgie* [1984] 1 All ER 1086; *Rapid Results College v Angell* (1986) 277 EG 856; *Straudley Investments v Barpress Ltd* (1987) 282 EG 1124; *Hatfield v Moss* (1988) 40 EG 112.
90 *Liverpool CC v Irwin* [1977] AC 239.

3.73 **'the installations in the dwelling-house'** The landlord is obliged to keep in repair and in working order the installations specifically mentioned in s11(1)(b) and (c). The provision also extends to all other installations for the supply of water/gas/electricity/ sanitation/heating/hot water. Thus water or gas pipes, electrical wiring, water tanks,[91] boilers, radiators and other space heating installations such as vents for underfloor heating will be within the repairing obligation.

3.74 It should be noted that the installations must normally be <u>in</u> the tenant's dwelling. However, some tenants (and particularly those in high rise flats) experience major problems as the result of the failure of installations serving blocks or estates but sited outside their homes, for example central heating boilers. The courts had declined to extend the benefit of the repairing covenant to such tenants. In the *Campden Hill Towers* case[92] Megaw LJ said:

> ... the installations in the physical confines of the flat must be kept in repair and capable, so far as their own structural and mechanical condition is concerned, of working properly. But no more than that.

3.75 The requirement that the defective installations must be <u>in</u> the dwelling has been lifted for more recent tenants. If the tenancy was granted on or after 15 January 1989 the obligation to repair and keep in proper working order is extended to any installation which (a) either directly or indirectly serves the dwelling and (b) is either owned by or under the control of the landlord or is part of a building owned by the landlord (s11(1A)), providing that the defect is in fact 'affecting the lessee's enjoyment' of his/her own dwelling house or of any common parts. This provision effectively overcomes the *Campden Hill Towers* case and gives these more recent tenants rights to require repairs to, for example, the communal heating boiler, the pump in the district heating system, the water tank on the roof of the tower block etc.

3.76 Apart from the installations specifically mentioned in the section, the repairing obligation does not extend to fixtures, fittings, and appliances for making use of water/gas/electricity and sanitation (s11(1)(b)).

3.77 In *Wycombe Area Health Authority v Barnet*[93] the Court of Appeal held that the obligations in s11(1)(b) and (c) to keep the installations

91 *Sheldon v West Bromwich Corporation* (1973) 13 HLR 23.
92 *Campden Hill Towers v Gardner* [1977] QB 823.
93 (1982) 5 HLR 84.

in the dwelling in proper working order did not impose a duty on the landlord to lag water tanks and pipes so as to avoid damage in exceptionally severe cold weather. The court did indicate, however, that a landlord would be liable if the pipes were prone to burst within the normal temperature range, and that since there was in any event no liability on the part of the tenant, any prudent landlord would insulate the pipes to avoid damage being caused to his/her reversion.

3.78   Even though the landlord will be presumed to know of disrepair affecting the parts of the property s/he retains, it is not certain that the courts will presume that the landlord knows of the effect on individual tenants. It is therefore advisable to ensure that the landlord has actual knowledge (preferably by notice) of both the defect and effect before proceeding for breach of s11(1A). It is a defence for the landlord to show in such proceedings that, despite using reasonable endeavours, s/he was unable to obtain the right to carry out the works to the particular part of the building concerned (eg, where the disrepair emanates from a flat of which the landlord is the freeholder but where the leaseholder is exercising the right to refuse access): s11(3A).

Standard for s11 repairs

3.79   The repairing obligations implied into tenancy agreements by s11 are subject to the important qualification that in determining the standard of repair to be required, regard is to be had to the age, character, and prospective life of the dwelling house and the locality in which it is situated (s11(3)). Reference to age, character and locality does no more than re-state the position which applies in any event at common law: see paragraph 3.14. At least where disrepair is materially affecting the tenant's comfortable enjoyment of the dwelling house its 'prospective life' is only relevant if demolition is imminent.[94] On the other hand, the fact that complete reconstruction is envisaged is a good reason for patch repairing the roof in the meantime even though ordinarily replacement would have been required.[95]

3.80   The standard of repair is no higher for a public sector landlord than it is in the private sector.[96]

---

94 *Newham LBC v Patel* (1978) 13 HLR 77; cf *McClean v Liverpool CC* (1987) 20 HLR 25.
95 *Dame Margaret Hungerford Charity Trustees v Beazeley* [1993] 2 EGLR 143.
96 *Wainwright v Leeds CC* (1984) 270 EG 1289.

Limitations of s11

3.81 The operation of s11 is circumscribed in a number of ways:

1) The provision applies only to tenancies commencing on or after HA 1961 s32, ie, 24 October 1961 (s13(1)).

2) It applies only to periodic tenancies and fixed-term leases of less than seven years. Lettings for longer periods are also covered where the landlord has an option to end the letting within seven years of commencement. But, by s13(2), lettings for less than seven years may fall outside s11 if the tenant can renew for a further term, making more than seven years in total. These provisions, together with those relating to renewed lettings, are somewhat complex and an adviser should pay close attention to the terms of ss12–15 before giving a conclusive opinion.

3) It does not apply to certain agricultural tenancies within the Agricultural Holdings Act 1948.

4) No liability can be imposed upon the landlord for breach of s11 until s/he has knowledge of the defects within the dwelling complained of and fails to effect repairs within a reasonable period of time (see below).

5) Except in the case of post-15 January 1989 tenancies, it does not extend to the common parts of the building, nor to parts of the premises retained by the landlord but which the tenant is permitted to use.

6) It does not extend to any item which the tenant is entitled to remove from the premises, nor does it relieve the tenant of the obligation to use the premises in a tenant-like manner, nor does it require the landlord to reinstate premises destroyed by act of God or inevitable accident etc (s11(2)).

7) It does not assist most business tenants (s32(2)).

8) It does not apply to certain properties let to local authorities and other public bodies (s14(4)).

9) It does not bind the Crown. It cannot therefore be relied on by the tenants of most government departments and agencies.

Important note for pre-1961 tenancies

3.82 Tenancies which would otherwise be outside s11 because they started before 24 October 1961 may nevertheless gain the benefit of the provision. For example, where a fair rent has been registered on the basis that the tenancy is subject to s11 and the landlord has accepted rent following that registration, the landlord will be bound by the repairing obligation.[97] Alternatively, a pre-1961 tenant may be able to show that s/he is covered by s11 because the earlier tenancy has been determined and replaced by one commencing after 1961. This will be the case for all local authority tenants because in the 1960s and 1970s council rent increases were achieved by a process of notice to quit and re-grant.[98] Pre-1961 tenants who are not covered by s11 may be able to rely on one of the implied terms described above.

Implied terms for the benefit of the landlord

The notice requirement

3.83　It is an implied term of all tenancy agreements which impose an obligation on the landlord to repair property rented out to a tenant that the landlord is not liable to carry out any repair unless and until s/he has been put on notice of the need for repair and has failed to carry out the repair within a reasonable period of time thereafter.[99] Although a 'common law' rule, it has been consistently held to apply where the repairing obligations are imposed by statute, eg, by LTA 1985 ss8 and 11.[100]

3.84　The landlord's knowledge of the defect must be proved even if the disrepair is latent, so that a tenant injured by the collapse of a ceiling which no one could have expected to be liable to fall, cannot recover damages from the landlord for breach of repairing obligations.[101]

3.85　It should be noted that it is the 'knowledge' of the landlord which is important. Usually this knowledge will arise from notice of disrepair given by the tenant. However, a landlord may be imputed with knowledge if the disrepair is brought to the attention of his/her workmen,[102] rent-collector or any other person (for example a resident caretaker) employed by the landlord and having express or implicit authority to receive complaints of disrepair on behalf of the landlord.

97　*Brikom Investments v Seaford* [1981] 1 WLR 863; *Johnstone v Charlton and Taylor* (1998) May *Legal Action* 21.

98　*Benson v Liverpool CC* (1989) March *Legal Action* 22.

99　*Makin v Watkinson* (1870) LR 6 Ex 25; *O'Brien v Robinson* [1973] AC 912; *Morris v Liverpool CC* (1987) 20 HLR 498.

100　Ibid.

101　*O'Brien v Robinson* [1973] AC 912.

102　*Sheldon v West Bromwich Corporation* (1973) 13 HLR 23.

3.86   The route by which the landlord receives knowledge of the disrepair is not significant, except that it has been suggested that the informant must be a 'responsible source'.[103] In *Dinefwr BC v Jones*,[104] the council was held to have actual notice of the disrepair seen at the property by an environmental health officer (EHO) even though the EHO was not from the housing department and was inspecting the property after complaints relating to cleanliness rather than disrepair. The EHO however was not treated as having implied knowledge on behalf of the council about defects other than those obviously visible (ie, not those which could have been discovered only on a thorough inspection). The *Jones* case also indicates that notice will be established where the landlord receives information about the defects in a property from an independent valuer (in that case from the valuation officer following a right-to-buy application). This was confirmed in *Hall v Howard*,[105] where the landlord received an offer of purchase from a private tenant accompanied by a surveyor's valuation report, listing (and costing) repairs needed. Receipt of the report was sufficient to fix the landlord with knowledge of the defects. Similarly, service by a local authority of some form of statutory repair notice is sufficient to establish knowledge on the part of the landlord and thus, liability.[106]

3.87   The information received by the landlord must be sufficient to put a reasonable person on enquiry as to whether works of repair are needed.[107] It will therefore be necessary for the tenant to make the landlord aware of the disrepair in question to be tackled, but the notice given need not particularise the degree or extent of the disrepair nor the remedial works required.[108] Where the tenant informs the landlord that s/he will be preparing a detailed list of items of disrepair and estimates for the works required, notice is not actually given until the list and estimates are served.[109] Save in the case of an inspection by an EHO or specialised tradesperson (see above), a tenant cannot necessarily rely on the proposition that

---

103 *Dinefwr BC v Jones* (1987) 19 HLR 445.
104 Ibid.
105 (1988) 20 HLR 566.
106 *McGreal v Wake* (1984) 13 HLR 107.
107 *O'Brien v Robinson* [1973] AC 912; *Sheldon v West Bromwich Corporation* (1973) 13 HLR 23; *British Telecommunications plc v Sun Life Assurance Society plc* [1995] 3 WLR 622.
108 *Griffen v Pillet* [1926] 1 KB 117.
109 *Al Hassani v Merrigan* (1988) 20 HLR 238.

because the premises were inspected by the landlord or landlord's agent, it follows that the landlord knew of the defects in the premises. It is for the tenant to show that the landlord or unqualified agent saw the defect.[110]

3.88   It is important to recognise that the implied term as to notice applies only to parts of a building which have been rented to the tenant. It does not apply to parts which have been retained in the ownership of the landlord. When there is disrepair to part of a building which (a) the landlord is contractually obliged to repair and (b) the landlord continues to own, then the landlord is liable immediately disrepair occurs whether or not s/he knows or could have known of the need for repairs.[111] Failure to complain in this type of case can in some circumstances be taken into account, however, as a failure to mitigate.[112]

3.89   Where no notice or knowledge can be established, DPA s4 may be helpful (see paragraphs 3.97–3.110). DPA s4 places landlords under a duty to take such care as is reasonable in all the circumstances to prevent personal injury to or damage to the property of all persons (including tenants) who might reasonably be expected to be affected by a failure on the part of the landlords to perform an obligation to repair or maintain the premises. DPA s4(2) provides that 'The said duty is owed if the landlord knows (whether as a result of being notified by the tenant or otherwise) or if he ought in all the circumstances to have known of the relevant defect'. The courts expect landlords to take positive steps to inspect for latent defects when the landlord is aware that a problem might exist, but not to inspect for unforeseeable dangers.[113] The landlord who fails to carry out repairs when he ought to have discovered the need for repair will be liable by virtue of DPA s4(2) even though he did not actually know of the disrepair, providing personal injury or property damage results.

3.90   In the case of gas installations the Gas Safety (Installation and Use) Regulations 1998[114] require landlords to inspect gas appliances

110   *Hughes v Liverpool CC* (1988) *Times* 30 March.
111   *Melles & Co v Holme* [1918] 2 KB 100; *Bishop v Consolidated London Properties Ltd* (1933) 102 LJKB 257; *Loria v Hammer* [1989] 2 EGLR 249; *British Telecommunications plc v Sun Life Assurance Society plc* [1995] 3 WLR 622; *Passley v Wandsworth LBC* (1996) 30 HLR 165.
112   *Minchburn v Peck* [1988] 1 EGLR 53.
113   *Kathleen Clarke v Taff-Ely BC* (1980) 10 HLR 44; *Preston BC v Fairclough* (1982) 8 HLR 75.
114   SI No 2451, see appendix F.

annually. Failure to inspect js likely to result in the court holding that a landlord 'ought to have known' of any defect causing personal injury or property damage for the purposes of DPA s4.

Access for the landlord

3.91 For the purposes of carrying out repairs or inspecting for repairs, landlords have rights of access at either common law or under statute.

Access at common law

3.92 The landlord who is subject to an express or implied duty to keep premises 'in repair' will have the right at common law to enter to carry out those works (but no others):

> I have construed that covenant to mean that he shall put them into good condition if necessary and it is my judgment that the covenant carries with it an implied licence to the lessor to enter upon premises of the lessee and to occupy them for a reasonable time to do what he has covenanted to do.[115]

The right to enter is subject to an obligation to give the tenant reasonable notice and must be exercised reasonably, although the tenant is not normally entitled to a copy of the specification of works.[116]

3.93 The landlord has the right to vacant possession in order to carry out repairs only when vacant possession is essential.[117]

3.94 In the case of periodic tenancies of dwelling-houses the landlord has an implied right to enter to repair defects which might cause personal injury.[118]

Access by statute

3.95 Most statutory repairing obligations carry within them express rights of entry for the landlord (see particularly the discussions of the LTA 1985 ss8 and 11 at paragraphs 3.46–3.82).

3.96 In addition, Rent Act 1977 s148 gives landlords an express right to enter for the purpose of carrying out repairs in the case of

---

115 *Saner v Bilton* (1878) 7 Ch D 815.
116 *Granada Theatres v Freehold Investment (Leytonstone) Ltd* [1959] Ch 592.
117 *McGreal v Wake* (1984) 13 HLR 134.
118 *McAuley v Bristol CC* [1992] QB 134.

protected or statutory tenancies. HA 1988 s16 gives the same right of access to the landlord of an assured tenant.

Statutory duties of care

Defective Premises Act 1972 s4

3.97   DPA s4 serves two distinct purposes which can be broadly summarised as follows: (a) in some circumstances it makes landlords liable for personal injury or property damage caused by disrepair even though the landlord did not have notice of the need for repair; and (b) in some circumstances it creates new obligations to prevent the condition of the dwelling causing personal injury or property damage. The full text of DPA s4 is set out at appendix A.

The basic duty

3.98   The DPA applies as from 1 January 1974 whether or not the tenancy began before that date: DPA s4(3). It applies to all of the land let not just the dwelling-house, eg, it applied to the patio at the rear of the dwelling-house in *Smith v Bradford MBC*.[119] It does not apply to land which is not let, eg, the common parts.

3.99   The duty is owed to 'all persons who might reasonably[120] be expected to be affected by defects in the state of the premises': that includes the tenant as well as the tenant's family members and visitors.[121]

3.100   The duty is a duty to 'take such care as is reasonable in all the circumstances' to see that the persons owed the duty are reasonably safe from personal injury or property damage caused by a 'relevant defect' of which the landlord knew or 'ought ... to have known'.

3.101   A 'relevant defect' is a defect which the landlord is either (a) bound to repair or maintain under the express or implied terms of the contract including LTA 1985 s11 or (b) bound to repair or maintain under DPA s4(4) (see below).

3.102   The landlord can not exclude or modify the duty: DPA s6(3).

---

119   (1982) P & CR 171.
120   *McDonagh v Kent AHA* (1984) 134 NLJ 567.
121   *Smith v Bradford MBC* see note 119.

The duty where the landlord ought to have known of the defect

3.103 Section 4(1), (2) and (3) creates no new repairing or maintaining obligations[122] but they do superimpose a duty to take care upon existing repairing obligations in such a way that the landlord can be liable for personal injury or damage to property when he 'ought ... to have known' of the likelihood of such injury or damage.

3.104 DPA s4(2) provides that:

> The said duty is owed if the landlord knows (whether as a result of being notified by the tenant or otherwise) or if he ought in all the circumstances to have known of the relevant defect.

3.105 The courts expect landlords to take positive steps to inspect for latent defects when the landlord is aware that a problem might exist, but not to inspect for unforeseeable dangers.[123]

3.106 Cases in which, on special facts, the landlord ought to have known of the risk of personal injury are: *Clarke v Taff-Ely BC*[124] (rotten floorboards) and *Smith v Bradford MBC*[125] (defective patio).

3.107 Cases in which, on the facts, personal injury was not reasonably foreseeable are: *Ryan v Camden LBC*[126] (unusually hot water pipes in flat), *Issit v Tower Hamlets LBC*[127] (defective catch to window), *Marsden v Havering LBC*[128] (door knocker falling off).

New duties

3.108 DPA s4(4) provides as follows:

> (4) Where premises are let under a tenancy which expressly or impliedly gives the landlord the right to enter the premises to carry out any description of maintenance or repairs of the premises, then, as from the time when he first is, or by notice, or otherwise can put himself, in a position to exercise the right and for so long as he is or can put himself in that position, he shall be treated for the purposes of subsections (1) to (3) above (but for not other purposes) as if he were under an obligation to the tenant for that description of maintenance or repair of the

122 *McNerny v Lambeth LBC* (1998) 21 HLR 188; *Boldack v East Lindsey DC* (1988) 31 HLR 41.
123 *Morley v Knowsley BC* (1998) May *Legal Action* 22.
124 (1980) 10 HLR 44.
125 (1982) P&CR 171.
126 (1982) 8 HLR 75.
127 (1983) 6 December, unreported, CA, Ub Transcript 1115.
128 (1983) 11 March, unreported, CA.

premises; but the landlord shall not owe the tenancy any duty by virtue of this subsection in respect of any defect in the state of the premises arising from, or continuing because of, a failure to carry out an obligation expressly imposed on the tenant by the tenancy.

3.109   This section has the result that where a landlord is expressly or impliedly permitted to enter the premises let to carry out a work of repair or maintenance s/he comes under a positive duty to ensure that his/her failure to carry out that type of repair or maintenance does not cause personal injury or property damage.

3.110   The scope of DPA s4(4) is potentially wide because the Court of Appeal held in *McAuley v Bristol CC*[129] that the landlord of a council house let on a periodic tenancy had an implied right to enter the dwelling house to carry out any works of repair which were necessary to remove a 'significant risk' of personal injury to the tenant, his/her family or visitors. By virtue of DPA s4(4) that right was converted into a duty, breach of which resulted in the landlord being held liable for personal injury to one of the tenants.

Occupiers' Liability Act 1957

3.111   Under the Occupiers' Liability Act 1957 (OLA) the 'occupier' owes a 'common duty of care' to all visitors except to the extent that he lawfully restricts liability. The 'common duty of care' is a duty to take such care as is reasonable in all the circumstances to ensure that the visitor will be reasonably safe when on the premises for the purpose for which invited: OLA s2(2) (1).

3.112   The landlord remains the occupier, for the purposes of the OLA of the common parts.[130]

---

129   (1991) 23 HLR 586.
130   *Wheat v E Lacon Ltd* [1966] AC 552; *Dear v Newham LBC* (1987) 19 HLR 391; *Jordan v Achara* (1988) 20 HLR 607; *Irving v London CC* (1965) 109 SJ 157; *Shortall v GLC* (1969) 210 EG 25.

CHAPTER 4

Civil remedies

For complete chapter contents, see overleaf

Introduction

4.1   Notwithstanding tenants' detailed legal rights under contract, in tort and by statute to secure repairs from landlords, large numbers of tenanted dwellings remain in exceptionally poor repair. For some occupiers, the only prospect of decent accommodation lies with use of the procedures available under the Environmental Protection Act 1990 (EPA) (see chapter 6) but for many others a range of civil remedies should be considered.

4.2   For the purposes of each of the avenues of redress discussed below three matters have been assumed:

1) The landlord is liable to undertake the appropriate type of repair.
2) The tenant has given notice of the existence of disrepair and the need for remedial works.
3) The landlord has failed to carry out the repairs within a reasonable period.

4.3   In such circumstances, the tenant has accrued a right to both financial compensation (damages) and an order requiring the landlord to discharge his/her obligations.

Preparing for legal action

4.4   Much preparatory work in disrepair cases may be undertaken using the Legal Advice and Assistance ('green form' or 'claim 10') scheme. This can cover initial research on the law, drafting of letters and notices, and advice to the tenant. Where necessary, extensions to the green form should be sought for preliminary reports from experts as to the cause of the disrepair and the scale of remedial works required. An initial medical report may also assist in identifying any past ill health or continuing health risk to the tenant caused by disrepair.

4.5   The Legal Aid Board has published guidelines as to what the green form should cover. The current guidelines are at appendix H but practitioners must be alert to possible changes.

4.6   The identity of an elusive landlord should be established as early as possible, using the Landlord and Tenant Act (LTA) 1985 s1, which requires the person to whom rent is paid to disclose the name and address of the landlord upon request or by obtaining office copy entries of the registered title from Her Majesty's Land Registry.

Direct action

Using rent to pay for repairs

4.7   Where landlords are in breach of their repairing obligations, tenants have a right at common law to (a) undertake the necessary repairs (either personally or by engaging a contractor) and (b) recover the costs of the repairs by deduction from future rent.

4.8   The origins of this right are to be found in precedents of considerable antiquity but its availability to tenants was reaffirmed in *Lee-Parker v Izzet*, decided in 1971.[1] A modern example is *Loria v Hammer*.[2]

4.9   The tenant has to establish that the repairs which s/he has paid for do fall within the landlord's repairing obligations as a matter of law, that the landlord was in default and that the tenant's expenditure was proper, eg, not extravagant. Accordingly, before exercising the right to use rent to pay for repairs in default, the prudent tenant will:

1) Inform the landlord of the intention to take this form of action if repairs are not carried out.
2) Allow a further reasonable period for the landlord to comply with the repairing obligations.
3) Obtain ideally three estimates for the cost of carrying out the remedial works and submit copies of these to the landlord with a 'final warning'.
4) Engage the contractor at the lowest tender and have the work carried out.
5) Submit a copy of the contractor's invoice to the landlord and request reimbursement.
6) If no money is forthcoming, recoup the cost by deduction from future rent.

4.10   If the matter is one of urgency then the above procedure will clearly have to be modified and the prudent tenant in such circumstances will wish to act in accordance with expert advice.

4.11   This right, which is wholly separate from the right to 'set-off against rent' (see below), will provide a tenant who is sued for unpaid rent, with a complete defence to the landlord's action to the extent of the money spent.

1   [1971] 1 WLR 1688.
2   [1989] 2 EGLR 249.

4.12   The right to recoup from rent (whether from future rent or arrears) is confined to the actual costs and expenses of remedial works. It includes VAT and where reasonable the cost of professional supervision and so forth; it does not allow for the recovery of monies for damage suffered as a result of disrepair. Also, given the length of time necessary to accumulate sufficient withheld rent to pay a contractor, the right is of only limited use to the poorer tenant suffering extensive disrepair.

4.13   The landlord can probably exclude this right by an express term in the tenancy agreement.[3] Such an exclusion clause is not apparently caught by the Unfair Contract Terms Act 1977.[4]

4.14   Where the tenant is receiving housing benefit, it will be advisable to inform the paying authority that this procedure is being used in order to avert the possibility of payment being withheld.[5]

4.15   Since 1 January 1986, secure tenants of local authorities and most housing associations have had access to a statutory scheme for the use of rent to pay for repairs. The scheme, which is in almost all respects more limited than the common law right, is to be found in HA 1985 s96 and is detailed in regulations.[6] Despite extensive literature on the potential application of s96, the statutory procedure is hardly ever used in practice. Its scope is limited to repair work costing up to £250 (in the opinion of the local authority), it requires the service of a multiplicity of forms and counter-notices, it involves the tenant discharging what are the landlord's responsibilities and provides for minimal amounts of compensation, worked out in accordance with complicated formulae. It is in all respects a less satisfactory remedy for tenants than the use of legal proceedings.

Withholding rent and rent strikes

4.16   The tenant has no right in law simply to withhold rent in protest at the landlord's failure to carry out repairs. In addition to inviting possession proceedings against themselves, tenants organising rent strikes may be guilty of unlawful interference with the contracts (ie,

3   *Connaught Restaurants Ltd v Indoor Leisure Ltd* [1993] 2 EGLR 108.
4   *Electricity Supply Nominees Ltd v I A F Group Ltd* [1993] 2 EGLR 95.
5   Housing Benefit (General) Regulations 1987 reg 95.
6   Secure Tenants of Local Housing Authorities (Right to Repair) Regulations 1994 SI No 133; Secure Tenants of Local Housing Authorities (Right to Repair) (Amendment) Regulations 1994 SI No 844 and Secure Tenants of Local Housing Authorities (Right to Repair) (Amendment) Regulations 1997 SI No 73.

tenancy agreements) of other tenants.[7] On the other hand, withholding rent can in some cases be a powerful weapon in persuading a recalcitrant landlord to carry out repairs. It can also result in the tenant being more likely to recoup some legal costs and damages when the landlord is thought to be impecunious.

4.17   Tenants are permitted to withhold service charges and service elements in rent, but only where the landlord is seeking to impose the expenses of remedial works on the tenant which by statute are the liability of the landlord, for example where the service charge includes an amount for LTA 1985 s11 repairs.[8]

4.18   In other circumstances advisers assisting those who have withheld rent should consider:

1) applying the accrued arrears towards the payment of a contractor to carry out works in default (see above); and/or

2) defending possession proceedings based on arrears of rent, on the ground that it would not be reasonable, given the circumstances of the tenant's action, to order possession; and/or

3) a defence of set-off (see below) and counterclaim to the landlord's proceedings for arrears of rent (this can include maintaining that rent arrears which are prima facie sufficiently high to establish a mandatory rent arrears ground – HA 1988 Sch 2 ground 8 – against an assured tenant are in fact subject to a set-off in equity).

4.19   The dangers of advising the tenant to withhold some or all payment to the landlord, on the basis that substantial balancing sums will be recoverable by a claim or counterclaim for damages are well illustrated by *Al Hassani v Merrigan*.[9] There, the counterclaim for damages was dismissed and the judge found it reasonable in the circumstances to grant a possession order for arrears of rent (see paragraphs 4.24–4.27 for further consideration of this type of case).

4.20   Where the tenant's claim would be dealt with under the small claims track, or where for other reasons the tenant is unlikely to obtain legal aid, withholding an appropriate amount of rent may be the tenant's only way of obtaining compensation. Where the tenant has no security of tenure, on the other hand, the decision as to what – if any – remedy to invoke is fraught with difficulty. This applies to most private sector tenancies entered into after 28 February 1997,

7   *Camden Nominees v Forcey* [1940] Ch 352.
8   *Campden Hill Towers v Gardner* [1977] 1 All ER 739.
9   (1988) 20 HLR 238.

the date that HA 1996 ss97–100 came into force making all new assured tenancies shortholds.

Set-off against rent

4.21   In many cases the tenant will seek to recover out of rent a sum equal to the damages and expenses to which s/he would be entitled as a result of the landlord's default (for example, the costs of future repairs not yet carried out but for which the tenant is saving up out of rent, the cost of redecoration or of replacement of damaged furniture) and also unliquidated claims, such as claims for compensation for distress or inconvenience caused by past disrepair which the landlord failed to remedy in breach of contract or tortiously.

4.22   In practice, such considerations usually arise where the landlord has commenced possession proceedings based on rent arrears, after the tenant has withheld the rent because of the landlord's failure to repair, or spent it on new furnishings etc.

4.23   The authorities were reviewed in *British Anzani (Felixstowe) Ltd v International Marine Management (UK) Ltd*,[10] where it was held that unliquidated claims in damages for breach of a contractual repairing obligation could be set-off against arrears of rent. Where the value of the damages to which the tenant is entitled matches or exceeds the rent arrears, the tenant is entitled to an equitable set-off amounting to a complete defence to the landlord's action.[11] The equitable set-off has the advantage over the common law right to recoup from rent discussed above, in that it goes beyond costs of remedial works to include ordinary damages to which the tenant is entitled by reason of the landlord's default.

4.24   The set-off should formally be raised in the defence to the landlord's claim, and will usually be accompanied by a counterclaim setting out the breach complained of and particularising the damage suffered.

4.25   It must be shown that the set-off arises under the tenancy and that it would be inequitable to allow the landlord to recover the amount claimed, in the face of the tenant's counterclaim; such conditions will usually be automatically satisfied in the case of damages resulting from the landlord's breach of a contractual repairing obligation.

10   [1980] QB 637; [1979] 2 All ER 1063.
11   *Melville v Grape Lodge Developments* [1978] 39 P&CR 179.

4.26   Levels of damages (see below) awarded in disrepair cases have, until recently, been notoriously low, but nowadays the tenant should be able to establish a set-off sufficient to amount to a complete defence to the landlord's claim in most disrepair cases. Where the tenant's set-off exceeds the rent arrears it would be 'plainly wrong' for the court to make a possession order. In such a case the tenant ought to be awarded the costs of both claim and set-off.[12] If at trial the tenant's bona fide set-off does not exceed the rent arrears claim a possession order will not be made if the tenant is able to make up the difference out of money put to one side or, unless the tenant has a poor rent payment history, make reasonable proposals for the repayment.[13] The judge did find it reasonable to make a possession order in *Al Hassani v Merrigan*,[14] but in that case the rent withheld was grossly disproportionate to the disrepair and the tenant was not able to pay the balance immediately or to make acceptable proposals. It should be noted that county court judges can not be expected to adjourn possession claims simply because the tenant makes general allegations about disrepair.[15]

4.27   Set-off is an equitable defence, therefore the usual time limits of the Limitation Act 1980 (LA) do not apply.[16]

Reduction in rent

4.28   A tenant paying a registered fair rent may apply to the rent officer for a reduction in the registered rent at any time if there has been a change 'in the condition of the dwelling' since the last assessment.[17] However, this right should be exercised only in a clear-cut case of substantial deterioration in condition, since such application allows a complete reassessment of the rent, not confined to the simple question of deterioration.[18]

4.29   In respect of council and housing association tenancies it is worth consulting the tenancy agreement to identify any available

---

12 *Televantos v McCulloch* (1990) 23 HLR 412; *British Anzani (Felixstowe) Ltd v International Marine Management (UK) Ltd* [1980] QB 637.

13 *Haringey LBC v Stewart* (1991) 23 HLR 557.

14 (1987) 20 HLR 238.

15 *Asco Developments Ltd v Gordon* (1978) 248 EG 683; *Agyeman v Boadi* [1996] EGCS 14.

16 LA s36(2); *Filross Securities Ltd v Midgeley* (1999) 31 HLR 465.

17 Rent Act 1977 s67(3)(a).

18 *London Housing and Commercial Properties v Cowan* [1977] QB 148.

'unusable rooms allowances' and rent reductions for lift or service failures. The express terms of secure tenancies are available for inspection from the appropriate local authority or housing association on request (HA 1985 s104).

Appointing a receiver or manager

4.30   Not infrequently, the reason for extensive disrepair will be persistent landlord neglect. In the private sector, situations commonly arise in which the present landlords are not known or cannot be traced and urgent repairs await attention. In such cases the common-sense solution is to have one person officially appointed to collect all the rents and then pay for the repairs from the money received. In legal terms, this process is known as the appointment of a receiver, and the High Court has power to implement the procedure in any case where it appears just and convenient to do so (Supreme Court Act 1981 s37(1)). The power has been exercised to the benefit of a group of private tenants where no repairs had been carried out and no rent collected for two or three years.[19] By virtue of s38 of the County Courts Act 1984 the county court has similar power to appoint receivers. The remedy of appointment of a receiver is not available to tenants of local authorities.[20] On the remuneration of the receiver, see *Evans v Clayhope Properties*.[21] In an appropriate case, a receiver may be appointed even if the landlord is known but s/he resists the application unsuccessfully.[22] Once the appointment has been made, the ability of the landlord to frustrate the order by selling the property can be avoided by registering the appointment as a caution or land charge.

4.31   For situations where there are two or more flats in a single block, the procedure for appointment of a manager is now codified in LTA 1987 Pt II as amended by HA 1996 ss85 and 86. This requires, in the usual case, that a preliminary 'warning notice' be served on the landlord or agent (s22). If this does not produce the required effect, the leasehold valuation tribunal may, on application, appoint a manager to take over and run the block (s24). The appointment can be registered against the title of the property or as a land charge to

---

19 *Hart v Emelkirk Ltd* [1983] 3 All ER 15; *Daiches v Bluelake Investments Ltd* (1985) 17 HLR 543; *Clayhope Properties v Evans* (1986) 18 HLR 361.
20 *Parker v Camden LBC* [1985] 2 All ER 141.
21 (1988) 20 HLR 176.
22 *Blawdziewcz v Diodon Establishment* (1988) 35 EG 83.

prevent the landlord avoiding the consequences of the order by selling-on (s24(8)).

4.32   Grounds for appointing a manager are that the landlord is in breach of his/her obligations, has delivered or is likely to deliver unreasonable service charge bills or has failed to comply with a code of practice issued under Leasehold Reform, Housing and Urban Development Act 1993 s87. In each case it must be 'just and convenient' for the appointment to be made. If the appointment of a manager would not be sufficient the court can go further and, on the tenants' application, make an order for the compulsory acquisition of the landlord's interest.[23]

Court proceedings

Limitation periods

4.33   The tenant contemplating use of legal action as a remedy for disrepair should ensure that proceedings are issued before the expiry of any relevant limitation period. The basic period is three years in personal injury claims and six years in other cases, running from when the cause of action accrues: LA ss5 and 11. Thus, the key date is that on which the cause of action accrues, which may vary, as follows.

4.34   **Claims in contract** The six-year cause of action accrues at the date of breach of the obligation to repair: LA s5. Where notice/delay is not a precondition for establishing a breach of contract the cause of action occurs as soon as there is disrepair. Where premises are in disrepair but notice is required before there is a breach of contract, breach occurs when the landlord has had notice of the disrepair and failed to remedy it within a reasonable period. If repairs are not carried out thereafter the cause of action is a continuing one but proceedings should be commenced within six years of the initial breach in order to ensure that the tenant is compensated for the whole period. If there has been a continuing breach of obligation for more than six years, the consideration of damages will be limited to the circumstances over the six years preceding the launch of proceedings.[24]

4.35   **Claims in negligence** The limitation period runs from the date of damage even though the landlord's negligent act (eg, letting the

---

23 *Gray v Standard Home and Counties Properties* [1994] 1 EGLR 119.
24 *Sturolson & Co v Mauroux* (1988) 20 HLR 332.

premises in dangerous condition) may have occurred many years earlier.[25] The limitation period for property damage caused by negligence is six years from the date of damage, or, if later, three years from the date of knowledge, subject to an overall long-stop of 15 years: LA ss2 and 14A.

4.36 **Personal injury actions** Where the action includes a claim 'in respect of personal injuries to the plaintiff or any other person' then the limitation period is three years from the date of injury or, if later, from knowledge, providing the personal injury was not caused deliberately but arose as the result of 'negligence, nuisance or breach of duty': LA s11. Criteria for determining when the plaintiff acquired sufficient 'knowledge' for the purposes of the Limitation Acts are set out in LA 1980 s14. There is, furthermore, an overriding discretion to extend the limitation period in personal injuries actions if it would be 'equitable' to do so having regard to the criteria set out in LA 1980 s33.

4.37 Many disrepair claims will contain elements of both personal injury (eg, ill health caused by dampness) as well as damage to property (damage to personal possessions etc). Even if only one of the plaintiffs is claiming damages in respect of personal injuries the whole action is caught by LA 1980 s11 and the three-year limitation period, but the court does have a discretion under LA 1980 s33 to extend that time limit, eg, to six years, either in respect of the action as a whole or, more realistically, in respect of the claims not involving personal injury.

Interim injunctions

4.38 In cases of really severe disrepair causing serious and continuing interference with the tenant's enjoyment of the property, an application for an interim injunction should be considered. An application for an interim injunction will ensure that the matter is brought before a judge in a matter of hours or days rather than months.

4.39 In order to ensure a successful application, a tenant should:

1) Unless the circumstances are extraordinary, make an application on notice to the landlord in accordance with the rules of court: Civil Procedure Rules (CPR) Parts 25 and 32 and Practice Directions (PDs) 25 and 32.

25 *Rimmer v Liverpool CC* [1984] 1 All ER 93.

2) Ensure that the evidence in support of the application notice includes the surveyor's or other experts' report. It is usual to ask the surveyor to attend the hearing so that the landlord's surveyor and the tenant's surveyor can assist the court by agreeing substantial parts of the evidence and drawing up a schedule of work at court. Although this seems to be general practice (certainly in London) it would be desirable if experts could at least narrow the surveying issues before the hearing.

3) Prepare a detailed draft order containing a realistic schedule of works of repair, a time scale and any subsidiary orders required.

4.40   The making of interim injunctions is essentially discretionary. Different factors may come into play in different cases, persuading a particular judge to grant or not grant the injunction. Nonetheless, general guidelines exist to assist the practitioner.

4.41   The basic guidelines for making all types of interlocutory relief are contained in *American Cyanamid Co v Ethicon Ltd*,[26] namely:

1) That there is a serious question to be tried (ie, a more than frivolous assertion that the landlord is in breach of a repairing obligation) and that either:

2) The balance of convenience (ie, comparative hardship should the order be wrongly granted or withheld) favours the tenant; or, alternatively,

3) Damages alone would not be adequate compensation (eg, because of a risk to health) or because the landlord would not be in a financial position to meet the damages to which the tenant would be entitled if the works were delayed; and

4) The tenant will be in a position to meet the costs incurred by the landlord in performing works required by the injunction, if it is later found that the order should not have been made.

4.42   An interim injunction requiring repairs to be carried out is a mandatory injunction. Mandatory injunctions in general are relatively onerous and involve the defendant in financial outlay – sometimes substantial. It is therefore usual for the courts to vary the *Cyanamid* guidelines when the tenant seeks a mandatory injunction in order to make the test harder for the tenant to satisfy. The leading authority in the disrepair context is *Parker v Camden LBC*.[27] In that case the Court of Appeal held that:

---

26 [1975] AC 396.
27 [1986] Ch 162.

1) The work required must be agreed between the parties or it must be clear what needs to be done (eg, there should not be a substantial dispute between the surveyors).
2) The circumstances must be exceptional, eg, there is an immediate risk to health and safety.

4.43   These are the authoritative guidelines, but they are only guidelines and different approaches can be taken where the facts and the interests of justice require. In many London county courts, for example, interim repairing injunctions are made routinely against London local authority landlords simply because in practice they rarely substantially dispute the need for the works sought to be carried out in any event, whatever the position ultimately is as to liability.[28]

4.44   In an interesting county court decision it was held that since one of the defects was within the *Parker v Camden LBC* criteria it would be invidious on the facts of that particular case not to order the landlord to carry out all of the works sought.[29]

4.45   It is also necessary for the draft order sought to be sufficiently detailed so that the landlord is made aware of exactly what remedial works have to be undertaken and by what date.[30]

4.46   If the application fails, the evidence put before the court suggesting risk to health or safety should at least found a direction for an early trial.

Specific performance

4.47   If the matter proceeds to trial with the dwelling-house remaining in disrepair, the tenant will first seek an order that the landlord carries out repairs. The order sought is of 'specific performance' of the express or implied terms of the tenancy agreement. For non-contractual repairing obligations the equivalent remedy will be a mandatory injunction. The duties imposed by Defective Premises Act 1972 s4 (see paragraphs 3.97–3.110) can also be enforced by injunction.[31]

4.48   Specific performance is a remedy available at common law[32] and by statute. The LTA 1985 s17 (see appendix D for text) provides:

28 See also *Office Overload v Gunn* [1977] FSR 39.
29 *Sheriden v Broadbridge* September 1995 *Legal Action* 16.
30 *Morris v Redland Bricks Ltd* [1970] AC 652, HL.
31 *Barrett v Lounova (1982) Ltd* [1990] QB 348.
32 *Jeune v Queens Cross Properties* [1974] Ch 97.

(1) In proceedings in which a tenant of a dwelling alleges a breach on the part of his landlord of a repairing covenant relating to any part of the premises in which the dwelling is comprised, the court may order specific performance of the covenant, whether or not the breach relates to a part of the premises let to the tenant and notwithstanding any equitable rule restricting the scope of the remedy, whether on the basis of a lack of mutuality or otherwise.

4.49　Several points arise:

1) For the purposes of s17, 'tenant' includes sub-tenants and statutory tenants (s17(2)).
2) Specific performance of obligations to maintain common parts can be ordered on the application of a single tenant.
3) It does not matter that the landlord may not be able to obtain specific performance of the tenant's obligations under the tenancy agreement (eg, that the contract does not contain mutually enforceable obligations).

4.50　The terms of an order of specific performance must be sufficiently clear for the defendant to know what must be done and by what time.[33]

4.51　It is (almost invariably) no defence for the landlord on an application for specific performance to raise the prospect of severe financial hardship as a result of the terms of the order.[34] If severe hardship going beyond financial difficulties would be likely to occur as a result of the order, and if the circumstances were 'extraordinary and persuasive' the court might not make the order.[35] That is how-ever unlikely ever to happen in a disrepair case.

Remedies for breach of an injunction or of an order for specific performance

4.52　Failure to perform works directed in an order of specific performance or by injunction is punishable by committal for contempt. If the landlord is a local authority or company, the initial injunction should be addressed personally to, or at least served on, an officer who can be committed for breach.[36] Proceedings to commit the landlord for contempt of court may provide an incentive

---

33　*Morris v Redland Bricks Ltd* [1970] AC 652.
34　*Francis v Cowliffe Ltd* (1976) 33 P&CR 368.
35　*Patel v Ali* [1984] Ch 283.
36　*R v Wandsworth County Court ex p Munn* (1994) 26 HLR 697.

for the landlord to do the repairs ordered. In *Bloombury v Lambeth LBC*[37] the local authority was fined £500 and ordered to pay costs on an indemnity basis after failing to comply with an interlocutory injunction.

4.53 As an alternative to the use of committal, RSC Order 45 r8 allows a court faced with breach of an order of specific performance to direct that the necessary action be taken by or on behalf of the plaintiff at the expense of the landlord defendant. The court may select and direct the individual or company which is to carry out the action required. The availability of Order 45 r8 (which is also applicable in the county court: County Courts Act 1984 s76) for repairs cases was confirmed in *Parker v Camden LBC*.[38] For a discussion of the procedure and subsequent cases in which it has been applied, see November 1989 *Legal Action* 19. The court may enforce the financial element of the Order 45 r8 procedure, either by directing a payment into court[39] or by an order of sequestration on the landlord's assets.[40] Such orders were made in *Hooker-Goodman v Cohane*[41] and *Cook v Horford Investment Ltd and Taj*.[42] The new Civil Procedure Rules preserve Order 45 r8.

Declarations

4.54 The county court has power to grant a declaration relating to rights over real property, even if it is the only relief sought (County Courts Act 1984 s38). Where a mandatory order is unlikely to be effective (either because it cannot be served or will not be complied with) and the tenant would prefer to carry out the works and recoup the costs from future rent, or simply where an injunction is refused, the grant of a declaration may be a useful alternative remedy. In a disrepair case the court should be invited to make a declaration providing that:

1) the landlord is in breach of a specified repairing obligation;
2) the tenant is entitled to do the necessary works of repair in default; and
3) the works may be financed by deduction from future rent; and
4) the tenant's compliance with stages (1) and (2) will not constitute

37 June 1995 *Legal Action* 23.
38 [1986] Ch 162.
39 *Barrett v Lounova (1982) Ltd* [1990] QB 348.
40 *Rose v Laskington Ltd* (1989) 139 NLJ 973.
41 September 1992 *Legal Action* 22.
42 September 1993 *Legal Action* 16.

breach by the tenant of any express terms of the tenancy agreement which prima facie prohibit such action.

4.55   Armed with such a declaration the tenant may in fact secure the performance of the works earlier than the date on which they would have been carried out by the landlord under a mandatory order. The court now has power to make interim declarations: CPR r25.1.

Damages

4.56   Where a tenant has succeeded in establishing breach of the landlord's repairing obligation or has shown that the landlord's negligence or breach of statutory duty has caused personal injury or damage to property, the appropriate remedy in most cases will be an award of substantial damages, ie, financial recompense. If the case has not yet come to trial but the claim for damages is clear, application may usefully be made for an interim payment under CPR r25.6.

4.57   Obviously, the landlord remains liable to compensate the tenant for damage suffered as the result of failure to repair in breach of the express or implied terms of the contract, or in breach of statutory duty, even though the landlord carries out repairs before judgment, or before the issue of proceedings: the tenant has an accrued cause of action as soon as the landlord's breach causes loss.

The purpose of damages

4.58   The fundamental principle in awarding damages in disrepair cases is that the amount allowed should as far as possible place the tenant in the position he would have occupied if he 'had not suffered the wrong complained of, be that wrong a tort or breach of contract'.[43]

4.59   It should be noted that the purpose of awarding damages will go no further than that. The object is not 'to punish the landlord but, so far as money can, to restore the tenant to the position he would have been in had there been no breach'.[44]

The approach to assessment

4.60   Bearing in mind the principle to be applied, the courts have offered only broad guidance on the assessment of damages, although the

---

43 *Dodd Properties (Kent) Ltd v Canterbury CC* [1980] 1 All ER 928.
44 *Calabar Properties Ltd v Stitcher* [1983] 3 All ER 759.

usual rule that both general and special damages will be available is applied in disrepair cases. An assessment cannot be achieved by applying one set of rules to all cases regardless of the circumstances of the particular case. The facts of each case must be looked at to see what damage the tenant has suffered and how they may be fairly compensated by a monetary award:

> So, the true measure of damages for persons ... occupying land, whether in tort or contract, depends on the position of the tenants and all the circumstances in which they have suffered loss and damage.[45]

General damages

4.61　In disrepair cases the award of general damages is assessed as the loss of value of the tenancy to the tenant.[46] The calculation of this 'loss of value' will vary according to the circumstances of the case.

Tenants who remain in occupation

4.62　If the tenant remains in residence during a period of disrepair, the general damages will be a substantial award for all the inconvenience, disappointment, discomfort, ill health and mental distress as well as loss of enjoyment suffered by the tenant.[47] The period attracting compensation runs from the date of landlord's knowledge of the disrepair in cases where knowledge is a precondition of liability up to the date of assessment or the carrying out of the repairs.

4.63　Sometimes it is appropriate to use the rent as an indicator of the level of general damages.[48] The court looks at the rent due under the letting and then awards as damages a 'discount' representing the extent of loss of use and enjoyment suffered by the tenant. For example, if the rent were £30 per week and the disrepair affected one-third of the property, a weekly figure of £10 might provide a starting point.

4.64　This rather artificial approach can result in compensation being underestimated, particularly where the rent is relatively low in

---

45　*Dodd Properties (Kent) Ltd. v Canterbury CC* [1980] 1 All ER 928.
46　*Hewitt v Rowlands* (1924) 93 LJKB 729.
47　*Calabar Properties Ltd v Stitcher* [1983] 3 All ER 759.
48　*McCoy v Clarke* (1982) 13 HLR 89.

comparison to the hardship suffered.[49] However, nowadays the courts are concerned to ensure that tenants affected by disrepair are awarded 'substantial sums' as opposed to 'nominal or cosmetic amounts'.[50] There are, accordingly, a number of cases in which, on the facts, it has been held erroneous in law to restrict the award of general damages by reference to the rent.[51]

4.65   Certainly, the court is not obliged to 'take account of the rent as a prima facie indication of the level of any proper award' and may instead just make a single global assessment of the general damages for inconvenience and distress.[52] Thus, the Court of Appeal would not interfere with an assessment of damages under that head at £30 per week where the contractual rent for the entire premises was only £8 per week.[53]

4.66   On the other hand, it is reasonable to perceive at least part of the tenant's loss as arising out of being contractually obliged to pay rent of, say, £80 per week, for a flat which, in its defective condition, is only worth £50 per week. In some cases it is fairest to seek to evaluate an award of compensation in respect of both the tenant's commercial loss (loss of rental value) and any discomfort, injury or inconvenience suffered.

4.67   For example, in *Sturolson & Co v Mauroux*[54] the Court of Appeal did not comment adversely upon the approach of a county court judge who first applied the 'discounting' method to assess the degree of loss of value to the tenant of the tenancy itself and then went on to add to it a substantial award for inconvenience, discomfort and injury to health (although the correctness of the county court judge's approach was not in that respect challenged). The fact that the rent had been registered as a fair rent and therefore in a sense had been fixed with regard to the state of repair did not affect the assessment.

49 See, eg, *Seal v Greenwich LBC* October 1981 *LAG Bulletin* 237; *Daejan Properties Ltd v Elliott* September 1977 *LAG Bulletin* 208; *Horrex v Pidwell* [1958] CLY 1461; *Ahmed v GLC, Mitchell v Brent LBC* and *May v Pooles Park Neighbourhood Co-op* all noted at May 1984 *Legal Action* 53–54 and *De Rosario v Dewing* August 1982 *LAG Bulletin* 91.

50 *Davies v Peterson* (1988) 21 HLR 63, CA, applying *Saunders v Edwards* [1987] 1 WLR 1116.

51 *Personal Representatives of Chiodi v de Marney* (1988) 21 HLR 6; *Credit Suisse v Beegas Nominees Ltd* [1994] 1 EGLR 76; *Hussein v Mehlman* [1992] 2 EGLR 87; *Wallace v Manchester CC* (1998) 30 HLR 1111.

52 *Personal Representatives of Chiodi v De Marney* (1988) 21 HLR 6, CA.

53 Ibid.

54 (1988) 20 HLR 332.

4.68   The county court judge followed the same approach in *Brent LBC v Carmel (Murphy)*.[55] The Court of Appeal refused to interfere with the level of damages awarded, either on the ground that it was excessive or on the basis that it was calculated on a wrong basis. Numerous other examples of county court judges adopting this approach can be found in the housing law updates published in *Legal Action* magazine.

4.69   If general damages are awarded on the basis, in part or whole, of loss of rental value it may be asked whether any reduction ought to be made where the rent was paid by way of housing benefit, particularly when the defendant landlord is also the local authority. In *Bell v Mazehead Ltd*[56] Mr Recorder Rayner James held that no such reduction ought to be made. That decision must be correct because irrespective of the basis of the court's technical approach to assessing general damages, the award is in principle personal compensation to the tenant for hardship.

4.70   In *Wallace v Manchester CC*[57] the Court of Appeal recently re-iterated that the loss for which the tenant is to be compensated in respect of time spent living in a dwelling in disrepair is the loss of comfort and convenience. While the method of determining the amount needed to compensate for that loss could involve a notional reduction in rent, it could also take the form of a global award for discomfort and inconvenience, or it could be a combination of the two. There was, however, no requirement to assess damages separately under the two heads as they were merely different methods of expressing the same concept.

4.71   In exceptional circumstances, a very low rent can properly result in a lower award of damages.[58]

4.72   If the tenant is required to move out (either temporarily while works are undertaken or, if conditions are sufficiently serious, before remedial work starts) any specific costs of removal or alternative accommodation can be recovered as special damages. However, a separate element of general damages will be awarded for the inconvenience of having to move and live for a time in temporary accommodation. Such award will be increased if undertakings as to

---

55   (1996) 28 HLR 203.
56   March 1996 *Legal Action* 14.
57   (1998) 30 HLR 1111.
58   *Newham LBC v Patel* (1978) 13 HLR 77.

the length of the stay in temporary housing are broken by the landlord.[59]

4.73   If it can be shown that the landlord's breach of contract or duty of care caused personal injury (mental or physical) then substantial damages for that injury can be recovered.[60]

Tenant not in occupation

4.74   If the tenant has rented the property for the purpose of sub-letting it (or is going away temporarily and wishes to sub-let) and as a result of disrepair is unable to sub-let it or can only sub-let for a reduced rent, the damages awarded will be measured by the loss of rental income from the sub-letting.[61]

4.75   If a long lessee is driven out of occupation by the disrepair and forced to sell the lease (or bought the lease intending to offer it for re-sale), then the damages awarded can be measured as the difference between the selling price and the price s/he would have obtained if the landlord had carried out the repairs.[62] Indeed, if it can be established that the landlord deliberately prepared the leasehold premises for sale in such a way as to disguise a serious repairing problem, the lessee may recover damages in deceit as well as for breach of contractual obligation.[63]

Conclusion

4.76   It will be obvious that certain of these heads represent compensation for quite specific loss. Accordingly, the courts will expect the tenant to give notice in the pleadings as to the loss suffered; it will not be sufficient just to claim 'damages'.[64] The tenant's claim may be exacerbated by the effects of the disrepair on other members of the tenant's family[65] although family members with a cause of action in

---

59   *Lubren v Lambeth LBC* (1988) 20 HLR 165, CA.

60   *McCoy & Co v Clark* (1992) 13 HLR 89; *Attia v British Gas plc* [1988] QB 304.

61   *Calabar Properties Ltd v Stitcher* [1983] 3 All ER 759; and see *Mira v Aylmer Square Investments Ltd* (1989) 21 HLR 284, QBD.

62   *Calabar Properties Ltd v Stitcher* [1983] 3 All ER 759; *City and Metropolitan Properties v Greycroft* [1987] 3 All ER 839 at 842–843; *Credit Suisse v Beegas Nominees Ltd* [1994] 1 EGLR 76.

63   *Gordon v Selico Co* [1986] 18 HLR 219, CA.

64   *Perestrello e Companhia Limitada v United Paint Co* [1969] 3 All ER 479, CA at 485.

65   *Jackson v Horizon Holidays Ltd* [1975] 3 All ER 92, CA.

their own right, eg, personal injury claims under s4 of the Defective Premises Act 1972 have to be joined to the action as plaintiffs.[66]

Special damages

4.77 The tenant is entitled to recover damages representing the loss in value of items of furniture and other personal belongings destroyed or damaged as a result of the landlord's failure to repair. The most common examples are carpets, furniture, curtains and clothing corrupted by dampness. Additionally, special damages may be sought for other specific loss capable of calculation in monetary terms, for example:

1) cleaning costs;

2) loss of earnings;

3) extra heating costs (eg, for 'drying-out' dampness);

4) costs of alternative accommodation (see below);

5) expenses of repairs, cleaning up and redecoration (see below);

6) travelling and medical costs (eg, arising from personal injury);

7) cost of eating out (eg, if food storage or cooking facilities have been damaged).

The above list is of examples only. Those acting for the tenant should ensure that consideration is given to pleading all losses which as a matter of fact are caused by the disrepair.

4.78 If the tenant actually has to carry out works of repair, clearing up or redecoration, damages will be awarded to compensate for any such expenses reasonably incurred.[67] Even if the works actually improve the property no reduction is made from the damages on account of this element of betterment, if the tenant was unable to make good the damage without betterment.[68] These specific costs may be pleaded as special damages. If VAT is payable on the repair work, the VAT may also be recoverable by the tenant.[69]

4.79 If the disrepair renders the premises uninhabitable, the tenant may recover as damages any expenses reasonably incurred in taking

---

66 *C (a minor) v Hackney LBC* [1996] 1 All ER 973.

67 *Calabar Properties Ltd v Stitcher* [1983] 3 All ER 759 and *Little v Glasgow DC* 1988 SCLR 482.

68 *McGreal v Wake* (1984) 13 HLR 107.

69 *Elite Investments Ltd v TI Bainbridge Silencers Ltd (No 2)* (1987) 283 EG 747 discussed at (1987) NLJ 869.

alternative accommodation from the date that the premises could no longer be occupied up to the date of assessment or repair.[70] Such damages will include the costs of any removals, storage of furniture etc. Such costs should be specifically pleaded as special damages.

4.80   Each specific item for which special damages are claimed must be identified in the pleadings and at trial it will be necessary to prove the loss in respect of each item. It is therefore vital that the tenant collects and retains where possible all receipts, accounts and invoices relating to items replaced or repaired. Where there is likely to be a dispute over the damages claimed the tenant would be well advised to retain (or at least photograph) any damaged item pending the trial.

Tenants' duty to mitigate loss

4.81   In an action for damages for breach of a contractual repairing obligation, it is important for tenants to show that they took whatever reasonable steps were available to mitigate or prevent loss or damage, for example, that a bucket was placed under a leak, rather than that dampness was allowed simply to rot the floorboards and carpets. Thus, if a tenant delayed giving notice of disrepair to the landlord so that the eventual damage was greater than it would otherwise have been, that tenant may see a reduction in damages on account of the failure to mitigate the loss.[71]

4.82   Refusal to permit access is a common allegation and can be treated as a failure to mitigate loss, or, more commonly, as an action which entirely suspends the landlord's liability.[72]

4.83   However, in cases where landlords have patently neglected to repair property, the duty to mitigate does not impose an obligation on tenants to do the work themselves.[73] Nor are tenants to be penalised for any refusal (other than a capricious one) to move to alternative accommodation.[74] But tenants can be expected to take reasonable measures, such as blocking up the source of draughts or temporarily covering broken window glazing.[75]

---

70 *Calabar Properties Ltd v Stitcher* [1983] 3 All ER 759.
71 *Minchburn v Peck* (1987) 20 HLR 392, CA.
72 *Granada Theatres Ltd v Freehold Investment (Leytonstone) Ltd* [1959] 1 WLR 570; *Empson v Forde* [1990] 1 EGLR 131.
73 *Sturolson & Co v Mauroux* (1988) 20 HLR 332.
74 *Lubren v Lambeth LBC* (1988) 20 HLR 165.
75 *Kearns v Liverpool CC* (1985) 22 February, unreported, Liverpool County Court.

Interest

4.84 As it is not unknown for disrepair cases to take months or years before the stage is reached for assessment of damages, advisers should ensure than any award for a retrospective period carries with it a claim for interest to be assessed under County Courts Act 1984 s69.

Using the ombudsmen

4.85 Council tenants aggrieved by their landlords' failure to carry out repairs, and private tenants concerned at the failure of local authorities to intervene to improve their housing conditions, may seek redress against the council concerned from the Commissioners for Local Administration or 'ombudsmen'. Ombudsmen have the power to investigate complaints of maladministration, delay or injustice made against local authorities by tenants and their associations. If there is a genuine dispute over the cause of disrepair or the appropriate remedy, the ombudsman may even appoint an independent surveyor to help in the investigation of a complaint.[76] Past investigations of repairs complaints have led to recommendations for compensation and public apologies equivalent to those which might have been obtained by seeking redress in the courts.

4.86 Even though the full investigation of a complaint can take over a year, the formal process of instituting a complaint is often sufficient to propel a recalcitrant local authority into action. The local ombudsmen have made it clear that they do not expect council tenants to take court action in order to get repairs done. Accordingly, they are prepared to investigate complaints even in cases where the tenant could clearly sue in damages. Indeed, the ombudsmen are ensuring that their recommendations for compensation awards reflect the amounts that are being awarded in comparable civil litigation.[77] The Commission for Local Administration has published a useful good practice guide on council housing repairs.[78]

4.87 Tenants of registered social landlords (principally housing

---

76 Investigation 315/L/85.
77 Luba 'Compensation for disrepair' September 1988 *Legal Action* 15.
78 Commission for Local Administration in England *Council housing repairs – guidance on good practice*, note no 3, 1993.

associations) have access to the Independent Housing Ombudsman (IHO).[79] The IHO service operates in broadly similar fashion to the local ombudsmen.

CHAPTER 5

How to bring a civil action

Initial preparation of the case

5.1   There is more than one way of preparing a case. Different advisers may have different, equally effective procedures. Different cases may call for different approaches. This chapter does not seek to provide a comprehensive blue print for disrepair litigation. It does, however, seek to give practical assistance in relation to some procedural issues that commonly arise.

5.2   Most advisers will take an initial statement, often while the client is on Claim 10, in order to make a legal aid application. Many firms already use questionnaires, while others prefer to take a more formal proof of evidence at the start. A sample initial statement questionnaire is included in appendix K.

5.3   Other steps which will be taken very early on will be a letter before action to the landlord, setting out the allegations or the principal allegations of disrepair, previous complaints and damage. An initial medical report might be obtained from the GP and a survey report commissioned. The client will be asked to obtain and produce all relevant documents – in particular the tenancy agreement, invoices, receipts, correspondence – and to start to think in detail about issues of notice, special damages and the possibility of obtaining statements from witnesses of fact.

5.4   If other occupiers besides the tenant(s) have suffered personal injury or property damage they will have their own cause of action, for example, under DPA s4. Their claims should be prepared at the same time as the tenant's claim, legal aid should be obtained (where appropriate) and the proceedings should include them as joint plaintiffs.[1]

5.5   The Civil Procedure Rules (CPR) contain a pre-action protocol for personal injury claims. Failure to comply with its provisions is likely to result in adverse costs consequences if proceedings are issued that 'might' have proven unnecessary and will be taken into account in any event both in relation to costs and when the court gives directions for the management of proceedings.[2]

5.6   There is no pre-action protocol for disrepair cases but paragraph 4 of the Pre-action Protocols Practice Direction (PD) records that the court expects the parties to act reasonably before the issue of proceedings, in accordance with the overiding objectives in CPR

---

1   *C v Hackney LBC* [1996] 1 All ER 973.
2   CPR r44.3, Part 3 and Pre-action Protocols PD.

r1.1, in exchanging documents and information and generally trying to avoid the necessity of proceedings.

The survey report

5.7 Most survey reports begin with a general description of the dwelling-house which gives the reader an impression of its age, character, locality and prospective life and assists him/her to understand its principal design features (see LTA 1985 s11(3)).

Description of defects

5.8 First and foremost the survey report will contain a schedule of defects or otherwise report on all observable defects at the dwelling-house.

5.9 It is essential that the description of defects is sufficiently detailed to enable the reader to understand clearly (a) what the defects are, (b) how serious they are, and (c) their likely effect on the occupier. For example:

1) Expressions such as 'defective windows' or 'defective plaster' should be avoided. Because the surveyor has not indicated in what respect(s) the windows or plaster are defective, the adviser is unable to advise whether or not the defect(s) result from an actionable breach of repairing obligations, whether they are very serious or completely trivial or what (if any) effect on the tenant their condition is likely to have had. The surveyor should have said, for example: 'front right-hand first-floor bedroom vertical sliding sash window will not stay open because the weights have become detached from their cords'.

2) Vague descriptions such as 'damp and mould to bathroom external wall' should also be avoided. The adviser needs to know: (a) the approximate location of the areas of damp and mould on the relevant wall(s); (b) the size of the affected area(s) (eg, is it an area of only about two square feet or is the entire wall affected?); (c) the severity, eg, moisture meter readings, and description of density of mould and so forth (because the damp could be slight or severe); and (d) whether the brickwork or plaster is affected and if so to what extent, or whether the damp and mould is merely affecting the decorations. Such information is vital if the adviser is to be able to advise confidently as to both liability and also quantum.

3) Where a dispute might arise, the surveyor should indicate whether specific building elements which are in disrepair are properly to be considered to be part of the structure or part of the exterior of the dwelling-house.

Tackling causation

5.10   Second, but equally important, a report which is to be used in civil proceedings must set out the surveyor's opinion as to the most probable cause of each defect. Where appropriate, all realistically possible causes should be set out, with brief reasons why one cause is preferred as the most likely. Where further investigation is required in order to establish the probable cause, the report should set out what further investigation is required and why it is required.

5.11   As part of this exercise, the surveyor should (a) ascertain what repairs or improvements the landlord has carried out in the past, and (b) consider whether those works might have alleviated some pre-existing condition about which complaint is made, or might be the cause of some current defect. An example might be the landlord who replaces old windows with sealed double glazed units and blocks up fireplaces, thereby causing the dwelling-house to suffer from condensation.

5.12   Without knowing the probable cause of the defect, it is in many cases not possible to determine whether the landlord is liable. For example, a flat in a block of flats might suffer from water penetration to an area of external wall in the bathroom. It might be that the render to the external wall has cracked as the result of thermal expansion and contraction and rainwater is penetrating through the brick solid wall behind the render (a clear case of breach of LTA 1985 s11). But the cause might be a blocked gutter two storeys up causing water to flood down the outside of the building, saturating and penetrating perfectly sound brickwork (clearly within LTA 1985 s11 as amended, but not within LTA 1985 s11 in its unamended form). Alternatively, the water might be from plumbing to the flat upstairs. On further enquiry, the flat upstairs might be (a) vacant and in the possession of the landlord (who will therefore be potentially liable in nuisance), (b) tenanted but the plumbing leak may be a result of the landlord's failure to comply with his/her repairing obligations (so the landlord will therefore be potentially liable in nuisance), or (c) tenanted with the water simply arising out of a defective washing machine connection (so the upstairs tenant and not the landlord will be liable).

5.13 Where condensation is occurring it is particularly important to establish the whole range of causes at play, especially if disrepair is contributing to the condensation, eg (a) rising or penetrating damp increasing humidity, reducing temperatures or reducing the insulating properties of the walls, (b) dilapidated windows reducing air temperature, (c) a broken heating system not allowing the tenant to maintain air temperatures and so forth.

5.14 Where relevant the surveyor should indicate what future damage is likely to be caused if defects are not remedied.

Effects of the disrepair

5.15 It is of considerable assistance if the surveyor indicates what damage the defects in question are likely to have caused, are likely to be causing and are likely to cause within the foreseeable future. The adviser will be concerned with (a) damage to the decorations, furnishings and tenant's belongings, (b) damage to other parts of the dwelling house, and (c) damage to the health or comfort of the occupiers.

5.16 It can be difficult to determine how long certain defects have been in existence, but, where possible, an indication of the likely duration from the surveyor can be of assistance.

The remedial works

5.17 The court will not make an order of specific performance or grant an injunction unless the order is sufficiently clear for the landlord to know exactly what he has to do. The surveyor should accordingly make every effort to include a specification of work which in itself will indicate to building contractors what needs to be done.

5.18 Where a range of repair options is possible, the court is likely to choose the most economical and practical option. Accordingly, should the surveyor recommend replacement rather than patch repair, for example of the roof covering, relevant reasons have to be given directed at: (a) the likely prospective life of the dwelling house, (b) the expected life of present roof when originally installed, (c) the expected life of new roof, (d) the approximate cost of roof replacement, (e) the approximate cost of patching, (f) the likelihood and frequency of further patching and the likely additional cost, (g) the degree of future disruption likely as the result of the patching option. It will generally be necessary to build a case that patching, or the other cheaper repair, is not merely not the best option, but is outside the range of a reasonable landlord's responses.

5.19   Orders for specific performance and injunctions must specify the period of time within which the landlord is to complete the works ordered. The period of time required is a matter of expert opinion as much as any other part of the survey report. It is accordingly essential that the surveyor indicates how long needs to be allowed for the landlord to complete the works, taking into account, where appropriate, the need to tender, to make arrangements for builders to attend, to arrange supervision and so forth as well as the duration of the works themselves.

5.20   The likely duration of the works will often depend on whether the occupiers remain in occupation while the works are carried out. If it is actually necessary for the occupiers to move out while the works are carried out, eg, because the works are so extensive that the landlord can not reasonably complete them without vacant possession, then the report should say so, with reasons. If the occupiers can remain in occupation then the report should contain time periods for the works (a) on the basis of vacant possession, (b) on the basis of continued occupation.

5.21   It may well be that the occupiers desire to move out while the works are completed and seek to recover the cost of alternative accommodation as damages, where the need to move out arises from the landlord's breach. If that is the case, the survey report should state why, in the particular circumstances of the case, although not essential, it is reasonable for the occupiers to wish to move out.

Form and content of the survey report

5.22   The expert's report must be addressed to the court and not to the tenant or the tenant's solicitors: PD 35 para 1.1. At the end of the expert's report there must be a statement that the expert understands his/her duty to the court and that s/he has complied with that duty: CPR r35.10. The expert's duty is to help the court and that duty overrides any duty owed to the tenant: CPR r35.3. The report must set out the material part of all written or oral instructions: CPR r35.10. The report must conclude with a statement of truth: 'I believe that the facts stated in this report are true and that the opinions I have expressed are correct' (PD 35 para 1.4). PD 35 contains other, detailed formal requirements.

Use of experts

5.23   The court has a duty to restrict expert evidence to that which is reasonably required to resolve the proceedings: CPR r35.1. In many disrepair cases, a dispute between experts is the essence of the claim and may have to be resolved in the traditional way. Nonetheless, it is clear that the court will try to avoid going down that route if it can. The tenant may not call an expert or put in an expert's report without the permission of the court: CPR r35.4. Even if permission is given for a report, the court will not direct an expert to attend trial in fast track cases unless it is necessary to do so in the interests of justice: CPR r35.5. The court has power to direct that evidence is given by a single expert: CPR r35.7. The parties can put written questions to the other side's expert: CPR r35.6, and the court can direct that without prejudice meetings of experts take place: CPR r35.12.

5.24   CPR Part 35 and PD 35 are at appendix G.

Cost of the works

5.25   Disrepair claims will not be allocated to the small claims track if, inter alia, they include a claim for works costing more than £1,000: CPR r26.6. Accordingly, the expert should say how much it would cost the tenant to carry out the remedial works that s/he considers appropriate.

Consequential work

5.26   The tenant will be entitled to recover the cost of consequential redecoration after the landlord has completed the works ordered. It would assist the tenant's advisers in obtaining quotations for the cost if the surveyor indicated what redecoration is likely to be required.

The medical report

5.27   It is increasingly rare, but one still encounters medical reports which go like this, in so far as they are legible: 'I feel sure that Mrs Smith's poor housing conditions may well have contributed towards her depression, asthma and failing eyesight. Please find enclosed my fee note for £35.00 and I would appreciate prompt settlement'. It is, of course, the responsibility of the adviser to make sure that the medical expert knows what is required, and provides it.

5.28   The first part of any medical report should, after setting out details such as the patient's name, address and date of birth, contain (a) a comprehensive account of the patient's treatment by the GP and by specialists (eg, dates of attendance, symptoms complained of, treatment provided); and (b) a detailed account of the patient's symptoms day to day (the medical expert may well have to interview the patient to obtain this information, which should include an account of the effect on the patient's home, work and social life).

5.29   The second part of the medical report should summarise the medical expert's understanding of the condition of the dwelling-house and the period of time involved, indicating the source of information, eg, home visits and/or survey reports.

5.30   The third part of the report should contain the expert's opinion as to whether, on the balance of probabilities (a) the condition of the dwelling-house caused any identified illness to occur; and/or (b) the condition of the dwelling-house caused a material exacerbation of any underlying illness (eg, caused an increase in frequency or severity of asthma attacks).

5.31   The first point to note is that the burden of proof in civil cases is the balance of probabilities. The medical expert should endeavour to ensure that each and every expression of opinion in the report addresses this test and not some irrelevant test, eg, 'might well have', 'could have', 'it is possible that', 'I am quite definite that it is possible'. Either it is more likely than not that, for example, the condition of the dwelling-house led to a material increase in the severity and frequency of a child's asthma attacks, or there is no case.

5.32   A minority of medical experts are too helpful, and seem to be happy to state that the condition of the dwelling-house was the sole cause of all sorts of conditions, from asthma and arthritis to heart disease. It should be pointed out to the expert at the outset that his/her function is (a) to assist the legal aid board and court more than the client, (b) that medical authorities should be referred to for justification of unusual conclusions, and (c) that the expert may have to justify his conclusions in court.

5.33   Virtually all reports which are positive, will be to the effect that the condition of the dwelling-house materially exacerbated illnesses such as arthritis, depression, asthma or upper respiratory tract infections. It is extremely difficult to do, but the expert should be asked to be as clear as possible as to (a) which housing defects are of chief significance and (b) the degree of exacerbation (eg, increased frequency or severity of attack).

5.34   Advisers should, of course, endeavour to build up a list of well qualified experts who prepare reports of an acceptable quality for housing purposes. Where symptoms are relatively minor the client's GP can provide the most cost-effective report. If the GP does not write adequate reports, or if the symptoms are relatively serious then a report should be obtained from a more specialist GP or from a hospital doctor or consultant.

5.35   The fourth part of the report should contain the expert's prognosis (a) on the basis that the dwelling-house is not repaired, and (b) on the basis that it is.

5.36   CPR Part 35 and PD 35 contain detailed provisions relating to expert evidence (see above paras 5.22–5.24 and appendix G).

Effect of the new Civil Procedure Rules

5.37   The most directly relevant Civil Procedure Rules and Practice Directions are contained in appendix H.

Before the claim is issued

5.38   Claims including a personal injury claim should comply with the personal injury Pre-action Protocol. Failure to comply with its provisions is likely to result in adverse costs consequences if proceedings are issued that 'might' have proved unnecessary and will be taken into account in any event both in relation to costs and when the court gives directions for the management of proceedings: CPR r44.3, CPR Part 3, and Pre-action Protocols PD.

5.39   There is no pre-action protocol for disrepair, but para 4 of the Pre-action Protocols PD states that in cases where there is no pre-action protocol: 'the court will expect the parties ... to act reasonably in exchanging information and documents relevant to the claim and generally in trying to avoid the necessity for the start of proceedings'.

Starting proceedings

5.40   CPR Part 7 applies to disrepair claims. A claim form in Form N1 complying with CPR Part 16 must be used. The statement of value required by CPR r16.3 will indicate which track will be allocated. The particulars of claim should annex a copy of the tenancy agreement if reliance is placed on any express terms (PD 16 para 9.3), any medical expert's report (PD 16 para 4.3) and be verified by a statement of truth: CPR Part 22 and PD 22.

5.41   The general rule is that disrepair claims will be allocated to the small claims track if the financial value of the claim is not more than £5,000: CPR r26.6(3).

5.42   Where, however, the tenant's claim includes a claim for an order requiring the landlord to carry out work to the dwelling, it will not be allocated to the small claims track if either (a) the cost of the works is estimated to be more than £1,000, or (b) the financial value of the rest of the claim is more than £1,000: CPR r26.6(1)(b).

5.43   Furthermore, claims including claims for damages for personal injury will not be allocated to the small claims track if the personal injury part of the claim has a financial value of more than £1,000: CPR r26.6(1)(a).

5.44   Disrepair claims will be allocated to the multi-track if they have a financial value of more than £15,000 or if the trial is likely to last for more than one day: CPR r26.6(4), (5) and (6).

Part 36 offers

5.45   Unless the claim has been allocated to the small claims track (CPR r36.2(5)) the tenant is able to make a 'Part 36 offer' to the landlord, either before issue, under CPR r36.10, or at any time after issue: CPR r36.2(4).

5.46   A Part 36 offer is an offer to settle the whole or part of the tenant's claim. It can be made in respect of the claim for damages and also in respect of any claim for an order requiring the landlord to carry out works. If accepted by the landlord, the tenant's claim will be stayed on the terms of the offer and the tenant will be entitled to costs: CPR r36.15. If the landlord does not accept the offer but the tenant does better than the offer at trial, then the tenant can expect to recover indemnity costs and interest on both costs and damages at a rate of up to 10% over base rate: CPR r36.21.

Legal aid

5.47   Relevant recent guidance on the circumstances in which legal aid will be available for housing disrepair cases is contained at appendix H.

The full statement and the witness statement

5.48   Before proceedings are issued it is necessary to take the client's
instructions on the survey report. The adviser should take
instructions on each of the defects identified by the surveyor as
follows: (a) date the client first noticed the defect, (b) date and
circumstances (see next paragraph) of first complaint about the
defect, (c) date and circumstances (see next paragraph) of other
notice to landlord of the defect, (d) attempts made by the landlord to
repair the defect (approximate dates and nature of attempts to
repair), (e) details of subsequent re-appearance or modified re-
appearance of the defect, complaint/notice and so forth, and (f) the
effect of the defect on the comfortable or convenient enjoyment of
the dwelling-house, or on health.

5.49   It is necessary to take full instructions as to the circumstances of
complaints or of other notice to the landlord of defects. Where an
allegation of complaint is made the landlord is always entitled to
know (a) who complained, (b) when the complaint was made, (c)
how and where the complaint was made (eg, telephone, writing, in
person at the neighbourhood housing office), (d) exactly who the
complaint was made to, (e) who else was present, (f) what was said
or done at the time by all present, in particular, precisely what the
complaint was. Where notice is alleged to have taken place as the
result of inspection, the landlord is always entitled to know (a) when
the inspection is alleged to have taken place, (b) who is alleged to
have inspected on behalf of the landlord, (c) precisely what defects it
is alleged that the person saw or had drawn to his/her attention. If
the landlord carries out works of repair which fail, it is of importance
to obtain full details of notice to the landlord that the repair did fail.

5.50   Works of repair or improvement have to be carried out with
reasonable care and skill. It seems however to be an increasingly
common complaint that landlords or their contractors carry out
works very poorly, eg, the repairs drag on for longer than was
necessary, they are poorly programmed so that unnecessary
disruption is caused (loss of washing, toilet or cooking facilities),
there are excessive amounts of dust and noise and there is often
substantial damage to the tenant's furnishings and other
belongings. Claims can result in substantial awards of damages but
are often difficult to substantiate fully. It is highly desirable that
tenants are advised to keep a full diary while works are being carried
out. Ideally the tenant should see the adviser regularly so that the

diary can be clarified where necessary before too much time elapses and of course so that the adviser can put the major complaints formally on record.

5.51   Special damages generally require considerably more attention than they receive. There ought to be a schedule containing the following information:

1) description of the belonging;
2) location of the belonging when damaged;
3) what damage was caused to the belonging (as precisely as possible);
4) what caused the damage to occur;
5) if the belonging was repaired or cleaned what was the cost (receipts should be provided if possible);
6) if the belonging has been ruined so as to require replacement (a) the date and approximate cost of acquisition (receipts should be provided where available), (b) explanation of why cleaning or repair was not possible, (c) whether the belonging has been disposed of, (d) whether the belonging has been replaced, if so at what cost (receipts to be provided if possible), (e) whether it is proposed to replace the belonging and if so what it will cost (evidence to be obtained);
7) description of the discomfort or inconvenience caused to the tenant by the damaged condition or the absence of the belonging.

5.52   The tenant's witness statement, formally exchanged, should contain all of the above information (although it could merely verify a detailed schedule of special damages already served). In addition, it must contain full instructions as to the defences raised by the landlord, in the light of the documents disclosed by the landlord. The additional instructions will generally relate to allegations by the landlord that the tenant has (a) failed to complain, (b) only complained about the minor disrepair which the landlord attended to timeously, (c) failed to fix appointments, (d) failed to give or refused access to surveyors or workmen, (e) caused condensation damp by poor lifestyle/use of calor gas heaters/use of tumble driers, (f) refused to move to alternative accommodation.

CHAPTER 6

Proceedings under the Environmental Protection Act 1990

For complete chapter contents, see overleaf

Introduction

6.1 Since the mid-19th century, parliament has sought to protect the general public from the worst effects of slum housing (ie, disease, overcrowding and dangerous buildings) through public health legislation. These laws were largely consolidated into the Public Health Act 1936 (PHA 1936), were amended subsequently and are now recast in the Environmental Protection Act 1990 (EPA) Pt III. See appendix E for the text of EPA ss79–82. These provisions replace those found in PHA 1936 ss91–100 and came into force on 1 January 1991: EPA s164(2).

6.2 Much of this legislation can be used by tenants and others to force landlords of bad housing to effect necessary repairs, and improve the condition of property which they own. The Acts are concerned with attacking the effects of bad housing, that is, the poor conditions in which occupiers and others are placed as a result of deterioration in the structure of dwellings and other housing defects.

6.3 The key to the use of environmental health legislation by tenants against bad housing is the concept of the 'statutory nuisance'.

Statutory nuisance

6.4 Statutory nuisances are defined as arising in the specific circumstances set out in the EPA and include:

1) 'any premises in such a state as to be prejudicial to health or a nuisance' (s79(1)(a));

2) 'any accumulation or deposit which is prejudicial to health or a nuisance' (s79(1)(e));

3) 'any tent, van, shed or similar structure used for human habitation which is in such a state or so overcrowded as to be prejudicial to health; or the use of which, by reason of the absence of proper sanitary accommodation or otherwise, gives rise, whether on the site or on other land, to a nuisance or to conditions prejudicial to health' (PHA 1936 s268 as amended by EPA Sch 15 para 4);

4) 'any well, tank, cistern or water-butt used for the supply of water for domestic purposes which is so placed, constructed or kept as to render the water therein liable to contamination prejudicial to health' (PHA 1936 s141 as amended by EPA Sch 15 para 4);

5) 'any pond, pool, ditch, gutter or watercourse which is so foul or

in such a state as to be prejudicial to health or a nuisance' (PHA 1936 s259 as amended by EPA Sch 15 para 4); and

6) 'noise emitted from premises so as to be prejudicial to health or a nuisance' (s79(1)(g)).

6.5   Each 'species' of statutory nuisance contains two distinct limbs, which are to be read disjunctively and treated quite separately, ie, 'prejudicial to health' or a 'nuisance'.

6.6   Several of the listed statutory nuisances deal with matters likely to be common in dwellings out of repair (blocked gutters, polluted water tanks, defective cisterns etc) but the statutory nuisance of most relevance to disrepair is contained in EPA s79(1)(a). Each element of s79(1)(a) requires close attention.

Elements of s79(1)(a)

'any premises'

6.7   Premises are defined by the EPA to include all land and vessels. Thus both private and public sector housing are covered. The courts have held that the Act directs attention to the condition of the premises, rather than to the way in which they are used.[1] Indeed, the premises may be temporarily unoccupied.[2]

6.8   In the case of a block of flats, the 'premises' for the purposes of s79 may be an individual flat or flats. It is possible to allege a statutory nuisance in relation to an entire block only if either the tenants are complaining of the condition of the common parts or there is a problem 'not confined to any one constituent unit in the block and which can only be related to the entire block'.[3]

6.9   An open site without any permanent buildings (eg, a travellers' site) may also be 'premises' for the purpose of s79. Thus the EPA powers may be used to eliminate statutory nuisances on caravan sites and other areas of land used for residential purposes.[4]

---

1   *Metropolitan Asylum District Managers v Hill* (1881) 6 App Cas 193; *Fulham Vestry v London CC* [1897] 2 QB 76.

2   See *Lambeth LBC v Stubbs* (1980) 255 EG 789; (1980) 78 LGR 650; *Coventry CC v Doyle* [1981] 1 WLR 1325.

3   *Birmingham DC v McMahon and Others* (1987) 19 HLR 452 at 457.

4   *R v Secretary of State for Environment ex p Ward* [1984] 2 All ER 556 at 560; *Day v Sheffield CC* (1988) August *Legal Action* 19.

'in such a state'

6.10   A statutory nuisance arises if the state of the premises as a whole is such as to be prejudicial to health or a nuisance. This may arise either from a single major item of disrepair (for example a collapsing ceiling) or from the accumulation of a number of minor items. It should be noted that it is the effect of the defects which gives rise to the nuisance rather than the simple fact of disrepair. An ill-fitting window frame may contribute to premises being a statutory nuisance, not because it constitutes an item in need of repair, but rather because it allows wind and rain penetration causing damp and draughts which may render premises prejudicial to health or a nuisance.

6.11   It has been said that s79(1)(a) is directed to the type of case in which,

> ... the premises themselves are decayed, dilapidated, dirty or out of order, as for instance ... where foul matter has been allowed to soak into walls or floors, or where they are so dilapidated as to be a source of danger to life and limb.[5]

However, premises may be 'in such a state' as to amount to a statutory nuisance even if the origins of the nuisance are outside the premises, eg, where, because of poor insulation, the noise of local traffic and trains permeates the premises,[6] or where dampness enters from outside.[7]

6.12   The danger of accidental physical injury is not within the scope of the EPA,[8] but the risk of infection because of wholly inadequate hand washing facilities can be.[9]

'prejudicial to health'

6.13   A statutory nuisance will arise where a dwelling is in such a state, through disrepair or otherwise, as to be 'prejudicial to health' defined by EPA s79(7) to mean 'injurious or likely to cause injury, to health'. Thus, both actual and potential ill health are covered.

6.14   The courts have held that the requirement of prejudice to health will be satisfied simply where it can be shown that the state of the

5   *R v Parlby* (1889) 22 QBD 520 at 525.
6   *Southwark LBC v Ince* (1989) 21 HLR 504, QBD.
7   *Pollway Nominees Ltd v Havering LBC* (1989) 21 HLR 462, QBD.
8   *R v Bristol CC ex p Everett* [1999] 1 WLR 92.
9   *Oakley v Birmingham CC* (1999) *Times* 8 January.

premises is such as would cause a well person to become ill or the health of a sick person to deteriorate further. Accordingly, a statutory nuisance exists where any premises are so defective as to cause potential or actual detriment to the health of the tenant or other occupiers. The test is, however, objective in the sense that no account is taken of any occupier's particular vulnerability.[10]

6.15   'Health', although not defined by the Act, should be interpreted broadly to include physical and mental health, particularly to incorporate the medically recognised stress associated with living in bad housing.[11] Mere interference with comfort will not bring a case within the 'health' limb[12] nor will defects which are merely decorative (such as stained wallpaper[13]) or simply constitute an 'eyesore'.[14] The tenant's general practitioner or hospital consultant should be able to identify premises which are prejudicial to health and most environmental health officers (EHOs) are trained to recognise them.[15]

6.16   Examples of premises which are 'prejudicial to health' include those suffering from dampness, condensation or mould growth. The risk of accidental injury is not included.[16] Neither is traffic noise.[17]

'or a nuisance'

6.17   The EPA does not define 'nuisance'. Initially, it was given the common-sense interpretation of 'anything which caused inter-ference with the personal comfort of the occupier of premises'.[18] A definition of this breadth extended the concept of statutory nuisance to all but the most trifling cases of disrepair, and greatly expanded the usefulness of the provision.

10 *Malton Urban Sanitary Authority v Malton Farmers Manure Co* (1879) 4 Ex D 302; *Cunningham v Birmingham CC* (1998) 30 HLR 158.
11 See Ros Franey 'Housing stress' March/April 1982 *Roof* 19.
12 *Salford CC v McNally* [1975] 3 WLR 87, HL.
13 *Springett v Harold* [1954] 1 All ER 568.
14 *Coventry CC v Cartwright* [1975] 1 WLR 845; [1975] 2 All ER 99, DC.
15 See Ormandy and Burridge *Environmental health standards in housing* (Sweet & Maxwell, 1988); and Ormandy 'Public health quarterly notes' (1977) September *LAG Bulletin* 206.
16 *R v Bristol CC ex p Everett* [1999] 1 WLR 92.
17 *Haringey LBC v Jowett* [1999] EGCS 64. Cf (a) noise caused by inadequate sound insulation: *Lambert Flat Management Ltd v Lomas* [1981] 1 WLR 898; (b) noisy premises: *Network Housing Association v Westminster CC* (1994) 27 HLR 189.
18 *Betts v Penge UDC* [1942] 2 KB 154.

6.18 However, in 1975 the House of Lords threw doubt on that approach and subsequently in *National Coal Board v Neath BC*,[19] the Divisional Court held that to fall within s79(1)(a), the 'nuisance' must be either a public nuisance at common law, or a private nuisance at common law.

6.19 At common law a public nuisance arises where an act or omission affects adversely the comfort or quality of life of the public generally, or a class of citizens.

6.20 At common law a private nuisance is a substantial interference by the owner or occupier of property with the use and enjoyment of neighbouring property.

6.21 Given this restrictive interpretation of 'nuisance' in s79, it follows that a statutory nuisance based on this limb '... cannot arise if what has taken place affects only the person or persons occupying the premises'.[20] Thus, if the conditions in the premises are a nuisance only to the tenant or other occupier, a 'statutory nuisance' will not arise unless the prejudice to health 'limb' can be satisfied as an alternative.

6.22 Moreover, only certain types of nuisance may be within the section. To constitute a nuisance at common law, it will generally be enough 'that the matter complained of renders the enjoyment of property and life uncomfortable'[21] for the occupiers of adjoining property. Consequently, the nuisance can arise in circumstances short of prejudice to health, so that offensive smells, noise and dirt may be within the definition. However, the courts have required, in addition, that the nuisance be of such a nature as to relate to matters of public health.[22]

6.23 It will be apparent that the *National Coal Board* decision (above) represented a considerable setback for tenants. It has restricted the use of the nuisance limb to those tenants affected by the disrepair of neighbouring or adjacent property and those who occupy premises in such a state as to cause a nuisance to passers-by. Thus, the position at present is that tenants may take action under the 'nuisance' limb if personal comfort is interfered with as a result of disrepair where that disrepair is in an adjacent property; action may be taken under the 'health' limb in respect of disrepair inside the

19 [1976] 2 All ER 478; [1976] 1 WLR 543, DC.
20 Per Watkins J in *National Coal Board v Thorne* [1976] 1 WLR 543 at 546.
21 *R v White and Ward* (1757) 1 Burr 333; and see *R v Neill* (1826) 2 Car & P 485.
22 *R v Bristol ex p Everett* [1999] 2 All ER 193.

premises, as well as on neighbouring property but this does not include disrepair causing mere interference with personal comfort.

6.24   Attempts were made during the passage of the Local Government (Miscellaneous Provisions) Act 1976 to reverse this judicial narrowing of the definition of nuisance, but the relevant amendments were withdrawn as the Government gave assurances to review the position. The subsequent Department of Environment consultation document recommended that a suitable amendment to 'plug the gap' should be incorporated into future legislation. This was achieved to a modest degree by the HA 1985 s190(1)(b) which gave local authorities a discretionary power to tackle disrepair causing discomfort to tenants (see chapter 7). However, research has indicated a continuing need for amendment of the EPA to tackle conditions which are inconvenient or of discomfort to tenants.[23]

6.25   Even within the narrow definition of a 'nuisance', action can be taken against 'statutory nuisance' arising from disrepair in immediately adjacent property (including common parts retained by the landlord). Examples include: leaking lavatory overflows, unhygienic rubbish chutes, backsurges of sewage, blocked pipes and gutters, falling slates and external cladding, and noisy central heating boilers.[24]

6.26   Where premises are in such a state as to cause potential or actual injury to health, or constitute a nuisance, the consequent statutory nuisance may be tackled, either by action by the local authority, or direct action by the occupier.

Action by local authorities

Abatement notices

6.27   The existence of statutory nuisances may be brought to the attention of local authorities either by their own systematic inspections[25] of districts (for example, in renewal areas) or, more commonly, by complaints from tenants and others. The investigation of statutory nuisances and enforcement of environmental protection legislation

---

23 Hawke and Taylor 'The compulsory repair of individual substandard housing: the law in practice' (1984) JSWL 129.

24 *Joyce v Hackney LBC* (1976) 24 June, unreported, Highbury Corner Magistrates' Court, noted at September 1976 *LAG Bulletin* 211.

25 Local authorities are under a duty to inspect regularly their districts to identify statutory nuisance (EPA s79).

are usually delegated to individual EHOs.[26] For these purposes, EHOs have a right to enter and inspect premises which may be in such a state as to be a statutory nuisance.[27]

6.28   Once satisfied of the existence of a statutory nuisance (or the likelihood of a statutory nuisance arising or recurring), a local authority is legally bound to take action,[28] using the powers available to it under the EPA. Although obliged to follow the statutory procedures to tackle statutory nuisances, some authorities will first give the landlord an 'informal notice' that EPA sanctions are being considered.

6.29   The first formal step is service by the local authority of an abatement notice on the person responsible for the nuisance.[29] The notice requires the person served (in practice, usually the landlord) to abate the nuisance (or prevent it arising or recurring) and execute 'such works, and the taking of such other steps as may be necessary' for that purpose. The notice also gives a time limit for completion of remedial works.[30]

6.30   The abatement notice must be sufficiently clear in all the circumstances of the case, bearing in mind the risk of exposure to penal sanctions for non-compliance. In straightforward cases the notice need not spell out precisely what works are required, but can simply require a certain result to be achieved. In more complex cases, however (for example, where sound insulation is required to abate a noise nuisance) the abatement notice, to be valid, must specify the works required, which works must be capable of remedying the nuisance.[31] The date of service of the abatement notice is the relevant date for the purpose of determining the validity of and justification for the notice.[32]

6.31   In cases of structural defects (for example, statutory nuisances arising from disrepair), the abatement notice must be served on the 'owner',[33] ie, the person who does (or would) receive the

---

26 Under Local Government Act 1972 s101.

27 EPA Sch 3 para 2.

28 *Cocker v Cardwell* (1869) LR 5 QB 15.

29 EPA s80(1).

30 See EPA s80(1) and *Bristol Corporation v Sinnot* [1918] 1 Ch 62.

31 *Kirklees MBC v Field* (1998) 30 HLR 869. *Network Housing Association v Westminster CC* (1994) 27 HLR 189. See also *Millard v Wastall* [1898] 1 QB 342; *Whatling v Rees* (1914) 84 LJKB 1122; *R v Wheatley* (1885) 16 QBD 34.

32 *SFI Group v Gosport BC* [1998] EHLR 23.

33 EPA s80(2)(b).

rent.[34] The authority will be able to identify the owner from the tenant's rent book, or by use of its statutory powers to obtain information about the ownership of property.[35]

6.32   If the person causing the nuisance cannot be found (as is frequently the case with property in very gross disrepair), the authority can serve notice on the owner or occupier.[36]

6.33   Unless the nuisance arises out of a structural defect or the person responsible for the nuisance cannot be found, the local authority is required to serve the abatement notice on 'the person responsible for the nuisance': s80(2)(a). This is defined by EPA s79(7) as being 'the person to whose act, default or sufferance the nuisance is attributable'.

6.34   Where more than one person is responsible for a statutory nuisance, notice may be served on each person whether or not his/her conduct alone would amount to a nuisance.[37]

6.35   The person served with an abatement notice has a right of appeal to a magistrates' court (to be exercised within 21 days of the date on which notice is served[38]) by way of complaint.[39] The grounds of appeal are set out in the Statutory Nuisance (Appeals) Regulations 1995.[40] The grounds include defect or error in the abatement notice and that the notice might lawfully have been served on a third party as well as the appellant. The magistrates have power to quash or vary the abatement notice or dismiss the appeal.

6.36   If the abatement notice is neither appealed nor complied with, the person served is guilty of an offence if the failure to comply is without reasonable excuse.[41] Under the former PHA 1936 provisions, local authorities were under a statutory duty to prosecute for non-compliance with abatement notices. The EPA imposes no such obligation and is silent as to whether prosecutions may be brought by occupiers directly, in place of local authorities unwilling to take action.

---

34   PHA 1936 s343(1) and see *Pollway Nominees Ltd v Havering LBC* (1989) 21 HLR 462, QBD.

35   Local Government (Miscellaneous Provisions) Act 1976 s16; and, for the EHO's power to inspect rent books, see HA 1985 s336 and Ormandy 'Housing repairs: what local authorities should be doing' (1978) July *LAG Bulletin* 164.

36   EPA s80(2)(c).

37   Ibid s81(1).

38   Ibid s80(3).

39   Ibid Sch 3 para 1(2).

40   1990 SI No 2644.

41   EPA s80(4).

6.37   If the offence of failure to comply is proven, the landlord or other person served is liable to a fine (up to level 5 on the standard scale) and a further fine of one-tenth the level 5 scale for each further day of non-compliance following conviction.[42] Under the old PHA 1936 procedure, the magistrates were required to issue a nuisance order directing the offender to carry out specified works. In the EPA process, the original abatement notice continues to bind the person served and the incentive for compliance with it is the prospect of incurring daily fines. There is accordingly no need for a nuisance order.

6.38   Whether or not it prosecutes for non-compliance, the authority can itself abate the nuisance 'and do whatever may be necessary' for execution of the original abatement notice.[43] It can then recover its costs from the person served or from the present owner of the property.[44]

High Court actions

6.39   If the local authority is satisfied that it would be inappropriate to deal with a statutory nuisance by using the magistrates' court procedure outlined above, it may take any necessary legal proceedings against the owner in the High Court.[45] Such proceedings have the advantage of giving access to broader equitable remedies, eg, injunctions, and wide-ranging means of enforcement and are useful where the owner persistently defaults or repeatedly delays the summary process before the magistrates' court. For the procedure on a High Court action, see *Warwick RDC v Miller-Mead.*[46]

Emergency procedure

6.40   Frequently the delays inherent in the enforcement procedures described above render them inappropriate in tackling situations of 'prejudice to health' etc. A streamlined procedure for these urgent cases is to be found in the Building Act 1984, ss76–83 of which is set out at appendix B.

6.41   Thus, where an authority is satisfied (usually as a result of an

---

42 EPA s80(5).
43 Ibid s81(3).
44 Ibid s81(4).
45 Ibid s81(5). See also *City of Bradford MC v Brown and Others* (1986) 19 HLR 16.
46 [1962] 2 WLR 284, CA.

urgent tenant complaint) that a statutory nuisance exists and that unreasonable delay[47] would be caused by following the summary procedure, it may serve the landlord with a notice stating its intention to do the remedial works and specifying the defects it intends to remedy.[48]

6.42   Nine days after service, the local authority may carry out all the necessary work identified in the notice and may recover its costs and expenses from the person on whom the notice is served.[49] Landlords can prevent this procedure taking effect only if, within seven days of service of the notice, they serve a counter-notice upon the authority that they intend to remedy the defects. The authority cannot act thereafter unless:

1) the landlord fails to start remedial works within a reasonable time, or

2) having been started, remedial works proceed unreasonably slowly or make no progress at all.[50]

6.43   In either of these circumstances, the local authority can proceed directly and carry out the works, and recover the full cost from the landlord.

6.44   Advisers assisting tenants in situations where disrepair is sufficiently gross to constitute a statutory nuisance by reason of prejudice to health, should always consider pressing the Environmental Health Department to use this 'nine-day notice' procedure.

Recurring nuisances

6.45   Under the former PHA 1936 provisions, difficulties arose in serving abatement notices in respect of premises which were intermittently in a condition amounting to a nuisance but not constantly so. The Public Health (Recurring Nuisances) Act 1969 sought to plug this gap by introducing a prohibition notice procedure to prevent nuisances recurring.

6.46   However, the provisions are wholly recast by the EPA and the 1969 Act has been repealed in its entirety. Under the EPA a local

---

47 *Celcrest Properties Ltd v Hastings BC* (1979) 29 October, unreported, ChD, noted in Arden *Manual of housing law* (Sweet & Maxwell, 6th edn, 1997).

48 Building Act 1984 s76(1) as amended by EPA Sch 15 para 24.

49 Building Act 1984 s76(2).

50 Ibid s76(3).

authority can serve an abatement notice requiring works, not only (a) when it is satisfied that a nuisance exists, but also (b) where it is satisfied that a nuisance is likely to occur.

6.47   The notice can either prohibit or restrict the nuisance arising or recurring and require the necessary works for those purposes.[51]

Action by tenants and other occupiers

Private sector

6.48   Private sector or housing association tenants will usually look to the EHOs employed by local authorities to take the necessary administrative and legal proceedings to eradicate statutory nuisances arising at their premises, using their powers described above.

6.49   Accordingly, advisers consulted by private tenants suffering prejudice to health or nuisance should immediately involve the local authority's EHO by requesting a visit and inspection of the tenant's property. Thereafter, the adviser should liaise closely with the EHO and ensure that the abatement procedures are fully used, including the nine-day notice procedure for urgent cases. In any subsequent prosecution of the landlord, the tenant may well be a witness for the local authority.

6.50   There are five situations, however, which may give rise to difficulty:

1) **The EHO fails to carry out an inspection, or there is an unreasonable delay before a visit is made**   A local authority is required to investigate individual complaints (s79(1)). In the event of a clear default, a complaint may be made to the Secretary of State[52] who may direct the authority to inspect; alternatively a complaint may be made to the local ombudsman. In the interim, an inspection should be arranged with an independent EHO.

2) **The EHO carries out an inspection but does not agree that a statutory nuisance has arisen**   In such circumstances, advisers should ask for the matter to be reconsidered, ensuring that the EHO is supplied with all the available medical information about

---

51   EPA s80(1).

52   The power to make formal complaint to the secretary of state under EPA Sch 3 para 4 should be exercised by addressing written representations to the Secretary of State for the Environment, DETR, 2 Marsham Street, London SW1.

the prejudice to the health of the tenant, or complaints from other tenants about the nuisance. An EHO may be persuaded to revisit if presented with a convincing report from an independent expert engaged by the tenant.

3) **The EHO is not prepared to find that premises constitute a statutory nuisance, even after reconsideration**   In this eventuality, the tenant will have to establish the existence of the nuisance by other means (eg, an inspection and report by an independent EHO, a medical report as to prejudice to health etc), and if satisfied that a statutory nuisance can be proved, take proceedings directly against the landlord using the s82 procedure (see below).

4) **The EHO agrees that there is a statutory nuisance, but fails to take remedial action within a reasonable time using the EPA procedures**   The duty of the local authority to serve an abatement notice is a mandatory statutory duty.[53] The tenant can challenge the failure to take action, if aggrieved by the breach of statutory duty, and move in the High Court for judicial review and prerogative orders directing the local authority to use the powers available to it.[54] Alternatively, complaint may be made to the local government ombudsman. This may, however, be secondary to the urgent need to remedy the statutory nuisance, in which case the tenant should initiate summary proceedings directly against the landlord in the magistrates' court, using the s82 procedure and secure the attendance of the EHO as a witness (see below).

5) **The EHO behaves improperly or unprofessionally**   If the difficulty for the tenant arises from the improper or unprofessional behaviour of the EHO (eg, where the tenant is subject to racist remarks or has some evidence of corruption), complaint should be made to the chief EHO of the authority concerned. If this produces no satisfaction, the matter should be raised with the professional association of EHOs, the Chartered Institute of Environmental Health.[55]

53 *Cocker v Cardwell* (1869) LR 5 QB 15; *McPhail v Islington LBC* [1970] 2 WLR 583, CA at 586.

54 EPA s80(1) and see generally De Smith *Judicial review of administrative action* (Sweet & Maxwell, 5th edn, 1995).

55 Chartered Institute of Environmental Health, Chadwick Court, 15 Hatfields, London SE1 8DJ (tel 0171 928 6006).

Public sector

6.51 Council tenants are largely outside the protection of the public health legislation simply because EHOs, as local government officers, can not serve public health notices upon their own local authorities.[56] Many will however serve 'informal abatement notices'. The council tenant must therefore use the enforcement procedure contained in EPA s82.

EPA s82 proceedings

6.52 The procedure for direct action by tenants against their local authority or private landlord is contained in EPA s82 (formerly PHA 1936 s99).[57]

6.53 Under this section, action may be taken against a local authority by a council tenant for the abatement of a statutory nuisance, even though the authority is providing the accommodation in exercise of its powers as a housing authority.[58] Similarly, s82 can be used by a private sector or housing association tenant where the local authority is not itself taking proceedings to compel the landlord to repair the property.

6.54 Proceedings may be initiated by any person aggrieved by the statutory nuisance. Although this will usually be the tenant or licensee, the provision extends to all other occupiers of the premises such as the tenant's family or lodgers.

6.55 Under s82, proceedings brought by individual tenants are criminal proceedings from the outset[59] even though the Act itself refers to an action started by way of complaint.[60] The reference

56 See *Cardiff CC v Cross* (1982) 6 HLR 1, CA.

57 For a review of the development of s99 as a repairing tool, see Hodge 'Tenants and s99' (1974) NLJ 1161; Hughes 'Public health legislation and improvement of housing conditions' 27 NILQ 1; Hughes 'What is a nuisance?' 27 NILQ 131; Haddon 'Public health and housing legislation' 27 NILQ 245; and Hughes 'Housing and public health' 28 NILQ 233.

58 *R v Epping (Waltham Abbey) JJ ex p Burlinson* [1947] 2 All ER 537; [1948] 1 KB 79.

59 *R v Inner London Crown Court ex p Bentham* [1989] 1 WLR 408, *Botross v Hammersmith and Fulham LBC* (1994) 27 HLR 179. See also *Northern Ireland Trailers v Preston CB* [1972] 1 All ER 260.

60 *R v Newham East JJ ex p Hunt* [1976] 1 All ER 839; [1976] 1 WLR 420; and Magistrates' Courts Act 1980 s50.

to 'complaint' remains in s82 even though the proceedings are criminal in nature throughout. The main change has been the introduction of a new requirement of formal written notice of intention to prosecute (see below). Provided that notice has been given, the occupier can prosecute the landlord responsible for the statutory nuisance. If successful, those proceedings produce a nuisance order under s82(2), breach of which constitutes a further criminal offence: s82(8).

6.56   Before the person aggrieved starts court proceedings s/he must give the landlord at least 21 days' notice and the notice must specify the matter complained of: s82(6) and (7). The notice must provide reasonable details of the allegations but need not be comprehensive or set out what remedial works are required.[61] The first stage of s82 proceedings is commenced by the laying of an information in the magistrates' court by a person aggrieved by the existence of a statutory nuisance (ie, in order to have jurisdiction the court must be satisfied that at the date of information there is a statutory nuisance rather than the prospect of a nuisance arising or recurring).[62] The function of magistrates, or the justices' clerk, when issuing a summons is judicial, ie, there is a discretion to issue or to refuse to issue the summons, which must be exercised judicially. It would however be wrong to refuse to issue a summons merely because the landlord also faced civil proceedings, at least when the scope of the civil proceedings is not co-extensive with the scope of the EPA proceedings.[63] It is permissible to lay an information immediately after expiry of the notice period under s82(6).[64]

6.57   The proceedings are brought against the person responsible for the nuisance or against the owner if either the nuisance arises from any defect of a structural character, or if the person responsible for the nuisance cannot be found.[65] The landlord will not be the 'person responsible' if the court decides that the real cause of the nuisance is the tenant's failure to use the heating system supplied or otherwise

---

61   *East Staffordshire BC v Fairless* (1998) EGCS 140; *Pearshouse v Birmingham CC* (1998) *Independent* 16 November.

62   EPA s82(1).

63   *R v Highbury Corner Magistrates' Court ex p Edwards* (1994) 26 HLR 682.

64   *R v Dudley MC ex p Hollis* [1998] 1 All ER 759.

65   EPA s82(4) and (5).

to behave reasonably.[66] Service must be effected in accordance with s160.[67]

6.58   If on the hearing of the information the court is satisfied that a nuisance exists it makes an order requiring the defendant to abate the nuisance within a specified time and to carry out the works necessary for that purpose.[68] If at the hearing date the nuisance has abated (whether naturally or as a result of remedial measures) but the court is satisfied that recurrence is likely, it makes an order prohibiting recurrence and requiring works to prevent recurrence.[69] It will be apparent that the court's powers at this stage mirror those of the authority itself to serve an abatement notice (save that the magistrates have no jurisdiction to prevent first occurrence of a nuisance). In order to secure the most appropriate orders, tenants and their advisers should have drafts available for the court to consider.

6.59   A conviction will be entered and costs will be awarded to the complainant if an order is made and the court is satisfied that proceedings have been properly brought. The complainant will also recover proper and reasonable costs if it is proved that there was a nuisance at the date of the complaint, even though it may have been abated by the time of the hearing: s82(12). Costs will not be recovered if the prosecution was brought under a contingency fee arrangement.[70] The parties should attempt to identify the costs issues prior to any hearing.[71]

Preparatory work

6.60   Legal aid is not available for either the private prosecution of criminal cases, nor the enforcement of orders made under s82. Accordingly, preparatory work will mainly be undertaken using the green form scheme and it may be necessary to apply for an extension at an early stage. Preparation will usually include:

66 *Dover DC v Farrar* (1980) 2 HLR 32; *GLC v Tower Hamlets LBC* (1984) 15 HLR 54; *Warner v Lambeth LBC* (1984) 15 HLR 42; *Carr v Hackney LBC* (1995) 28 HLR 747.
67 *Baker and Others v Birmingham CC and Others* (1999) 149 NLJ 122.
68 EPA s82(2).
69 Ibid s82(2)(b).
70 *British Waterways Board v Norman* (1993) 22 HLR 232; *Thai Trading Co v Taylor* (1998) 2 WLR 893; *Hughes v Kingston-upon-Hull CC* [1999] 2 All ER 49.
71 *Taylor v Walsall & District PICL* (1998) 30 HLR 1062.

1) The engagement of an independent EHO to inspect the premises and prepare a report.[72]
2) Gathering of medical evidence, and preparation of a medical report, if the case is to proceed on the 'prejudice to health' limb.
3) The photographing of the premises, including the particular items said to contribute to the nuisance or prejudice to health.
4) The copying and collation of correspondence passing between the tenant, EHO and the local authority/landlord concerning the disrepair. If an EHO is unwilling to disclose documents, a witness summons should be issued requiring attendance at court with all documents relevant and available.
5) Preparation of statements of the tenant and other members of the household relating to conditions at the premises, including statements which may be submitted under the Criminal Justice Act 1967 s9.
6) Preparation of a schedule of items destroyed or damaged by disrepair, including other financial loss, to be submitted for consideration of a compensation order.

6.61   It is important that the tenant has sufficient evidence to show that the statutory nuisance existed at the date on which the information is laid, and that the tenant was 'aggrieved' by the statutory nuisance at that date.[73] Thus, it may be necessary to be selective about the stage at which it is decided to launch the proceedings. However, at least one magistrates' court has been prepared to accept that a statutory nuisance arises from the state of premises which are structurally prone to be prejudicial to health, even though not actually prejudicial to health at the date the information was laid.[74]

Procedure

6.62   Before the person aggrieved starts court proceedings s/he must give the landlord at least 21 days' notice and the notice must specify the matter complained of: s82(6) and (7). The notice must provide

---

72 Law centres, solicitors and legal advice agencies have access to the Health and Housing Group's panel of independent EHOs (Health and Housing Group, 120 Wilton Road, London SW1 1JZ. Tel: 0171 233 7780).
73 *Hilton v Hopwood* (1899) 44 SJ 96.
74 *Brunyee v Lambeth LBC* (1981) 13 November, unreported, Camberwell Green Magistrates' Court, noted at January/February 1982 *Roof* 25. (An appeal to the Divisional Court on this point was withdrawn.)

reasonable details of the allegations but need not be comprehensive or set out what remedial works are required.[75]

6.63   The first step is the laying of the information in the local magistrates' court. This is a straightforward process involving completion of a standard form or a simple written application. The information laid should disclose:

1) An indication of the capacity in which the defendant is to be served (ie, as 'owner' if the nuisance arises from a structural defect, or otherwise as the person responsible for the nuisance).

2) That the statutory nuisance arises under s79(1)(a) (prejudice to health or a nuisance) rather than one of the other subsections (smoke, effluvia, noise and so forth).

3) The nature of the alleged nuisance in as much detail as possible.

6.64   It would be usual for the tenant to be in occupation of the premises at the date the information is laid, but the absence of the tenant (perhaps driven to live elsewhere temporarily by the poor conditions) is not fatal to an application.[76]

6.65   Although many metropolitan magistrates' courts were familiar with applications made under PHA 1936 s99, advisers should be careful not to take the issue of a summons under EPA s82 for granted in other areas. It is good practice to ensure that the information is accompanied by a statement from the tenant, a copy of EPA s82 and a request for an early hearing date. Strictly, the issue of the summons is a judicial and not merely an administrative act, although the scope for refusing to issue a summons will be small.[77]

6.66   If the magistrate or clerk is satisfied that the information is properly laid, the court will issue a summons to the defendant to appear on a specified hearing date and, with it, will send a copy of the information and any supporting statement from the tenant.

6.67   In cases relying on 'prejudice to health', advisers should always press for an early hearing date, but in negotiating this with the court, it is essential to be realistic about the likely duration of the hearing, so that inconvenience to the tenant caused by repeated adjournments is avoided. Although the procedure up to the hearing date is comparatively straightforward, it can be intimidating to the

---

75 *East Staffordshire BC v Fairless* (1998) EGCS 140; *Pearshouse v Birmingham CC* (1998) *Independent* 16 November.

76 *Lambeth LBC v Stubbs* [1980] 2 EGLR 135; *Jones v Public Trustee* September 1988 *Legal Action* 21.

77 *R v Highbury Corner Magistrates' Court ex p Edwards* (1994) 26 HLR 682.

litigant in person[78] and may prove frustrating in a busy magistrates' court with a recalcitrant defendant.[79]

6.68 As well as taking all necessary preparatory steps prior to the hearing, advisers should endeavour to discover in advance whether the landlord or local authority will be pleading guilty and is agreeable to an order being made. Even if the remedial works are commenced after the laying of the information, the tenant and adviser should attend on the hearing date to secure an order for costs (see below). The case could also proceed to hearing even if the tenants have been rehoused, since removing the tenant does not remedy the statutory nuisance.[80]

6.69 Advisers may well find that on the hearing date notified in the summons, the case appears in a list of many other actions, on the basis that it will be effective only if there is a guilty plea and agreement as to matters such as the works to be covered by an order. If this is not the case, a fresh trial date will be set. It is unlawful for the court to adjourn simply in order to enable the landlord to carry out remedial work and so avoid conviction and the possibility of a fine or compensation order.[81]

6.70 At the substantive hearing, the proceedings before the magistrates will turn mainly on factual and expert information about 'prejudice to health' or 'nuisance'. The use of expert EHOs, architects and others as witnesses to give specialist evidence is growing. Indeed, the whole case may turn on 'scientific' evidence.[82] Recently, convictions have been overturned on appeal where tenants were unable to produce independent expert evidence of conditions relied upon before the justices.[83] On the other hand, the magistrates are not entitled to reject the evidence of expert witnesses called on behalf of the tenant unless that evidence is challenged or contradicted by witnesses for the respondent: '... when it comes to deciding whether the condition of premises is or is not liable or likely to be injurious to health one is moving outside the field where a tribunal is entitled to draw on its own experience. That is a matter

78 C Blood 'One woman's fight for a damp-free home' September 1979 *Roof* 162.

79 'Using s99' letter from Brixton Law Centre' November 1982 *LAG Bulletin* 82.

80 *Lambeth LBC v Stubbs* (1980) 255 EG 789, followed and applied in *Coventry CC v Doyle* [1981] 2 All ER 184.

81 *R v Dudley MC ex p Hollis* [1998] 1 All ER 759.

82 See, eg, *R v Fenny Stratford JJ ex p Watney Mann* [1976] 2 All ER 888.

83 *GLC v Feroushos* (1982) March, unreported, Inner London Crown Court, noted in *South London Press* 9 March 1982.

upon which the tribunal needs informed expert evidence.'[84] At the very least, cogent evidence given on behalf of the tenant by an independent EHO and/or building surveyor will establish that there is a case for the landlord to answer.[85] The proceedings are criminal, so proof has to be beyond reasonable doubt.[86]

6.71   Legal advisers attending the hearing with tenants whom they have been assisting under the green form scheme, can no longer invite the court to grant an extension to cover the costs of representation. It is worth checking that not only are none of the sitting justices members of the local authority if it is the defendant,[87] but also that none of them are in any obvious way likely to be associated with the interests of the defendant.[88]

Nuisance orders

6.72   At the close of the evidence, the justices are required to make certain findings, including:

1) The actual condition of the premises (a) at the date of the tenant's laying of the information and (b) at the date of hearing.
2) Whether the condition at the date of the laying of the information constitutes a statutory nuisance, and whether the statutory nuisance still exists.
3) Whether the statutory nuisance is found by reason of 'prejudice to health' or 'nuisance' or both.
4) Identifying the person responsible for the statutory nuisance, or the owner.

6.73   The existence of a statutory nuisance and the cause of that nuisance have to be proved to the criminal standard of proof, ie, beyond reasonable doubt.[89] The fact that the matter complained of does not arise from any breach of the landlord's statutory obligation to repair may be persuasive in showing that it was not caused by any act or default of the landlord, but is not conclusive.[90] However, where the

---

84   *Patel v Mehtab* (1982) 5 HLR 78 per Donaldson LJ at 82.
85   *McCorley v Birmingham DC* (1984) 12 January, unreported, DC, noted at D Pollard *Social Welfare Law* (Longman) para C.6063.
86   *Birmingham CC v Kelly* [1986] 2 EGLR 239.
87   Justices of the Peace Act 1979 s64.
88   *R v Smethwick JJ ex p Hands* (1980) *Times* 4 December, DC.
89   PHA 1936 s99 procedures were also criminal throughout.
90   *Birmingham DC v Kelly and Others* (1985) 17 HLR 572 at 579.

nuisance arises from any defect of a structural nature (eg, dampness resulting from a hole in the roof), the landlord is liable in the capacity of 'owner' irrespective of repairing obligations[91] (s82(4)(b)) once a statutory nuisance is proved.

6.74   If matters are found in favour of the tenant,[92] the court must make an order against the defendant local authority or landlord requiring:[93]

1) such work as the court considers necessary to abate the nuisance and prevent its recurrence, within a stipulated time limit; or
2) sufficient works to prevent a recurrence of the nuisance within a stipulated time limit.

6.75   The justices must be specific as to the work required in the nuisance order.[94] Thus, advisers should ensure that the court is supplied with a full and detailed draft order. Where there has been agreement as to the facts, advisers should arrange that the fullest possible order is agreed in advance with the landlord and put before the justices. Much may be achieved through hard bargaining on the terms of orders 'at the door of the court'. Whether or not the order is agreed, evidence in support of it must be given, since the decision as to the extent of the works necessary to abate the nuisance should be made by the court itself.[95] The order, may properly require works to be done which go beyond the terms of any other repairing obligation on the landlord. The order can, for instance, require improvement work or the installation of fixtures, fittings and facilities not present at the commencement of the tenancy.[96]

6.76   The court has a wide discretion as to the form and content of the order, and, in considering the remedial works to be specified, can properly have regard to the future life of the property. The justices must 'look at the whole circumstances of the case and try and make an order which is in its terms sensible and just, having regard to the entire prevailing situation',[97] and this may include consideration of

---

91 *Coventry CC v Doyle* [1981] 2 All ER 184.
92 Or other informant.
93 *R v Camberwell Green Magistrates' Court ex p Healey* (1984) 10 October, unreported, QBD, noted at December 1985 *Legal Action* 171.
94 *R v Horrocks ex p Boustead* (1900) 69 LJQB 688, *R v Secretary of State for Environment ex p Watney Mann (Midlands)* [1976] JPL 368, *R v Wheatley* (1885) 16 QBD 34, *Network Housing Association v Westminster CC* (1994) 27 HLR 189.
95 *Birmingham DC v Kelly and Others* (1985) 17 HLR 572.
96 Ibid at 582.
97 *Nottingham Corporation v Newton* [1974] 2 All ER 760.

the overlapping provisions of the Housing Act (see chapter 7). If the order is being made against a local authority, the court is also entitled to have regard to the general obligations that the council owes to its tenants and to the extent of its resources.[98]

6.77 Although in many cases, there will be an attempt to convince the court that simple 'patch' repairs will cure the statutory nuisance, advisers should be bold in pressing for substantial orders for work sufficient to prevent recurrence of the nuisance. With the assistance of expert witnesses, tenants have been able to persuade courts to make formidable orders for remedial works. Examples include:

1) Provision of new roof covering, installation of full gas central heating, insulation of walls, ceiling and floors, and complete electrical rewiring and renovation of electrical fittings.[99]

2) Re-pointing of external brickwork, replacement of defective sink and draining board (further works of installation of central heating and internal dry-lining having been agreed by the respondent).[100]

3) The provision of thermal insulation, installation of mechanical ventilation, and the overhaul of an inefficient heating system.[101]

4) Insulation of walls, floors and ceilings, renewal of defective windows, installation of ventilators and provision of night storage heaters.[102]

5) Installation of gas fired central heating, secondary double glazing, roof insulation, filling of cavity walls and electrical re-wiring.[103]

6.78 Where the only effective way to abate the statutory nuisance is to have the whole property demolished, a nuisance order requiring

---

98   *Salford CC v McNally* [1975] 3 WLR 87, HL; *Birmingham DC v Kelly and Others* (1985) 17 HLR 572; and *Southwark LBC v Ince* (1989) 21 HLR 504, QBD.

99   *Christou v Islington LBC* (1980) unreported, Inner London Crown Court, noted at 51 *Community Action* 10.

100 *Tusting v Kensington and Chelsea RLBC* (1975) 3 January, unreported, Inner London Crown Court, noted at 27 NILQ 16 and *Municipal Journal* 17 January 1975.

101 *Brunyee v Lambeth LBC* (1981) 13 November, unreported, Camberwell Green Magistrates' Court.

102 *Ali v Hackney LBC* (1985) 9 September, unreported, Highbury Magistrates' Court, noted at December 1985 *Legal Action* 171.

103 *Birmingham DC v Kelly and Others* (1985) 17 HLR 572.

demolition may be made.[104] Where the property is unfit the court can prohibit occupation (see below).

6.79 Alternatively, if the only means of abating the nuisance is the provision of facilities or installations, the nuisance order may direct that such provision be made.[105]

6.80 Usually the terms of the nuisance order will be complied with before expiry of the time stated in the order. If there is a failure without reasonable excuse to comply with 'any requirement' of an order made in s82 proceedings, the person subject to the order (usually the landlord) commits a further criminal offence: EPA s82(8). The tenant may then bring a prosecution for that non-compliance in the same magistrates' court where the order was made. Indeed, if the order in the earlier part of s82 proceedings was made against a private or housing association landlord, the local authority could bring the further prosecution even though it was the tenant who first obtained the order in default of the authority acting. The prosecution is launched by the laying of an information. If prima facie satisfied that an offence has occurred, the magistrates' court (or its clerk) will issue a summons requiring the attendance of the landlord for trial. Tenants should press for early hearing dates as the daily fine, which is the real pressure on the landlord to comply with the order, bites only from the date of conviction not from when the order is breached or the information laid.

6.81 Tenants should endeavour to establish in advance whether the landlord will be pleading guilty or not guilty. In particular tenants should be alive to the prospect of the defendant relying on the 'reasonable excuse' defence for non-compliance. This is undefined and potentially very wide ranging.

6.82 If the magistrates are satisfied as to non-compliance or there is a guilty plea, a further conviction will be entered. Penalties are described below.

6.83 The court may direct the local authority for the area (if not itself the defendant) to carry out the works (or any part of them) specified in the original notice. Before making such an order the justices must give the authority an opportunity to be heard: s82(8). In order to undertake the works the authority can call in aid considerable powers to enter private property: Sch 3 para 23.

---

104 *Brown v Biggleswade Union* (1879) 43 JP 554.
105 *Whittaker v Derby Urban SA* (1885) 55 (ns) LJ MC 8; *Hammersmith and Fulham LBC and Kensington and Chelsea RLBC v Ward* (1983) 7 November, unreported, Knightsbridge Crown Court, noted at May/June 1984 *Roof* 18.

Penalties

6.84 Where the initial prosecution under s82(1) results in a nuisance order, the court enters a conviction and may impose a fine of up to level 5 on the standard scale: s82(2). The penalty for failure to comply with a nuisance order made by the court is a fine of up to level 5 on the standard scale plus one-tenth of that scale for each subsequent day on which compliance remains outstanding (s82(8)).[106] In assessing the fine, the court will be assisted by any information about the defendant's earlier convictions relating to other properties owned.

Compensation

6.85 In addition to any penalty, a compensation order may be made in favour of the tenant for damage suffered to person and property. In a 'prejudice to health' case, actual ill health will usually have been proved and recompense should follow. A compensation order provides a 'speedy, summary and cheap' method of obtaining financial compensation without the need to bring separate civil proceedings.[107] Full details of any personal injury should be provided[108] although in the absence of such evidence an award for anxiety and distress can be made.[109] Up to £5,000 may be awarded by magistrates (there is no limit in the Crown Court), but the court should be assisted to make a proper assessment of loss.[110] It is not necessary to show that the landlord would have been liable in civil proceedings to pay compensation,[111] but some evidence of the actual loss suffered must be available: mere representations are insufficient.[112]

6.86 Prior to 1996 it was not unusual for a magistrates' court both to impose a substantial fine and to award the maximum amount of

106 Nuisance fines' March 1977 *Roof* 60; and see *emPHASis* No 67, 28 January 1977 and *Savizon v Lambeth LBC* (1985) unreported, Camberwell Green Magistrates' Court, noted at June 1986 *Legal Action* 81.

107 *R v Dorton* [1988] Crim LR 254, CA.

108 *R v Cooper* [1982] Crim LR 308, CA.

109 *Bond v Chief Constable of Kent* [1983] 1 All ER 456.

110 Powers of Criminal Courts Act 1973 s35 (see *R v Vivian* [1975] 1 All ER 48, CA).

111 *R v Chappell* [1984] Crim LR 574, CA.

112 *R v Horsham Justices ex p Richards* [1985] 2 All ER 1114; *R v Amey* [1983] 1 All ER 865, CA and Criminal Justice Act 1982 s67.

compensation,[113] although the Divisional Court in *Herbert v Lambeth LBC*[114] gave a clear warning that compensation orders were intended only for simple and clear cases where no great amount of money is at stake. In *R v Liverpool Crown Court ex p Cooke*[115] the Divisional Court approved the reduction by the Crown Court of a compensation order from £3,000 to £250 on the basis that magistrates were not entitled to take into account the whole period for which the nuisance existed. They could only take into account the statutory nuisance in so far as it existed at the date specified in the complaint, providing that such date is not before whichever is the later of (a) the date the statutory notice expired, (b) a date six months before the complaint was made. The Divisional Court reiterated that the power to make compensation orders should be exercised only in simple and clear cases.

6.87   Although the Divisional Court indicated in *Cooke* that in the context of the new, relatively short period of liability 'many, if not most' claims ought to be simple and straightforward, the Divisional Court in *Davenport v Walsall MBC*[116] dismissed an appeal from magistrates who refused to make a compensation order on the ground that the case was too complicated, even though it was a relevant factor that there was likely to be no civil remedy. It was a feature of the case that the defendant had pleaded guilty: so the magistrates did not already have a substantial pool of information about the case. The Divisional Court indicated that it did not wish to encourage magistrates to be 'over-eager to resort to assertions of complexity' but that it would only interfere if the 'decision falls outside the scope of their legitimate discretion'.

6.88   Magistrates are required to give reasons if refusing to award compensation, whether or not an application has been made.[117]

6.89   Care should be taken in identifying the actual loss in respect of which compensation is sought because, in any subsequent civil action for damages, credit will have to be given for the amount of the compensation order where the award is for the same 'injury, loss or

113 *Oliver v Islington LBC* (1987) 24 July, unreported, Highbury Corner Magistrates' Court, noted at September 1987 *Legal Action* 12; and similar cases noted in *Legal Action* in September 1988 (p15), December 1988 (p21) and March 1989 (p23).

114 (1991) 24 HLR 299.

115 [1996] 4 All ER 589.

116 (1995) 28 HLR 754.

117 Criminal Justice Act 1988 s104.

damage'.[118] The magistrates should therefore be asked to award compensation for those items which will not attract civil damages.

Appeals

6.90　An appeal against conviction may be made to the Crown Court.[119] Indeed, any 'person aggrieved' by the outcome of the proceedings before the magistrates may appeal and therefore a tenant, unsuccessful with a prosecution, may appeal to the Crown Court.[120] The appeal takes the form of a rehearing but the Court concerns itself only with the matters as at the date of the hearing before the justices.[121] Appeal also lies to the Divisional Court of the Queen's Bench Division by way of case stated. Alternatively, the procedure for judicial review by the High Court is available. Judicial review may be necessary, eg, to compel the magistrates in EPA proceedings to prepare a case stated for the purposes of an appeal.[122] Any order made by the magistrates' court to take effect before an appeal can be heard, must be complied with.[123]

Costs and legal aid

6.91　Under the old-style PHA 1936 s99 proceedings no specific provision was made for costs orders. Although it had long been thought that s94(3) operated to ensure automatic entitlement to costs if a statutory nuisance were proven, the award of costs was actually a matter for the discretion of the court.[124] The EPA now makes specific provision for costs awards in s82 proceedings. Where the court is satisfied that the statutory nuisance alleged existed at the date the information was laid then, irrespective of whether the nuisance still exists or is likely to recur, the court must order the defendant to pay

---

118　Criminal Justice Act 1988 s105.

119　PHA 1936 s301.

120　*Cook v Southend BC* (1989) 11 CL 323, CA; *Josiah v Thames Housing Association* (1989) 7 July, unreported, Knightsbridge Crown Court, noted at (1989) December *Legal Action* 16.

121　*Northern Ireland Trailers v Preston* CB [1972] 1 All ER 260.

122　*R v Wells Street Magistrates' Court ex p Morrissey* (1988) 18 July, unreported, QBD.

123　*Hammersmith LBC v Magnum Automated Forecourts* [1977] 1 All ER 401, CA.

124　*Sandwell MBC v Bujok* (1989) 22 HLR 87, DC.

the costs. The sum ordered to be paid to the occupier is 'such amount as the court considers reasonably sufficient to compensate him for any expenses properly incurred by him in the proceedings'.[125]

6.92   These should be sufficient to cover experts' fees, legal costs, tenant's loss of earnings etc. £1,200 costs awarded in *Ali v Hackney LBC*[126] included fees of an independent EHO, a heating engineer, medical reports, attendance by a GP and three sets of photographs. In one case, heard over four days, the tenant was awarded costs 'limited to £4,000'.[127] Costs are not usually taxed, but simply assessed from rates of costs and charges put to the court by the tenant's representative.

6.93   Costs remain 'properly incurred' when the complainant pursues an application for a compensation order at an adjourned hearing, even though the magistrates decide not to make a compensation order, providing the application was proper, eg, it was not 'doomed from the outset'.[128]

6.94   Costs will be 'properly incurred' only if the complainant is actually liable to pay those costs to the solicitor. They are not properly incurred if there is an unlawful contingency fee arrangement.[129] The adviser can of course reserve the right to waive payment of fees, but there must be a letter of retainer setting out the client's liability to pay costs, win or lose, together with applicable rates. Unless the magistrates are handed a letter of authority, costs (as with compensation) will be sent direct to the client, rather than to the adviser.

6.95   The parties should attempt to identify the costs issues prior to any hearing.[130]

6.96   Although legal aid is not available to tenants in the magistrates' court, it is available to the tenant to resist any appeal to the Crown Court,[131] or to the Divisional Court.

6.97   Even if the tenant loses a case, if it can be shown that proceedings

---

125 EPA s82(12).

126 (1985) 9 September, unreported, Highbury Corner Magistrates' Court.

127 *Day v Sheffield CC* August 1988 *Legal Action* 19.

128 *Davenport v Walsall MBC* (1995) 28 HLR 754.

129 *British Waterways Board v Norman* (1993) 26 HLR 232; *Thai Trading Co v Taylor* (1998) 2 WLR 893; *Hughes v Kingston-upon-Hull CC* [1999] 2 All ER 49.

130 *Taylor v Walsall & District PICL* (1998) 30 HLR 1062.

131 Legal Aid Act 1988 ss8 and 21; and *R v Inner London Crown Court ex p Bentham* (1988) 21 HLR 171, QBD.

had been reasonably commenced, an order may exceptionally be made for the payment of costs out of central funds.[132]

EPA 1990 and Housing Act 1985

6.98   As has been seen, local authorities have a statutory duty to take action where premises are in such a state as to be a statutory nuisance, under the EPA. However, if any premises are in such severe disrepair as to be unfit for human habitation, the local authority has a statutory duty to take action under the Housing Act 1985 (see chapter 7) Where premises are sufficiently out of repair to constitute a statutory nuisance and are unfit for human habitation, the courts have made it clear that local authorities should not use the statutory nuisance procedure to force full-scale repairs on landlords of unfit housing,[133] but must instead use the Housing Act procedure.[134]

6.99   On the other hand, the fact that council property is unfit (even to the extent of simply awaiting demolition) is no bar to the tenant taking proceedings under s82, although in such cases justices are invited to take into account, in drawing up orders, the prospective life of the property.[135] Indeed, the HA 1985 s203(3) makes it clear that the use of Housing Act powers does not prejudice use by tenants or local authorities of other procedures including those under the EPA.

Note of warning

6.100   Despite the attractions of the EPA procedures in providing a swift and straightforward remedy for bad housing and in imposing salutary penalties on landlords, including local authorities, several problems are relevant to tenants considering such action.

6.101   EPA s82 proceedings are criminal proceedings and carry a higher burden of proof. Advisers should be certain of their evidence before laying informations. If the proceedings finally result in the acquittal

---

132   Costs in Criminal Cases Act 1973; and see *Dover DC v Farrar* (1982) 2 HLR 32, DC.

133   *Salisbury Corporation v Roles* [1948] WN 412; (1948) 92 SJ 618, DC.

134   *R v Kerrier DC ex p Guppys (Bridport)* (1976) 32 P&CR 411, CA.

135   *Salford CC v McNally* [1975] 3 WLR 87, HL.

of the respondent, the tenant may be landed with a heavy bill for costs.[136]

6.102   The court may be persuaded that 'patch' repairs will suffice to abate the nuisance, or will allow such a long period for the completion of works that the tenant receives little immediate benefit.

6.103   The prosecution may result in a finding of unfitness and an order from the court prohibiting occupation of the property: s82(3). This would prevent the tenant returning to the property until it was made fit.

6.104   If, as the result of EPA proceedings, repairs are carried out, that may make it impossible to bring civil proceedings for compensation, eg, when the cost of the works would have exceeded £1,000 and the remaining damages claim does not exceed £5,000: CPR r26.6. In some cases, use of the EPA proceedings will result in the tenant not being able to pursue civil proceedings for recovery of compensation.

Final note

6.105   This chapter is concerned only with the relationship between public health and environmental protection legislation and housing disrepair. The Public Health Acts and related regulations have a wide ranging application to a large number of matters touching upon housing standards, and should not be overlooked. Reference may usefully be made to Arden and Partington *Housing Law* (1994 looseleaf edition, Sweet & Maxwell, updated).

---

136 *Williamson v Kirklees DC* (1975) 25 June, unreported, Huddersfield Crown Court, noted at 44 *Community Action* 10.

CHAPTER 7

Bad housing and the Housing Act 1985

Introduction

7.1   The 1996 *English House Condition Survey*[1] confirms that about 1.5 million dwellings are 'unfit for human habitation'. Notwithstanding the decline in the country's housing stock, for many years there has been a welter of law applicable to housing standards and conditions, most of it unused. This legislation covers the whole housing spectrum from compulsory improvement to slum clearance programmes and redevelopment.[2]

7.2   In this chapter, those aspects of the housing legislation of most assistance to the individual tenant and adviser will be considered. The Housing Acts will be discussed in their application to three standards of accommodation: unfit housing, housing in substantial disrepair, and housing in sufficient disrepair to cause discomfort to tenants.

7.3   Before turning, however, to the detail of the provisions, it is important to note that the judiciary has sanctioned policies of bold use of the Housing Acts in attempts to eradicate bad housing. Lord Denning MR said:[3]

> It seems to me that the policy of Parliament was to make the owners of houses keep them in proper repair. Not only so as to keep up the stock of houses, but also to see that protected tenants should be able to have their houses properly kept up. It would be deplorable if there were no means of compelling owners of old houses to keep them in proper repair; or if the owners could let them fall into disrepair as a means of evicting tenants. Of course, if the state of the house is so bad that it should be condemned whoever was occupying it then let it be demolished or closed or purchased. But if it is worth repairing, then it should be repaired, no matter whether it is occupied by a protected tenant or an unprotected tenant.

7.4   Readers should note that the provisions of the consolidating Housing Act (HA) 1985 have in turn been extensively re-cast by HA 1988 and the Local Government and Housing Act 1989 (LGHA). What amounts to an almost wholly new regime was introduced from 1 April 1990. In operating this scheme, local authorities are required by HA 1985 s604A to have regard to guidance issued by the Secretary

---

1   *English House Condition Survey 1996* (1998, HMSO).
2   The standard reference work, *Encyclopedia of Housing Law* ed A Arden (Sweet & Maxwell), now runs to five substantial volumes.
3   *Hillbank Properties v Hackney LBC* (1982) 3 HLR 73 at 82.

of State for the Environment. Relevant guidance is principally contained in DoE Circular 17/96. Circular 17/96 emphasises the advantages of dealing with unfitness on an area basis rather than a property-by-property basis. Important additions to the statutory scheme are contained in the Housing Grants, Construction and Regeneration Act 1996 (HGCRA) Chapter IV.

Housing unfit for human habitation

7.5 Part VI of HA 1985 as amended, sets out a code for tackling individual properties which are unfit for human habitation. The code, which is enforced by local authorities under the guidance of the Secretary of State for the Environment, requires that whenever an unfit property is identified, some form of action must be taken unless the local authority determines to defer action.

Identifying unfit property

7.6 All local housing authorities are under a statutory duty to consider annually what action should be taken concerning housing conditions in their area, particularly with regard to, inter alia, properties that are unfit.[4] More commonly, individual properties are brought to the attention of authorities by complaints from tenants and their advisers. Once identified, an inspection must be carried out by an EHO in order to determine the condition of the property (see also paras 7.51–7.58.) If the EHO is satisfied that the property is 'unfit' (see below), s/he must report that fact in writing to the committee or officer of the council with the delegated power to decide what action should be taken (HA 1985 s606(1)).

The meaning of 'unfit'

7.7 HA 1985 s604 sets out the definition of unfitness for these purposes:

(1) Subject to subsection (2) below, a dwelling-house is fit for human habitation for the purposes of this Act unless, in the opinion of the local housing authority, it fails to meet one or more of the requirements in paragraphs (a) to (i) below and, by reason of that failure, is not reasonably suitable for occupation,

4 HA 1985 s605 as substituted by Local Government and Housing Act 1989 Sch 9 para 85; see also Circular 17/96.

(a) it is structurally stable;

(b) it is free from serious disrepair;

(c) it is free from dampness prejudicial to the health of the occupants (if any);

(d) it has adequate provision for lighting, heating and ventilation;

(e) it has an adequate piped supply of wholesome water;

(f) there are satisfactory facilities in the dwelling-house for the preparation and cooking of food, including a sink with a satisfactory supply of hot and cold water;

(g) it has a suitably located water-closet for the exclusive use of the occupants (if any);

(h) it has, for the exclusive use of the occupants (if any), a suitably located fixed bath or shower and wash-hand basin each of which is provided with a satisfactory supply of hot and cold water; and

(i) it has an effective system for the drainage of foul, waste and surface water;

and any reference to a dwelling-house being unfit for human habitation shall be construed accordingly.

(2) Whether or not a dwelling-house which is a flat satisfies the requirements in subsection (1), it is unfit for human habitation for the purposes of this Act if, in the opinion of the local housing authority, the building or a part of the building outside the flat fails to meet one or more of the requirements in paragraphs (a) to (e) below and, by reason of that failure, the flat is not reasonably suitable for occupation,

(a) the building or part is structurally stable;

(b) it is free from serious disrepair;

(c) it is free from dampness;

(d) it has adequate provision for ventilation; and

(e) it has an effective system for the draining of foul, waste and surface water.

(3) Subsection (1) applies in relation to a house in multiple occupation with the substitution of a reference to the house for any reference to a dwelling-house.

(4) Subsection (2) applies in relation to a flat in multiple occupation with the substitution for any reference to a dwelling-house which is a flat of a reference to the flat in multiple occupation.

7.8   As can be seen, the provisions start from the presumption that premises are fit. Houses and flats which are unfit are those that fail to meet one or more of the nine requirements or standards in s604(1) and which by reason of that failure are not reasonably suitable for occupation.

7.9   The relevant standards for dwelling-houses are set out in s604(1). This is an exhaustive list and other matters, which might, in colloquial terms, render a home unfit, are not relevant to the statutory definition. If the property is a flat however, it may be unfit either for failing the standard in s604(1) or the alternative standard in s604(2) or both. In the case of flats it is important to note that any defects in the common parts relied upon must render the flat unsuitable for continued occupation as distinct from making the other parts of the block or building unsafe. The same factors or requirements apply for the purpose of determining fitness of houses in multiple occupation (s604(3)) or flats in multiple occupation (s604(4)).

7.10 The new s604 definition was in preparation for some considerable time and aspects of it are criticised as being unduly restrictive or representing little progress over the standards it replaced.[5] It should be noted that although premises may be deemed 'unfit for human habitation' at common law (eg, by reason of infestation by bugs), this is irrelevant to statutory unfitness. Nor are premises 'unfit' by reason of failure to be supplied with gas or electricity or otherwise to conform to building regulations or modern standards for new housing.[6] Nor is this definition of unfitness the same as that used in Landlord and Tenant Act 1985 for the purposes of the landlord's obligation to let and keep premises in fit condition (see paragraph 3.46).

7.11 In many cases, premises will be unfit by reference to more than one of the nine points. The section is so drafted however that the dwelling must completely fail at least one of the specified requirements, rather than being close to failing two or more of the requirements. It must be *that* failure which makes the dwelling not reasonably suitable for occupation. It is worth noting that the cause of the unfitness need not arise from within the premises themselves, for example, premises may become unfit where the supply of water or natural light is obstructed externally.

7.12 In considering fitness, the first port of call is DoE Circular 17/96 which at Appendix A contains *Guidance Notes on the Standard of Fitness for Human Habitation*. Advisers should have a copy of this guidance to hand when negotiating with local authority officers, who refer to it routinely.

7.13 At the end of the day, however, whether or not premises are unfit is a question of fact to be determined by the local authority. In *Jones*

---

5   See Ormandy 1985 *Housing Aid* 33 p11 and Parkinson 'Still not a fit standard' (1985) 34 *Housing Review* 190.
6   *Birchall v Wirral UDC* (1953) 117 JP 384.

v Green[7] it was held that 'it is only required that the place must be decently fit for human beings to live in'. In *Hall v Manchester Corporation*[8] the House of Lords held that the standard was that of the ordinary reasonable man. Thus, when considering the application of unfitness legislation, the local authority should ask, 'would the reasonable man hold these premises to be not reasonably suitable for occupation, by reason of a defect or combination of defects covered by the nine listed factors?'

7.14   In *Morgan v Liverpool Corporation*,[9] which would now have relevance to the interpretation of 'serious disrepair', Atkin LJ said that:

> ... if the state of repair of a house is such that by ordinary user damage may naturally be caused to the occupier, either in respect of personal injury to life or limb or injury to health, then the house is not in all respects fit for human habitation.

7.15   This test was approved expressly by the House of Lords in *Summers v Salford Corporation*.[10] In *Dover DC v Sherred and Tarling*,[11] the Court of Appeal confirmed that in considering questions of fitness 'the "Atkinian test" of ordinary user still applies'. Their lordships approved a statement by Luxmore LJ, namely that:

> The usual method of providing ventilation for a room in a dwelling is by a window or windows, which is or are constructed so as to open and shut without danger to the person opening or shutting it or them. If a room, especially a bedroom, has only one window and that window cannot be opened or shut without danger to the person seeking to perform that operation, that room may in my opinion be said not to be fit for human habitation.

7.16   The court held that presence in one room of defects covered by s604 may be sufficient to render the whole of the dwelling unfit. *Summers* also demonstrates that in order to qualify as 'unfit', premises need not be dirty, dilapidated and generally in appalling disrepair; unfitness was found on the basis of a single broken sashcord. The fact that the defects could quickly, easily and cheaply be remedied is irrelevant to the question of whether they render the premises unfit:

---

7   [1925] 1 KB 659 (a case under LTA 1985 s8).
8   [1915] LJ Ch 732.
9   [1927] 2 KB 131.
10   [1943] AC 283.
11   (1997) 29 HLR 864.

It must not be measured by the magnitude of the repairs required. A burst or leaking pipe, a displaced slate or tile, a stopped drain, a rotten stairtread, may each of them make a house unfit to live in, though each of them may quickly and easily be repaired.[12]

7.17 The question of whether or not premises are unfit is initially determined by the local authority. If it holds premises to be statutorily unfit as a result of defects other than those in s604, the finding would be quashed.[13] The authority will, however, be justified in having regard to factors which are present in addition to the statutorily relevant defects.[14] On an appeal to the county court, expert evidence can be called to assist the court in relation to technical matters but ultimately it is a question of fact and common sense for the court in the light of all of the evidence expert and factual whether premises are unfit. No expert can answer that question for the court.[15]

Selecting the appropriate action

7.18 Once a local authority accepted that a property was unfit, it was, until the enactment of the HGCRA, bound by the statutory code to tackle that unfitness. Under the pre-1990 arrangements this was simply a question of either serving notices for the repair of the premises or preventing their further occupation. A test of whether the work could be carried out at reasonable expense[16] determined which alternative was to be pursued. Not surprisingly a considerable body of case-law[17] developed around this criterion of reasonable expense.[18]

7.19 With effect from the coming into force of LGHA on 1 April 1990 the arrangements completely changed. On the face of it, there was no longer an issue as to reasonable expense, although Circular 17/96

---

12 [1943] AC 283, per Lord Atkin.
13 *Estate & Trust Co v Singapore Improvement Trust* [1937] 3 All ER 324, PC.
14 *Steele v Minister of Housing and Local Government and West Ham County BC* (1956) 168 EG 37, CA.
15 *Dover DC v Sherred and Tarling* (1997) 29 HLR 864.
16 See further D Morgan 'Unfit housing: the issue of reasonable cost' (1979) Conv 414; Hadden 'Compulsory repairs and improvements' SSRC 1978 App F; and Arden 'Reasonable expense under the Housing Acts' (1982) 3 HLR (introduction).
17 Starting with *Cohen v West Ham Corporation* [1933] Ch 814 and *Bacon v Grimsby Corporation* [1950] 1 KB 272, and cases up to and including *Cole v Swansea CC* (1988) 21 HLR 468, CA.
18 The reported cases are usefully gathered in *Housing Law Reports*, Vol 3.

reiterates its relevance. The local authority, faced with premises which were unfit, could select from a range of remedial measures prescribed by HA 1985 s604A. These were, and remain principally, as follows:

1) repair notices HA 1985 s189 or s190, with group repair schemes under s190A and HGCRA s60);
2) closing order (HA 1985 s264);
3) demolition order (HA 1985 s265);
4) declaration of housing action area (HA 1985 s239) or improvement area (HA 1985 s253);
5) area clearance (HA 1985 s289); and
6) with effect from 17 December 1996, the further option of the deferred action notice (HGCRA s81).

7.20   In determining which route to pursue, the authority is required to have regard to guidance issued by the Secretary of State for the Environment: currently contained at DoE Circular 17/96 Annex B. The guidance emphasises the advantages of dealing with unfitness by way of an area strategy, rather than on a property-by-property basis. The guidance recommends that before a decision is made as to how to deal with an individual property identified as being unfit, the local authority should assess the effect of the various courses of action (repairs notice, closure, demolition, clearance or deferred action) within the context of the whole area. The purpose of such a neighbourhood renewal assessment is to ensure that (a) economic, social and environmental factors are taken into account in determining the most satisfactory course of action, (b) the long-term consequences of any action are considered, and (c) action on unfit premises takes into account any effect of neighbouring premises.

7.21   After the neighbourhood renewal assessment has been carried out, local authorities are advised to consider:

1) each option within the context of their private sector renewal strategy and the resources available for taking the strategy forward;
2) the practicality of the option having regard to the physical condition of the premises and of any premises which they abut;
3) the life expectancy of the premises if repaired;
4) the relationship of the premises with neighbouring properties and the condition of those properties;
5) proposals for the future of the area in which the premises are situated including: whether the premises are within a

conservation or renewal area or area which is proposed as a renewal area or whether there are longer term plans for clearance; the need for the particular type of premises both in the short and longer term;

6) the owner(s) and occupants of the premises including their circumstances and wishes and any proposals they may have for the future of the premises;

7) in the case of rented premises, the management record of the landlord;

8) the effect of each option on the community in the area;

9) the manner in which each of the options will affect the local environment and overall appearance of the locality.

7.22 By virtue of HCGRA s86 and the Housing (Fitness Enforcement Procedures) Order 1996, the local housing authority must serve a 'minded to take action notice' before it takes any enforcement action, ie, service of a deferred action notice or renewal thereof, s189 or s190 repairs notice, s264 closing order or s265 demolition order. The notice must state what action the local authority is minded to take and must give the local authority's reasons. The person served has at least 14 days to make representations, which the local authority must consider. Clearly the information provided by the 'minded to take action' notice must give the person served sufficient information to enable proper representations to be made: there would seem to be no good reason in the normal case not to serve at least a copy of the draft proposed notice together with the full specification of any remedial works to be required. Failure to serve such notice is a ground of appeal (paragraph 4 of the 1996 Order). Circular 17/96 sets out at Annex B further considerations to which the authority must have regard in deciding whether to take any particular kind of action, ie, repairs notice, deferred action notice, closing order, demolition order or clearance area declaration.

7.23 A landlord disappointed by the authority's selection of the most appropriate action will have a right of appeal and the possibility of persuading the court to prefer a different option (see below). The implications for the tenants and other occupiers arising from the choice made by the authority are considerable (see below). While such tenants have no statutory right of appeal, they might have sufficient interest in such a decision to seek to challenge it by way of judicial review on the usual administrative law principles (eg, failure to take into account some relevant consideration).[19] In *R v Southwark LBC ex p Cordwell*,[20] however, the Court of Appeal indicated that relief by way of judicial review would be granted only in exceptional cases. It was for the local authority to decide on 'the most satisfactory course of action' for the purposes of HA 1985 s604A. The court would not conduct a fine analysis of what was of necessity an inherently imprecise process of evaluation of relevant material, in order to form a different view from the local authority as to the reasonableness of one course over another.

The repairs procedure

7.24   If it decides that the most satisfactory course of action is the restoration of the property to a state of fitness, the local authority must[21] unless it serves a deferred action notice under HGCRA s81 or includes the premises in a group repair scheme under HA 1985 s502, (a) serve a 'minded to take action notice' (see paragraph 7.22), then (b) serve[22] a repair notice on the person having control of the premises (usually the owner or managing agent)[23] (HA 1985 s189). If the property is a house occupied by more than one household, the notice may be served on the person managing the house instead of on the person having control (HA 1985 s189(1B)). If the property is a flat or a flat in multiple occupation and the reason for its unfitness is the defective condition of some other part of the building, the notice should be served on the person having control of that part (HA 1985 s189(1A)).

7.25   The notice requires the execution of stated works considered by the authority sufficient to render the premises fit and provides for a specific completion period. The notice is not confined to specifying 'repair work'. It may also require work or improvement, eg, the installation of a heating system or provision of a hot water supply (HA 1985 s189(2)(a)). The works are usually spelt out in a schedule to the notice and must be sufficiently detailed to enable the owner to see exactly what is required.[24] (Advisers should identify the officer

---

19 *Melhuish v Adams* (1996) March *Legal Action* 15.

20 (1994) 27 HLR 594.

21 *R v Kerrier DC ex p Guppys (Bridport) Ltd* (1976) 32 P&CR 411, CA.

22 As to service of HA notices see (1978) July *LAG Bulletin* 164.

23 See, for 'person in control', HA 1985 s207 and *Pollway Nominees Ltd v Croydon LBC* (1986) 18 HLR 443, HL.

24 *Cohen v West Ham Corporation* [1933] Ch 814. *Church of Our Lady of Hal v Camden LBC* (1980) 255 EG 991; *Maurice v Willesden Corporation* [1953] 2 QB 1.

within the authority responsible for drafting these schedules, and stress the need for the widest possible range of improvement and remedial works.) The authority must supply copies of the notices to freeholders, mortgagees, leaseholders, and, most importantly, tenants (HA 1985 s189(3)). Advisers acting for licensees and other occupiers should always request one, and if refused should check for any notices recorded in the land charges register or district land registry.[25]

7.26   The notice will specify not only the works required, but also the date by which works must start and be completed.[26] The commencement date cannot be earlier than 28 days from the date of service of the notice (HA 1985 s189(2)(a)). This should give the landlord sufficient opportunity to engage contractors (and, where relevant, apply for a local authority grant). Alternatively, the landlord may invite the authority serving the notice to agree to undertake the work at the landlord's expense (HA 1985 s191A).

7.27   If the works are not carried out as required, the local authority may undertake work in default (HA 1985 s193). This is, however, a discretionary power, rather than a mandatory duty.[27] It is exercisable where (a) work has not been started by the commencement date specified, (b) the work has not been completed by the specified completion date or (c) work is under way but 'reasonable progress is not being made' towards compliance with the notice (HA 1985 s193(2) and (2A)). Of course advisers should ensure that authorities are given maximum possible impetus for undertaking works in default.

7.28   If the authority decides to exercise its default powers, it may enter the premises for these purposes, if it has given notice of its intention to do so, and any obstruction by the owner or their agents will be a criminal offence (HA 1985 s194). The cost of carrying out the necessary remedial works[28] can thereafter be recouped from the owner as a debt, or by collection from rent that would otherwise be paid by tenants or as a charge upon the property (HA 1985 Sch 10 paras 1, 2, 4 and 6A). Interest is also recoverable if the sum is not paid on demand.

25 HA 1985 s189(5).
26 For what is reasonable in terms of time, see *Ryall v Cubitt Heath* [1922] 1 KB 275.
27 *Elliott v Brighton BC* (1981) 79 LGR 506.
28 For what is 'necessary' see *Adams v Tuer* (1923) 22 LGR 88; and *Hodgson v Sunderland Corporation* (1937) LJNCCR 187.

7.29　Any person aggrieved[29] by service of a repair notice or a demand for recovery of expenses may appeal to the county court (HA 1985 s191). The bringing of an appeal suspends the operation of the notice: HA 1985 s191(4). If no appeal is entered, the notice becomes final and effective 21 days after service and may not thereafter be impugned in proceedings.[30] On an appeal, the appellant may challenge the decisions of the authority on unfitness or on the terms of the notice.

7.30　There is specific provision for the landlord to argue that either (a) a different owner of the property or building should more properly be served with the notice (HA 1985 s191A) or (b) a more satisfactory way of dealing with the unfitness would have been the making of a demolition or closing order (HA 1985 s191(1B)). In the former case, the landlord is obliged to join other owners in the proceedings (HA 1985 s191(3A)–(3C)) and in the latter case the court must have regard to the DoE code of guidance on dealing with unfit housing (HA 1985 s191(1B)).

7.31　No ground of appeal is excluded, however, so that it appears that the appeal can be brought on any proper ground, including any ground impugning the validity of the notice[31] or raising a public law matter.[32]

7.32　A typical appeal would raise the issue of whether the premises were in fact unfit. Expert evidence can be called to assist the court in relation to technical matters relevant to that question but ultimately it is a question of fact and common sense for the court in the light of all of the evidence, expert and factual, whether premises are unfit and no expert can answer that question for the court.[33] It remains likely that 'unreasonable expense' can be relevant to appeals,[34] having regard to Circular 17/96.

7.33　The judge has power to confirm, quash or vary the notice or demand challenged (HA 1985 s191(2)). The notice may be quashed even if in some respects it is agreeable to the owner.[35] On the appeal,

---

29　This may include the tenant.

30　HA 1985 s189(4); but see *Re Falmouth Clearance Order* [1937] 3 All ER 308; *Graddage v Haringey LBC* [1975] 1 All ER 224; and *Pollway Nominees Ltd v Croydon LBC* [1987] AC 79.

31　*Elliott v Brighton BC* (1980) 258 EG 441.

32　*Wandsworth LBC v Winder* [1985] AC 461; *Nolan v Leeds CC* (1990) 23 HLR 135.

33　*Dover DC v Sherred and Tarling* (1997) 29 HLR 864.

34　See *Hillbank v Hackney LBC* (1978) 3 HLR 73; *Kenny v Kingston upon Thames RLBC* (1985) 17 HLR 344.

35　*Cochrane v Chanctonbury RDC* [1950] 2 All ER 1134.

the judge deals with all matters and questions with which the local authority itself could have dealt.[36] If the appeal is allowed (in whole or in part) because demolition or closure is a more satisfactory course of action than repair, the court may be required to make a finding to that effect (HA 1985 s191(3)). For the authority, this finding has the advantage that it may then, with confidence, make a demolition or closing order. The local authority can no longer ask for a finding which authorises compulsory purchase (HA 1985 s192 has been repealed).

7.34   In the past, repair notices have proved virtually ineffective when served on recalcitrant landlords. They were often either simply ignored or, worse still (from the tenant's point of view), work was half-heartedly started and abandoned part way through. Now, however, the intentional failure to comply with such a notice is a criminal offence (HA 1985 s198A). 'Failure to comply' can arise either from not starting work by the commencement date or not finishing it by the completion date. The landlord may be prosecuted irrespective of whether the local authority is carrying out, or intends to carry out, works in default. In addition to a conviction and fine (not exceeding level 4 on the standard scale), the landlord may be ordered to pay compensation to a tenant or other occupier affected by the offence (Powers of Criminal Courts Act 1973 s35).

The closure/demolition procedure

7.35   Where the local authority is satisfied (as the result of its own investigation, or the combination of its own investigation and findings by the county court judge on a repairs notice appeal) that premises would most reasonably be dealt with by being closed it must make a closing order (HA 1985 s264) in respect of the house or house in multiple occupation (HMO). If one or more flats in a block are unfit, the closing notice may require closure of the whole or of parts of the block (HA 1985 s264(2)).

7.36   If the authority decides that the most satisfactory course of action is demolition, it must serve a demolition order (HA 1985 s265). Where the unfit properties are some or all of the flats in a block, the notice can require the demolition of the entire block (HA 1985 s265(2)). Tenants are not generally given a copy of the notice, but the owner or mortgagee of the property is served with notice (HA 1985 s268(1)). If the order relates to the whole or part of a block of flats,

36   *Fletcher v Ilkeston Corporation* (1931) 96 JPLGR 7.

the building owner and the flat owners must be served (HA 1985 s268(2)).

7.37   Under the pre-1990 regime, an authority considering making a closing or demolition order was required to go through an elaborate procedure of consultation with the landlord and, in certain circumstances, an order could be avoided by an undertaking to carry out works. These statutory consultation requirements are now replaced by the DoE's code of guidance on dealing with unfit properties (HA 1985 s604A). Having declared a property 'unfit', the authority may prefer closure or demolition to the other alternatives of repair or area clearance (see generally DoE circular 17/96).

7.38   A demolition order requires the owner to demolish the premises after they have been vacated and clear the site, and gives rise to powers to demolish in default and recover expenses. A closing order prohibits the use of the premises for any purpose other than one approved by the local authority (HA 1985 s267(2)).

7.39   If the local authority considers that it could use the premises for temporary accommodation it may purchase the property instead of making a demolition or closing order (HA 1985 s300(1)). Notwithstanding that the premises are, a priori, unfit for human habitation and that it has earlier resolved that they are best dealt with by being closed or demolished, the authority is entitled to carry out patch repairs to the purchased property and let it to tenants,[37] who are necessarily deprived of the protection of the implied covenant of fitness at LTA 1985 s8 (HA 1985 s302(a) and (c)).

7.40   Premises retained under HA 1985 s300(1) are notoriously used as 'short life' accommodation or as 'transit' lettings to homeless families. Any attempt by the authority to retain such purchased property as a permanent part of the housing stock will, however, be struck down by the courts.[38]

7.41   If the premises are not capable of providing temporary accommodation and are therefore not purchased, the authority must take further steps including service of notices, leading to either the demolition of the property or its closure.[39] Closure and demolition both give rise to rehousing and compensatory obligations on the part

---

36 *Fletcher v Ilkeston Corporation* (1931) 96 JPLGR 7.
37 Who will not usually be secure: HA 1985 Sch 1 para 3.
38 *Victoria Square Property Co v Southwark LBC* [1978] 2 All ER 281; and see *R v Birmingham CC ex p Sale* (1983) 9 HLR 33.
39 *R v Epsom and Ewell Corporation ex p RB Property Investments (Eastern)* [1964] 2 All ER 832.

of the authority towards displaced tenants. Furthermore, the authority may board up any premises, which have become dangerous, pending demolition or closure.[40]

7.42   Closing and demolition orders may be challenged by a 'person aggrieved' by appeal to the county court (HA 1985 s269). Tenants whose leases have less than three years to run have no right of appeal (HA 1985 s269(2)). It is a ground of appeal that service of the closing or demolition order was not the most satisfactory course of action (HA 1985 s269(2A)(a)). On the hearing of the appeal, the judge may confirm, quash or vary the notice challenged, but may not vary it in such a way as would frustrate the purposes of the legislation, for example, by postponing the date of demolition for several years.[41]

7.43   No ground of appeal is excluded, however, so that it appears that the appeal can be brought on any proper ground, including any ground impugning the validity of the notice[42] or raising a public law matter.[43]

7.44   If the appeal is allowed, the court may, on the application of either party, issue a finding that one of the alternative notices would be more appropriate (HA 1985 s269(3A)). This enables the local authority to serve such alternative notice with some assurance.

7.45   It should be noted that, although most tenants do not have a right of appeal, if the local authority decision is unreasonable under administrative law principles, tenants may challenge such a decision by way of judicial review.[44] Such an application would only succeed if the local authority had made some clear error.[45]

Deferred action notices

7.46   If the local housing authority is satisfied that premises are unfit for human habitation but that service of a deferred action notice is the most satisfactory course of action, it must serve a deferred action notice (HGCRA s81). Such a notice must state that the premises are unfit, specify the necessary works and set out the local authority's options.

7.47   Such notices must be preceded by 'minded to take action' notices

---

40 Local Government (Miscellaneous Provisions) Act 1976 s8.
41 *Pocklington v Melksham UDC* [1964] 2 All ER 862.
42 *Elliott v Brighton BC* (1980) 258 EG 441.
43 *Wandsworth LBC v Winder* [1985] AC 461; *Nolan v Leeds CC* (1990) 23 HLR 135.
44 *R v Ealing LBC ex p Richardson* (1982) 4 HLR 125.
45 *R v Southwark LBC ex p Cordwell* (1994) 27 HLR 594.

under HGCRA s87 and the Housing (Fitness Enforcement Procedures) Order 1996 (see above paragraph 7.22). The person served has the right to appeal within 21 days (there is no power to extend time). Otherwise the notice remains a local land charge while operative.

7.48   The local authority may review the deferred action notice at any time and must review it at intervals of no greater than two years (HGCRA s84(1)). A review must be preceded by an inspection (HGCRA s84(2)). If the local authority considers that a deferred action notice remains the most appropriate course of action it must first serve a 'minded to take action notice' (see above at paragraph 7.22) and then, if appropriate, renew the notice and serve notice of its decision (HGCRA 1985 s84(3)) whereupon the appeal procedures revive.

7.49   In determining whether a deferred action notice is the most satisfactory course of action the local authority is required to have regard to central government guidance,[46] currently at DoE Circular 17/96.

7.50   There is no provision for any appeal to be brought by tenants, but judicial review remains a possibility, providing the case is exceptional.[47]

Mobilising the local authority

7.51   ... a majority of the authorities investigated maintained that it was the presence of a local voluntary housing advice centre or law centre which encouraged strictest compliance with statutory powers.[48]

7.52   Although authorities have substantial powers to eradicate unfit housing, as can be seen above, a frequent difficulty for advisers is mobilising an authority into taking action. Accordingly, advisers must be prepared to argue forcefully with the authority the need for action. Initially, this may take the form of letters and telephone calls to the Housing and Environmental Health Departments, and approaches to local councillors.

7.53   If such pressure produces no response within a reasonable period, advisers should consider obtaining a magistrate's complaint.

---

46 HGCRA s85.
47 *R v Southwark LBC ex p Cordwell* (1994) 27 HLR 594.
48 Hawke and Taylor 'Compulsory repair of individual physically substandard housing' (1984) JSWL 129 at 132.

Under HA 1985 s606(2), reproduced at appendix C, a justice of the peace for the area may complain to the local authority that certain premises are unfit. On receipt of such complaint, the authority is bound to (a) inspect the premises, (b) obtain a report from the officers, and (c) consider the question of 'unfitness'.

7.54　　A similar complaint may be made by a parish or community council, with like effect (HA 1985 s606(2)(b)). See appendix L for a draft complaint.

7.55　　It is not procedurally difficult to arrange for such a complaint to be made. Advisers can draft all necessary documents themselves[49] and need only satisfy a JP on the basis of either a personal inspection or written report, that certain premises are unfit.[50] Practice varies considerably in arrangements made by courts for dealing with these cases, but most justices' clerks will simply make an ad hoc arrangement for a magistrate to be available. The speediest method is to set up an inspection on an informal basis with a JP known to the adviser or tenant.

7.56　　Complaints received by local authorities under HA 1985 s606 usually prompt an immediate inspection and officer's report, and find their way on to Housing Committee agendas.[51]

7.57　　If a local authority is satisfied that premises are unfit but is dilatory in taking action, the remedy of judicial review and mandamus should be considered by advisers, since the HA 1985 code compels the authority to act[52] unless it:

1) serves a deferred action notice under HGCRA s81, or
2) determines that the premises will qualify for inclusion in a group repair scheme (HA 1985 s190A) due to be prepared within 12 months (in which case the duty to take action relates only to works which will not form part of the group repair scheme).

7.58　　In certain cases, complaint to the local ombudsman may be worthwhile. Failure to act when it is known that a property is unfit is maladministration, notwithstanding the resource implications for local authorities.[53]

49　See appendix L and 'Unfitness' Shelter Practice Note No 2 for standard forms.
50　See case discussed at (1973) June *LAG Bulletin* 117.
51　See 'Action Notes on s157' in 48 *Community Action* 26–28; and for the use of s606 (formerly HA 1957 s157) in Manchester see 53 *Community Action* 4, and in Newham see *Municipal Engineering* 11 February 1977, and March 1977 *Roof*.
52　*R v Kerrier DC ex p Guppys (Bridport) Ltd* (1976) P&CR 411.
53　Investigation No 171/C/84.

Tenants' rights to rehousing

7.59   Persons who are displaced as the result of a closing or demolition order are, generally, entitled to monetary compensation and rehousing.[54]

7.60   Where a person is displaced from residential accommodation as a result of a demolition or closing order and suitable alternative accommodation is not available, the local authority is under a duty to provide accommodation (Land Compensation Act 1973 s39). However, the duty is for the local authority to 'do its best', and it can offer temporary accommodation until permanent accommodation is available and the permanent accommodation need not be offered on the same terms as those on which the previous accommodation was held.[55] Nevertheless, use of the HA procedures may prove attractive to a would-be council tenant not otherwise in a priority group for the allocation of council housing.

Implications for tenants

7.61   Before taking any action in respect of individual unfit properties, advisers should be careful to clarify precisely the instructions given by the tenant/client. If the tenant wishes to have the premises put in repair, the adviser should press for use of the repair notice procedure (HA 1985 s189) and, if necessary, prosecution for non-compliance and works in default. If the process is upset by the owner establishing on appeal that the premises are more satisfactorily dealt with by closure or demolition, the adviser should ensure that the court makes a formal finding, and thereafter serves the appropriate notice in respect of the property (HA 1985 s191).

7.62   Alternatively, the tenants of a landlord successful in a repair notice appeal may prefer and be able to seek other means of redress (see chapters 3–6) rather than lose their homes under closure or demolition procedures.

7.63   If, on the other hand, the tenant wishes to be rehoused, usually into local authority accommodation, the approach will differ. The adviser will be pressing for a finding that the premises are most satisfactorily dealt with by closure, demolition or clearance. Thereafter, the making of a closing or demolition order will entitle the tenant to alternative housing and certain compensatory

---

54 Land Compensation Act 1973 ss29–39.
55 *R v Bristol Corporation ex p Hendy* [1974] 1 All ER 1047, CA.

payments (see above). However, note that the accommodation need not necessarily be permanent housing of the type sought by the tenant.[56] Advisers should also be alert to the possibility of the authority acquiring the property for temporary accommodation and carrying out patch repairs (HA 1985 s300(1)).

7.64 Advisers should note that, although once served with a copy of the demolition or closing order the tenant is required to give up occupation (HA 1985 s270 demolition orders, s277 closing orders), that does not usually cause the tenancy to end. Special provision is made under s317 for either landlord or tenant to apply to the county court for an order terminating or varying the lease. This gives the court the opportunity, inter alia, to award compensation and damages if the tenancy should be terminated as a result of the local authority notice.[57] Statutory Rent Act tenants, however, do not enjoy the benefit of this procedure as the Rent Acts cannot prevent the recovery of possession under a demolition or closing order (HA 1988 ss270 and 276), other than by showing either that they have not received notice of the order or that it has not become operative.[58]

7.65 Whichever course is adopted, advisers should ensure that they are familiar with the way in which their own authority has delegated the exercise of Housing Act powers and duties, and at what level the principal decisions such as 'unfitness' and the most satisfactory course of action are determined. In at least one London borough, the powers to make these decisions and serve notices have been delegated to individual EHOs.[59]

7.66 Exercise of HA powers does not interfere with the tenant's rights to take alternative action as a result of default by landlords (HA 1985 s203(3)). But the tenant has no right to withhold rent[60] unless recouping the cost of repairs or exercising a set-off (see chapter 4).

7.67 Application may be made to reduce any current registered rent, but the rent officer need not register a nil or nominal rent in respect of unfit property[61] although a lower registered rent may be anticipated.[62]

56 *R v Bristol Corporation ex p Hendy* [1974] 1 All ER 1047, CA.
57 HA 1985 s317(2) and *Malik v Politi* [1964] CLY 1703.
58 *Beaney v Branchett* (1987) 19 HLR 471, CA.
59 Under Local Government Act 1972 s101.
60 *Stevenson (Westminster) v Mock* [1954] JPL 275.
61 *Williams v Khan* (1981) 258 EG 554, CA.
62 See D Ormandy 'Conditions and rent' April 1978 *LAG Bulletin* 91.

Council tenants

7.68   The position of private sector and housing association tenants is as described above. Similarly, if a council tenant rents from one authority but lives within the area of another, there is no bar to the exercise of HA powers by the latter against the landlord authority.

7.69   However, where the council tenant's landlord is the local authority itself, it has been held that as a local authority cannot properly serve HA notices upon itself and it cannot apply HA 1985 Pt VI in respect of its own properties.[63] Nevertheless, the authority is obliged to consider complaints of unfitness from both tenants and magistrates (see paras 7.51–7.52). In the latter case an inspection and report must be made (HA 1985 s606(2)).

7.70   Modern government guidance[64] has encouraged local authorities to make local arrangements to deal with unfit council housing. It urges them to introduce and publish arrangements whereby, if a council tenant seeks the help of an EHO about the condition of a property which, in the EHO's opinion is such that, if it were private property, action under the HA would be necessary, the EHO will give notice to the Director of Housing who should ensure that necessary works are carried out within a reasonable period. Advisers should accordingly obtain copies of the relevant authorities' published arrangements and have regard to the guidance issued to EHOs as to implementation.[65]

7.71   Where council property is transferred to a housing action trust (HA 1988 Pt III), the Secretary of State may, by order, give the trust powers to deal with unfit property in substitution for, or concurrent with, those of the authority (HA 1988 s65). If no such order is made, the property conveyed to the trust is vulnerable to the unfitness procedures of local authorities in just the same way as property owned by private landlords.

Housing in need of substantial repair

7.72   Not all disrepair will be sufficiently serious to make a property statutorily unfit. Yet tenants may experience severe hardship as a

---

63   *R v Cardiff CC ex p Cross* (1983) 6 HLR 1, CA.
64   DoE Circular 21/84 para 117; WO Circular 42/84.
65   See Ormandy *Housing Aid* 30 p6 and 32 p18.

result of that disrepair. Since 1969[66] local authorities have had the power to act in such circumstances. The HA 1985 s190(1)(a) provides that where a local authority is satisfied that:

> ... a dwelling-house or house in multiple occupation is in such a state of disrepair that although it is not unfit for human habitation, substantial repairs are required to bring it up to a reasonable standard ...

it may serve a notice on the person having control of the house (usually the landlord/owner rather than the tenant[67]) requiring the performance of specified remedial works. If the building is an HMO, notice can be served on the manager (s190(1C)). Copies of the notice must be served on any freeholder, mortgagee and, most importantly, tenants (s190(3)), although there is no requirement to serve copies on other occupiers.

7.73   By virtue of HGCRA s86 and the Housing (Fitness Enforcement Procedures) Order 1996 (SI 1996 No 2885) the local authority is required to serve a 'minded to take action notice' (see above at paragraph 7.22) before serving a s190 repairs notice under HA 1985.

7.74   The only express limitations on what may be included in the notice itself are that it cannot compel works of internal decorative repairs (HA 1985 s190(2)). The prohibition of internal decorative repair should cause no difficulty for the tenant since the landlord's performance of the other works of repair specified in the notice will in any event carry with it an obligation to make good any decoration disturbed or destroyed).[68] The authority is required to draft the notice in sufficient detail for the owner to see exactly what remedial works are required.[69]

7.75   If the tenant occupies a flat in a block, and it is disrepair in the other parts of the building which is causing problems, the authority may serve the s190 notice on the person having control of that part of the building concerned (HA 1985 s190(1A)). Thus, in securing the comprehensive repair of a building containing flats, the council will serve notices on leaseholders of the individual flats as well as on the freeholder (in respect of the common parts).[70]

7.76   For s190 to apply, the property concerned must either be situated

---

66 HA 1969 s72.
67 S207 and see *White v Barnet LBC* (1989) 21 HLR 346, CA.
68 *McGreal v Wake* (1984) 13 HLR 107, CA; and *Bradley v Chorley BC* (1985) 17 HLR 305, CA.
69 *Church of Our Lady of Hal v Camden LBC* (1980) 255 EG 991, CA.
70 DoE Circular 1/89 para 9.

in a renewal area (see chapter 8) or have an 'occupying tenant' (HA 1985 s190(1B)). An 'occupying tenant' is either a contractual or statutory tenant or a licensee with a restricted contract or a protected or assured agricultural occupier (HA 1985 s207).

7.77 Any appeal must be brought within 21 days after the date of service of the notice (HA 1985 s191(1)): there is no power to extend time. There are no prescribed limits to the grounds on which an appeal may be brought. Many appeals are on the basis that the premises are not 'in disrepair' or that 'substantial repairs' are not 'necessary to bring it up to a reasonable standard'. Appeals can however turn on the validity of the notice itself[71] or raise public law issues.[72]

7.78 If the owner subsequently appeals, the county court judge, in considering whether to uphold the appeal, may take into account all relevant matters including the cost of the work, the value of the property, the circumstances of the owner etc[73] and, indeed, all relevant central government guidance, eg, DoE Circular 17/96. It is however important to keep in mind that the policy of parliament is to make the owners of houses keep them in proper repair (see paragraph 7.3).

7.79 The court may quash, vary (eg, as to the amount of work required[74] or confirm the notice (HA 1985 s191(2). If an appeal is allowed at least in part because the court is satisfied that a closing order or a demolition order would be 'the most satisfactory course of action' the judge shall include a finding to that effect in his judgment, if requested to do so by local authority or appellant prior to entry of judgment (HA 1985 s191(3)).

7.80 It is also a ground of appeal that some other owner is more properly served than the appellant (HA 1985 s191(1A)). If such appeal is allowed, the court may vary the notice so as to require the works to be carried out by some other owner of the property (HA 1985 s191(3A)).

7.81 If the owner fails to commence the work or complete it by the commencement or completion dates specified in the notice, or starts work but does not make reasonable progress, the authority may

---

71 *Elliott v Brighton BC* (1980) 258 EG 441.
72 *Wandsworth LBC v Winder* [1985] AC 461; *Nolan v Leeds CC* (1990) 23 HLR 135.
73 S191 and *Hillbank Properties v Hackney LBC*; *Kenny v Kingston upon Thames RLBC* (1985) 17 HLR 344. See H Wilkinson 'Capable of being rendered fit' 1985 NLJ 831.
74 *Cochrane v Chanctonbury RDC* [1950] 2 All ER 1134.

enter the premises and carry out the works in default, with the same rights as to recovery of expenses as in relation to s189 repair notices. The owner retains a right of appeal under HA 1985 s191.

7.82   The courts have supported the use by local authorities of the s190 provision to stop bad housing from slipping into unfitness.[75] In particular, the Court of Appeal has allowed county court judges, in dealing with appeals against s190 notices, to have regard to the policy considerations behind the legislation and weigh them against the burdens falling upon landlords who allow their properties to fall into substantial disrepair.[76]

7.83   Advisers should encourage their local authority into positive use of s190 and in particular to prosecute (see below) and carry out works in default. Landlords can no longer frustrate or avoid enforcement action by selling-on properties subject to notice, as notices must be registered as local land charges when they become operative (HA 1985 s190(5)).

7.84   Intentional failure to comply with a s190 notice constitutes a summary criminal offence. Authorities should be encouraged to prosecute defaulting landlords and, in appropriate cases, tenants should apply for criminal compensation orders against landlords who will also be convicted and fined (HA 1985 s198A).

Fit houses in disrepair

7.85   Local authorities have further powers to take action in respect of premises which are neither unfit for human habitation nor in severe disrepair. HA 1985 s190(1)(b) provides that where a local authority is satisfied that:

> ... a dwelling-house or house in multiple occupation is in such state of disrepair that, although it is not unfit for human habitation, the condition is such as to interfere materially with the personal comfort of occupying tenants or in the case of a house in multiple occupation, the persons occupying it (whether as tenants or licensees) ...,

it may serve a notice on the owner requiring the execution of specified remedial works. If the tenant occupies a flat and it is part of the building outside the flat, which is interfering with the personal

---

75 See note 73.
76 *Kenny v Kingston upon Thames LBC* (1985) 274 EG 395, (1985) 17 HLR 344.

comfort of the tenant, notice may be served on the owner of those (common) parts (HA 1985 s190(1A)(b)).

7.86   Exercise of this power is discretionary and the authority may act either on its own initiative or, for example, in response to a complaint from a tenant occupying the whole or part of the property. For these purposes, 'tenant' includes statutory tenants and those with restricted contracts (HA 1985 s207).

7.87   Experience indicates that the s190 provision is under-employed as a weapon to tackle bad housing, even though it can be used to compel landlords to undertake repairs. In default, the authority has the same power to enter the property, do the work, recover its expenses and/or prosecute the landlord as it does for other repair notices (see above).

7.88   The Act does not require the authority to have regard to the age, character and locality of the dwelling. However, the discomfort must arise from the condition of the property itself and external factors are probably thereby excluded unless they arise from common parts.

7.89   Almost all forms of disrepair will cause some interference with the personal comfort of occupiers, and if this discomfort is sufficiently 'material' advisers should encourage authorities to use their powers under this provision.

'Houses'

7.90   Throughout Pt VI of HA 1985, the term 'house' has been replaced by the term 'dwelling-house' or 'premises' to describe the type of property subject to the unfitness and repairs procedure. For these purposes, 'dwelling-house' is defined to include 'any yard, garden, outhouse and appurtenances belonging to it or usually enjoyed with it'.[77] Thus, if a backyard is in such a state of disrepair as to constitute a danger to the tenant, the property as a whole may be deemed unfit and subject to the Housing Act code. Furthermore, for the purposes of Pts VI and IX, the statutory powers extend to flats which are dwelling-houses (HA 1985 s207) and, as seen above, notices may be served in respect of buildings containing flats. The post-1990 scheme also includes both HMOs and flats in multiple occupation (HA 1985 s345). The revision of these technical references was made necessary by continued difficulty with the use of the word 'house' in

77   HA 1985 s207 and see *R v Camden LBC ex p Rowton* [1984] LGR 614.

the previous statute and case-law.[78] However, because of the improved fitness standard, the possibility of using HA 1988 notices on temporary[79] and movable structures has been withdrawn (HA 1985 s205 has been repealed). The plethora of cases on the meaning of 'multiple occupation' and 'house' can be looked up in any annotated version of HA 1985 s207 and 345.

Conclusion

7.91 The procedures for dealing with statutorily unfit properties constitute a double-edged sword. They may just as easily leave an owner with vacant possession or a cleared site, as provide the tenant with a repaired home. Even those tenants who would qualify for rehousing by the local authority may languish in unfit property for substantial periods awaiting an offer of accommodation, notwithstanding the statutory priorities.[80] It is for these reasons that advisers should be pressing authorities to use powers under HA 1985 s190 to tackle bad housing before it sinks into unfitness. It is worth remembering that the courts are not necessarily anxious to prevent slum landlords from making a profit out of their own failure to carry out repairing obligations.[81]

78 In *Pollway Nominees Ltd v Croydon LBC* [1987] AC 79, it was accepted, for the purposes of the appeal, that s189 might be applied to a 'house' consisting of a purpose-built block of flats.

79 See the 'henhouse' declared unfit by Caradon DC *Times* 15 October 1980.

80 HA 1996 Part VI.

81 *Buswell v Goodwin* [1971] 1 WLR 92.

CHAPTER 8

Housing conditions

For complete chapter contents, see overleaf

Introduction

8.1 This chapter notes other housing conditions related to disrepair: its purpose is to draw readers' attention to problems which are likely to be encountered when advising tenants. There is no attempt here to go into detail; the intention is solely to give pointers to more appropriate sources where specialised and comprehensive information can be obtained.

Area action

8.2 In addition to dealing with unsatisfactory individual houses and flats through the Housing Act 1985 (HA 1985) (chapter 7) and the Environmental Protection Act 1990 (EPA) (chapter 6), housing authorities may resolve to tackle areas of unsatisfactory housing, by using powers under HA 1985, as amended/extended by the Local Government and Housing Act 1989 (LGHA) and the Housing Grants, Construction and Regeneration Act 1996 (HGCRA). The following powers are available:

1) Declaration of a clearance area under HA 1985 ss289–306, where the most satisfactory course of action is the clearance of unsatisfactory housing.
2) Declaration of a renewal area under LGHA ss89–100, where rehabilitation of housing is the most effective way of dealing with an area of primarily unsatisfactory housing.
3) Preparation of a group repair scheme under HGCRA ss60–75 to repair the exterior of a group of houses ('enveloping').

Clearance areas under HA 1985 ss289–306

8.3 A clearance area is an area which is to be cleared of all buildings (s289(1)) on the ground that the local housing authority is satisfied that the dwellings in the area are unfit for human habitation or dangerous/injurious to health by reason of 'bad arrangement' and that demolition of all the buildings in the area is the most satisfactory course of action(s289(2)).

8.4 Declaration by the authority of a clearance area leads to a process of acquisition by compulsory purchase of the properties in that area and their subsequent demolition. The cleared site is then available to the authority for its own purposes, usually the provision of new housing. The authority must:

1) ensure that owners and occupiers are formally notified at an early stage and consult with them (s289(2A), (2B) and (2C));
2) ensure that it has sufficient resources to carry the scheme through and to rehouse any displaced persons who are unable to secure their own suitable accommodation (s289(4));
3) take account of a wide range of factors before declaring a clearance area (s604A and the code of guidance issued thereunder, DoE Circular 17/96);
4) pay compensation paid to displaced owners (Pt XVII as extensively amended).

8.5   There has been no improvement in the rights of displaced tenants, indeed, 'well maintained' payments, formerly available to some displaced tenants have been abolished (HA 1985 Schs 23 and 24 have been repealed).

8.6   The authority has to pass a resolution defining a clearance area by reference to a map, which must exclude dwellings which are not unfit or dangerous/injurious to health (s289(3)). It then purchases all of the dwellings in that area, by agreement or by using its compulsory purchase powers (subject to the consent of the Secretary of State)(s290). The authority can then clear the area itself or sell the land subject to conditions relating to its clearance (s291). Dwellings capable of providing adequate accommodation for the time being can be used for the provision of interim accommodation (ss300–302).

Renewal areas under LGHA ss89–100

8.7   A local housing authority may resolve that an area of land be defined on a map and declared to be a renewal area if it is satisfied that the area is primarily residential and that living conditions are unsatisfactory and that those conditions can be most effectively dealt with by declaring the area to be a renewal area (s89(1)).

8.8   The authority may not make such a resolution before it has consulted locally (s89(5)), had regard to central government guidance (DoE Circulars 6/90 and 17/96) (s89(4)) and considered a report particularising living conditions in the area, improvement proposals, the powers available to the housing authority, detailed proposals for the exercise of those powers, the cost and the resources available from whatever source (including contributions from the secretary of state under s96)(s89(3)).

8.9   A renewal area must contain at least 300 dwellings, at least 75%

of which must be privately owned and at least 75% of which must be unfit or able to qualify for repairs grants under LGHA ss112, 113 or 115 (s90 and directions thereunder found at DoE Circular 17/96 Annex C.1). Renewal areas are initially for ten years (s89(6)).

8.10   Once a renewal area has come into existence, the housing authority is required to publicise the action it proposes to take and the assistance which is available, providing an information and advice service to persons wishing to carry out works to housing accommodation (ss91, 92). Assistance is generally in the form of repairs and improvement grants, which used to be found in LGHA Pt VIII but which are now found in HGCRA Chapter 1: but there is a very wide power to provide grants and other assistance under LGHA s93(5).

Group repair schemes under HGCRA ss60–74

8.11   Group repair schemes are commonly known as 'enveloping': 'Enveloping is the renovation of the external fabric and curtilage of dwellings which have deteriorated beyond the scope of routine maintenance ... It includes such items as repair or renewal of roof and chimneys, rainwater goods, work to external walls, repair or replacement of doors and windows and improvements to the curtilages. Whole terraces or blocks are dealt with simultaneously' (DoE Circular 29/82).

8.12   Local housing authorities have a discretion to prepare a group repair scheme to put the exterior of buildings comprised in the scheme into reasonable repair, or to render them structurally stable (s60(1)). Buildings are 'qualifying buildings' if their exterior is not in reasonable repair, or they are structurally unstable (s61; Group Repair (Qualifying Buildings) Regulations 1996).[1]

8.13   The authority has to prepare a specification of 'scheme works' (s62). If the group repair scheme is approved by the Secretary of State then the authority may, with the consent of persons participating in the scheme, enter into agreements for the work to be carried out (s63). The persons who participate in the scheme are the owners of the relevant buildings (s64) and they must consent to the scheme (s65). Owners are liable to pay a percentage of the cost of the work but the percentage would not normally exceed the higher of (a) the sum that would be paid if the owner had obtained a means-tested renovation grant, (b) 25% of the cost of the works (if the dwelling is

1   SI No 2883.

in a renewal area) or 50% of the cost of the works (otherwise) (s67).

8.14   References

Arden and Hunter *Encyclopedia of Housing Law and Practice* (Sweet
& Maxwell, updated).
Hughes and Lowe *Social Housing Law and Policy* (Butterworths,
1995, chapter 7).
Burridge and Ormandy *Unhealthy Housing* (Routledge & Chapman,
1993) chapters 14, 15 and 16)
DoE Circular 17/96.

Asbestos

8.15   Asbestos, and building materials containing asbestos, have been
used in the construction and modernisation of housing for more
than a generation. Asbestos and its derivatives may be found, for
example, in insulation boards used for panels or in the form of
sprayed-on insulation coverings as well as in some older types of
textured paint. It was heavily used in system-built blocks of flats
where industrialised building techniques were employed and has
been extensively applied in pipelining.

8.16   It is widely recognised that asbestos fibres released in air may
prove prejudicial to human health. Indeed, having regard to the
weight of widely published expert opinion as to the dangers of
asbestos, a contractor who, ignorant of the health risk involved,
carries out remedial work resulting in dangerous levels of asbestos
contamination, will be held to have failed to work with reasonable
care and skill.[2] It was reasonably foreseeable as early as 1925 that
exposure to asbestos dust could result in pulmonary injury, including
mesothelioma.[3]

8.17   Tenants with homes containing asbestos or suspected asbestos
will be best advised initially to contact their local EHO. According to
the circumstances it may be possible to take such action as will cause
the removal of the asbestos by the landlord. Technical support and

2   *Barclays Bank plc v Fairclough Building Ltd (No 2)* 44 Con LR 35, 76 BLR 1,
   [1995] IRLR 605, [1995] EGCS 10, (1995) *Times* 15 February; see also Control
   of Asbestos at Work Regulations 1987 SI No 2115.
3   *Margereson v J W Roberts Ltd* [1996] PIQR P358, [1996] Env LR 304, (1996)
   Times 17 April.

assistance may be available from the London Hazards Centre, Interchange Studios, Dalby Street, London NW5 3NQ.

8.18   Asbestos fibres loose in air as a result of disrepair are very probably prejudicial to health.[4] Accordingly, action may be taken either under the EPA (chapter 6) or directly under other repairing obligations or the obligation to carry out remedial or improvement work with reasonable care and skill (chapters 3 and 4).

8.19   **References**

Health and Safety Executive *Asbestos dust: the hidden killer! Are you at risk?* (Published in series IND(G)187 6/96 C500).
R Widdison 'Asbestos in the home' October 1982 *LAG Bulletin* 114.
Asbestos materials in buildings (forthcoming, DETR, TSO).
Dalton and Summers 'Asbestos: killer dust' Jan/Feb 1981 *Roof* 10.
'Danger asbestos' 46 and 47 *Community Action*.
Church v Ministry of Defence (1984) NLJ 623.
C Hughes '£2 billion needed to make asbestos safe' *Times* 10 September 1985.
'Fighting the invisible enemy' May/June 1984 *Roof* 20.

Condensation dampness

8.20   The DETR English House Condition survey of 1996 revealed that over 300,000 people suffer from condensation, rising and/or penetrating damp to their homes.

8.21   Condensation dampness brings with it conditions of mould growth, excessive humidity and, often, insect infestation. The grave effects of these conditions on the health and well-being of tenants have now been extensively documented.

8.22   In very basic terms, condensation dampness arises when a dwelling is incapable of dealing with normal levels of water vapour due to: lack of insulation, lack of ventilation, inadequate heat input, or a combination of such factors. Its presence is observed as condensed water on cooled surfaces, mould spores, damp wall coverings and plaster, infestation by house mites and destruction of soft furnishings in severe cases.

---

4   *Morganite Crucible Ltd v Nurse* [1989] AC 692, [1989] 2 WLR 82, [1989] 1 All ER 113; *Gotech Industrial and Environmental Services v Friel* Env L M 1996 5(2), 6–8 and cases in footnotes 2 and 3.

8.23   For some time tenants and their advisers have been using legal remedies among others to seek redress in such circumstances. The following short summary deals with various legal remedies and the condensation dampness problem.

Terms of the tenancy agreement

8.24   Express terms often oblige the landlord to do no more than remedy structural defects. Frequently however, the obligation is more extensive. An obligation to keep 'premises' (eg, as a whole) in 'habitable repair' means that they must be kept 'in all respects reasonably fit for human habitation'.[5]

8.25   A number of cases decide that an obligation to keep a dwelling in 'good condition' is more onerous than an obligation to keep a dwelling in 'good repair'.[6]

8.26   Accordingly, in *Jones v Joseph*[7] the obligation to keep and deliver up the premises 'in as good repair and condition' as at the commencement of the tenancy was broken when the premises became infested with bugs. In *Johnson v Sheffield CC*[8] the court held that a requirement to keep the dwelling 'fit to live in' meant that the landlord was liable for condensation damp and mould caused by the inherently defective condition of the dwelling. A similar result was achieved in *Arnold v Greenwich LBC*[9] where the obligation was 'to maintain the dwelling in good condition and repair'.

8.27   It is sometimes possible to imply terms into the tenancy agreement. For example, if the tenant is obliged to decorate internally, it may be implied that the landlord is obliged to prevent the defective condition of the dwelling giving rise to condensation and mould, destructive of the decorations.[10] Furnished lettings are subject to the implied term as to fitness for habitation.[11]

5   *Summers v Salford Corporation* [1943] AC 283; *Belcher v Mackintosh* (1839) 2 Moo & R 186.

6   *Lurcott v Wakely and Wheeler* [1911] 1 KB 905; *Credit Suisse v Beegas Nominees Ltd* [1994] 4 All ER 804.

7   [1918] KB 510.

8   August 1994 *Legal Action* 16.

9   May 1998 *Legal Action* 21.

10 See by analogy *Barrett v Lounova (1982) Ltd* [1990] 1 QB 348.

11 *Hart v Windsor* (1844) 12 M & W 68.

LTA 1985 s11 or DPA 1972 s4

8.28 The more traditional contractual and common law remedies against landlords (see chapters 3 and 4) are difficult to apply in condensation cases due to the need to show specific disrepair to the structure or fabric of a building rather than a design problem or planning defect.

8.29 In *Quick v Taff-Ely BC*[12] the Court of Appeal decided that s11 cannot provide a remedy for a tenant suffering the effects of condensation dampness unless there is actual disrepair to the structure or exterior of the dwelling. Where such disrepair can be shown (for example because the condensation has corrupted woodwork or caused plaster to crumble) it will become actionable.[13] In such cases, the court is likely to be satisfied that the only sensible way of remedying the s11 disrepair involves tackling the underlying defects giving rise to condensation.[14] Conversely, where disrepair falling within s11 is causing or materially contributing to condensation, it is also actionable.[15]

8.30 Because DPA 1972 s4(1)–(3) spring from an obligation to repair or maintain the property, these provisions by themselves are of limited usefulness in the absence of actual damage to the structure or 'fabric' of the property.[16] Section 4(4) provides however that where a landlord is 'expressly or impliedly' entitled to enter to carry out 'any description of maintenance or repair' then the landlord is treated as being under a duty to take reasonable care to ensure that a failure to so repair or maintain does not cause personal injury or property damage.[17] There can be little doubt that by virtue of s4(4) the express or implied rights to enter to repair or maintain found in some tenancy agreements can give rise to liability for personal injury or property damage caused by condensation.

8.31 If work to rectify condensation fails to eradicate it, a possible action may lie in negligence.[18] If the dwelling was negligently designed or constructed so as to generate condensation, an action may lie in negligence against the landlord or designer or builder (see chapter 3 para 3.38).

---

12 [1985] 3 All ER 321.

13 *Staves & Staves v Leeds CC* (1991) 23 HLR 107; *Switzer v Law* [1998] 7 CL 380.

14 *Elmcroft Developments v Tankersley-Sawyer* (1984) 15 HLR 63; [1984] 1 EGLR 47; *Stent v Monmouth DC* (1987) 19 HLR 269; [1987] 1 EGLR 59.

15 *Lloyd v Rees* [1996] CLY 3725; *Switzer v Law* [1998] 7 CL 380.

16 *Abdullah and Others v South Tyneside BC* September 1987 *Legal Action* 12.

17 *McAuley v Bristol CC* [1992] QB 134.

18 *Ball v London CC* [1949] 2 KB 159; *Billings (AC) & Sons v Riden* [1957] 3 All ER 1.

EPA 1990 s82

8.32   In recent years public health and environmental protection legislation has increasingly been recognised as a satisfactory means of securing redress, since acute condensation dampness invariably gives rise to conditions which are 'prejudicial to health' and thus a statutory nuisance (see chapter 6). The period between 1975 and 1980 saw extensive use of PHA 1936 s99 (and now EPA s82) proceedings in condensation cases in the magistrates' courts.[19] Indeed, by 1980/81 it had become well recognised that dampness was prejudicial to health and that condensation dampness itself was capable of potential or actual injury to health.[20]

8.33   However, in order to establish a successful prosecution the tenant must be able to show that (unless the problem arises from structural defects) the conditions are the responsibility of the landlord. Thus in *Dover DC v Farrar*[21] a conviction was quashed on appeal where the housing authority landlord successfully established that the dwellings concerned had been constructed by it in accordance with prevailing standards and that with sufficient use of the supplied heating system, the provision made for ventilation and insulation was adequate to avoid condensation. The fact that fuel price increases subsequent to construction meant that the tenants were unable to use the heating system was held not to be the responsibility of the landlord authority.

8.34   Regrettably, the *Dover* case has been used by housing authorities and other landlords to persuade tenants, their advisers and magistrates that s82 proceedings could not be founded on condensation dampness. In fact the contrary is the case. The *Dover* decision is clear authority for the proposition that landlords can be prosecuted in relation to condensation dampness. Later cases have shown that with the careful use of specialist written evidence and expert witnesses (especially independent EHOs) it is possible to prove in the majority of condensation cases that the dampness does arise from the landlord's failure to get the

---

19   *Portsmouth v Treleavan* (1975) unreported, noted at January 1976 *Roof* 21; *Fitzpatrick v Dawnray* (1976) unreported, noted at May 1976 *Roof* 2; *Piper v GLC* (1977) unreported, noted at July 1977 *Roof* 122.

20   *Patel v Mehtab* (1982) 5 HLR 78; *Dover DC v Farrar* (1982) 2 HLR 32; DoE Circular 6/90 annex A5

21   (1982) 2 HLR 32.

condensation   equation   (heat/moisture/ventilation/insulation)
right.[22]

8.35   In *Tower Hamlets LBC v GLC*[23] the Divisional Court dismissed an
appeal against a conviction in relation to condensation dampness.
The tenants and prosecuting authority claimed that the dwellings
were insufficiently ventilated and insulated and that the inability of
the flats to cope with normal moisture led to condensation for which
the landlord was responsible. Considering the *Dover* case, Griffiths
LJ said he did not read it as authority for the proposition that tenants
should be required to use wholly abnormal quantities of fuel to avert
condensation. The court held that 'a landlord is required to apply his
mind to the necessity of ventilation and, if need be, to insulation and
heating. The landlord must provide a combination of these factors to
make a house habitable for the tenant'.

8.36   Applying these authorities, the Divisional Court in *Birmingham
DC v Kelly and Others*[24] was able to uphold convictions even though
the landlord was not in breach of any contractual or other obligation
to repair. Liability for the condensation dampness was established
from the evidence that there was some default by the council in
relation to the design of the premises which caused the condensation
difficulties and thus the mould.

Ombudsmen

8.37   The local government ombudsmen have regularly accepted that
failures to investigate properly or to resolve complaints of
condensation dampness amount to maladministration. Their reports
frequently contain not only strong recommendations for compensatory payments but also useful guidance on the proper approach to be
adopted by councils in condensation cases. See, for example, the
report on Investigation 746/1/84 noted at (1986) March *Legal Action*
33.

22 *Lawton v East Devon DC* (1982) unreported, noted at July/August 1982 *Roof* 28;
    McGourlick v Renfrew DC (1982) unreported, noted at 1982 *Scolag* 182 and
    1986 *Scolag* 83.
23 (1983) 15 HLR 54, QBD, applied in *Law v Hillingdon LBC* December 1989
    Legal Action 16.
24 (1985) 17 HLR 572, QBD.

8.38   ## References

Tenants' Resource & Information Service *Action on Damp Homes* (1995, from the Newcastle Tenants Federation, First Floor, 1 Pink Lane, Newcastle upon Tyne NE1 5DW).
BS 5250: 1989 *Control of Condensation in Buildings*, from BSI Customer Services, 389 Chiswick High Road, London W4 4AL.
Ormandy *The Law of Statutory Nuisance* (1997, CIEH).
Burridge and Ormandy *Unhealthy Housing* (Routledge & Chapman, 1993).
Platt et al 'Damp housing, mould growth and symptomatic health state' (1989) 298 BMJ 1673.

Dampness

8.39   This increasingly common form of housing disrepair now affects millions of tenants. It may take the form of penetrating dampness, construction damp, rising damp or condensation (see above).

8.40   As has been shown, legal remedies for tenants suffering the effects of dampness as a result of disrepair are available both under contractual and common law rights (chapters 3 and 4) and through enforcement of statutory obligations under the Environmental Protection and Housing Acts (see chapters 6 and 7).

8.41   ## References

English House Condition Survey 1996 (DETR, 1998).
Oxley and Gobert *Dampness in Buildings* (2nd edn, 1994, Butterworth-Heinemann).
Platt et al 'Damp housing, mould growth and symptomatic health state' (1989) 298 BMJ 1673.

Dangerous buildings

8.42   Not infrequently a property will be in such poor repair as to represent a danger not only to those within it but also to people using adjacent streets. Once notified of such a situation a local housing authority may either take urgent remedial action itself or may follow a procedure requiring the owner to remedy the dangerous condition or demolish the building (Building Act 1984 ss77–83).

8.43   No express provision is made for the removal or compensation of any tenant although rehousing may, according to the circumstances, be achieved under HA 1996 Pt VII. Tenants displaced in such circumstances would have a remedy against the landlord arising from the breach of repairing obligation which led to the dangerous condition of the property.

8.44   Where the landlord is civilly liable for the building's dangerous condition an interim injunction can be obtained in the county court within hours (see chapter 4).

8.45 ## References

Arden and Partington *Housing Law* (1994 looseleaf edition, Sweet & Maxwell, updated) chapter 9 'Obstructive, dangerous and dilapidated buildings'.

Dilapidated buildings

8.46   A property in very serious disrepair may fall within the statutory definition of 'dilapidated', ie, one which by reason of its ruinous or dilapidated condition is seriously detrimental to the amenities of the neighbourhood (Building Act 1984 s79).

8.47   When notified of a property in such condition the housing authority for the area may require the owner either to repair/restore the property or demolish it. In default of compliance the housing authority may itself undertake the necessary work.

8.48   Again, in addition to the tenant's ordinary remedies in civil proceedings or under EPA s82 (chapters 3 and 6), the tenant may be able to obtain speedy interlocutory relief in civil proceedings (chapter 4).

8.49 ## References

Arden and Partington *Housing Law* chapter 9 (see para 8.45)

Drains and sewers

8.50   A 'drain' means a drain used for the drainage of one building, while a 'sewer' means all drains used for the drainage of more than one building. The law does not distinguish between foul and surface water sewers. A public sewer is a sewer vested in the local water authority[25].

8.51   Tenants may be caused serious inconvenience by the blockage, disrepair or overflow of drains as a result of their landlord's failure to repair or maintain them.

8.52   Landlord and Tenant Act 1985 s11 makes landlords responsible for keeping in repair the structure and exterior of the dwelling house 'including drains'. It seems logical to assume that the draftsman meant that a drain forms part of the dwelling house for the purposes of s11 up to the point it enters the public sewer.

8.53   The local water authority is responsible for public sewers but the housing authority is usually responsible for day to day maintenance pursuant to arrangements made under Water Act 1973 s15. Accordingly, generally both water authority and housing authority can be responsible for damage caused by nuisance or negligence in connection with the maintenance of sewers.[26]

8.54   Local authorities have extensive powers to require owners (and occupiers) to take remedial action where a drain or sewer is prejudicial to health or a nuisance (Building Act 1984 ss21 and 59). In default, the council may itself carry out the necessary work and recover its costs thereafter.

8.55   Similarly, a housing authority may by notice secure the performance of repairs if a drain or sewer is insufficiently maintained or repaired (PHA 1961 s17).[27]

8.56   ## References

Garner and Bailey *The Law of Sewers and Drains* (8th edn, 1995, Shaw & Sons).

Fire precautions

8.57   The powers available to require landlords to take fire precautions are abysmally poor. Although contractual and common law rights (chapter 3) will usually require a landlord to *maintain* an existing fire

---

25   *Dear v Thames Water plc* (1994) 33 Con LR 43.
26   *Dear v Thames Water plc* (1994) 33 Con LR 43.
27   *Rotherham MBC v Dodds* [1986] 2 All ER 867.

escape or stairway retained in his/her possession, they cannot be used to compel the landlord to *provide* such facilities.

8.58 The Fire Precautions Act 1971 s3 which would require fire certificates for certain houses has yet to be brought into force. The Act does, however, make a certificate mandatory where the property provides sleeping accommodation for staff or guests in a boarding house (s1). The term 'boarding house' for these purposes was construed widely in *R v Mabbot*[28] to cover premises such as hostels which provide overnight sleeping accommodation.

8.59 Local authorities have extensive powers in relation to houses in multiple occupation and common lodging houses to require the provision of means of escape from fire or alternatively to make a closing order or accept an undertaking not to use the premises residentially (HA 1985 ss365–368).[29] Local authorities are under a positive duty to exercise these powers in the case of larger HMOs. If a resident is displaced by a closing order or undertaking, the housing authority has to provide him/her with compensation and suitable alternative residential accommodation on reasonable terms, if he has nowhere else to go (Land Compensation Act 1973 ss29 and 39).

8.60 Local councils also have power to require fire precautions to be taken in certain multistorey blocks of flats, tenements and boarding houses (Building Act 1984 s72).

8.61 ## References

Arden and Partington *Housing Law* (see para 8.45) chapter 8 'Statutory nuisance and related powers', para 8–44 'Fire precautions'.

David Ormandy 'Fire precautions' February 1979 *LAG Bulletin* 66; August 1979 *LAG Bulletin* 190.

David Ormandy 'Housing can seriously damage your health: 2' October 1994 *Legal Action* 13.

Shelter Housing Advice Factsheet H8 *Houses in Multiple Occupation* (April 1997).

DoE Circular 12/92 *Improvement notices under HA 1985 s352*.

Berg v Trafford BC (1988) 20 HLR 47, CA.

Zenca and Others v Pouyiouros September 1989 *Legal Action* 24, QBD.

---

28 (1987) *Times* 4 August, CA.
29 On undertakings, see *Desmond v Bromley LBC* (1996) 28 HLR 518.

Improvements

8.62   This book is primarily concerned with housing in need of repair rather than improvement. However, in a variety of circumstances either landlord or tenant may wish to improve property in addition to or in place of carrying out repairs.

8.63   A wide variety of grants are available under HGCRA Chapters 1 and 3.

Voluntary improvement

8.64   A secure tenant has a statutory right to carry out certain improvements subject to the consent of the landlord (HA 1985 ss97–98). Other tenants will have only such rights as are contained in their tenancy agreements.

8.65   Where the landlord wishes to carry out improvement to occupied property the ability to do so will be governed by the terms of letting or any further agreement entered into between landlord and tenant.[30] The landlord does not have the right to enter to carry out improvements, except perhaps where necessary to prevent personal injury.[31]

Compulsory improvement

8.66   Local authorities have long had power to secure certain improvement works from the landlords of property in poor condition. The statutory process (consolidated in HA 1985 Pt VII) was initiated by the authority of its own volition in a housing action area or general improvement area (see 'Area action' above) and in other cases upon receipt by the authority of written representations from a tenant.

8.67   From 1 April 1990, the compulsory improvement scheme is replaced in part by the incorporation, within the new statutory definition of unfitness, of aspects which formerly would have been addressed by HA 1985 Pt VII (repealed by LGHA s165(2)). Thus the failure to have sufficient heating, hot water supply or sanitary installations may render a house 'unfit' and compel the housing authority, on hearing of the condition of the property, to take the 'most satisfactory course' of remedial action.

---

30 *McDougall v Easington DC* [1989] 1 EGLR 93.
31 *McGreal v Wake* (1984) 13 HLR 134; *McAuley v Bristol CC* [1992] QB 134.

8.68   References

Arden and Partington *Housing Law* (see para 8.45) chapter 11
'Improvements and alterations'.

Home improvements Office of Fair Trading (tel: 0870 606321).

FFF Estates Ltd v Hackney LBC [1981] QB 503.

Multi-occupied property

8.69   Some of the worst instances of landlord neglect and disrepair are to
be found in properties subject to more than one tenancy or
occupancy, eg, houses converted into 'bedsits', hostels, hotels, and
houses converted into two or more 'flatlets'. Although these are the
most obvious types of multi-occupied property, any house or flat is
in multiple occupation if it contains two or more households.[32]

8.70   Local housing authorities (through EHOs) have extensive powers
to control: (a) the provision of facilities in such properties (HA 1985
s352); (b) the number of occupants (HA 1985 ss35–47); and (c) the
means of escape from fire (HA 1985 ss36–58).[33]

8.71   In addition, the authority has power to bring proceedings under
EPA s80 (see chapter 6) and to intervene where there are problems
of disrepair, lack of maintenance and other unsatisfactory aspects to
the state of the property because the Housing Act codes in relation
to unfitness and housing in poor repair, described in chapter 7, apply
to houses and flats in multiple occupation. Also, the authority may
act to enforce management regulations (HA 1985 s369) setting out
the landlord's responsibilities and the work necessary to bring the
property up to standard. Failure to comply may result in prosecution
and the authority may do the necessary works in default and recoup
its costs.

8.72   Where conditions are so poor as to represent a danger to the
health, safety or welfare of the occupants, the authority may impose
a control order (HA 1985 ss379–400). This gives the authority the
power to run the property itself and carry out the necessary work,

---

32   *Living Waters Christian Centres Ltd v Conwy CBC* (1999) 77 P&CR 54; *Norwich
CC v Billings* (1997) 29 HLR 679; *Thrasyvoulou v Secretary of State for
Environment and Hackney LBC* (1986) HLR 370; *Okereke v Brent LBC* [1967] QB
42; *R v Camden LBC ex p Rowton* [1984] LGR 614; *Simmons v Pizzey* [1977] 2
All ER 432.

33   See *Pearson v Glasgow DC* (1994) SCLR 444.

collect the rents etc. There is an appeal to the county court. Ultimately, the authority may compulsorily purchase the property.[34]

8.73   ## References

DoE Circular 5/90 *Revised controls over houses in multiple occupation.*
Tenants' rights in shared housing National Homeless Alliance.
Arden and Partington *Housing Law* (see para 8.45) chapter 10 'Overcrowding, multiple occupation and common lodging houses'.
Ormandy 'Standards, enforcement and improvement' May 1990 *Legal Action* 14 and (letter) August 1990 *Legal Action.*
McLoughlin 'Houses in multiple occupation' (1986) LS Gaz 1382.
Shelter Housing Advice Factsheet H8 *Houses in Multiple Occupation* (April 1997).
Hammersmith and Fulham LBC v Gill, Same v Abrahams June 1989 *Legal Action* 24.
Hammersmith and Fulham LBC v Gamble March 1989 *Legal Action* 24.

Neighbouring property

8.74   The effects of disrepair are often felt beyond their immediate location. The ramifications of a structure or installation out of repair may lead to injury to health or damage to neighbouring property. Indeed, one of the most common sights in areas of high density housing is the scarring effect on a number of properties of a defective WC cistern overflow in an upperfloor flat.

8.75   If the neighbouring property or building in disrepair is owned by the landlord, the tenant may be able to take action under one or more of the implied covenants contained in all letting agreements (see chapter 3): (a) the covenant to repair common parts; (b) the covenant of quiet enjoyment; (c) the covenant of non-derogation from grant.

8.76   If the property is in other hands, the neighbouring tenant may involve the EHO of the housing authority either on the basis that the property is a statutory nuisance (see chapter 6) or that it is dangerous

---

34   *R v Secretary of State for Environment ex p Kensington and Chelsea RLBC* (1987) 19 HLR 161; *Wandsworth LBC v Orakpo* (1987) 19 HLR 57; *Webb v Secretary of State for Environment* (1990) 22 HLR 274; *Orakpo v Wandsworth LBC* (1992) 24 HLR 370.

or dilapidated (see paragraphs 8.42 and 8.46). In either case, the tenant should be able to take proceedings in nuisance.[35]

8.77 It is now possible to apply to court for an order permitting access onto neighbouring land in order to carry out works to the dominant land which are reasonably necessary to preserve the whole or part of the dominant land and which cannot be carried out, or would be substantially more difficult to carry out, without access.[36]

Noise

8.78 Very substantial distress and inconvenience may be caused by noise nuisance. In modern housing this is commonly exacerbated by the lack of good insulation of party walls or between flats. Often the tenant will be able to restrain the continuation of any excessive noise by using the procedures under EPA Pt III or by an action in private nuisance (tort), brought against the perpetrator of the noise.

8.79 However, if the source of noise is simply normal usage of a property, the most appropriate challenge is one addressed to the landlord responsible for letting a dwelling insufficiently insulated against normal domestic noise.

8.80 Criminal proceedings against landlords in which tenants have successfully obtained orders for insulation work have been brought under the Control of Pollution Act 1974 s59 (now EPA s82),[37] and under the Public Health Act 1936 s99 or EPA s82.[38]

8.81 Action has also been taken successfully in private law actions alleging nuisance[39] although not breach of the covenant for quiet enjoyment.[40] Unfortunately, the Court of Appeal recently held that

---

35 *Spicer v Smee* [1946] 1 All ER 489; *Mint v Good* [1951] 1 KB 517, *Stone v Bolton* [1949] 1 All ER 237 and see generally Stephen Knafler *Remedies for Disrepair and other Building Defects*, Sweet and Maxwell, 1996 chapter 12.

36 See Access to Neighbouring Land Act 1992; *Williams v Edwards* [1997] CLY 561.

37 *Joyce v Hackney LBC* September 1976 *LAG Bulletin* 211; *Lambert Flat Management v Lomas* [1981] 1 WLR 898; *Rossall v Southwark LBC* (1985) unreported, noted at (1986) 8 *IEHO Housing Law Newsletter* 7.

38 *Southwark LBC v Ince* (1989) 21 HLR 504, QBD; *Network Housing Association v Westminster CC* (1994) 27 HLR 189; *A Lambert Flat Management v Lomas* [1981] 2 All ER 280.

39 *Sampson v Hodson-Pressinger* [1981] 3 All ER 710; *Toff v McDowell* (1993) 25 HLR 650); *Baxter v Camden LBC* (1998) 30 HLR 501

40 *Southwark LBC v Mills* [1998] 3 WLR 49 (subject to appeal).

the principle of 'caveat lessee' meant that landlords were not liable to tenants in nuisance resulting from poor sound insulation.[41]

8.82   If the noise results from disrepair, eg, broken floorboards, tenants can take civil proceedings.[42] There may also be a remedy under the DPA 1972 if the noise results from negligent building or conversion works (see chapter 3).

8.83   ## References

Dymond 'Noise at night: the new offence' October 1997 *Legal Action* 26.

Overcrowding

8.84   Experience suggests a degree of correlation between properties in disrepair and those which landlords permit to become overcrowded. Statutory limits are imposed as to the maximum number of persons permitted to occupy a dwelling and enforcement is the responsibility and duty of the housing authority for the area (HA 1985 Pt X).

8.85   Overcrowding is measured by two standards and failure to comply with either or both will render the overcrowding illegal. The first of the standards is based on the number of rooms, the number of occupants and their ages. The second test is based on the size and number of rooms, the occupiers and their ages. The statutory code permits strictly limited exceptions.

8.86   Illegal overcrowding may bring to an end any Rent Act security of tenure and may lead to homelessness (and possible rehousing by the council).

8.87   Enforcement by housing authorities is mandatory and may lead to the prosecution of the landlord. Overcrowding in council property is equally illegal and the code may be enforced by council tenants by a relator action with the fiat of the Attorney-General.[43]

---

41 *Baxter v Camden LBC* [1999] 2 WLR 566 (subject to appeal).
42 *Guinan v Enfield LBC* June 1990 *Legal Action* 16.
43 See *DPP v Carrick* (1985) 31 *Housing Aid* 5.

8.88 ## References

Arden and Partington *Housing Law* (see para 8.45) chapter 10 'Overcrowding, multiple occupation and common lodging houses'.
Shelter Housing Advice Factsheet H8 *Houses in Multiple Occupation* (April 1997).
David Ormandy 'Overcrowding' October 1973 *LAG Bulletin* 218.

Refuse

8.89 Accumulations of rubbish may not only attract vermin (see below) but may also themselves constitute a danger to residents.[44] The former right of tenants to require a housing authority to remove house refuse (PHA 1936 s72) was repealed on 6 June 1988[45] and a new code of refuse disposal is to be found in the Control of Pollution Act 1974 (see Collection and Disposal of Waste Regulations 1988).[46] This makes 'collection authorities' responsible for clearing rubbish, but EHOs retain the power to require removal of 'accumulations' which are a public health hazard (see chapter 5).

8.90 In multi-storey blocks of flats, difficulties may be caused if the rubbish chutes and collection bins are not regularly cleared. A tenant living in a flat adjacent to a blocked chute or overspilled collection bin may have an action in private nuisance against the landlord.[47]

8.91 It is an implied term that landlords take reasonable steps to keep such facilities in repair.[48]

Sanitary installations

8.92 Where a landlord has permitted sanitary installations to fall out of repair or proper working order the tenant may take action under contractual or common law repairing obligations (chapter 3) and if conditions have become prejudicial to health or a nuisance should involve the EHO to take action under the Public Health and Environmental Protection Acts (chapter 6).

44 See, eg, *Dear v Newham LBC* (1988) 20 HLR 348, CA.
45 Control of Pollution Act 1974 (Commencement No 19) Order 1988 SI No 818.
46 1988 SI No 819.
47 *Sillitoe v Liverpool CC* (1998) 29 November, unreported, Liverpool County Court, HHJ Stannard.
48 *Liverpool CC v Irwin* [1977] AC 239.

8.93   Additional powers are given to housing authorities to deal with situations where there are insufficient sanitary conveniences in a dwelling or the existing ones require replacement.

8.94   ## References

Arden and Partington *Housing Law* (see para 8.45) chapter 8 'Statutory nuisance and related powers', para 8–61 'Sanitary accommodation'.

Services (gas, water and electricity)

8.95   Under the covenant implied in most tenancies by LTA 1985 s11, a landlord is required to keep in repair and proper working order the installations in the dwelling for the supply of gas, electricity and water (s11(1)(b), (c)) or, in respect of certain tenancies, the installations serving the dwelling, wherever situated (see chapter 3 para 3.74).

8.96   However, problems commonly arise where, although the installations themselves are in good order, the landlord has caused loss of supply of the services themselves, eg, by failing to pay fuel bills. In these circumstances, upon receipt of a complaint from the occupiers, a housing authority can make the necessary arrangements with the relevant boards to ensure reconnection of the supply. Most authorities have delegated the power to carry out this service to EHOs or tenancy relations officers. Once supply is re-established the authority can thereafter recover any necessary costs from the landlord (Local Government (Miscellaneous Provisions) Act 1976 s33).

8.97   ## References

Ormandy 'Housing can seriously damage your health: 1' August 1994 *Legal Action* 10.
Ormandy 'Housing can seriously damage your health: 2' October 1994 *Legal Action* 13.
Critchley and Greenan 'Carbon monoxide: a hidden cause for action' January 1997 *Legal Action* 15.
A Hoffland and N Nicol *Fuel Rights Handbook* (10th edn, 1996, CPAG).

Vandalism

8.98 Where disrepair results from the deliberate or negligent act of a stranger rather than from the activities of the landlord or tenant or their visitors, responsibility for repair of the damage will lie on either or neither party according to respective repairing obligations. For example, where the landlord is liable to repair the 'exterior' this requires the replacement of glazing in a window smashed by the act of a third party. Obviously, where the third party can be identified the landlord will seek redress from him/her.

8.99   In certain limited circumstances a landlord may be liable for acts of vandalism by unknown third parties which cause injury or damage to tenants. For example, the landlord of a number of adjoining properties may be liable in negligence if one property is left vacant and unsecured against vandals who destroy pipework and cause thereby flooding to the neighbouring tenanted properties, providing the damage was highly foreseeable or the case was exceptional.[49] Where damage is caused by third parties as the result of the landlord's failure to comply with his repairing obligations, the damage need only be foreseeable.[50]

8.100 References

Ward v Cannock Chase DC [1985] 3 All ER 537.
Lamb v Camden LBC [1981] QB 625.
Perl (Exporters) Ltd v Camden LBC [1984] QB 342.
Hoath 'Damage caused by vandalism: responsibility as between landlord and tenant' February 1986 *Legal Action* 22.
Coley v Camden LBC (1983) 12 September, unreported, Bloomsbury and Marylebone County Court, but noted at *Times* 13 September.
King v Liverpool CC [1986] 1 WLR 890, CA.

Vermin

8.101 One of the least pleasant consequences of disrepair or of poor building design may be the incursion of vermin. These not only cause distress but also damage to personal possessions and in certain

49 *Smith v Littlewoods Organisation Ltd* [1987] AC 241.
50 *Morris v Liverpool CC* (1987) 20 HLR 498.

cases to the fabric of the property. Even in more modern, system-built dwellings infestation by ants or cockroaches is not uncommon.[51]

8.102   If the landlord lets premises infested by vermin those premises may be unfit for human habitation at common law (see chapter 3). If after a letting, a landlord negligently fails to deal with the vermin or the incursion is a nuisance for which the landlord is responsible, the tenant may have other remedies at common law (see chapter 3).

8.103   In addition, housing authorities have extensive powers to take action in case of pest infestation (Prevention of Damage by Pests Act 1949 and Public Health Act 1936 Pt II).

8.104   Premises infested with vermin are very likely to constitute a 'statutory nuisance' (chapter 6) as they are prejudicial to health. If it can be shown that the incursion or infestation is caused by the 'act, default or sufferance' of the landlord, the tenant may rely on the processes of the EPA and, where necessary, prosecute the landlord using s82.[52]

8.105   ## References

Arden and Partington *Housing Law* (see para 8.45) chapter 8 'Statutory nuisance and related powers', para 8–93 'Vermin'.

A Spackman 'The plague in all our houses' *Sunday Times* 3 November 1985.

David Ormandy 'Vermin, drains and garbage' June 1975 *LAG Bulletin* 152.

Bob Young 'Infestation' July/August 1980 *Roof* 110.

M O'Dwyer 'Pest control' (1986) June *LCF News* 10.

'Fighting the beetles and bugs' *Independent* 7 April 1990.

---

51 See, eg, *Hudson v Kensington and Chelsea RLBC* (1986) unreported, but noted at (1986) *Daily Hazard* 1; December 1985 *Legal Action* 171.

52 As in *White v Hackney LBC* March 1989 *Legal Action* 24 (ants).

Damages awards for disrepair

Awards for inconvenience and discomfort

Awards exceeding £2,000 per annum when updated

Court of Appeal

9.1   *Elmcroft Developments Ltd v Tankersley-Sawyer*
(1984) 15 HLR 63; [1984] 1 EGLR 47; (1984) 270 EG 140, CA

£2,600 to a single, female plaintiff for two years of severe rising damp throughout a basement flat in an expensive and fashionable part of London.

9.2   *Personal Representatives of Chiodi v De Marney*
(1988) 21 HLR 6; [1988] 2 EGLR 64; [1988] 41 EG 80, CA

£1,560 to a single woman in her early 30s. Between 1980 and 1983 the flat suffered from water penetration, the hot water supply ceased, there were frequent electrical problems, some windows were very rotten and one was broken. The judge made a further award of £1,500 for aggravation of the plaintiff's arthritis and a number of colds and influenza symptoms suffered by her.

9.3   *Brent LBC v Carmel (Murphy)*
(1996) 28 HLR 203, CA

£2,750 per annum for water penetration throughout the flat from 1981. The central heating system was 'wholly inadequate'. In the winter, one and sometimes two out of the three bedrooms were uninhabitable. The plaintiff's teenage boy and girl had to share her bedroom, while their clothes were stored in the living room.

9.4   *Ezekiel v McDade*
[1995] 2 EGLR 107; [1995] 47 EG 150, CA

£4,000 for the physical discomfort of having to occupy temporary accommodation: the plaintiff, his wife and their three children were in a one-bedroom bed and breakfast hotel for ten weeks, and in a two-bedroomed house for about ten months with only a gas fire in the living room, no other heating and cramped conditions.

High Court

9.5 *Sampson v Wilson*
(1994) 26 HLR 486, ChD

The dwelling was in substantial disrepair. The landlord was an absentee and his agents carried out works of repair in such a manner as to deliberately make matters worse and drive out the tenants. Because works were carried out without permission or exceeding any permission, there was a trespass (in addition to a breach of contract) thereby permitting an award of exemplary damages to be made. The judge awarded the full amount of the rent to each tenant (£25 and £40 per week) and made an exemplary award of £2,000.

County court

9.6 *Walker v Lambeth LBC*
September 1992 *Legal Action* 21, Lambeth County Court

£3,750 to a single, female tenant, who had a young child and for half the period of 18 months in question was pregnant. During this time, one of two lifts was out of operation and the other was subject to frequent breakdowns. The tenant was on the 15th floor of a 21-storey block, was on one occasion trapped in the lift and frequently had to use the stairs.

9.7 *Foster v Donaghey*
[1994] CLY 1454, Huddersfield County Court

£2,000 to a single, male tenant for eight months in a two-bedroom house with extensive rising and penetrating damp, windows which did not keep out the elements, a gas fire which emitted fumes, a toilet which did not flush and only one operable tap (cold). The damages included compensation for two minor incidents of harassment.

9.8 *Adam v Melhuish and Kensey*
August 1994 *Legal Action* 17, Guildford County Court

£2,080 per annum to a single male tenant where there had been serious water penetration affecting every room of an old house causing the plaster to become saturated and mouldy throughout.

9.9 *Bell v Mazehead Ltd*
March 1996 *Legal Action* 14, Shoreditch County Court

£15,250 for five years of water penetration through the roof and other dampness.

9.10   *Hardy v Maund*

December 1995 *Legal Action* 22, Stockport County Court

£2,475 to a single male tenant for six months of very severe rising and penetrating damp in all parts of a modest bedsit.

9.11   *Symons v Warren*

[1995] CLY 3039, Clerkenwell County Court

£2,470 per annum when the light and extractor fan in the bathroom/toilet did not work.

9.12   *Banton v Lambeth LBC*

December 1995 *Legal Action* 22, Lambeth County Court

£12,000 to a single, male tenant for damp penetration from a leaking central heating pipe in the flat above which spread and got worse over a seven-year period to the point where the walls in the hall, bathroom and lounge became wet and the whole flat smelt musty. Additionally, for two winters the central heating and hot water were inoperable.

9.13   *Essapen v Jouaneau*

June 1995 *Legal Action* 22, Bow County Court

£10,240 for 33 months of water penetration around the windows, which were inoperable, and through the roof; the electrical installation was defective and there was only intermittent heating.

9.14   *Rayson v Sanctuary Housing Association Ltd*

March 1996 *Legal Action* 15, Ipswich County Court

£4,750 to a single, female tenant for two years of severe, unsightly and worrying structural cracking.

9.15   *Southwark LBC v Bente*

[1998] 2 CL 181, Lambeth County Court

£2,500 for family's home subject to leaks, dampness and a dangerous garden wall.

Awards between £1,000 and £2,000 per annum when updated

Court of Appeal

9.16 *Calabar Properties Ltd v Stitcher*

[1984] 1 WLR 287; [1983] 3 All ER 759; (1983) 11 HLR 20; (1983) 268 EG 697, CA

£3,000 for five years of water penetration. External woodwork began to rot, mastic sealing around the windows perished and there was substantial water penetration. The tenant's husband suffered two attacks of pleurisy and one of bronchitis. Eventually the tenant and her husband left the flat to live permanently on the Isle of Man.

9.17 *Lubren v Lambeth LBC*

(1988) 20 HLR 165, CA

£4,000 to a mother with two adult sons for five years of cold and damp as the result of unspecified disrepair, deteriorating from a reasonable condition at the outset to being 'appalling'. In the last two years the hot water heating system worked intermittently and caused significant additional inconvenience. £500 for a period of 14 months when the plaintiff was in alternative accommodation waiting for the works to be completed, when the defendant had undertaken that the works would take only three months.

9.18 *Sturolson & Co v Mauroux*

(1988) 20 HLR 332; [1988] 1 EGLR 66; [1988] 24 EG 102, CA

£5,895 to an elderly male plaintiff for about 11 years of disrepair. There had been water penetration through external walls of the flat and around the windows, insufficient hot water for washing and for the radiators, poorly lit corridors, an electrical system which was often unusable, blocked drains and defective bath and sink.

9.19 *Davies v Peterson*

(1989) 21 HLR 63; [1989] 06 EG 130, CA

£1,000 to a single, female plaintiff for about 12 months of damp which severely affected one bedroom and the living room.

9.20 *Watts v Morrow*

[1991] 1 WLR 1421; [1991] 4 All ER 937; (1991) 23 HLR 608; [1991] 2 EGLR 152; [1991] 43 EG 121, CA

£750 each to a professional couple for having to occupy (during the weekends) their expensive weekend cottage for a period of about eight months while substantial repairs were carried out to it.

9.21   *Staves and Staves v Leeds CC*
(1991) 23 HLR 107, CA

£5,000 for four years in which condensation and some penetrating damp through the ceiling had caused damp and mould to the gable walls in the bedrooms so that the plaster deteriorated. The plaintiffs were a married couple with three young children.

9.22   *Wallace v Manchester CC*
(1998) 30 HLR 1111, CA

£3,500 for three years of intermittent rat infestation, rotten windows, falling plaster and intermittent rising damp in the living room and a leaking gutter.

High Court

9.23   *Loria v Hammer*
[1989] 2 EGLR 249, ChD

£900 to a single, female plaintiff for five months of rainwater penetration through the roof which caused severe damp to the plaster of the flat.

9.24   *Arnold v Greenwich LBC*
[1998] CLY 3618, QBD

£8,750 for almost six years of modest condensation damp and mould, smells from refuse storage area and noise from communal rubbish shute.

County court

9.25   *Hussein v Mehlman*
[1992] 2 EGLR 87; [1992] 32 EG 59, Wood Green Trial Centre

£600 to one tenant for the landlord's failure put three gas heaters into working order over the 1989/90 winter. The tenant did buy calor gas fires which mitigated the discomfort to an extent. £1,250 to the three tenants jointly for eight months in which one bedroom had had a collapsed ceiling letting in damp and cold draughts to the rest of the house and there was a bulging sitting room ceiling for about 13 months.

9.26 **Tuoma v Raad**
August 1994 *Legal Action* 17, Central London Court

£1,820 per annum for water dripping into the tenant's bathroom from the flat above causing some plaster to fall and leaving him without a fixed light fitting in the bathroom.

Awards under £1,000 per annum when updated

Court of Appeal

9.27 **Taylor v Knowsley BC**
(1985) 17 HLR 376, CA

£32 to a young single man for being without hot water for five months and without a central light in the living room for three months. Also £59 for eight months' dripping from a pipe in the bathroom ceiling.

9.28 **Minchburn v Peck**
(1988) 20 HLR 392; [1988] 1 EGLR 53, CA

£800 to a single man for two years of water penetration as a result of defective roof slates and three to four years of cracks to the party walls which spoilt the decorations.

9.29 **Sella House Ltd v Mears**
(1989) 21 HLR 147; [1989] 1 EGLR 65; [1989] 12 EG 67, CA

£1,250 to a single, male plaintiff occupying a fairly high class flat for seven years in which the condition of the hall and stairs in the common parts became 'fairly shabby'.

9.30 **Joyce v Liverpool CC; Wynne v Liverpool CC**
[1995] 3 All ER 110; (1995) 27 HLR 548; [1995] NPC 74, CA

Tenant could not reasonably expect to receive more than £718 for two years of two badly spalled bricks, a blocked side gully and missing grid, warped casement windows in one room, minor decay to external casement timbers, a broken power socket and insecure switch, some missing and loose vinyl floor tiles in the kitchen and bathroom, deteriorated sink base, constant blocking of sink waste outlet, missing ceramic tiles behind sink, seizing of bedroom window casements and defective hinges, not all of which fell within the landlord's repairing covenants.

County court

9.31 *Makan v British Gas plc*

[1994] CLY 1466, Epsom County Court

£2,000 for negligently causing a hot water cylinder to flood a living room causing the ceiling to collapse. The plaintiffs lost the use of the living room for about nine months.

9.32 *Hallett v Camden LBC*

August 1994 *Legal Action* 17, Central London County Court

£300 per annum for draughty windows which were 'low in the scale of possible defects'.

9.33 *Newham LBC v Hewitt*

June 1995 *Legal Action* 23; [1995] CLY 1563, Bow County Court

£850 per annum to a single, male tenant in his 50s when the bedroom and hallway radiators and one of the living room radiators failed to work so that, during the winter months, the tenant had to wear a coat in the living room and go to bed in his clothes. A further £600 because the cold made the tenant's bad foot feel 'dead'.

9.34 *Lewin v Brent LBC*

[1995] CLY 1574, Central London County Court

£600 per annum for an ineffective rubbish collection service, grass in common areas not kept clean and service areas in disrepair. £800 per annum when sewers had overflowed from time to time.

Awards for noise nuisance

9.35 *Sampson v Hodson-Pressinger*

[1981] 3 All ER 710; (1984) 12 HLR 40; (1982) 261 EG 891, CA

£2,000 for noise nuisance consisting of footsteps and conversations which could be heard from above in the plaintiff's sitting room between August 1978 to August 1980.

9.36 *Power v Hammersmith and Fulham LBC*

March 1993 *Legal Action* 14, Central London County Court

£1,000 per annum for poor sound insulation resulting in the single male tenant being able to hear normal domestic noise from the flat above.

9.37 *Toff v McDowell*
(1993) 25 HLR 650; (1995) 69 P&CR 535; [1993] NPC 114, ChD

£2,000 per annum for unreasonable household noise; £1,000 per annum thereafter.

Awards for personal injury

Pneumonia

9.38 *McCoy & Co v Clark*
(1982) 13 HLR 89, CA

£200 for left lower lobe pneumonia, spending nine days in hospital in considerable pain and five to six weeks afterwards feeling ill. Damages were reduced by 50% owing to the tenant's failure to look after himself properly

Depression

9.39 *Yilmaz v Hackney LBC*
March 1995 *Legal Action* 15, Shoreditch County Court

£500 for depression caused in part (about 20%) by disrepair.

Asthma

9.40 *Bygraves v Southwark LBC,*
(1990) Kemp & Kemp @ F2-035/2

£5,000 to a child five years old at the time of the award for material exacerbation of very severe asthma since birth. £5,000 for future pain and suffering.

9.41 *McCaffery v Lambeth LBC*
August 1994 *Legal Action* 18; [1994] CLY 1635; Kemp & Kemp @ F2-045/3, Wandsworth County Court

£600 per annum to a young girl who suffered upper respiratory tract infections and asthma over a period of four and a half years, including nine full-blown attacks but no hospital treatment, mainly suffering from wheezing and shortness of breath. £450 per annum to a young girl who suffered a large number of colds over a five-and-a-half-year period and developed asthma, requiring treatment from her GP on a number of occasions. £400 per annum to a young girl who suffered intermittently from chest problems and wheeziness sometimes requiring antibiotics.

9.42   *Stone v Redair Mersey Agencies*
May 1997 *Legal Action* 18; [1996] CLY 2244, Liverpool County Court

£2,000 for six-year-old girl who had suffered four years of constant chest infections and mild asthma exacerbated by damp and draughts.

9.43   *Alienus v Tower Hamlets LBC*
[1998] CLY 2987, Central London County Court

£11,000 to a child who contracted and suffered acute asthma for a seven-year period.

Awards for infestations

Cockroaches

9.44   *Brent LBC v Roberts*
April 1991 *Legal Action* 21, Willesden County Court

£5,000 for a cockroach infestation of varying severity for four years.

9.45   *Hodder v Tower Hamlets LBC*
August 1994 *Legal Action* 17; [1993] CLY 1371, Shoreditch County Court

£1,500 per annum over a seven-year period for a severe cockroach infestation.

9.46   *Lambeth LBC v Wright*
August 1994 *Legal Action* 18, Wood Green Trial Centre

£1,440 per annum for a heavy cockroach infestation.

9.47   *Clark v Wandsworth LBC*
June 1994 *Legal Action* 15, Wandsworth County Court

£3,500 per annum for a heavily infested flat.

9.48   *McGuigan v Southwark LBC*
March 1996 *Legal Action* 14; [1996] CLY 3721, Central London County Court

Awards ranging from between £1,000 per annum to £3,500 per annum for light to very severe cockroach infestations.

Mice and rats

9.49 *Dadd v Christian Action (Enfield) Housing Association*
December 1994 *Legal Action* 18, Central London County Court

£2,090 per annum for a rat infestation.

Ants

9.50 *McGuigan v Southwark LBC*
March 1996 *Legal Action* 14; [1996] CLY 3721, Central London County Court

£3,000 for a severe one-year ant infestation with some cockroaches (see para 9.48).

9.51 *Ryan v Islington LBC*
(1996) 21 February, HHJ Marr Johnson

£2,500 per annum for infestation by pharoah ants.

APPENDICES

A   Defective Premises Act 1972 ss1–4

B   Building Act 1984 ss76–83

C   Housing Act 1985 ss604 and 606

D   Landlord and Tenant Act 1985 ss8 and 11–17

E   Environmental Protection Act 1990 ss79–82

F   Gas Safety (Installation and Use) Regulations 1998 Parts E and F

G   Civil Procedure Rules 1999 Parts 1, 16, 26, 35 and 36

H   Legal Aid Board Housing Guidance, March 1999

I   Control of Condensation in Buildings BS 5250: 1989 (extracts)

J   'Damp housing, mould growth and symptomatic health state', British Medical Journal, 24 June 1989

K   Client questionnaire

L   Precedents

Defective Premises Act 1972 ss1–4

Duty to build dwellings properly

1 (1) A person taking on work for or in connection with the provision of a dwelling (whether the dwelling is provided by the erection or by the conversion or enlargement of a building) owes a duty –

(a) if the dwelling is provided to the order of any person, to that person; and

(b) without prejudice to paragraph (a) above, to every person who acquires an interest (whether legal or equitable) in the dwelling;

to see that the work which he takes on is done in a workman-like or, as the case may be, professional manner, with proper materials and so that as regards that work the dwelling will be fit for habitation when completed.

(2) A person who takes on any such work for another on terms that he is to do it in accordance with instructions given by or on behalf of that other shall, to the extent to which he does it properly in accordance with those instructions, be treated for the purposes of this section as discharging the duty imposed on him by subsection (1) above except where he owes a duty to that other to warn him of any defects in the instructions and fails to discharge that duty.

(3) A person shall not be treated for the purposes of subsection (2) above as having given instructions for the doing of work merely because he has agreed to the work being done in a specified manner, with specified materials or to a specified design.

(4) A person who –

(a) in the course of a business which consists of or includes providing or arranging for the provision of dwellings or installations in dwellings; or

(b) in the exercise of a power of making such provision or arrangements conferred by or by virtue of any enactment;

arranges for another to take on work for or in connection with the provision of a dwelling shall be treated for the purposes of this section as included among the persons who have taken on the work.

(5) Any cause of action in respect of a breach of the duty imposed by this section shall be deemed, for the purposes of the Limitation Act 1939, the Law Reform (Limitation of Actions, &c) Act 1954 and the Limitation Act 1963, to have accrued at the time when the dwelling was completed, but if after that time a person who has done work for or in connection with the provision of the dwelling does further work to rectify the work he has already done, any such cause of action in respect of that further work shall be deemed for those purposes to have accrued at the time when the further work was finished.

Cases excluded from the remedy under section 1

2 (1) Where –

(a) in connection with the provision of a dwelling or its first sale or letting for habitation any rights in respect of defects in the state of the dwelling are conferred by an approved scheme to which this section applies on a person having or acquiring an interest in the dwelling; and

(b) it is stated in a document of a type approved for the purposes of this section that the requirements as to design or construction imposed by or under the scheme have, or appear to have, been substantially complied with in relation to the dwelling;

no action shall be brought by any person having or acquiring an interest in the dwelling for breach of the duty imposed by section 1 above in relation to the dwelling.

(2) A scheme to which this section applies –

(a) may consist of any number of documents and any number of agreements or other transactions between any number of persons; but

(b) must confer, by virtue of agreements entered into with persons having or acquiring an interest in the dwellings to which the scheme applies, rights on such persons in respect of defects in the state of the dwellings.

(3) In this section 'approved' means approved by the Secretary of State, and the power of the Secretary of State to approve a scheme or document for the purposes of this section shall be exercisable by order, except that any requirements as to construction or design imposed under a scheme to which this section applies may be approved by him without making any order or, if he thinks fit, by order.

(4) The Secretary of State –

(a) may approve by a scheme or document for the purposes of this section with or without limiting the duration of his approval; and

(b) may by order revoke or vary a previous order under this section or, without such an order, revoke or vary a previous approval under this section given otherwise than by order.

(5) The production of a document purporting to be a copy of an approval given by the Secretary of State otherwise than by order and certified by an officer of the Secretary of State to be a true copy of the approval shall be conclusive evidence of the approval, and without proof of the handwriting or official position of the person purporting to sign the certificate.

(6) The power to make an order under this section shall be exercisable by statutory instrument which shall be subject to annulment in pursuance of a resolution by either House of Parliament.

(7) Where an interest in a dwelling is compulsorily acquired –

(a) no action shall be brought by the acquiring authority for breach of the duty imposed by section 1 above in respect of the dwelling; and

(b) if any work for or in connection with the provision of the dwelling was done otherwise than in the course of a business by the person in occupation of the dwelling at the time of the compulsory acquisition, the acquiring authority and not that person shall be treated as the person who took on the work and accordingly as owing that duty.

Duty of care with respect to work done on premises not abated by disposal of premises

3 (1) Where work of construction, repair, maintenance or demolition or any other work is done on or in relation to premises, any duty of care owed, because of the doing of the work, to persons who might reasonably be expected to be affected by the defects in the state of the premises created by the doing of the work shall not be abated by the subsequent disposal of the premises by the person who owed the duty.

(2) This section does not apply –

(a) in the case of premises which are let, where the relevant tenancy of the premises commenced, or the relevant tenancy agreement of the premises was entered into, before the commencement of this Act;

(b) in the case of premises disposed of in any other way, when the disposal of the premises was completed, or a contract for their disposal was entered into, before the commencement of this Act; or

(c) in either case, where the relevant transaction disposing of the premises is entered into in pursuance of an enforceable option by which the consideration for the disposal was fixed before the commencement of this Act.

Landlord's duty of care in virtue of obligation or right to repair premises demised

4 (1) Where premises are let under a tenancy which puts on the landlord an obligation to the tenant for the maintenance or repair of the premises, the landlord owes to all persons who might reasonably be expected to be affected by defects in the state of the premises a duty to take such care as is reasonable in all the circumstances to see that they are reasonably safe from personal injury or from damage to their property caused by a relevant defect.

(2) The said duty is owed if the landlord knows (whether as the result of being notified by the tenant or otherwise) or if he ought in all the circumstances to have known of the relevant defect.

(3) In this section 'relevant defect' means a defect in the state of the premises existing at or after the material time and arising from, or continuing because of, an act or omission by the landlord which constitutes or would if he had had notice of the defect, have constituted a failure by him to carry out his obligation to the tenant for the maintenance or repair of the premises; and for the purposes of the foregoing provision 'the material time' means –

(a) where the tenancy commenced before this Act, the commencement of this Act; and

(b) in all other cases, the earliest of the following times, that is to say –

(i) the time when the tenancy commences;

(ii) the time when the tenancy agreement is entered into;

(iii) the time when possession is taken of the premises in contemplation of the letting.

(4) Where premises are let under a tenancy which expressly or impliedly gives the landlord the right to enter the premises to carry out any description of maintenance or repair of the premises, then, as from the time when he first is, or by notice or otherwise can put himself, in a position to exercise the right

and so long as he is or can put himself in that position, he shall be treated for the purposes of subsections (1) to (3) above (but for no other purpose) as if he were under an obligation to the tenant for that description of maintenance or repair of the premises; but the landlord shall not owe the tenant any duty by virtue of this subsection in respect of any defect in the state of the premises arising from, or continuing because of, a failure to carry out an obligation expressly imposed on the tenant by the tenancy.

(5) For the purposes of this section obligations imposed or rights given by any enactment in virtue of a tenancy shall be treated as imposed or given by the tenancy.

(6) This section applies to a right of occupation given by contract or any enactment and not amounting to a tenancy as if the right were a tenancy, and 'tenancy' and cognate expressions shall be construed accordingly.

Building Act 1984 ss76–83

Defective premises

76 (1) If it appears to a local authority that –

(a) any premises are in such a state (in this section referred to as a 'defective state') as to be prejudicial to health or a nuisance, and

(b) unreasonable delay in remedying the defective state would be occasioned by following the procedure prescribed by [section 80 of the Environmental Protection Act 1990],

the local authority may serve on the person on whom it would have been appropriate to serve an abatement notice under the said section 93 (if the local authority had proceeded under that section) a notice stating that the local authority intend to remedy the defective state and specifying the defects that they intend to remedy.

(2) Subject to subsection (3) below, the local authority may, after the expiration of nine days after service of a notice under subsection (1) above, execute such works as may be necessary to remedy the defective state, and recover the expenses reasonably incurred in so doing from the person on whom the notice was served.

(3) If, within seven days after service of a notice under subsection (1) above, the person on whom the notice was served serves a counter-notice that he intends to remedy the defects specified in the first-mentioned notice, the local authority shall take no action in pursuance of the first-mentioned notice unless the person who served the counter-notice –

(a) fails within what seems to the local authority a reasonable time to begin to execute works to remedy the said defects, or

(b) having begun to execute such works fails to make such progress towards their completion as seems to the local authority reasonable.

(4) In proceedings to recover expenses under subsection (2) above, the court (a) shall inquire whether the local authority were justified in concluding that the premises were in a defective state, or that unreasonable delay in remedying the defective state would have been occasioned by following the procedure prescribed by [section 80 of the Environmental Health Act 1990], and

(b) if the defendant proves that he served a counter-notice under subsection (3) above, shall inquire whether the defendant failed to begin the works to remedy the defects within a reasonable time, or failed to make reasonable progress towards their completion,

and if the court determines that –
    (i) the local authority were not justified in either of the conclusions mentioned in paragraph (a) of this subsection, or
    (ii) there was no failure under paragraph (b) of this subsection,
the local authority shall not recover the expenses or any part of them.

(5) Subject to subsection (4) above, in proceedings to recover expenses under subsection (2) above, the court may –
    (a) inquire whether the said expenses ought to be borne wholly or in part by some person other than the defendant in the proceedings, and
    (b) make such order concerning the expenses or their apportionment as appears to the court to be just,
but the court shall not order the expenses or any part of them to be borne by a person other than the defendant in the proceedings unless the court is satisfied that that other person has had due notice of the proceedings and an opportunity of being heard.

(6) A local authority shall not serve a notice under subsection (1) above, or proceed with the execution of works in accordance with a notice so served, if the execution of the works would, to their knowledge, be in contravention of a building preservation order under section 29 of the Town and Country Planning Act 1947.

(7) The power conferred on a local authority by subsection (1) above may be exercised notwithstanding that the local authority might instead have proceeded under [Part VI of the Housing Act 1985 (repair notices)].

Amendment

The words in square brackets in subss(1)(b) and (4)(a) were substituted by Environmental Protection Act 1990 Sch 15 para 24. The words in square brackets in subs(7) were substituted by Housing (Consequential Provisions) Act 1985 Sch 2 para 57.

Dangerous building

77 (1) If it appears to a local authority that a building or structure, or part of a building or structure, is in such a condition, or is used to carry such loads, as to be dangerous, the authority may apply to a magistrates' court, and the court may –
    (a) where danger arises from the condition of the building or structure, make an order requiring the owner thereof –
        (i) to execute such work as may be necessary to obviate the danger or,
        (ii) if he so elects, to demolish the building or structure, or any dangerous part of it, and remove any rubbish resulting from the demolition, or
    (b) where danger arises from overloading of the building or structure, make an order restricting its use until a magistrates' court, being satisfied that any necessary works have been executed, withdraws or modifies the restriction.

(2) If the person on whom an order is made under subsection (1)(a) above fails to comply with the order within the time specified, the local authority may –
    (a) execute the order in such manner as they think fit, and

(b) recover the expenses reasonably incurred by them in doing so from the person in default,

and, without prejudice to the right of the authority to exercise those powers, the person is liable on summary conviction to a fine not exceeding level 1 on the standard scale.

Dangerous building – emergency measures

78 (1) If it appears to a local authority that –

    (a) a building or structure, or part of a building or structure, is in such a state, or is used to carry such loads, as to be dangerous, and

    (b) immediate action should be taken to remove the danger,

they may take such steps as may be necessary for that purpose.

(2) Before exercising their powers under this section, the local authority shall, if it is reasonably practicable to do so, give notice of their intention to the owner and occupier of the building, or of the premises on which the structure is situated.

(3) Subject to this section, the local authority may recover from the owner the expenses reasonably incurred by them under this section.

(4) So far as expenses incurred by the local authority under this section consist of expenses of fencing off the building or structure, or arranging for it to be watched, the expenses shall not be recoverable in respect of any period –

    (a) after the danger has been removed by other steps under this section, or

    (b) after an order made under section 77(1) above for the purpose of its removal has been complied with or has been executed as mentioned in subsection (2) of that section.

(5) In proceedings to recover expenses under this section, the court shall inquire whether the local authority might reasonably have proceeded instead under section 77(1) above, and, if the court determines that the local authority might reasonably have proceeded instead under that subsection, the local authority shall not recover the expenses or any part of them.

(6) Subject to subsection (5) above, in proceedings to recover expenses under this section, the court may –

    (a) inquire whether the expenses ought to be borne wholly or in part by some person other than the defendant in the proceedings, and

    (b) make such order concerning the expenses or their apportionment as appears to the court to be just,

but the court shall not order the expenses or any part of them to be borne by any person other than the defendant in the proceedings unless it is satisfied that that other person has had due notice of the proceedings and an opportunity of being heard.

(7) Where in consequence of the exercise of the powers conferred by this section the owner or occupier of any premises sustains damage, but section 106(1) below does not apply because the owner or occupier has been in default –

    (a) the owner or occupier may apply to a magistrates' court to determine whether the local authority were justified in exercising their powers under this section so as to occasion the damage sustained, and

    (b) if the court determines that the local authority were not so justified, the owner or occupier is entitled to compensation, and section 106(2) and (3) below applies in relation to any dispute as regards compensation arising under this subsection.

(8) The proper officer of a local authority may, as an officer of the local authority, exercise the powers conferred on the local authority by subsection (1) above.

(9) This section does not apply to premises forming part of a mine or quarry within the meaning of the Mines and Quarries Act 1954.

Ruinous and dilapidated buildings and neglected sites

79 (1) If it appears to a local authority that a building or structure is by reason of its ruinous or dilapidated condition seriously detrimental to the amenities of the neighbourhood, the local authority may by notice require the owner thereof –

(a) to execute such works of repair or restoration, or

(b) if he so elects, to take such steps for demolishing the building or structure, or any part thereof,

and removing any rubbish or other material resulting from or exposed by the demolition, as may be necessary in the interests of amenity.

(2) If it appears to a local authority that –

(a) rubbish or other material resulting from, or exposed by, the demolition or collapse of a building or structure is lying on the site or on any adjoining land, and

(b) by reason thereof the site or land is in such a condition as to be seriously detrimental to the amenities of the neighbourhood,

the local authority may by notice require the owner of the site or land to take such steps for removing the rubbish or material as may be necessary in the interests of amenity.

(3) Sections 99 and 102 below apply in relation to a notice given under subsection (1) or (2) above, subject to the following modifications –

(a) section 99(1) requires the notice to indicate the nature of the works of repair or restoration and that of the works of demolition and removal of rubbish or material, and

(b) section 99(2) authorises the local authority to execute, subject to that subsection, at their election either the works of repair or restoration or the works of demolition and removal of rubbish or material.

(4) This section does not apply to an advertisement as defined in [section 3A(1) of the Town and Country Planning Act 1990].

Amendment

The words in square brackets in subs(4) were substituted by Planning (Consequential Provisions) Act 1990 Sch 2 para 67(4).

Notice to local authority of intended demolition

80 (1) This section applies to any demolition of the whole or part of a building except –

(a) a demolition in pursuance of a demolition order [[or obstructive building order]] made under [Part IX of the Housing Act 1985], and

(b) a demolition –

(i) of an internal part of a building, where the building is occupied and it is intended that it should continue to be occupied,

    (ii) of a building that has a cubic content (as ascertained by external measurement) of not more than 1750 cubic feet, or, where a greenhouse, conservatory, shed or prefabricated garage forms part of a larger building, of that greenhouse, conservatory, shed or prefabricated garage, or

    (iii) without prejudice to sub-paragraph (ii) above, of an agricultural building (as defined in section 26 of the General Rate Act 1967), unless it is contiguous to another building that is not itself an agricultural building or a building of a kind mentioned in that sub-paragraph.

(2) No person shall begin a demolition to which this section applies unless –
  (a) he has given the local authority notice of his intention to do so, and
  (b) either –
    (i) the local authority have given a notice to him under section 81 below, or
    (ii) the relevant period (as defined in that section) has expired.

(3) A notice under subsection (2) above shall specify the building to which it relates and the works of demolition intended to be carried out, and it is the duty of a person giving such a notice to a local authority to send or give a copy of it to –
  (a) the occupier of any building adjacent to the building,
  (b) the British Gas Corporation, and
  (c) the Area Electricity Board in whose area the building is situated.

(4) A person who contravenes subsection (2) above is liable on summary conviction to a fine not exceeding level 4 on the standard scale.

Amendment
The words in square brackets in subs(1) were substituted by Housing (Consequential Provisions) Act 1985 Sch 2 para 57. The words in double square brackets in subs(1) were added by Housing and Planning Act 1986 Sch 5 para 11.

Local authority's power to serve notice about demolition
81 (1) A local authority may give a notice under this section to –
  (a) a person on whom a demolition order [[or obstructive building order]] has been served under [Part IX of the Housing Act 1985],
  (b) a person who appears to them not to be intending to comply with an order made under section 77 above or a notice given under section 79 above, and
  (c) a person who appears to them to have begun or to be intending to begin a demolition to which section 80 above otherwise applies.

(2) Nothing contained in a notice under this section prejudices or affects the operation of any of the relevant statutory provisions, as defined in section 53(1) of the Health and Safety at Work etc Act 1974; and accordingly, if a requirement of such a notice is inconsistent with a requirement imposed by or under the said Act of 1974, the latter requirement prevails.

(3) Where –
  (a) a person has given a notice under section 80 above, or
  (b) the local authority have served a demolition order [[or obstructive building

order]] on a person under [Part IX of the Housing Act 1985],
a notice under this section may only be given to the person in question within
the relevant period.

(4) In this section and section 80 above, 'the relevant period' means –
  (a) in a case such as is mentioned in subsection (3)(a) above, six weeks from
      the giving of the notice under section 80 above, or such longer period as
      the person who gave that notice may in writing allow, and
  (b) in a case such as is mentioned in subsection (3)(b) above, seven days after
      the local authority served a copy of the demolition order [[or obstructive
      building order]] in accordance with [Part IX of the Housing Act 1985], or
      such longer period as the person on whom the copy was served may in
      writing allow.

(5) It is the duty of the local authority to send or give a copy of a notice under
    this section to the owner and occupier of any building adjacent to the building
    to which the notice relates.

(6) It is also the duty of the local authority to send or give a copy of a notice under
    this section –
  (a) if it contains such a requirement as is specified in section 82(1)(h) below,
      to the statutory undertakers concerned, and
  (b) if it contains such a requirement as is specified in section 82(1)(i)
      below –
    (i) to the fire authority, if they are not themselves the fire authority, and
    (ii) to the Health and Safety Executive, if the premises are special
         premises.

(7) In this section and section 82 below, 'special premises' means premises for
    which a fire certificate is required by virtue of regulations under the Health
    and Safety at Work etc Act 1974.

Amendments

The words in square brackets in subss(1), (3) and (4) were substituted by
Housing (Consequential Provisions) Act 1985 Sch 2 para 57. The words in
double square brackets in subss(1), (3) and (4) were added by Housing and
Planning Act 1986 Sch 5 para 11.

Notices under section 81

82 (1) A notice under section 81(1) above may require the person to whom it is given
–

  (a) to shore up any building adjacent to the building to which the notice
      relates,
  (b) to weatherproof any surfaces of an adjacent building that are exposed by
      the demolition,
  (c) to repair and make good any damage to an adjacent building caused by
      the demolition or by the negligent act or omission of any person engaged
      in it,
  (d) to remove material or rubbish resulting from the demolition and
      clearance of the site,
  (e) to disconnect and seal, at such points as the local authority may
      reasonably require, any sewer or drain in or under the building,

(f) to remove any such sewer or drain, and seal any sewer or drain with which the sewer or drain to be removed is connected,

(g) to make good to the satisfaction of the local authority the surface of the ground disturbed by anything done under paragraph (e) or (f) above,

(h) to make arrangements with the relevant statutory undertakers for the disconnection of the supply of gas, electricity and water to the building,

(i) to make such arrangements with regard to the burning of structures or materials on the site as may be reasonably required –

   (i) if the building is or forms part of special premises, by the Health and Safety Executive and the fire authority, and

   (ii) in any other case, by the fire authority, and

(j) to take such steps relating to the conditions subject to which the demolition is to be undertaken, and the condition in which the site is to be left on completion of the demolition, as the local authority may consider reasonably necessary for the protection of the public and the preservation of public amenity.

(2) No one shall be required under paragraph (c), (e) or (f) of subsection (1) above to carry out any work in land outside the premises on which the works of demolition are being carried out if he has no right to carry out that work, but, subject to section 101 below, the person undertaking the demolition, or the local authority acting in his default, may break open any street for the purpose of complying with any such requirement.

(3) Before a person complies with a requirement under paragraph (e), (f) or (g) of subsection (1) above, he shall give to the local authority –

(a) at least 48 hours' notice, in the case of a requirement under paragraph (e) or (f), or

(b) at least 24 hours' notice, in the case of a requirement under paragraph (g),

and a person who fails to comply with this subsection is liable on summary conviction to a fine not exceeding level 2 on the standard scale.

(4) This section does not authorise interference with apparatus or works of statutory undertakers authorised by an enactment to carry on an undertaking for the supply of electricity [or gas or with apparatus or works of a water undertaker or sewerage undertaker].

(5) Without prejudice to the generality of subsection (4) above, this section does not exempt a person from –

(a) the obligation to obtain any consent required under [section 167 of the Water Act 1989 (interference with water supplies or with waterworks)],

(b) criminal liability under any enactment relating to the supply of gas or electricity, or

(c) the requirements of regulations under section 31 of the Gas Act 1972 (public safety).

(6) Section 99 below applies in relation to a notice given under section 81(1) above.

Amendments

The words in square brackets in subss(4) and (5)(a) were substituted by Water Act 1989 Sch 25 para 70.

Appeal against notice under s81

83 (1) Section 102 below applies in relation to a notice given under section 81 above.

(2) Among the grounds on which an appeal may be brought under section 102 below against such a notice are –

(a) in the case of a notice requiring an adjacent building to be shored up, that the owner of the building is not entitled to the support of that building by the building that is being demolished, and ought to pay, or contribute towards, the expenses of shoring it up,

(b) in the case of a notice requiring any surfaces of an adjacent building to be weatherproofed, that the owner of the adjacent building ought to pay, or contribute towards, the expenses of weatherproofing those surfaces.

(3) Where the grounds on which an appeal under section 102 below is brought include a ground specified in subsection (2) above –

(a) the appellant shall serve a copy of his notice of appeal on the person or persons referred to in that ground of appeal, and

(b) on the hearing of the appeal the court may make such order as it thinks fit –

(i) in respect of the payment of, or contribution towards, the cost of the works by any such person, or

(ii) as to how any expenses that may be recoverable by the local authority are to be borne between the appellant and any such person.

Housing Act 1985 ss604 and 606

GENERAL PROVISIONS RELATING TO HOUSING CONDITIONS
Fitness for human habitation

604 (1) Subject to subsection (2) below, a dwellinghouse is fit for human habitation for the purposes of this Act unless, in the opinion of the local housing authority, it fails to meet one or more of the requirements in paragraphs (a) to (i) below and, by reason of that failure, is not reasonably suitable for occupation, –

(a) it is structurally stable;
(b) it is free from serious disrepair;
(c) it is free from dampness prejudicial to the health of the occupants (if any);
(d) it has adequate provision for lighting, heating and ventilation;
(e) it has an adequate piped supply of wholesome water;
(f) there are satisfactory facilities in the dwellinghouse for the preparation and cooking of food, including a sink with a satisfactory supply of hot and cold water;
(g) it has a suitably located watercloset for the exclusive use of the occupants (if any);
(h) it has, for the exclusive use of the occupants (if any), a suitably located fixed bath or shower and washhand basin each of which is provided with a satisfactory supply of hot and cold water; and
(i) it has an effective system for the draining of foul, waste and surface water;

and any reference to a dwellinghouse being unfit for human habitation shall be construed accordingly.

(2) Whether or not a dwellinghouse which is a flat satisfies the requirements in subsection (1), it is unfit for human habitation for the purposes of this Act if, in the opinion of the local housing authority, the building or a part of the building outside the flat fails to meet one or more of the requirements in paragraphs (a) to (e) below and, by reason of that failure, the flat is not reasonably suitable for occupation, –

(a) the building or part is structurally stable;
(b) it is free from serious disrepair;
(c) it is free from dampness;
(d) it has adequate provision for ventilation; and
(e) it has an effective system for the draining of foul, waste and surface water.

(3) Subsection (1) applies in relation to a house in multiple occupation with the substitution of a reference to the house for any reference to a dwellinghouse.

(4) Subsection (2) applies in relation to a flat in multiple occupation with the substitution for any reference to a dwellinghouse which is a flat of a reference to the flat in multiple occupation.

(5) The Secretary of State may by order amend the provisions of subsection (1) or subsection (2) in such manner and to such extent as he considers appropriate; and any such order –

    (a) may contain such transitional and supplementary provisions as the Secretary of State considers expedient; and

    (b) shall be made by statutory instrument which shall be subject to annulment in pursuance of a resolution of either House of Parliament.

Amendment

This section was substituted by Local Government and Housing Act 1989 Sch 9 para 83.

Reports on particular houses or areas

606 (1) The proper officer of the local housing authority shall make a report in writing to the authority whenever he is of the opinion –

    (a) that a [dwelling-house or house in multiple occupation] in their district is unfit for human habitation, or

    (b) that an area in their district should be dealt with as a clearance area;

and the authority shall take into consideration as soon as may be any such report made to them.

(2) If a complaint in writing that a [dwelling-house or house in multiple occupation] is unfit for human habitation, or that an area should be dealt with as a clearance area, is made to the proper officer of the local housing authority by –

    (a) a justice of the peace having jurisdiction in any part of their district, or

    (b) a parish or community council for a parish or community within their district,

the officer shall forthwith inspect the [dwelling-house or house in multiple occupation] or area and make a report to the authority stating the facts of the case and whether in his opinion the [dwelling-house or house in multiple occupation] is unfit for human habitation or the area should be dealt with as a clearance area.

(3) The absence of a complaint under subsection (2) does not excuse the proper officer of the authority from inspecting a [dwelling-house or house in multiple occupation] or area or making a report on it under subsection (1).

Amendment

The words in square brackets in subss(2) and (3) were substituted by Local Government and Housing Act 1989 Sch 9 para 86.

Landlord and Tenant Act 1985 ss8 and 11–17

Implied terms as to fitness for human habitation

8 (1) In a contract to which this section applies for the letting of a house for human habitation there is implied, notwithstanding any stipulation to the contrary –
   (a) a condition that the house is fit for human habitation at the commencement of the tenancy, and
   (b) an undertaking that the house will be kept by the landlord fit for human habitation during the tenancy.

(2) The landlord, or a person authorised by him in writing, may at reasonable times of the day, on giving 24 hours' notice in writing to the tenant or occupier, enter premises to which this section applies for the purpose of viewing their state and condition.

(3) This section applies to a contract if –
   (a) the rent does not exceed the figure applicable in accordance with subsection (4), and
   (b) the letting is not on such terms as to the tenant's responsibility as are mentioned in subsection (5).

(4) The rent limit for the application of this section is shown by the following Table, by reference to the date of making of the contract and the situation of the premises:

TABLE

Date of making of contract	Rent limit
Before 31st July 1923.	In London: £40. Elsewhere: £26 or £16 (see Note 1).
On or after 31st July 1923 and before 6th July 1957.	In London: £40. Elsewhere: £26.
On or after 6th July 1957.	In London: £80. Elsewhere: £52.

NOTES

1 The applicable figure for contracts made before 31st July 1923 is £26 in the case of premises situated in a borough or urban district which at the date of the contract had according to the last published census a population of 50,000 or more. In the case of a house situated elsewhere, the figure is £16.

2 The references to 'London' are, in relation to contracts made before 1st April 1965, to the administrative county of London and, in relation to contracts made on or after that date, to Greater London exclusive of the outer London boroughs.

(5) This section does not apply where a house is let for a term of three years or more (the lease not being determinable at the option of either party before the expiration of three years) upon terms that the tenant puts the premises into a condition reasonably fit for human habitation.

(6) In this section 'house' includes –

(a) a part of a house, and

(b) any yard, garden, outhouses and appurtenances belonging to the house or usually enjoyed with it.

Repairing obligations in short leases

11 (1) In a lease to which this section applies (as to which, see sections 13 and 14) there is implied a covenant by the lessor –

(a) to keep in repair the structure and exterior of the dwelling-house (including drains, gutters and external pipes),

(b) to keep in repair and proper working order the installations in the dwelling-house for the supply of water, gas and electricity and for sanitation (including basins, sinks, baths and sanitary conveniences, but not other fixtures, fittings and appliances for making use of the supply of water, gas or electricity), and

(c) to keep in repair and proper working order the installations in the dwelling-house for space heating and heating water.

[(1A) If a lease to which this section applies is a lease of a dwelling-house which forms part only of a building, then, subject to subsection (1B), the covenant implied by subsection (1) shall have effect as if –

(a) the reference in paragraph (a) of that subsection to the dwelling-house included a reference to any part of the building in which the lessor has an estate or interest; and

(b) any reference in paragraphs (b) and (c) of that subsection to an installation in the dwelling-house included a reference to an installation which, directly or indirectly, serves the dwelling-house and which either –

(i) forms part of any part of a building in which the lessor has an estate or interest; or

(ii) is owned by the lessor or under his control.]

(1B) Nothing in subsection (1A) shall be construed as requiring the lessor to carry out any works or repairs unless the disrepair (or failure to maintain in working order) is such as to affect the lessee's enjoyment of the dwelling-house or of any common parts, as defined in section 60(1) of the Landlord and Tenant Act 1987, which the lessee, as such, is entitled to use.]

(2) The covenant implied by subsection (1) ('the lessor's repairing covenant') shall not be construed as requiring the lessor –

(a) to carry out works or repairs for which the lessee is liable by virtue of his duty to use the premises in a tenant-like manner, or would be so liable but for an express covenant on his part,

(b) to rebuild or reinstate the premises in the case of destruction or damage by fire, or by tempest, flood or other inevitable accident, or

(c) to keep in repair or maintain anything which the lessee is entitled to remove from the dwelling-house.

(3) In determining the standard of repair required by the lessor's repairing covenant, regard shall be had to the age, character and prospective life of the dwelling-house and the locality in which it is situated.

[(3A) In any case where –
- (a) the lessor's repairing covenant has effect as mentioned in subsection (1A), and
- (b) in order to comply with the covenant the lessor needs to carry out works or repairs otherwise than in, or to an installation in, the dwelling-house, and
- (c) the lessor does not have a sufficient right in the part of the building or the installation concerned to enable him to carry out the required works or repairs,

then, in any proceedings relating to a failure to comply with the lessor's repairing covenant, so far as it requires the lessor to carry out the works or repairs in question, it shall be a defence for the lessor to prove that he used all reasonable endeavours to obtain, but was unable to obtain, such rights as would be adequate to enable him to carry out the works or repairs.]

(4) A covenant by the lessee for the repair of the premises is of no effect so far as it relates to the matters mentioned in subsection (1)(a) to (c), except so far as it imposes on the lessee any of the requirements mentioned in subsection (2)(a) or (c).

(5) The reference in subsection (4) to a covenant by the lessee for the repair of the premises includes a covenant –
- (a) to put in repair or deliver up in repair,
- (b) to paint, point or render,
- (c) to pay money in lieu of repairs by the lessee, or
- (d) to pay money on account of repairs by the lessor.

(6) In a lease in which the lessor's repairing covenant is implied there is also implied a covenant by the lessee that the lessor, or any person authorised by him in writing, may at reasonable times of the day and on giving 24 hours' notice in writing to the occupier, enter the premises comprised in the lease for the purpose of viewing their condition and state of repair.

Restriction on contracting out of s11

12 (1) A covenant or agreement, whether contained in a lease to which section 11 applies or in an agreement collateral to such a lease, is void in so far as it purports –
- (a) to exclude or limit the obligations of the lessor or the immunities of the lessee under that section, or
- (b) to authorise any forfeiture or impose on the lessee any penalty, disability or obligation in the event of his enforcing or relying upon those obligations or immunities, unless the inclusion of the provision was authorised by the county court.

(2) The county court may, by order made with the consent of the parties, authorise the inclusion in a lease, or in an agreement collateral to a lease, of provisions excluding or modifying in relation to the lease, the provisions of section 11 with respect to the repairing obligations of the parties if it appears to the court that it is reasonable to do so, having regard to all the

circumstances of the case, including the other terms and conditions of the lease.

Leases to which s11 applies: general rule

13 (1) Section 11 (repairing obligations) applies to a lease of a dwelling-house granted on or after 24th October 1961 for a term of less than seven years.

(2) In determining whether a lease is one to which section 11 applies –

(a) any part of the term which falls before the grant shall be left out of account and the lease shall be treated as a lease for a term commencing with the grant,

(b) a lease which is determinable at the option of the lessor before the expiration of seven years from the commencement of the term shall be treated as a lease for a term of less than seven years, and

(c) a lease (other than a lease to which paragraph (b) applies) shall not be treated as a lease for a term of less than seven years if it confers on the lessee an option for renewal for a term which, together with the original term, amounts to seven years or more.

(3) This section has effect subject to –

section 14 (leases to which section 11 applies: exceptions), and

section 32(2) (provisions not applying to tenancies within Part II of the Landlord and Tenant Act 1954).

Leases to which s11 applies: exceptions

14 (1) Section 11 (repairing obligations) does not apply to a new lease granted to an existing tenant, or to a former tenant still in possession, if the previous lease was not a lease to which section 11 applied (and, in the case of a lease granted before 24th October 1961, would not have been if it had been granted on or after that date).

(2) In subsection (1) –

'existing tenant' means a person who is when, or immediately before, the new lease is granted, the lessee under another lease of the dwelling-house;

'former tenant still in possession' means a person who –

(a) was the lessee under another lease of the dwelling-house which terminated at some time before the new lease was granted, and

(b) between the termination of that other lease and the grant of the new lease was continuously in possession of the dwelling-house or of the rents and profits of the dwelling-house; and

'the previous lease' means the other lease referred to in the above definitions.

(3) Section 11 does not apply to a lease of a dwelling-house which is a tenancy of an agricultural holding within the meaning of the [Agricultural Holdings Act 1986] [[and in relation to which that Act applies or to a farm business tenancy within the meaning of the Agricultural Tenancies Act 1995]].

(4) Section 11 does not apply to a lease granted on or after 3rd October 1980 to –

a local authority,

a new town corporation,

an urban development corporation,

the Development Board for Rural Wales,

a [[registered social landlord]],

a co-operative housing association, or

an educational institution or other body specified, or of a class specified, by regulations under section 8 of the Rent Act 1977 [or paragraph 8 of Schedule 1 to the Housing Act 1988] (bodies making student lettings).

(5) Section 11 does not apply to a lease granted on or after 3rd October 1980 to –

(a) Her Majesty in right of the Crown (unless the lease is under the management of the Crown Estate Commissioners), or

(b) a government department or a person holding in trust for Her Majesty for the purposes of a government department.

Amendments

In subs(3), the words in square brackets were substituted by Agricultural Holdings Act 1986 Sch 14 para 64 and the words in double square brackets were added by Agricultural Tenancies Act 1995 Sch para 31. In subs(4), the words in square brackets were added by Local Government and Housing Act 1989 Sch 11 para 89 and the words in double square brackets were substituted by Housing Act 1996 (Consequential Provisions) Order 1996 SI No 2325 Sch 2 para 16(2).

Jurisdiction of county court

15   The county court has jurisdiction to make a declaration that section 11 (repairing obligations) applies, or does not apply, to a lease –

(a) whatever the net annual value of the property in question, and

(b) notwithstanding that no other relief is sought than a declaration.

Meaning of 'lease' and related expressions

16   In sections 11 to 15 (repairing obligations in short leases) –

(a) 'lease' does not include a mortgage term;

(b) 'lease of a dwelling-house' means a lease by which a building or part of a building is let wholly or mainly as a private residence, and 'dwelling-house' means that building or part of a building;

(c) 'lessee' and 'lessor' mean, respectively, the person for the time being entitled to the term of a lease and to the reversion expectant on it.

Specific performance of landlord's repairing obligations

17 (1) In proceedings in which a tenant of a dwelling alleges a breach on the part of his landlord of a repairing covenant relating to any part of the premises in which the dwelling is comprised, the court may order specific performance of the covenant whether or not the breach relates to a part of the premises let to the tenant and notwithstanding any equitable rule restricting the scope of the remedy, whether on the basis of a lack of mutuality or otherwise.

(2) In this section –

(a) 'tenant' includes a statutory tenant,

(b) in relation to a statutory tenant the reference to the premises let to him is to the premises of which he is a statutory tenant,

(c) 'landlord', in relation to a tenant, includes any person against whom the tenant has a right to enforce a repairing covenant, and

(d) 'repairing covenant' means a covenant to repair, maintain, renew, construct or replace any property.

Environmental Protection Act 1990 ss79–82

PART III – STATUTORY NUISANCES AND CLEAN AIR STATUTORY NUISANCES: ENGLAND AND WALES

Statutory nuisances and inspections therefor

79 (1) [Subject to subsections (2) to (6A) below], the following matters constitute 'statutory nuisances' for the purposes of this Part, that is to say –

(a) any premises in such a state as to be prejudicial to health or a nuisance;

(b) smoke emitted from premises so as to be prejudicial to health or a nuisance;

(c) fumes or gases emitted from premises so as to be prejudicial to health or a nuisance;

(d) any dust, steam, smell or other effluvia arising on industrial, trade or business premises and being prejudicial to health or a nuisance;

(e) any accumulation or deposit which is prejudicial to health or a nuisance;

(f) any animal kept in such a place or manner as to be prejudicial to health or a nuisance;

(g) noise emitted from premises so as to be prejudicial to health or a nuisance;

[(ga) noise that is prejudicial to health or a nuisance and is emitted from or caused by a vehicle, machinery or equipment in a street;]

(h) any other matter declared by any enactment to be a statutory nuisance; and it shall be the duty of every local authority to cause its area to be inspected from time to time to detect any statutory nuisances which ought to be dealt with under section 80 below [or sections 80 and 80A below] and, where a complaint of a statutory nuisance is made to it by a person living within its area, to take such steps as are reasonably practicable to investigate the complaint.

(2) Subsections (1)(b) and (g) above do not apply in relation to premises –

(a) occupied on behalf of the Crown for naval, military or air force purposes or for the purposes of the department of the Secretary of State having responsibility for defence, or

(b) occupied by or for the purposes of a visiting force; and 'visiting force' means any such body, contingent or detachment of the forces of any country as is a visiting force for the purposes of any of the provisions of the Visiting Forces Act 1952.

(3) Subsection (1)(b) above does not apply to –

(i)   smoke emitted from a chimney of a private dwelling within a smoke control area,

(ii) dark smoke emitted from a chimney of a building or a chimney serving the furnace of a boiler or industrial plant attached to a building or for the time being fixed to or installed on any land,

(iii) smoke emitted from a railway locomotive steam engine, or

(iv) dark smoke emitted otherwise than as mentioned above from industrial or trade premises.

(4) Subsection (1)(c) above does not apply in relation to premises other than private dwellings.

(5) Subsection (1)(d) above does not apply to steam emitted from a railway locomotive engine.

(6) Subsection (1)(g) above does not apply to noise caused by aircraft other than model aircraft.

[(6A) Subsection (1)(ga) above does not apply to noise made –

(a) by traffic,

(b) by any naval, military or air force of the Crown or by a visiting force (as defined in subsection (2) above), or

(c) by a political demonstration or a demonstration supporting or opposing a cause or campaign.]

(7) In this Part –

'chimney' includes structures and openings of any kind from or through which smoke may be emitted;

'dust' does not include dust emitted from a chimney as an ingredient of smoke;

['equipment' includes a musical instrument;]

'fumes' means any airborne solid matter smaller than dust;

'gas' includes vapour and moisture precipitated from vapour;

'industrial, trade or business premises' means premises used for any industrial, trade or business purposes or premises not so used on which matter is burnt in connection with any industrial, trade or business process, and premises are used for industrial purposes, where they are used for the purposes of any treatment or process as well as where they are used for the purposes or manufacturing;

'local authority' means, subject to subsection (8) below, –

(a) in Greater London, a London borough council, the Common Council of the City of London and, as respects the Temples, the Sub-Treasurer of the Inner Temple and the Under-Treasurer of the Middle Temple respectively;

(b) outside Greater London, a district council;

[(bb) in Wales, a county or county borough council;] and

(c) the Council of the Isles of Scilly;

'noise' includes vibration;

['person responsible' –

(a) in relation to a statutory nuisance, means the person to whose act, default or sufferance the nuisance is attributable;

(b) in relation to a vehicle, includes the person in whose name the vehicle is for the time being registered under the Vehicles (Excise) Act 1971 and any other person who is for the time being the driver of the vehicle;

(c) in relation to machinery or equipment, includes any person who is for the time being the operator of the machinery or equipment;]

'prejudicial to health' means injurious, or likely to cause injury, to health;

'premises' includes land and, subject to subsection (12) [and section 81A(9)] below, any vessel;

'private dwelling' means any building, or part of a building, used or intended to be used, as a dwelling;

'smoke' includes soot, ash, grit and gritty particles emitted in smoke;

['street' means a highway and any other road, footway, square or court that is for the time being open to the public;]

and any expressions used in this section and in [[the Clean Air Act 1993]] have the same meaning in this section as in that Act and [[section 3 of the Clean Air Act 1993]] shall apply for the interpretation of the expression 'dark smoke' and the operation of this Part in relation to it.

(8) Where, by an order under section 2 of the Public Health (Control of Disease) Act 1984, a port health authority has been constituted for any port health district, the port health authority shall have by virtue of this subsection, as respects its district, the functions conferred or imposed by this Part in relation to statutory nuisances other than a nuisance falling within paragraph (g) [or (ga)] of subsection (1) above and no such order shall be made assigning those functions; and 'local authority' and 'area' shall be construed accordingly.

(9) In this Part 'best practicable means' is to be interpreted by reference to the following provisions –

(a) 'practicable' means reasonably practicable having regard among other things to local conditions and circumstances, to the current state of technical knowledge and to the financial implications;

(b) the means to be employed include the design, installation, maintenance and manner and periods of operation of plant and machinery, and the design, construction and maintenance of buildings and structures;

(c) the test is to apply only so far as compatible with any duty imposed by law;

(d) the test is to apply only so far as compatible with safety and safe working conditions, and with the exigencies of any emergency or unforeseeable circumstances;

and, in circumstances where a code of practice under section 71 of the Control of Pollution Act 1974 (noise minimisation) is applicable, regard shall also be had to guidance given in it.

(10) A local authority shall not without the consent of the Secretary of State institute summary proceedings under this Part in respect of a nuisance falling within paragraph (b), (d) or (e) of subsection (1) above if proceedings in respect thereof might be instituted under Part 1 of the Alkali &c Works Regulation Act 1906 or section 5 of the Health and Safety at Work etc Act 1974.

(11) The area of a local authority which includes part of the seashore shall also include for the purposes of this Part the territorial sea lying seawards from

that part of the shore; and subject to subsection (12) [and section 81A(9)] below, this Part shall have effect, in relation to any area included in the area of a local authority by virtue of this subsection –

(a) as if references to premises and the occupier of premises included respectively a vessel and the master of a vessel; and

(b) with such other modifications, if any, as are prescribed in regulations made by the Secretary of State.

(12) A vessel powered by steam reciprocating machinery is not a vessel to which this Part of this Act applies.

Amendments

The words in square brackets in subss(1) and (8), the whole of subs(6A), and the definitions of 'equipment' and 'street', were added by and the definition of 'person responsible' substituted by Noise and Statutory Nuisance Act 1993 s2. The words in square brackets in subss(7) and (11) were added by s10 of the same Act. The words in double square brackets in subs(7) were substituted by Clean Air Act 1993 Sch 4 para 4. Subsection (7)(bb) was added by Local Government (Wales) Act 1994 Sch 9 para 17(5).

Summary proceedings for statutory nuisances

80 (1) Where a local authority is satisfied that a statutory nuisance exists, or is likely to occur or recur, in the area of the authority, the local authority shall serve a notice ('an abatement notice') imposing all or any of the following requirements –

(a) requiring the abatement of the nuisance or prohibiting or restricting its occurrence or recurrence;

(b) requiring the execution of such works, and the taking of such other steps, as may be necessary for any of those purposes,

and the notice shall specify the time or times within which the requirements of the notice are to be complied with.

(2) [Subject to section 80A(1) below, the abatement notice] shall be served –

(a) except in a case falling within paragraph (b) or (c) below, on the person responsible for the nuisance;

(b) where the nuisance arises from any defect of a structural character, on the owner of the premises;

(c) where the person responsible for the nuisance cannot be found or the nuisance has not yet occurred, on the owner or occupier of the premises.

(3) [A person served with an abatement notice] may appeal against the notice to a magistrates' court within the period of twenty-one days beginning with the date on which he was served with the notice.

(4) If a person on whom an abatement notice is served, without reasonable excuse, contravenes or fails to comply with any requirement or prohibition imposed by the notice, he shall be guilty of an offence.

(5) Except in a case falling within subsection (6) below, a person who commits an offence under subsection (4) above shall be liable on summary conviction to a fine not exceeding level 5 on the standard scale together with a further fine of an amount equal to one-tenth of that level for each day on which the offence continues after the conviction.

(6) A person who commits an offence under subsection (4) above on industrial,

trade or business premises shall be liable on summary conviction to a fine not exceeding £20,000.

(7) Subject to subsection (8) below, in any proceedings for an offence under subsection (4) above in respect of a statutory nuisance it shall be a defence to prove that the best practicable means were used to prevent, or to counteract the effects of, the nuisance.

(8) The defence under subsection (7) above is not available –

    (a) in the case of a nuisance falling within paragraph (a), (d), (e), (f) or (g) of section 79(1) above except where the nuisance arises on industrial, trade or business premises;

    [(aa) in the case of a nuisance falling within paragraph (ga) of section 79(1) above except where the noise is emitted from or caused by a vehicle, machinery or equipment being used for industrial, trade or business purposes;]

    (b) in the case of a nuisance falling within paragraph (b) of section 79(1) above except where the smoke is emitted from a chimney; and

    (c) in the case of a nuisance falling within paragraph (c) or (h) of section 79(1) above.

(9) In proceedings for an offence under subsection (4) above in respect of a statutory nuisance falling within paragraph (g) [or (ga)] of section 79(1) above where the offence consists in contravening requirements imposed by virtue of subsection (1)(a) above it shall be a defence to prove –

    (a) that the alleged offence was covered by a notice served under section 60 or a consent given under section 61 or 65 of the Control of Pollution Act 1974 (construction sites, etc); or

    (b) where the alleged offence was committed at a time when the premises were subject to a notice under section 66 of that Act (noise reduction notice), that the level of noise emitted from the premises at that time was not such as to constitute a contravention of the notice under that section; or

    (c) where the alleged offence was committed at a time when the premises were not subject to a notice under section 66 of that Act, and when a level fixed under section 67 of that Act (new buildings liable to abatement order) applied to the premises, that the level of noise emitted from the premises at that time did not exceed that level.

Paragraphs (b) and (c) of subsection (9) above apply whether or not the relevant notice was subject to appeal at the time when the offence was alleged to have been committed.

Amendments

The words in square brackets in subss(2) and (3) were substituted and subs(8)(aa) and the words in square brackets in subs(9) were added by Noise and Statutory Nuisance Act 1993 s3.

[Abatement notice in respect of noise in street

80A(1) In the case of a statutory nuisance within section 79(1)(ga) above that –

    (a) has not yet occurred, or

    (b) arises from noise emitted from or caused by an unattended vehicle or unattended machinery or equipment, the abatement notice shall be served in accordance with subsection (2) below.

(2) The notice shall be served –

    (a) where the person responsible for the vehicle, machinery or equipment can be found, on that person;

    (b) where that person cannot be found or where the local authority determines that this paragraph should apply, by fixing the notice to the vehicle, machinery or equipment.

(3) Where –

    (a) an abatement notice is served in accordance with subsection (2)(b) above by virtue of a determination of the local authority, and

    (b) the person responsible for the vehicle, machinery or equipment can be found and served with a copy of the notice within an hour of the notice being fixed to the vehicle, machinery or equipment, a copy of the notice shall be served on that person accordingly.

(4) Where an abatement notice is served in accordance with subsection (2)(b) above by virtue of a determination of the local authority, the notice shall state that, if a copy of the notice is subsequently served under subsection (3) above, the time specified in the notice as the time within which its requirements are to be complied with is extended by such further period as is specified in the notice.

(5) Where an abatement notice is served in accordance with subsection (2)(b) above, the person responsible for the vehicle, machinery or equipment may appeal against the notice under section 80(3) above as if he had been served with the notice on the date on which it was fixed to the vehicle, machinery or equipment.

(6) Section 80(4) above shall apply in relation to a person on whom a copy of an abatement notice is served under subsection (3) above as if the copy were the notice itself.

(7) A person who removes or interferes with a notice fixed to a vehicle, machinery or equipment in accordance with subsection (2)(b) above shall be guilty of an offence, unless he is the person responsible for the vehicle, machinery or equipment or he does so with the authority of that person.

A person who commits an offence under subsection (7) above shall be liable on summary conviction to a fine not exceeding level 3 on the standard scale.]

Amendment

Section 80A was inserted by Noise and Statutory Nuisance Act 1993 s3(6).

Supplementary provisions

81 (1) [Subject to subsection (1A) below, where] more than one person is responsible for a statutory nuisance section 80 above shall apply to each of those persons whether or not what any one of them is responsible for would by itself amount to a nuisance.

[(1A) In relation to a statutory nuisance within section 79(1)(ga) above for which more than one person is responsible (whether or not what any one of those persons is responsible for would by itself amount to such a nuisance), section 80(2)(a) above shall apply with the substitution of 'any one of the persons' for 'the person'.]

[(1B) In relation to a statutory nuisance within section 79(1)(ga) above caused by noise emitted from or caused by an unattended vehicle or unattended machinery or equipment for which more than one person is responsible, section 80A above shall apply with the substitution –
- (a) in subsection (2)(a), of 'any of the persons' for 'the person' and of 'one such person' for 'that person',
- (b) in subsection (2)(b), of 'such a person' for 'that person',
- (c) in subsection (3), of 'any of the persons' for 'the person' and of 'one such person' for 'that person',
- (d) in subsection (5), of 'any person' for 'the person', and
- (e) in subsection (7), of 'a person' for 'the person' and of 'such a person' for 'that person'.]

(2) Where a statutory nuisance which exists or has occurred within the area of a local authority, or which has affected any part of that area, appears to the local authority to be wholly or partly caused by some act or default committed or taking place outside the area, the local authority may act under section 80 above as if the act or default were wholly within that area, except that any appeal shall be heard by a magistrates' court having jurisdiction where the act or default is alleged to have taken place.

(3) Where an abatement notice has not been complied with the local authority may, whether or not they take proceedings for an offence under section 80(4) above, abate the nuisance and do whatever may be necessary in execution of the notice.

(4) Any expenses reasonably incurred by a local authority in abating, or preventing the recurrence of, a statutory nuisance under subsection (3) above may be recovered by them from the person by whose act or default the nuisance was caused and, if that person is the owner of the premises, from any person who is for the time being the owner thereof; and the court may apportion the expenses between persons by whose acts or defaults the nuisance is caused in such manner as the court consider fair and reasonable.

(5) If a local authority is of opinion that proceedings for an offence under section 80(4) above would afford an inadequate remedy in the case of any statutory nuisance, they may, subject to subsection (6) below, take proceedings in the High Court for the purpose of securing the abatement, prohibition or restriction of the nuisance, and the proceedings shall be maintainable notwithstanding the local authority have suffered no damage from the nuisance.

(6) In any proceedings under subsection (5) above in respect of a nuisance falling within paragraph (g) [or (ga)] of section 79(1) above, it shall be a defence to prove that the noise was authorised by a notice under section 60 or a consent under section 61 (construction sites) of the Control of Pollution Act 1974.

(7) The further supplementary provisions in Schedule 3 to this Act shall have effect.

Amendments
The words in square brackets in subss(1) and (6) and the whole of subss(1A) and (1B) were added by Noise and Statutory Nuisance Act 1993 s4.

[Expenses recoverable from owner to be a charge on premises

81A (1) Where any expenses are recoverable under section 81(4) above a person who is the owner of the premises there mentioned and the local authority serves a notice on him under this section –

(a) the expenses shall carry interest, at such reasonable rate as the local authority may determine, from the date of service of the notice until the whole amount is paid, and

(b) subject to the following provisions of this section, the expenses and accrued interest shall be a charge on the premises.

(2) A notice served under this section shall –

(a) specify the amount of the expenses that the local authority claims is recoverable,

(b) state the effect of subsection (1) above and the rate of interest determined by the local authority under that subsection, and

(c) state the effect of subsections (4) to (6) below.

(3) On the date on which a local authority serves a notice on a person under this section the authority shall also serve a copy of the notice on every other person who, to the knowledge of the authority, has an interest in the premises capable of being affected by the charge.

(4) Subject to any order under subsection (7)(b) or (c) below, the amount of any expenses specified in a notice under this section and the accrued interest shall be a charge on the premises –

(a) as from the end of the period of twenty-one days beginning with the date of service of the notice, or

(b) where an appeal is brought under subsection (6) below, as from the final determination of the appeal, until the expenses and interest are recovered.

(5) For the purposes of subsection (4) above, the withdrawal of an appeal has the same effect as a final determination of the appeal.

(6) A person served with a notice or copy of a notice under this section may appeal against the notice to the county court within the period of twenty-one days beginning with the date of service.

(7) On such an appeal the court may –

(a) confirm the notice without modification,

(b) order that the notice is to have effect with the substitution of a different amount for the amount originally specified in it, or

(c) order that the notice is to be of no effect.

(8) A local authority shall, for the purpose of enforcing a charge under this section, have all the same powers and remedies under the Law of Property Act 1925, and otherwise, as if it were a mortgagee by deed having powers of sale and lease, of accepting surrenders of leases and of appointing a receiver.

(9) In this section –

'owner', in relation to any premises, means a person (other than a mortgagee not in possession) who, whether in his own right or as trustee for any other person, is entitled to receive the rack rent of the premises or, where the premises are not let at a rack rent, would be so entitled if they were so let, and

'premises' does not include a vessel.]

Amendment

> Section 81A was inserted by Noise and Statutory Nuisance Act 1993 s10(2).

[Payment of expenses by instalments

81B(1) Where any expenses are a charge on premises under section 81A above, the local authority may by order declare the expenses to be pay-able with interest by instalments within the specified period, until the whole amount is paid.

(2) In subsection (1) above –

'interest' means interest at the rate determined by the authority under section 81A(1) above, and

'the specified period' means such period of thirty years or less from the date of service of the notice under section 81A above as is speci-fied in the order.

(3) Subject to subsection (5) below, the instalments and interest, or any part of them, may be recovered from the owner or occupier for the time being of the premises.

(4) Any sums recovered from an occupier may be deducted by him from the rent of the premises.

(5) An occupier shall not be required to pay at any one time any sum greater than the aggregate of –

  (a) the amount that was due from him on account of rent at the date on which he was served with a demand from the local authority together with a notice requiring him not to pay rent to his landlord without deducting the sum demanded, and

  (b) the amount that has become due from him on account of rent since that date.]

Amendment

> Section 81B was inserted by Noise and Statutory Nuisance Act 1993 s10(2).

Summary proceedings by persons aggrieved by statutory nuisances

82 (1) A magistrates' court may act under this section on a complaint made by any person on the ground that he is aggrieved by the existence of a statutory nuisance.

(2) If the magistrates' court is satisfied that the alleged nuisance exists, or that although abated it is likely to recur on the same premises [or, in the case of a nuisance within section 79(1)(ga) above, in the same street], the court shall make an order for either or both of the following purposes –

  (a) requiring the defendant to abate the nuisance, within a time specified in the order, and to execute any works necessary for that purpose;

  (b) prohibiting a recurrence of the nuisance, and requiring the defendant, within a time specified in the order, to execute any works necessary to prevent the recurrence;

and may also impose on the defendant a fine not exceeding level 5 on the standard scale.

(3) If the magistrates' court is satisfied that the alleged nuisance exists and is such as, in the opinion of the court, to render premises unfit for human habitation, an order under subsection (2) above may prohibit the use of the premises for human habitation until the premises are, to the satisfaction of the court, rendered fit for that purpose.

(4) Proceedings for an order under subsection (2) above shall be brought –

    (a) except in a case falling within [paragraph (b), (c) or (d) below], against the person responsible for the nuisance;

    (b) where the nuisance arises from any defect of a structural character, against the owner of the premises;

    (c) where the person responsible for the nuisance cannot be found, against the owner or occupier of the premises;

    [(d) in the case of a statutory nuisance within section 79(1)(ga) above caused by noise emitted from or caused by an unattended vehicle or unattended machinery or equipment, against the person responsible for the vehicle, machinery or equipment.]

(5) [Subject to subsection (5A) below, where] more than one person is responsible for a statutory nuisance, subsections (1) to (4) above shall apply to each of those persons whether or not what any one of them is responsible for would by itself amount to a nuisance.

[(5A) In relation to a statutory nuisance within section 79(1)(ga) above for which more than one person is responsible (whether or not what any one of those persons is responsible for would by itself amount to such a nuisance), subsection (4)(a) above shall apply with the substitution of 'each person responsible for the nuisance who can be found' for 'the person responsible for the nuisance'.]

[(5B) In relation to a statutory nuisance within section 79(1)(ga) above caused by noise emitted from or caused by an unattended vehicle or unattended machinery or equipment for which more than one person is responsible, subsection (4)(d) above shall apply with the substitution of 'any person' for 'the person'.]

(6) Before instituting proceedings for an order under subsection (2) above against any person, the person aggrieved by the nuisance shall give to that person such notice in writing of his intention to bring the proceedings as is applicable to proceedings in respect of a nuisance of that description and the notice shall specify the matter complained of.

(7) The notice of the bringing of proceedings in respect of a statutory nuisance required by subsection (6) above which is applicable is –

    (a) in the case of a nuisance falling within paragraph (g) [or (ga)] of section 79(1) above, not less than three days' notice; and

    (b) in the case of a nuisance of any other description, not less than twenty-one days' notice;

but the Secretary of State may, by order, provide that this subsection shall have effect as if such period as is specified in the order were the minimum period of notice applicable to any description of statutory nuisance specified in the order.

(8) A person who, without reasonable excuse, contravenes any requirement or prohibition imposed by an order under subsection (2) above shall be guilty of an offence and liable on summary conviction to a fine not exceeding level 5 on the standard scale together with a further fine of an amount equal to one-tenth of that level for each day on which the offence continues after the conviction.

(9) Subject to subsection (10) below, in any proceedings for an offence under subsection (8) above in respect of a statutory nuisance it shall be a defence to prove that the best practicable means were used to prevent, or to counteract the effects of, the nuisance.

(10) The defence under subsection (9) above is not available –

    (a) in the case of a nuisance falling within paragraph (a), (d), (e), (f) or (g) of section 79(1) above except where the nuisance arises on industrial, trade or business premises;

   [(aa) in the case of a nuisance falling within paragraph (ga) of section 79(1) above except where the noise is emitted from or caused by a vehicle, machinery or equipment being used for industrial, trade or business purposes;]

    (b) in the case of a nuisance falling within paragraph (b) of section 79(1) above except where the smoke is emitted from a chimney;

    (c) in the case of a nuisance falling within paragraph (c) or (h) of section 79(1) above; and

    (d) in the case of a nuisance which is such as to render the premises unfit for human habitation.

(11) If a person is convicted of an offence under subsection (8) above, a magistrates' court may, after giving the local authority in whose area the nuisance has occurred an opportunity of being heard, direct the authority to do anything which the person convicted was required to do by the order to which the conviction relates.

(12) Where on the hearing of proceedings for an order under subsection (2) above it is proved that the alleged nuisance existed at the date of the making of the complaint, then, whether or not at the date of the hearing it still exists or is likely to recur, the court shall order the defendant (or defendants in such proportions as appears fair and reasonable) to pay to the person bringing the proceedings such amount as the court considers reasonably sufficient to compensate him for any expenses properly incurred by him in the proceedings.

(13) If it appears to the magistrates' court that neither the person responsible for the nuisance nor the owner or occupier of the premises [or (as the case may be) the person responsible for the vehicle, machinery or equipment] can be found the court may, after giving the local authority in whose area the nuisance has occurred an opportunity of being heard, direct the authority to do anything which the court would have ordered that person to do.

Amendments

The words in square brackets in subss(2), (7) and (13) and the whole of subss(4)(d), (5A), (5B) and (10)(aa) were added, and the words in square brackets in subss(4)(a) and (5) substituted by Noise and Statutory Nuisance Act 1993 s5.

Gas Safety (Installation and Use) Regulations 1998 SI No 2451 Parts E and F

PART E: GAS APPLIANCES
Interpretation of Part E

25 In this Part –

'flue pipe' means a pipe forming a flue but does not include a pipe built as a lining into either a chimney or a gas appliance ventilation duct;

'operating pressure', in relation to a gas appliance, means the pressure of gas at which it is designed to operate.

Gas appliances – safety precautions

26 (1) No person shall install a gas appliance unless it can be used without constituting a danger to any person.

(2) No person shall connect a flued domestic gas appliance to the gas supply system except by a permanently fixed rigid pipe.

(3) No person shall install a used gas appliance without verifying that it is in a safe condition for further use.

(4) No person shall install a gas appliance which does not comply with any enactment imposing a prohibition or restriction on the supply of such an appliance on grounds of safety.

(5) No person carrying out the installation of a gas appliance shall leave it connected to the gas supply unless –
(a) the appliance can be used safely; or
(b) the appliance is sealed off from the gas supply with an appropriate fitting.

(6) No person shall install a gas appliance without there being at the inlet to it means of shutting off the supply of gas to the appliance unless the provision of such means is not reasonably practicable.

(7) No person shall carry out any work in relation to a gas appliance which bears an indication that it conforms to a type approved by any person as complying with safety standards in such a manner that the appliance ceases to comply with those standards.

(8) No person carrying out work in relation to a gas appliance which bears an indication that it so conforms shall remove or deface the indication.

(9) Where a person performs work on a gas appliance he shall immediately thereafter examine –
(a) the effectiveness of any flue;
(b) the supply of combustion air;

(c) its operating pressure or heat input or, where necessary, both;

(d) its operation so as to ensure its safe functioning,

and forthwith take all reasonable practicable steps to notify any defect to the responsible person and, where different, the owner of the premises in which the appliance is situated or, where neither is reasonably practicable, in the case of an appliance supplied with liquefied petroleum gas, the supplier of gas to the appliance, or, in any other case, the transporter.

(10) Paragraph (9) shall not apply in respect of –

(a) the direct disconnection of the gas supply of a gas appliance; or

(b) the purging of gas or air from an appliance or its associated pipework or fittings in any case where that purging does not adversely affect the safety of that appliance, pipe or fitting.

Flues

27 (1) No person shall install a gas appliance to any flue unless the flue is suitable and in a proper condition for the safe operation of the appliance.

(2) No person shall install a flue pipe so that it enters a brick or masonry chimney in such a way that the seal between the flue pipe and the chimney cannot be inspected.

(3) No person shall connect a gas appliance to a flue which is surrounded by an enclosure unless that enclosure is so sealed that any spillage of products of combustion cannot pass from the enclosure to any room or internal space other than the room or internal space in which the appliance is installed.

(4) No person shall install a power operated flue system for a gas appliance unless it safely prevents the operation of the appliance if the draught fails.

(5) No person shall install a flue other than in a safe position.

Access

28   No person shall install a gas appliance except in such a manner that it is readily accessible for operation, inspection and maintenance.

Manufacturer's instructions

29   Any person who installs a gas appliance shall leave for the use of the owner or occupier of the premises in which the appliance is installed all instructions provided by the manufacturer accompanying the appliance.

Room-scaled appliances

30 (1) No person shall install a gas appliance in a room used or intended to be used as a bathroom or a shower room unless it is a room-sealed appliance.

(2) No person shall install a gas fire, other gas space heater or a gas water heater of more than 14 kilowatt gross heat input in a room used or intended to be used as sleeping accommodation unless the appliance is a room-sealed appliance.

(3) No person shall install a gas fire, other gas space heater or a gas water heater of 14 kilowatt gross heat input or less in a room used or intended to be used as sleeping accommodation and no person shall install an instantaneous water heater unless (in each case) –

(a) it is a room-sealed appliance; or

(b) it incorporates a safety control designed to shut down the appliance before there is a build up of a dangerous quantity of the products of combustion in the room concerned.

(4) The references in paragraphs (1) to (3) to a room used or intended to be used for the purpose therein referred to includes a reference to –

(a) a cupboard or compartment within such a room; or

(b) a cupboard, compartment or space adjacent to such a room if there is an air vent from the cupboard, compartment or space into such a room.

Suspended appliances

31   No person shall install a suspended gas appliance unless the installation pipework to which it is connected is so constructed and installed as to be capable of safety supporting the weight imposed on it and the appliance is designed to be so supported.

Flue dampers

32 (1) Any person who installs an automatic damper to serve a gas appliance shall –

(a) ensure that the damper is so interlocked with the gas supply to the burner that burner operation is prevented in the event of failure of the damper when not in the open position; and

(b) immediately after installation examine the appliance and the damper to verify that they can be used together safely without constituting a danger to any person.

(2) No person shall install a manually operated damper to serve a domestic gas appliance.

(3) No person shall install a domestic gas appliance to a flue which incorporates a manually operated damper unless the damper is permanently fixed in the open position.

Testing of appliances

33 (1) Where a person installs a gas appliance at a time when gas is being supplied to the premises in which the appliance is installed, he shall immediately thereafter test its connection to the installation pipework to verify that it is gastight and examine the appliance and the gas fittings and other works for the supply of gas and any flue or means of ventilation to be used in connection with the appliance for the purpose of ascertaining whether –

(a) the appliance has been installed in accordance with these Regulations;

(b) the operating pressure is as recommended by the manufacturer;

(c) the appliance has been installed with due regard to any manufacturer's instructions provided to accompany the appliance; and

(d) all gas safety controls are in proper working order.

(2) Where a person carries out such testing and examination in relation to a gas appliance and adjustments are necessary to ensure compliance with the requirements specified in sub-paragraphs (a) to (d) of paragraph (1) above, he shall either carry out those adjustments or disconnect the appliance from the gas supply or seal off the appliance from the gas supply with an appropriate fitting.

(3) Where gas is not being supplied to any premises in which any gas appliance is installed –
   (a) no person shall subsequently permit gas to pass into the appliance unless he has caused such testing, examination and adjustment as is specified in paragraphs (1) and (2) above to be carried out; and
   (b) a person who subsequently provides a gas supply to those premises shall, unless he complies with sub-paragraph (a) above, ensure that the appliance is sealed off from the gas supply with an appropriate fitting.

Use of appliances

34 (1) The responsible person for any premises shall not use a gas appliance or permit a gas appliance to be used if at any time he knows or has reason to suspect that it cannot be used without constituting a danger to any person.

(2) For the purposes of paragraph (1) above, the responsible person means the occupier of the premises, the owner of the premises and any person with authority for the time being to take appropriate action in relation to any gas fitting therein.

(3) Any person engaged in carrying out any work in relation to a gas main, service pipe, service pipework, gas storage vessel or gas fitting who knows or has reason to suspect that any gas appliance cannot be used without constituting a danger to any person shall forthwith take all reasonably practicable steps to inform the responsible person for the premises in which the appliance is situated and, where different, the owner of the appliance or, where neither is reasonably practicable, in the case of an appliance supplied with liquefied petroleum gas, the supplier of gas to the appliance, or, in any other case, the transporter.

(4) In paragraph (3) above the expression 'work' shall be construed as if, in the definition of 'work' in regulation 2(1) above, every reference to a gas fitting were a reference to a gas main, service pipe, service pipework, gas storage vessel or gas fitting.

PART F: MAINTENANCE
Duties of employers and self-employed persons

35   It shall be the duty of every employer or self-employed person to ensure that any gas appliance, installation pipework or flue installed at any place of work under his control is maintained in a safe condition so as to prevent risk of injury to any person.

Duties of landlords

36 (1) In this regulation –
   'landlord' means –
   (a) in England and Wales –
      (i) where the relevant premises are occupied under a lease, the person for the time being entitled to the reversion expectant on that lease or who, apart from any statutory tenancy, would be entitled to possession of the premises; and
      (ii) where the relevant premises are occupied under a licence, the

licensor, save that where the licensor is himself a tenant in respect of those premises, it means the person referred to in paragraph (i) above;

(b) in Scotland, the person for the time being entitled to the landlord's interest under a lease;

'lease' means –

(a) a lease for a term of less than 7 years; and

(b) a tenancy for a periodic term; and

(c) any statutory tenancy arising out of a lease or tenancy referred to in subparagraphs (a) or (b) above, and in determining whether a lease is one which falls within sub-paragraph (a) above –

   (i) in England and Wales, any part of the term which falls before the grant shall be left out of account and the lease shall be treated as a lease for a term commencing with the grant;

   (ii) a lease which is determinable at the option of the lessor before the expiration of 7 years from the commencement of the term shall be treated as a lease for a term of less than 7 years;

   (iii) a lease (other than a lease to which sub-paragraph (b) above applies) shall not be treated as a lease for a term of less than 7 years if it confers on the lessee an option for renewal for a term which, together with the original term, amounts to 7 years or more; and

   (iv) a 'lease' does not include a mortgage term;

'relevant gas fitting' means –

(a) any gas appliance (other than an appliance which the tenant is entitled to remove from the relevant premises) or any installation pipework installed in any relevant premises; and

(b) any gas appliance or installation pipework which, directly or indirectly, serves the relevant premises and which either –

   (i) is installed in any part of premises in which the landlord has an estate or interest; or

   (ii) is owned by the landlord or is under his control,

except that it shall not include any gas appliance or installation pipework exclusively used in a part of premises occupied for non-residential purposes.

'relevant premises' means premises or any part of premises occupied, whether exclusively or not, for residential purposes (such occupation being in consideration of money or money's worth) under –

(a) a lease; or

(b) a licence;

'statutory tenancy' means –

(a) in England and Wales, a statutory tenancy within the meaning of the Rent Act 1977 and the Rent (Agriculture) Act 1976; and

(b) in Scotland, a statutory tenancy within the meaning of the Rent (Scotland) Act 1984, a statutory assured tenancy within the meaning of the Housing (Scotland) Act 1988 or a secure tenancy within the meaning of the Housing (Scotland) Act 1987;

'tenant' means a person who occupies relevant premises being –

(a) in England and Wales –

   (i) where the relevant premises are so occupied under a lease, the person for the time being entitled to the term of that lease; and

      (ii) where the relevant premises are so occupied under a licence, the licensee;

   (b) in Scotland, the person for the time being entitled to the tenant's interest under a lease.

(2) Every landlord shall ensure that there is maintained in a safe condition –

   (a) any relevant gas fitting; and

   (b) any flue which serves any relevant gas fitting,

so as to prevent the risk of injury to any person in lawful occupation of relevant premises.

(3) Without prejudice to the generality of paragraph (2) above, a landlord shall –

   (a) ensure that each appliance and flue to which that duty extends is checked for safety within 12 months of being installed and at intervals of not more than 12 months since it was last checked for safety (whether such check was made pursuant to these Regulations or not);

   (b) in the case of a lease commencing after the coming into force of these Regulations, ensure that each appliance and flue to which the duty extends has been checked for safety within a period of 12 months before the lease commences or has been or is so checked within 12 months after the appliance or flue has been installed, whichever is later; and

   (c) ensure that a record in respect of any appliance or flue so checked is made and retained for a period of 2 years from the date of that check, which record shall include the following information –

      (i) the date on which the appliance or flue was checked;

      (ii) the address of the premises at which the appliance or flue is installed;

      (iii)the name and address of the landlord of the premises (or, where appropriate, his agent) at which the appliance or flue is installed;

      (iv) a description of and the location of each appliance or flue checked;

      (v) any defect identified;

      (vi) any remedial action taken;

      (vii) confirmation that the check undertaken complies with the requirements of paragraph (9) below;

      (viii)the name and signature of the individual carrying out the check; and

      (ix) the registration number with which that individual, or his employer, is registered with a body approved by the Executive for the purposes of regulation 3(3) of these Regulations.

(4) Every landlord shall ensure that any work in relation to a relevant gas fitting or any check of a gas appliance or flue carried out pursuant to paragraphs (2) or (3) above is carried out by, or by an employee of, a member of a class of persons approved for the time being by the Health and Safety Executive for the purposes of regulation 3(3) of these Regulations.

(5) The record referred to in paragraph (3)(c) above, or a copy thereof, shall be made available upon request and upon reasonable notice for the inspection of any person in lawful occupation of relevant premises who may be affected by the use or operation of any appliance to which the record relates.

(6) Notwithstanding paragraph (5) above, every landlord shall ensure that –

   (a) a copy of the record made pursuant to the requirements of paragraph (3)(c) above is given to each existing tenant of premises to which the record relates within 28 days of the date of the check; and

(b) a copy of the last record made in respect of each appliance or flue is given to any new tenant of premises to which the record relates before that tenant occupies those premises save that, in respect of a tenant whose right to occupy those premises is for a period not exceeding 28 days, a copy of the record may instead be prominently displayed within those premises.

(7) Where there is no relevant gas appliance in any room occupied or to be occupied by the tenant in relevant premises, the landlord may, instead of ensuring that a copy of the record referred to in paragraph (6) above is given to the tenant, ensure that there is displayed in a prominent position in the premises (from such time as a copy would have been required to have been given to the tenant under that paragraph), a copy of the record with a statement endorsed on it that the tenant is entitled to have his own copy of the record on request to the landlord at an address specified in the statement; and on any such request being made, the landlord shall give to the tenant a copy of the record as soon as is practicable.

(8) A copy of the record given to a tenant pursuant to paragraph (6)(b) above need not contain a copy of the signature of the individual carrying out the check if the copy of the record contains a statement that another copy containing a copy of such signature is available for inspection by the tenant on request to the landlord at an address specified in the statement, and on any such request being made the landlord shall make such a copy available for inspection as soon as is practicable.

(9) A safety check carried out pursuant to paragraph (3) above shall include, but shall not be limited to, an examination of the matters referred to in sub-paragraphs (a) to (d) of regulation 26(9) of these Regulations.

(10) Nothing done or agreed to be done by a tenant of relevant premises or by any other person in lawful occupation of them in relation to the maintenance or checking of a relevant gas fitting or flue in the premises (other than one in part of premises occupied for non-residential purposes) shall be taken into account in determining whether a landlord has discharged his obligations under this regulation (except in so far as it relates to access to that gas fitting or flue for the purposes of such maintenance or checking).

(11) Every landlord shall ensure that in any room occupied or to be occupied as sleeping accommodation by a tenant in relevant premises there is not fitted a relevant gas fitting of a type the installation of which would contravene regulation 30(2) or (3) of these Regulations.

(12) Paragraph (11) above shall not apply in relation to a room which since before the coming into force of these Regulations has been occupied or intended to be occupied as sleeping accommodation.

Civil Procedure Rules

Parts 1, 16, 26, 35 and 36

PART 1: OVERRIDING OBJECTIVE
The overriding objective

1.1 (1) These Rules are a new procedural code with the overriding objective of enabling the court to deal with cases justly.

(2) Dealing with a case justly includes, so far as is practicable –
   (a) ensuring that the parties are on an equal footing;
   (b) saving expense;
   (c) dealing with the case in ways which are proportionate –
      (i) to the amount of money involved;
      (ii) to the importance of the case;
      (iii) to the complexity of the issues; and
      (iv) to the financial position of each party;
   (d) ensuring that it is dealt with expeditiously and fairly; and
   (e) allotting to it an appropriate share of the court's resources, while taking into account the need to allot resources to other cases.

Application by the court of the overriding objective

1.2 The court must seek to give effect to the overriding objective when it –
   (a) exercises any power given to it by the Rules; or
   (b) interprets any rule.

Duty of the parties

1.3 The parties are required to help the court to further the overriding objective.

Court's duty to manage cases

1.4 (1) The court must further the overriding objective by actively managing cases.

(2) Active case management includes –
   (a) encouraging the parties to co-operate with each other in the conduct of the proceedings;
   (b) identifying the issues at an early stage;
   (c) deciding promptly which issues need full investigation and trial and accordingly disposing summarily of the others;
   (d) deciding the order in which issues are to be resolved;
   (e) encouraging the parties to use an alternative dispute resolution procedure if the court considers that appropriate and facilitating the use of such procedure;
   (f) helping the parties to settle the whole or part of the case;

(g) fixing timetables or otherwise controlling the progress of the case;
(h) considering whether the likely benefits of taking a particular step justify the cost of taking it;
(i) dealing with as many aspects of the case as it can on the same occasion;
(j) dealing with the case without the parties needing to attend at court;
(k) making use of technology; and
(l) giving directions to ensure that the trial of a case proceeds quickly and efficiently.

PART 16: STATEMENTS OF CASE

Part not to apply where claimant uses Part 8 procedure

16.1   This Part does not apply where the claimant uses the procedure set out in Part 8 (alternative procedure for claims).

Contents of the claim form

16.2(1) The claim form must –
(a) contain a concise statement of the nature of the claim;
(b) specify the remedy which the claimant seeks;
(c) where the claimant is making a claim for money, contain a statement of value in accordance with rule 16.3; and
(d) contain such other matters as may be set out in a practice direction.

(2) If the particulars of claim specified in rule 16.4 are not contained in, or are not served with the claim form, the claimant must state on the claim form that the particulars of claim will follow.

(3) If the claimant is claiming in a representative capacity, the claim form must state what that capacity is.

(4) If the defendant is sued in a representative capacity, the claim form must state what that capacity is.

(5) The court may grant any remedy to which the claimant is entitled even if that remedy is not specified in the claim form.

(Part 22 requires a claim form to be verified by a statement of truth)

Statement of value to be included in the claim form

16.3 (1) This rule applies where the claimant is making a claim for money.

(2) The claimant must, in the claim form, state –
(a) the amount of money which he is claiming;
(b) that he expects to recover –
(i) not more than £5,000;
(ii) more than £5,000 but not more than £15,000; or
(iii)more than £15,000; or
(c) that he cannot say how much he expects to recover.

(3) In a claim for personal injuries, the claimant must also state in the claim form whether the amount which he expects to recover as general damages for pain, suffering and loss of amenity is –
(a) not more than £1,000; or
(b) more than £1,000.

(4) In a claim which includes a claim by a tenant of residential premises against his landlord where the tenant is seeking an order requiring the landlord to carry out repairs or other work to the premises, the claimant must also state in the claim form –

    (a) whether the estimated costs of those repairs or other work is –
        (i) not more than £1,000; or
        (ii) more than £1,000; and
    (b) whether the financial value of any other claim for damages is –
        (i) not more than £1,000; or
        (ii) more than £1,000.

(5) If the claim form is to be issued in the High Court it must, where this rule applies –

    (a) state that the claimant expects to recover more than £15,000;
    (b) state that some other enactment provides that the claim may be commenced only in the High Court and specify that enactment;
    (c) if the claim is a claim for personal injuries state that the claimant expects to recover £50,000 or more; or
    (d) state that the claim is to be in one of the specialist High Court lists and state which list.

(6) When calculating how much he expects to recover, the claimant must disregard any possibility –

    (a) that he may recover –
        (i) interest;
        (ii) costs;
    (b) that the court may make a finding of contributory negligence against him;
    (c) that the defendant may make a counterclaim or that the defence may include a set-off; or
    (d) that the defendant may be liable to pay an amount of money which the court awards to the claimant to the Secretary of State for Social Security under section 6 of the Social Security (Recovery of Benefits) Act 1997.

(7) The statement of value in the claim form does not limit the power of the court to give judgment for the amount which it finds the claimant is entitled to.

Contents of the particulars of claim

16.4(1) Particulars of claim must include –

    (a) a concise statement of the facts on which the claimant relies;
    (b) if the claimant is seeking interest, a statement to that effect and the details set out in paragraph (2);
    (c) if the claimant is seeking aggravated damages or exemplary damages, a statement to that effect and his grounds for claiming them;
    (d) if the claimant is seeking provisional damages, a statement to that effect and his grounds for claiming them; and
    (e) such other matters as may be set out in a practice direction.

(2) If the claimant is seeking interest he must –

    (a) state whether he is doing so –
        (i) under the terms of a contract;

    (ii) under an enactment and if so which; or

    (iii) on some other basis and if so 'what that basis is; and

  (b) if the claim is for a specified amount of money, state –

    (i) the percentage rate at which interest is claimed;

    (ii) the date from which it is claimed;

    (iii) the date to which it is calculated, which must not be later than the date on which the claim form is issued;

    (iv) the total amount of interest claimed to the date of calculation; and

    (v) the daily rate at which interest accrues after that date.

(Part 22 requires particulars of claim to be verified by a statement of truth)

Contents of defence

16.5(1) In his defence, the defendant must state –

  (a) which of the allegations in the particulars of claim he denies;

  (b) which allegations he is unable to admit or deny, but which he requires the claimant to prove; and

  (c) which allegations he admits.

(2) Where the defendant denies an allegation –

  (a) he must state his reasons for doing so; and

  (b) if he intends to put forward a different version of events from that given by the claimant, he must state his own version.

(3) A defendant who –

  (a) fails to deal with an allegation; but

  (b) has set out in his defence the nature of his case in relation to the issue to which that allegation is relevant, shall be taken to require that allegation to be proved.

(4) Where the claim includes a money claim, a defendant shall be taken to require that any allegation relating to the amount of money claimed be proved unless he expressly admits the allegation.

(5) Subject to paragraphs (3) and (4), a defendant who fails to deal with an allegation shall be taken to admit that allegation.

(6) If the defendant disputes the claimant's statement of value under rule 16.3 he must –

  (a) state why he disputes it; and

  (b) if he is able, give his own statement of the value of the claim.

(7) If the defendant is defending in a representative capacity, he must state what that capacity is.

(8) If the defendant has not filed an acknowledgment of service under Part 10, he must give an address for service.

(Part 22 requires a defence to be verified by a statement of truth)

(Rule 6.5 provides that an address for service must be within the jurisdiction)

Defence of set-off

16.6 Where a defendant –

  (a) contends he is entitled to money from the claimant; and

  (b) relies on this as a defence to the whole or part of the claim, the contention may be included in the defence and set off against the claim, whether or not it is also a Part 20 claim.

Reply to defence

16.7(1) A claimant who does not file a reply to the defence shall not be taken to admit the matters raised in the defence.

(2) A claimant who –
(a) files a reply to a defence; but
(b) fails to deal with a matter raised in the defence,
shall be taken to require that matter to be proved.

(Part 22 requires a reply to be verified by a statement of truth)

Court's power to dispense with statements of case

16.8 If a claim form has been –
(a) issued in accordance with rule 7.2; and
(b) served in accordance with rule 7.5,
the court may make an order that the claim will continue without any other statement of case.

(Other rules about the contents of statements of case can be found –
(a) in Schedule 1, in the following RSC – Order 77 (proceedings against the Crown); 0rder 82 (defamation claims); Order 88 (mortgage claims); Order 97 (claims under section 1 of the Landlord and Tenant Act 1927); and
(b) in Schedule 2, in the following CCR – Order 6 (recovery of land; mortgage claims; mortgage claims – dwelling house and hire purchase); Order 42 (proceedings against the Crown); Order 43 (applications under sections 13 or 24 of the Landlord and Tenant Act 1954 and sections 24, 29, 30 or 40 of the Landlord and Tenant Act 1987); Order 49 (applications under various statutes).)

PRACTICE DIRECTION 16: STATEMENTS OF CASE

This Practice Direction supplements CPR Part 16

General

1.1 The provisions of Part 16 do not apply to claims in respect of which the Part 8 procedure is being used.

1.2 In relation to specialist proceedings (see CPR Part 49) in respect of which special provisions for statements of case are made by the rules and practice directions applicable to those claims, the provisions of Part 16 and of this practice direction apply only to the extent that they are not inconsistent with those rules and practice directions.

The claim form

2 Rule 16.2 refers to matters which the claim form must contain. Where the claim is for money, the claim form must also contain the statement of value referred to in rule 16.3.

(For information about how and where a claim may be started see Part 7 and the practice direction which supplements it.)

Particulars of claim

3.1 If practicable, the particulars of claim should be set out in the claim form.

3.2 Where the claimant does not include the particulars of claim in the claim form, particulars of claim may be served separately:
(1) either at the same time as the claim form, or
(2) within 14 days after service of the claim form[1] provided that the service of the particulars of claim is not later than 4 months from the date of issue of the claim form[2] (or 6 months where the claim form is to be served out of the jurisdiction[3]).

3.3 If the particulars of claim are not included in or have not been served with the claim form, the claim form must also contain a statement that particulars of claim will follow.[4]

3.4 Particulars of claim which are not included in the claim form must be verified by a statement of truth, the form of which is as follows:
'[1 believe][the claimant believes] that the facts stated in these particulars of claim are true.'

3.5 Attention is drawn to rule 32.14 which sets out the consequences of verifying a statement of case containing a false statement without an honest belief in its truth.

3.6 The full particulars of claim must include:
(1) the matters set out in rule 16.4, and
(2) where appropriate, the matters set out in practice directions relating to specific types of claims.

3.7 Attention is drawn to the provisions of rule 16.4(2) in respect of a claim for interest.

3.8 Particulars of claim served separately from the claim form must also contain:
(1) the name of the court in which the claim is proceeding,
(2) the claim number,
(3) the title of the proceedings, and
(4) the claimant's address for service.

Matters which must be included in the particulars of claim in certain types of claim

Personal injury claims

4.1 The particulars of claim must contain:
(1) the claimant's date of birth, and
(2) brief details of the claimant's personal injuries.

4.2 The claimant must attach to his particulars of claim a schedule of details of any past and future expenses and losses which he claims.

4.3 Where the claimant is relying on the evidence of a medical practitioner the claimant must attach to or serve with his particulars of claim a report from

---

1   See rule 7.4(10).
2   See rules 7.4(2) and 7.50.
3   See rule 7.50.
4   See rule 16.20.

a medical practitioner about the personal injuries which he alleges in his claim.

4.4 In a provisional damages claim the claimant must state in his particulars of claim:

(1) that he is seeking an award of provisional damages under either section 32A of the Supreme Court Act 1981 or section 51 of the County Courts Act 1984,

(2) that there is a chance that at some future time the claimant will develop some serious disease or suffer some serious deterioration in his physical or mental condition, and

(3) specify the disease or type of deterioration in respect of which an application may be made at a future date.

(Part 41 and the practice direction which supplements it contain information about awards for provisional damages.)

Fatal accident claims

5.1 In a fatal accident claim the claimant must state in his particulars of claim:

(1) that it is brought under the Fatal Accidents Act 1976,

(2) the dependants on whose behalf the claim is made,

(3) the date of birth of each dependent, and

(4) details of the nature of the dependency claim.

5.2 A fatal accident claim may include a claim for damages for bereavement.

5.3 In a fatal accident claim the claimant may also bring a claim under the Law Reform (Miscellaneous Provisions) Act 1934 on behalf of the estate of the deceased.

(For information on apportionment under the Law Reform (Miscellaneous Provisions) Act 1934 and the Fatal Accidents Act 1976 or between dependants see Part 37 and the practice direction which supplements it.)

Recovery of land

6 In a claim for recovery of land the particulars of claim must:

(1) identify the land sought to be recovered,

(2) state whether the claim relates to residential premises,

(3) if the claim relates to residential premises, and the tenancy is one which otherwise would be a protected tenancy within the meaning of the Rent Act 1977, state whether the rateable value of the premises on every day specified by section 4(2) of the Rent Act 1977 in relation to the premises exceeds the sum so specified or whether the rent for the time being payable in respect of the premises exceeds the sum specified in section 4(4)(b) of the Act,

(4) where the claim relates to residential premises and is for non-payment of rent, state –

(a) the amount due at the start of the proceedings,

(b) details of all payments which have been missed,

(c) details of any history of late or under-payment,

(d) any previous steps taken to recover the arrears of rent with full details of any court proceedings, and

(e) any relevant information about the defendants circumstances, in particular whether any payments are made on his behalf directly to the claimant under the Social Security Contributions and Benefits Act 1992,

(5) give details about the agreement or tenancy, if any, under which the land was held, stating when it determined and the amount of money payable by way of rent or licence fee,

(6) in a case to which section 138 of the County Courts Act 1984 applies (forfeiture for non-payment of rent), state the daily rate at which the rent in arrear is to be calculated,

(7) state the ground on which possession is claimed whether statutory or otherwise, and

(8) in a case where the claimant knows of any person entitled to claim relief against forfeiture as underlessee (including a mortgagee) under section 146(4) of the Law of Property Act 1925 (or in accordance with section 38 of the Supreme Court Act 1981), give the name and address of that person.

(See also further rules about recovery of land in RSC Orders 88 and 113 (Schedule 1 to the CPR) and CCR Orders 6 and 24 (Schedule 2 to the CM).

Hire purchase claims

7.1 Where the claim is for the delivery of goods let under a hire-purchase agreement or conditional sale agreement to a person other than a company or other corporation, the claimant must state in the particulars of claim:

(1) the date of the agreement,

(2) the parties to the agreement,

(3) the number or other identification of the agreement,

(4) where the claimant was not one of the original parties to the agreement, the means by which the rights and duties of the creditor passed to him,

(5) whether the agreement is a regulated agreement, and if it is not a regulated agreement, the reason why,

(6) the place where the agreement was signed by the defendant,

(7) the goods claimed,

(8) the total price of the goods,

(9) the paid-up sum,

(10) the unpaid balance of the total price,

(11) whether a default notice or a notice under section 76(1) or 98(1) of the Consumer Credit Act 1974 has been served on the defendant, and if it has, the date and method of service,

(12) the date when the right to demand delivery of the goods accrued,

(13) the amount (if any) claimed as an alternative to the delivery of goods, and

(14) the amount (if any) claimed in addition to –

    (a) the delivery of the goods, or

    (b) any claim under (13) above,

with the grounds of each claim.

(if the agreement is a regulated agreement the procedure set out in the practice direction relating to consumer credit act claims (which supplements Part 7) should be used).

7.2 Where the claim is not for the delivery of goods, the claimant must state in his particulars of claim:

(1) the matters set out in paragraph 7.1(1) to (6) above,

(2) the goods let under the agreement,

(3) the amount of the total price,

(4) the paid-up sum,

(5) the amount (if any) claimed as being due and unpaid in respect of any instalment or instalments of the total price, and

(6) the nature and amount of any other claim and how it arises.

Defamation

8.1 If the claim form starting a claim:

(1) for libel does not include or have served with it the full particulars of claim, at least sufficient detail must be given of the publications which are the subject of the claim to enable them to be identified, and

(2) for slander does not include or have served with it the full particulars of claim, at least sufficient detail must be given of the words complained of, including to whom they were spoken and when, to enable them to be identified.

8.2 Where in a claim for libel or slander the claimant alleges that the words or matters complained of were used in a defamatory sense other than their ordinary meaning, the particulars of claim must describe that defamatory sense.

8.3 Where a defendant to a claim for libel or slander alleges that the words complained of are true, or are fair comment on a matter of public interest, or similar, the claimant must serve a reply specifically admitting or denying the allegation and giving the facts on which he relies, unless they are set out elsewhere.

8.4 In a claim for libel or slander the claimant need not set out specific details of malice in his particulars of claim. However, if the defendant contends that any of the words or matters:

(1) are fair comment on a matter of public interest, or

(2) were published on a privileged occasion,

and the claimant intends to allege that the defendant acted with express malice, the claimant must serve a reply giving details of the facts or matters relied on.

8.5 A claimant must give full details of the facts and matters on which he relies in support of his claim for damages and of any conduct of the defendant which the claimant alleges has increased the loss suffered (and see rule 16.4(1k) in respect of aggravated or exemplary damages).

8.6 In a claim for slander the precise words used and the names of the persons to whom they were spoken must be set out in the particulars of claim.

8.7 RSC Order 82 (Schedule 1 to the CPR) contains additional requirements relating to defamation claims.

Other matters to be included in particulars of claim

9.1 Where a claim is made for an injunction or declaration in respect of or relating to any land or the possession, occupation, use or enjoyment of any land the particulars of claim must:

(1) state whether or not the injunction or declaration relates to residential premises, and

(2) identify the land (by reference to a plan where necessary).

9.2 Where a claim is brought to enforce a right to recover possession of goods the particulars of claim must contain a statement showing the value of the goods.

9.3 Where a claim is based upon a written agreement:

(1) a copy of the contract or documents constituting the agreement should be attached to or served with the particulars of claim and the original(s) should be available at the hearing, and

(2) any general conditions of sale incorporated in the contract should also be attached (but where the contract is or the documents constituting the agreement are bulky this practice direction is complied with by attaching or serving only the relevant parts of the contract or documents).

9.4 Where a claim is based upon an oral agreement, the particulars of claim should set out the contractual words used and state by whom, to whom, when and where they were spoken.

9.5 Where a claim is based upon an agreement by conduct, the particulars of claim must specify the conduct relied on and state by whom, when and where the acts constituting the conduct were done.

9.6 In a claim issued in the High Court relating to a Consumer Credit Agreement, the particulars of claim must contain a statement that the action is not one to which section 141 of the Consumer Credit Act 1974 applies.

Matters which must be specifically set out in the particulars of claim if relied on

10.1 A claimant who wishes to rely on evidence:

(1) under section 11 of the Civil Evidence Act 1968 of a conviction of an offence, or

(2) under section 12 of the above-mentioned Act of a finding or adjudication of adultery or paternity,

must include in his particulars of claim a statement to that effect and give the following details:

(1) the type of conviction, finding or adjudication and its date,

(2) the court or Court-Martial which made the conviction, finding or adjudication, and

(3) the issue in the claim to which it relates.

10.2 The claimant must specifically set out the following matters in his particulars of claim where he wishes to rely on them in support of his claim:

(1) any allegation of fraud,

(2) the fact of any illegality,

(3) details of any misrepresentation,

(4) details of all breaches of trust,

(5) notice or knowledge of a fact,

(6) details of unsoundness of mind or undue influence,

(7) details of wilful default, and

(8) any facts relating to mitigation of loss or damage.

General

11.1 Where a claim is for a sum of money expressed in a foreign currency it must expressly state:

(1) that the claim is for payment in a specified foreign currency,

(2) why it is for payment in that currency,

(3) the Sterling equivalent of the sum at the date of the claim, and

(4) the source of the exchange rate relied on to calculate the Sterling equivalent.

11.2 A subsequent statement of case must not contradict or be inconsistent with an earlier one; for example a reply to a defence must not bring in a new claim. Where new matters have come to light the appropriate course may be to seek the court's permission to amend the statement of case.

The defence

General

12.1 Rule 16.5 deals with the contents of the defence.

12.2 A defendant should deal with every allegation in accordance with rule 16.5(1) and (2).

12.3 Rule 16.50, (4) and (5) sets out the consequences of not dealing with an allegation.

Statement of truth

13.1 Part 22 requires a defence to be verified by a statement of truth.

13.2 The form of the statement of truth is as follows:

'[I believe][the defendant believes] that the facts stated in the defence are true.'

13.3 Attention is drawn to rule 32.14 which sets out the consequences of verifying a statement of case containing a false statement without an honest belief in its truth.

Matters which must be included in the defence

Personal injury claims

14.1 Where the claim is for personal injuries and the claimant has attached a medical report in respect of his alleged injuries, the defendant should:

(1) state in his defence whether he –

(a) agrees,

(b) disputes, or

(c) neither agrees nor disputes but has no knowledge of, the matters contained in the medical report,

(2) where he disputes any part of the medical report, give in his defence his reasons for doing so, and

(3) where he has obtained his own medical report on which he intends to rely, attach it to his defence.

14.2 Where the claim is for personal injuries and the claimant has included a schedule of past and future expenses and losses, the defendant should include in or attach to his defence a counter-schedule stating:

(1) which of those items he –
  (a) agrees,
  (b) disputes, or
  (c) neither agrees nor disputes but has no knowledge of, and
(2) where any items are disputed, supplying alternative figures where appropriate.

Defamation

15 Where in a claim for libel or slander a defendant alleges that the words complained of are true or are fair comment on a matter of public interest he must give specific details in support of that allegation. RSC Order 82 (Schedule 1 to the CPR) contains requirements relating to defamation claims.

Other matters

16.1 The defendant must give details of the expiry of any relevant limitation period relied on.

16.2 Rule 37.3 and paragraph 2 of the practice direction which supplements Part 37 contains information about a defence of tender.

16.3 A party may:
  (1) refer in his statement of case to any point of law on which his claim or defence, as the case may be, is based,
  (2) give in his statement of case the name of any witness he proposes to call, and
  (3) attach to or serve with this statement of case a copy of any document which he considers is necessary to his claim or defence, as the case may be (including any expert's report to be filed in accordance with Part 35).

PART 26: CASE MANAGEMENT – PRELIMINARY STAGE
Scope of this part

26.1(1) This Part provides for –
  (a) the automatic transfer of some defended cases between courts; and
  (b) the allocation of defended cases to case management tracks.

(2) There are three tracks –
  (a) the small claims track;
  (b) the fast track; and
  (c) the multi-track.

(Rule 26.6 sets out the normal scope of each track. Part 27 makes provision for the small claims track. Part 28 makes provision for the fast track. Part 29 makes provision for the multi-track)

Automatic transfer

26.2(1) This rule applies to proceedings where –
  (a) the claim is for a specified amount of money;
  (b) the claim was commenced in a court which is not the defendant's home court;
  (c) the claim has not been transferred to another defendant's home court

under rule 13.4 (application to set aside or vary default judgment – procedure) or rule 14.12 (admission – determination of rate of payment by judge); and

(d) the defendant is an individual.

(2) This rule does not apply where the claim was commenced in a specialist list.

(3) Where this rule applies, the court will transfer the proceedings to the defendant's home court when a defence is filed, unless paragraph (4) applies.

(Rule 2.3 defines 'defendant's home court')

(4) Where the claimant notifies the court under rule 15. 10 or rule 14.5 that he wishes the proceedings to continue, the court will transfer the proceedings to the defendant's home court when it receives that notification from the claimant.

(Rule 15.10 deals with a claimant's notice where the defence is that money claimed has been paid)

(Rule 14.5 sets out the procedure where the defendant admits part of a claim for a specified amount of money)

(5) Where –

(a) the claim is against two or more defendants with different home courts; and

(b) the defendant whose defence is filed first is an individual,

proceedings are to be transferred under this rule to the home court of that defendant.

(6) The time when a claim is automatically transferred under this rule may be varied by a practice direction in respect of claims issued by the Production Centre.

(Rule 7.10 makes provision for the Production Centre)

Allocation questionnaire

26.3(1) When a defendant files a defence the court will serve an allocation questionnaire on each party unless –

(a) rule 15.10 or rule 14.5 applies; or

(b) the court dispenses with the need for a questionnaire.

(2) Where there are two or more defendants and at least one of them files a defence, the court will serve the allocation questionnaire under paragraph (1) –

(a) when all the defendants have filed a defence; or

(b) when the period for the filing of the last defence has expired,

whichever is the sooner.

(Rule 15.4 specifies the period for filing a defence)

(3) Where proceedings are automatically transferred to the defendant's home court under rule 26.2, the court in which the proceedings have been commenced will serve an allocation questionnaire before the proceedings are transferred.

Where –

(a) rule 15.10 or rule 14.5 applies; and

(b) the proceedings are not automatically transferred to the defendant's home court under rule 26.2,

the court will serve an allocation questionnaire on each party when the claimant files a notice indicating that he wishes the proceedings to continue.

(5) The court may, on the application of the claimant, serve an allocation questionnaire earlier than it would otherwise serve it under this rule.

(6) Each party must file the completed allocation questionnaire no later than the date specified in it, which shall be at least 14 days after the date when it is deemed to be served on the party in question.

(7) The time when the court serves an allocation questionnaire under this rule may be varied by a practice direction in respect of claims issued by the Production Centre.

(Rule 7. 10 makes provision for the Production Centre)

(Rule 6.7 specifies when a document is deemed to be served)

Stay to allow for settlement of the case

26.4(1) A party may, when filing the completed allocation questionnaire, make a written request for the proceedings to be stayed while the parties try to settle the case by alternative dispute resolution or other means.

(2) Where –
(a) all parties request a stay under paragraph (1); or
(b) the court, of its own initiative, considers that such a stay would be appropriate,

the court will direct that the proceedings be stayed for one month.

(3) The court may extend the stay until such date or for such specified period as it considers appropriate.

(4) Where the court stays the proceedings under this rule, the claimant must tell the court if a settlement is reached.

(5) If the claimant does not tell the court by the end of the period of the stay that a settlement has been reached, the court will give such directions as to the management of the case as it considers appropriate.

Allocation

26.5(1) The court will allocate the claim to a track –
(a) when every defendant has filed an allocation questionnaire, or
(b) when the period for filing the allocation questionnaires has expired,

whichever is the sooner, unless it has –
(i) stayed the proceedings under rule 26.4; or
(ii) dispensed with the need for allocation questionnaires.

(Rules 12.7 and 14.8 provide for the court to allocate a claim to a track where the claimant obtains default judgment on request or judgment on admission for an amount to be decided by the court)

(2) If the court has stayed the proceedings under rule 26.4, it will allocate the claim to a track at the end of the period of the stay.

(3) Before deciding the track to which to allocate proceedings or deciding whether to give directions for an allocation hearing to be fixed, the court may order a party to provide further information about his case.

(4) The court may hold an allocation hearing if it thinks it is necessary.

(5) If a party falls to file an allocation questionnaire, the court may give any direction it considers appropriate.

Scope of each track

26.6(1) The small claims track is the normal track for –

    (a) any claim for personal injuries where –

        (i) the financial value of the claim is not more than £5,000; and

        (ii) the financial value of any claim for damages for personal injuries is not more than £1,000;

    (b) any claim which includes a claim by a tenant of residential premises against his landlord where –

        (i) the tenant is seeking an order requiring the landlord to carry out repairs or other work to the premises (whether or not the tenant is also seeking some other remedy);

        (ii) the cost of the repairs or other work to the premises is estimated to be not more than £1,000; and

        (iii)the financial value of any other claim for damages is not more than £1,000.

    (Rule 2.3 defines 'claim for personal injuries' as proceedings in which there is a claim for damages in respect of personal injuries to the claimant or any other person or in respect of a person's death)

(2) For the purposes of paragraph (1) 'damages for personal injuries' means damages claimed as compensation for pain, suffering and loss of amenity and does not include any other damages which are claimed.

(3) Subject to paragraph (1), the small claims track is the normal track for any claim which has a financial value of not more than £5,000.

    (Rule 26.7(4) provides that the court will not allocate to the small claims track certain claims in respect of harassment or unlawful eviction)

(4) Subject to paragraph (5), the fast track is the normal track for any claim –

    (a) for which the small claims track is not the normal track; and

    (b) which has a financial value of not more than £15,000.

(5) The fast track is the normal track for the claims referred to in paragraph (4) only if the court considers that –

    (a) the trial is likely to last for no longer than one day; and

    (b) oral expert evidence at trial will be limited to –

        (i) one expert per party in relation to any expert field; and

        (ii) expert evidence in two expert fields.

(6) The multi-track is the normal track for any claim for which the small claims track or the fast track is not the normal track.

General rule for allocation

26.7(1) In considering whether to allocate a claim to the normal track for that claim under rule 26.6, the court will have regard to the matters mentioned in rule 26.8(1).

(2) The court will allocate a claim which has no financial value to the track which it considers most suitable having regard to the matters mentioned in rule 26.8(1).

(3) The court will not allocate proceedings to a track if the financial value of any claim in those proceedings, assessed by the court under rule 26.8, exceeds the limit for that track unless all the parties consent to the allocation of the claim to that track.

(4) The court will not allocate a claim to the small claims track, if it includes a claim by a tenant of residential premises against his landlord for a remedy in respect of harassment or unlawful eviction.

Matters relevant to allocation to a track

26.8(1) When deciding the track for a claim, the matters to which the court shall have regard include –
   (a) the financial value, if any, of the claim;
   (b) the nature of the remedy sought;
   (c) the likely complexity of the facts, law or evidence;
   (d) the number of parties or likely parties;
   (e) the value of any counterclaim or other Part 20 claim and the complexity of any matters relating to it;
   (f) the amount of oral evidence which may be required;
   (g) the importance of the claim to persons who are not parties to the proceedings;
   (h) the views expressed by the parties; and
   (i) the circumstances of the parties.

(2) It is for the court to assess the financial value of a claim and in doing so it will disregard –
   (a) any amount not in dispute;
   (b) any claim for interest;
   (c) costs; and
   (d) any contributory negligence.

(3) Where –
   (a) two or more claimants have started a claim against the same defendant using the same claim form; and
   (b) each claimant has a claim against the defendant separate from the other claimants,
   the court will consider the claim of each claimant separately when it assesses financial value under paragraph (1).

Notice of allocation

26.9(1) When it has allocated a claim to a track, the court will serve notice of allocation on every party.

(2) When the court serves notice of allocation on a party, it will also serve –
   (a) a copy of the allocation questionnaires filed by the other parties; and
   (b) a copy of any further information provided by another party about his case (whether by order or not).
   (Rule 26.5 provides that the court may, before allocating proceedings, order a party to provide further information about his case)

Re-allocation

26.10 The court may subsequently re-allocate a claim to a different track.

PRACTICE DIRECTION 26: CASE MANAGEMENT – PRELIMINARY STAGE: ALLOCATION AND RE-ALLOCATION

This practice direction supplements CPR Part 26

Reminders of important rule provisions other than Parts 26–29

1 Attention is drawn in particular to the following provisions of the Civil Procedure Rules:

Part 1 The Overriding Objective (defined in Rule 1.1).

The duty of the court to further that objective by actively managing cases (set out in Rule 1.4).

The requirement that the parties help the court to further that objective (set out in Rule 1.3).

Part 3 The court's case management powers (which may be exercised on application or on its own initiative) and the sanctions which it may impose.

Part 24 The court's power to grant summary judgment.

Parts 32–35 Evidence, especially the court's power to control evidence.

Attention is also drawn to the practice directions which supplement those Parts and Parts 27–29, and to those which relate to the various specialist jurisdictions.

The allocation questionnaire

2.1 **Form**

The allocation questionnaire referred to in Part 26 will be in Form N150.

Attention is drawn to the Costs Practice Direction, paragraph 4.5(1) which requires an estimate of costs to be filed and served when an allocation questionnaire is filed.

2.2 **Provision of Extra Information**

(1) This paragraph sets out what a party should do when he files his allocation questionnaire if he wishes to give the court information about matters which he believes may affect its decision about allocation or case management.

(2) The general rule is that the court will not take such information into account unless the document containing it either:

(a) confirms that all parties have agreed that the information is correct and that it should be put before the court, or

(b) confirms that the party who has sent the document to the court has delivered a copy to all the other parties.

(3) The following are examples of information which will be likely to help the court:

(a) a party's intention to apply for summary judgment or some other order that may dispose of the case or reduce the amount in dispute or the number of issues remaining to be decided,

(b) a party's intention to issue a Part 20 claim or to add another party,

(c) the steps the parties have taken in the preparation of evidence (in particular expert evidence), the steps they intend to take and whether those steps are to be taken in co-operation with any other party,

(d) the directions the party believes will be appropriate to be given for the management of the case,

(e) about any particular facts that may affect the timetable the court will set,

(f) any facts which may make it desirable for the court to fix an allocation hearing or a hearing at which case management directions will be given.

2.3 Consultation

(1) The parties should consult one another and co-operate in completing the allocation questionnaires and giving other information to the court.

(2) They should try to agree the case management directions which they will invite the court to make. Further details appear in the practice directions which supplement Parts 28 and 29.

(3) The process of consultation must not delay the filing of the allocation questionnaires.

2.4 Hearings Before Allocation

Where a court hearing takes place (for example on an application for an interim injunction or for summary judgment under Part 24) before the claim is allocated to a track, the court may at that hearing:

(1) dispense with the need for the parties to file allocation questionnaires, treat the hearing as an allocation hearing, make an order for allocation and give directions for case management, or

(2) fix a date for allocation questionnaires to be filed and give other directions.

2.5 Consequences of Failure to File an Allocation Questionnaire

(1) If no party files an allocation questionnaire within the time specified by Form N152:

(a) the file will be referred to a judge for his directions,

(b) the judge will usually order that unless an allocation questionnaire is filed within 3 days from service of that order the claim and any counterclaim will be struck out, but he may make a different order.

(2) Where a party files an allocation questionnaire but another party does not, the court may:

(a) allocate the claim to a track if it considers that it has enough information to do so, or

(b) order that an allocation hearing is listed and that all or any parties must attend.

Stay to allow for settlement of the case

3.1 Procedure for the parties to apply to extend the stay

(1) (a) The court will generally accept a letter from any party or from the solicitor for any party as an application to extend the stay under rule 26.4.

(b) The letter should –

(i) confirm that the application is made with the agreement of all parties, and

(ii) explain the steps being taken and identify any mediator or expert assisting with the process.

(2) (a) An order extending the stay must be made by a judge.

(b) The extension will generally be for no more than 4 weeks unless clear reasons are given to justify a longer time.

(3) More than one extension of the stay may be granted.

3.2 Position at the end of the stay if no settlement is reached

(1) At the end of the stay the file will be referred to a judge for his directions.

(2) He will consider whether to allocate the claim to a track and what other directions to give, or may require any party to give further information or fix an allocation hearing.

3.3 Any party may apply for a stay to be lifted.

3.4 Position where settlement is reached during a stay

Where the whole of the proceedings are settled during a stay, the taking of any of the following steps will be treated as an application for the stay to be lifted:

(1) an application for a consent order (in any form) to give effect to the settlement,

(2) an application for the approval of a settlement where a party is a person under a disability,

(3) giving notice of acceptance of money paid into court in satisfaction of the claim or applying for money in court to be paid out.

Allocation, re-allocation and case management

4.1 The court's general approach

The Civil Procedure Rules lay down the overriding objective, the powers and duties of the court and the factors to which it must have regard in exercising them. The court will expect to exercise its powers as far as possible in cooperation with the parties and their legal representatives so as to deal with the case justly in accordance with that objective.

4.2 Allocation to track

(1) In most cases the court will expect to have enough information from the statements of case and allocation questionnaires to be able to allocate the claim to a track and to give case management directions.

(2) If the court does not have enough information to allocate the claim it will generally make an order under rule 26.5(3) requiring one or more parties to provide further information within 14 days.

(3) Where there has been no allocation hearing the notice of allocation will be in Forms N154 (fast track), N155 (multi-track) or N157–160 (small claims).

(4) (a) The general rule is that the court will give brief reasons for its allocation decision, and these will be set out in the notice of allocation.

(b) The general rule does not apply where all the allocation question-naires which have been filed have expressed the wish for the claim to be allocated to the track to which the court has allocated it.

(5) Paragraph 6 of this practice direction deals with allocation hearings and Paragraph 7 deals with allocation principles.

(6) Paragraph 11 of this practice direction deals with re-allocation.

4.3 The practice directions supplementing Parts 27, 28 and 29 contain further information about the giving of case management directions at the allocation stage.

Summary judgment or other early termination

5.1 Part of the court's duty of active case management is the summary disposal of issues which do not need full investigation and trial (rule 1.4(2)(c)).

5.2 The court's powers to make orders to dispose of issues in that way include:

(a) under rule 3.4, striking out a statement of case, or part of a statement of case, and

(b) under Part 24, giving summary judgment where a claimant or a defendant has no reasonable prospect of success.

The court may use these powers on an application or on its own initiative. The practice direction 'Summary Disposal of Claims' contains further information.

5.3 (1) A party intending to make such an application should do so before or when filing his allocation questionnaire.

(2) Where a party makes an application for such an order before a claim has been allocated to a track the court will not normally allocate the claim before the hearing of the application.

(3) Where a party files an allocation questionnaire stating that he intends to make such an application but has not done so, the judge will usually direct that an allocation hearing is listed.

(4) The application may be heard at that allocation hearing if the application notice has been issued and served in sufficient time.

5.4 (1) This paragraph applies where the court proposes to make such an order of its own initiative.

(2) The court will not allocate the claim to a track but instead it will either:

(a) fix a hearing, giving the parties at least 14 days notice of the date of the hearing and of the issues which it is proposed that the court will decide, or

(b) make an order directing a party to take the steps described in the order within a stated time and specifying the consequence of not taking those steps.

5.5 Where the court decides at the hearing of an application or a hearing fixed under paragraph 5.4(2)(a) that the claim (or part of the claim) is to continue it may:

(1) treat that hearing as an allocation hearing, allocate the claim and give case management directions, or

(2) give other directions.

Allocation hearings

6.1 **General Principle**

The court will only hold an allocation hearing on its own initiative if it considers that it is necessary to do so.

6.2 **Procedure**

Where the court orders an allocation hearing to take place:

(1) it will give the parties at least 7 days notice of the hearing in Form N153, and

(2) Form N153 will give a brief explanation of the decision to order the hearing.

6.3 Power to treat another hearing as an allocation hearing

Where the court may treat another hearing as an allocation hearing it does not need to give notice to any party that it proposes to do so.

6.4 The notice of allocation after an allocation hearing will be in Forms N154, N155 or N157.

6.5 **Representation**

A legal representative who attends an allocation hearing should, if possible, be the person responsible for the case and must in any event be familiar with the case, be able to provide the court with the information it is likely to need to take its decisions about allocation and case management, and have sufficient authority to deal with any issues that are likely to arise.

6.6 **Sanctions**

(1) This paragraph sets out the sanctions that the court will usually impose for default in connection with the allocation procedure, but the court may make a different order.

(2) (a) Where an allocation hearing takes place because a party has failed to file an allocation questionnaire or to provide further information which the court has ordered, the court will usually order that party to pay on the indemnity basis the costs of any other party who has attended the hearing, summarily assess the amount of those costs, and order them to be paid forthwith or within a stated period.

(b) The court may order that if the party does not pay those costs within the time stated his statement of case will be struck out.

(3) Where a party whose default has led to a fixing of an allocation hearing is still in default and does not attend the hearing the court will usually make an order specifying the steps he is required to take and providing that unless he takes them within a stated time his statement of case will be struck out.

Allocation principles

7.1 Rules 26.6, 26.7 and 26.8

(1) Rule 26.6 sets out the scope of each track,

(2) Rule 26.7 states the general rule for allocation, and

(3) Rule 26.8 sets out the matters relevant to allocation to a track.

7.2 **Objective of this paragraph**

The object of this paragraph is to explain what will be the court's general approach to some of the matters set out in rule 26.8.

7.3 **'the financial value of the claim'**
  (1) Rule 26.8(2) provides that it is for the court to assess the financial value of a claim.
  (2) Where the court believes that the amount the claimant is seeking exceeds what he may reasonably be expected to recover it may make an order under rule 26.50 directing the claimant to justify the amount.

7.4 **'any amount not in dispute'**
In deciding, for the purposes of rule 26.8(2), whether an amount is in dispute the court will apply the following general principles:
  (1) Any amount for which the defendant does not admit liability is in dispute,
  (2) Any sum in respect of an item forming part of the claim for which judgment has been entered (for example a summary judgment) is not in dispute,
  (3) Any specific sum claimed as a distinct item and which the defendant admits he is liable to pay is not in dispute,
  (4) Any sum offered by the defendant which has been accepted by the claimant in satisfaction of any item which forms a distinct part of the claim is not in dispute.

It follows from these provisions that if, in relation to a claim the value of which is above the small claims track limit of £5,000, the defendant makes, before allocation, an admission that reduces the amount in dispute to a figure below £5,000 (see CPR Part 14), the normal track for the claim will be the small claims track. As to recovery of pre-allocation costs, the claimant can, before allocation, apply for judgment with costs on the amount of the claim that has been admitted (see CPR rule 14.3 but see also paragraph 5.1(3) of the Costs Directions relating to CPR Part 44 under which the court has a discretion to allow pre-allocation costs).

7.5 **'the views expressed by the parties'**
The court will treat these views as an important factor, but the allocation decision is one for the court, to be taken in the light of all the circumstances, and the court will not be bound by any agreement or common view of the parties.

7.6 **'the circumstances of the parties'**
See paragraph 8.

7.7 **'the value of any counterclaim or other Part 20 claim'**
Where the case involves more than one money claim (for example where there is a Part 20 claim or there is more than one claimant each making separate claims) the court will not generally aggregate the claims. Instead it will generally regard the largest of them as determining the financial value of the claims.

The small claims track – allocation and case management

8.1 **Allocation**

    (1) (a) The small claims track is intended to provide a proportionate procedure by which most straightforward claims with a financial value of not more than £5,000 can be decided, without the need for substantial pre-hearing preparation and the formalities of a traditional trial, and without incurring large legal costs. (Rule 26.6 provides for a lower financial value in certain types of case.)

       (b) The procedure laid down in Part 27 for the preparation of the case and the conduct of the hearing are designed to make it possible for a litigant to conduct his own case without legal representation if he wishes.

       (c) Cases generally suitable for the small claims track will include consumer disputes, accident claims, disputes about the ownership of goods and most disputes between a landlord and tenant other than those for possession.

       (d) A case involving a disputed allegation of dishonesty will not usually be suitable for the small claims track.

    (2) Rule 26.70 and rule 27.14(5)

       (a) These rules allow the parties to consent to the allocation to the small claims track of a claim the value of which is above the limits mentioned in rule 26.60 and, in that event, the rules make provision about costs.

       (b) The court will not allocate such a claim to the small claims track, notwithstanding that the parties have consented to the allocation, unless it is satisfied that it is suitable for that track.

       (c) The court will not normally allow more than one day for the hearing of such a claim.

       (d) The court will give case management directions to ensure that the case is dealt with in as short a time as possible. These may include directions of a kind that are not usually given in small claim cases, for example, for Scott Schedules.

8.2 **Case management**

    (1) Directions for case management of claims allocated to the small claims track will generally be given by the court on allocation.

    (2) Rule 27.4 contains further provisions about directions and the practice direction supplementing Part 27 sets out the standard directions which the court will usually give.

The fast track

9.1 **Allocation**

    (1) Where the court is to decide whether to allocate to the fast track or the multi-track a claim for which the normal track is the fast track, it will allocate the claim to the fast track unless it believes that it cannot be dealt with justly on that track.

    (2) The court will, in particular, take into account the limits likely to be placed on disclosure, the extent to which expert evidence may be

necessary and whether the trial is likely to last more than a day.
(3) (a) When it is considering the likely length of the trial the court will regard a day as being a period of 5 hours, and will consider whether that is likely to be sufficient time for the case to be heard.

(b) The court will also take into account the case management directions (including the fixing of a trial timetable) that are likely to be given and the court's powers to control evidence and to limit cross-examination.

(c) The possibility that a trial might last longer than one day is not necessarily a conclusive reason for the court to allocate or to re-allocate a claim to the multi-track.

(d) A claim may be allocated to the fast track or ordered to remain on that track although there is to be a split trial.

(e) Where the case involves a counterclaim or other Part 20 claim that will be tried with the claim and as a result the trial will last more than a day, the court may not allocate it to the fast track.

9.2 Case management

(1) Directions for the case management of claims which have been allocated to the fast track will be given at the allocation stage or at the listing stage (in either case with or without a hearing) or at both, and if necessary at other times. The trial judge may, at or before the trial, give directions for its conduct.

(2) The practice direction supplementing Part 28 contains further provisions and contains standard directions which the court may give.

The multi-track

10.1 The following paragraphs do not apply to a claim which is being dealt with at the Royal Courts of Justice.

10.2 Venue for allocation and case management

(1) The case management of a claim which is allocated to the multi-track will normally be dealt with at a Civil Trial Centre.

(2) In the case of a claim to which Part 49 (specialist proceedings) applies, case management must be dealt with at a Civil Trial Centre. Sub-paragraphs (4) to (10) do not apply to such a claim. The claim will be allocated to the multi-track irrespective of its value, and must be transferred to a Civil Trial Centre for allocation and case management if not already there.

(3) Where a claim is issued in or automatically transferred to a Civil Trial Centre it will be allocated and managed at that court.

(4) The following sub-paragraphs apply to a claim which is issued in or automatically transferred to a court which is not a Civil Trial Centre. Such a court is referred to as a 'feeder court'.

(5) Where a judge sitting at a feeder court decides, on the basis of the allocation questionnaires and any other documents filed by the parties, that the claim should be dealt with on the multi-track he will normally make an order:

(a) allocating the claim to that track,

(b) giving case management directions, and

(c) transferring the claim to a Civil Trial Centre.

(6) If he decides that an allocation hearing or some pre-allocation hearing is to take place (for example to strike out a statement of case under Part 3 of the Rules) that hearing will take place at the feeder court.

(7) If, before allocation, a hearing takes place at a feeder court and in exercising his powers under paragraph 2.4(1) above the judge allocates the claim to the multi-track, he will also normally make an order transferring the claim to a Civil Trial Centre.

(8) A judge sitting at a feeder court may, rather than making an allocation order himself, transfer the claim to a Civil Trial Centre for the decision about allocation to be taken there.

(9) When, following an order for transfer, the file is received at the Civil Trial Centre, a judge sitting at that Centre will consider it and give any further directions that appear necessary or desirable.

(10) Where there is reason to believe that more than one case management conference may be needed and the parties or their legal advisers are located inconveniently far from the Civil Trial Centre, a judge sitting at a feeder court may, with the agreement of the Designated Civil Judge and notwithstanding the allocation of the case to the multi-track, decide that in the particular circumstances of the case it should not be transferred to a Civil Trial Centre, but should be case managed for the time being at the feeder court.

(11) A Designated Civil Judge may at any time make an order transferring a claim from a feeder court to a Civil Trial Centre and he may do so irrespective of the track, if any, to which it has been allocated.

(12) No order will be made by a feeder court fixing a date for a hearing at a Civil Trial Centre unless that date has been given or confirmed by a judge or listing officer of that Centre.

10.3 **Case management**

Part 29 of the Rules and the practice direction supplementing that Part set out the procedure to be adopted.

Re-allocation of claims and the variation of directions

11.1 (1) Where a party is dissatisfied with an order made allocating the claim to a track he may appeal or apply to the court to re-allocate the claim.

(2) He should appeal if the order was made at a hearing at which he was present or represented, or of which he was given due notice.

(3) In any other case he should apply to the court to re-allocate the claim.

11.2 Where there has been a change in the circumstances since an order was made allocating the claim to a track the court may re-allocate the claim. It may do so on application or on its own initiative. The practice directions supplementing Parts 28 and 29 contain provisions about the variation of case management directions.

Allocation and case management of assessments of damages and allied proceedings

12.1   **Scope**

(1) In the following paragraphs a 'relevant order' means an order or judgment of the court which requires the amount of money to be paid by one party to another to be decided by the court.

(2) A relevant order may have been obtained:

(a) by a judgment in default under Part 12,

(b) by a judgment on an admission under Part 14,

(c) on the striking out of a statement of case under Part 3,

(d) on a summary judgment application under Part 24,

(e) on the determination of a preliminary issue or on a trial as to liability, or

(f) at trial.

(3) A relevant order includes an order for an amount of damages or interest to be decided by the court, an order for the taking of an account or the making of an inquiry as to any sum due, and any similar order.

(4) A relevant order does not include an order for the assessment of costs except where the court has made an order for the assessment of costs payable under a contract other than a contract between a solicitor and client for legal services.

12.2   **Directions**

(1) Directions which may be given under the following paragraphs may include:

(a) a direction allocating or re-allocating the claim,

(b) a direction that allocation questionnaires be filed by a specified date,

(c) a direction that a date be fixed for a hearing or a further hearing,

(d) an order that the claim be stayed while the parties try to settle the case by alternative dispute resolution or other means.

(2) Directions may specify the level or type of judge before whom a hearing or a further hearing will take place and the nature and purpose of that hearing.

12.3   **Allocation**

Where a claim has not been allocated to a track at the, time a relevant order is made, the court will not normally consider it to be appropriate to allocate it to a track (other than the small claims track) unless the amount payable appears to be genuinely disputed on grounds which appear to be substantial. It may instead direct that a disposal hearing (referred to in paragraph 12.8) be listed.

12.4   **Orders and judgments made at hearings**

Where a relevant order is made by a judge at a hearing, the judge should at the same time give such directions as the information about the case available to him enables him to give.

12.5   **Orders made by consent without a bearing**

(1) Where a relevant order is made by consent without a hearing a judge will give directions.

(2) The parties should where possible file with the draft consent order agreed directions which they invite the court to give.

12.6   Judgments entered on admissions without a hearing

(1) Where a relevant order is a judgment entered without a hearing under Part 14 the court will give directions.

(2) The court may in particular direct that a disposal hearing be listed.

12.7 Judgments entered in default

(1) This paragraph applies where the relevant order is a judgment entered under Part 12 without a hearing.

(2) On the entry of the judgment the court will list a disposal hearing.

12.8 Disposal hearings

(1) At a disposal hearing the court may give directions or decide the amount payable in accordance with this sub-paragraph.

(2) If the financial value of the claim (determined in accordance with Part 26) is such that the claim would, if defended, be allocated to the small claims track, the court will normally allocate it to that track and may treat the disposal hearing as a final hearing in accordance with Part 27.

(3) If the court does not give directions and does not allocate the claim to the small claims track, it may nonetheless order that the amount payable is to be decided there and then without allocating the claim to another track.

(4) Rule 32.6 applies to evidence at a disposal hearing unless the court otherwise directs.

(5) The court will not exercise its powers under sub-paragraph 12.8(3) unless any written evidence on which the claimant relies has been served on the defendant at least 3 days before the disposal hearing.

12.9 Costs

(1) Attention is drawn to the costs practice directions and in particular to the court's power to make a summary assessment of costs.

(2) Attention is drawn to rule 44.13(1) which provides that if an order makes no mention of costs, none are payable in respect of the proceedings to which it relates.

(3) Attention is drawn to rule 27.14 (special rules about costs in cases allocated to the small claims track).

(4) Attention is drawn to Part 45 (fixed trial costs in cases which have been allocated to the fast track). Part 45 will not apply to a case dealt with at a disposal hearing whatever the financial value of the claim. So the costs of a disposal hearing will be in the discretion of the court.

12.10 Jurisdiction of Masters and district judges

Unless the court otherwise directs, a Master or a district judge may decide the amount payable under a relevant order irrespective of the financial value of the claim and of the track to which the claim may have been allocated.

PART 35: EXPERTS AND ASSESSORS
Duty to restrict expert evidence

35.1   Expert evidence shall be restricted to that which is reasonably required to resolve the proceedings.

Interpretation

35.2   A reference to an 'expert' in this Part is a reference to an expert who has been instructed to give or prepare evidence for the purpose of court proceedings.

Experts – overriding duty to the court

35.3(1)   It is the duty of an expert to help the court on the matters within his expertise.

(2)   This duty overrides any obligation to the person from whom he has received instructions or by whom he is paid.

Court's power to restrict expert evidence

35.4(1)   No party may call an expert or put in evidence an expert's report without the court's permission.

(2)   When a party applies for permission under this rule he must identify –
(a)   the field in which he wishes to rely on expert evidence; and
(b)   where practicable the expert in that field on whose evidence he wishes to rely.

(3)   If permission is granted under this rule it shall be in relation only to the expert named or the field identified under paragraph (2).

(4)   The court may limit the amount of the expert's fees and expenses that the party who wishes to rely on the expert may recover from any other party.

General requirement for expert evidence to be given in a written report

35.5(1)   Expert evidence is to be given in a written report unless the court directs otherwise.

(2)   If a claim is on the fast track, the court will not direct an expert to attend a hearing unless it is necessary to do so in the interests of justice.

Written questions to experts

35.6(1)   A party may put to –
(a)   an expert instructed by another party; or
(b)   a single joint expert appointed under rule 35.7,
written questions about his report.

(2)   Written questions under paragraph (1) –
(a)   may be put once only;
(b)   must be put within 28 days of service of the expert's report; and
(c)   must be for the purpose only of clarification of the report,
unless in any case –
(i)   the court gives permission; or
(ii)   the other party agrees.

(3)   An expert's answers to questions put in accordance with paragraph (1) shall

be treated as part of the expert's report.

(4) Where –
   (a) a party has put a written question to an expert instructed by another party in accordance with this rule; and
   (b) the expert does not answer that question,

the court may make one or both of the following orders in relation to the party who instructed the expert –
   (i) that the party may not rely on the evidence of that expert; or
   (ii) that the party may not recover the fees and expenses of that expert from any other party.

Court's power to direct that evidence is to be given by a single joint expert

35.7(1) Where two or more parties wish to submit expert evidence on a particular issue, the court may direct that the evidence on that issue is to given by one expert only.

(2) The parties wishing to submit the expert evidence are called 'the instructing parties'.

(3) Where the instructing parties cannot agree who should be the expert, the court may –
   (a) select the expert from a list prepared or identified by the instructing parties; or
   (b) direct that the expert be selected in such other manner as the court may direct.

Instructions to a single joint expert

35.8(1) Where the court gives a direction under rule 35.7 for a single joint expert to be used, each instructing party may give instructions to the expert.

(2) When an instructing party gives instructions to the expert he must, at the same time, send a copy of the instructions to the other instructing parties.

(3) The court may give directions about –
   (a) the payment of the expert's fees and expenses; and
   (b) any inspection, examination or experiments which the expert wishes to carry out.

(4) The court may, before an expert is instructed –
   (a) limit the amount that can be paid by way of fees and expenses to the expert; and
   (b) direct that the instructing parties pay that amount into court.

(5) Unless the court otherwise directs, the instructing parties are jointly and severally liable for the payment of the expert's fees and expenses.

Power of court to direct a party to provide information

35.9 Where a party has access to information which is not reasonably available to the other party, the court may direct the party who has access to the information to –
   (a) prepare and file a document recording the information; and
   (b) serve a copy of that document on the other party.

Contents of report

35.10(1) An expert's report must comply with the requirements set out in the relevant practice direction.

(2) At the end of an expert's report there must be a statement that –
  (a) the expert understands his duty to the court; and
  (b) he has complied with that duty.

(3) The expert's report must state the substance of all material instructions, whether written or oral, on the basis of which the report was written.

(4) The instructions referred to in paragraph (3) shall not be privileged against disclosure but the court will not, in relation to those instructions –
  (a) order disclosure of any specific document; or
  (b) permit any questioning in court, other than by the party who instructed the expert,

unless it is satisfied that there are reasonable grounds to consider the statement of instructions given under paragraph (3) to be inaccurate or incomplete.

Use by one party of expert's report disclosed by another

35.11   Where a party has disclosed an expert's report, any party may use that expert's report as evidence at the trial.

Discussions between experts

35.12(1) The court may, at any stage, direct a discussion between experts for the purpose of requiring the experts to –
  (a) identify the issues in the proceedings; and
  (b) where possible, reach agreement on an issue.

(2) The court may specify the issues which the experts must discuss.

(3) The court may direct that following a discussion between the experts they must prepare a statement for the court showing –
  (a) those issues on which they agree; and
  (b) those issues on which they disagree and a summary of their reasons for disagreeing.

(4) The content of the discussion between the experts shall not be referred to at the trial unless the parties agree.

(5) Where experts reach agreement on an issue during their discussions, the agreement shall not bind the parties unless the parties expressly agree to be bound by the agreement.

Consequence of failure to disclose expert's report

35.13   A party who fails to disclose an expert's report may not use the report at the trial or call the expert to give evidence orally unless the court gives permission.

Expert's right to ask court for directions

35.14(1) An expert may file a written request for directions to assist him in carrying out his function as an expert.

(2) An expert may request directions under paragraph (1) without giving notice to any party.

(3) The court, when it gives directions, may also direct that a party be served with –
   (a) a copy of the directions; and
   (b) copy of the request for directions.

Assessors

35.15 (1) This rule applies where the court appoints one or more persons (an 'assessor') under section 70 of the Supreme Court Act 1981 or section 63 of the County Courts Act 1984.

(2) The assessor shall assist the court in dealing with a matter in which the assessor has skill and experience.

(3) An assessor shall take such part in the proceedings as the court may direct and in particular the court may –
   (a) direct the assessor to prepare a report for the court on any matter at issue in the proceedings; and
   (b) direct the assessor to attend the whole or any part of the trial to advise the court on any such matter.

(4) If the assessor prepares a report for the court before the trial has begun –
   (a) the court will send a copy to each of the parties; and
   (b) the parties may use it at trial.

(5) The remuneration to be paid to the assessor for his services shall be determined by the court and shall form part of the costs of the proceedings.

(6) The court may order any party to deposit in the court office a specified sum in respect of the assessor's fees and, where it does so, the assessor will not be asked to act until the sum has been deposited.

(7) Paragraphs (5) and (6) do not apply where the remuneration of the assessor is to be paid out of money provided by Parliament.

PRACTICE DIRECTION 35: EXPERTS AND ASSESSORS

This practice direction supplements CPR Part 35

Part 35 is intended to limit the use of oral expert evidence to that which is reasonably required. In addition, where possible, matters requiring expert evidence should be dealt with by a single expert. Permission of the court is always required either to call an expert or to put an expert's report in evidence.

Form and content of expert's reports

1.1 An expert's report should be addressed to the court and not to the party from whom the expert has received his instructions.

1.2 An expert's report must:
   (1) give details of the expert's qualifications,
   (2) give details of any literature or other material which the expert has relied on in making the report,
   (3) say who carried out any test or experiment which the expert has used for the report and whether or not the test or experiment has been carried out under the expert's supervision,
   (4) give the qualifications of the person who carried out any such test or experiment, and

(5) where there is a range of opinion on the matters dealt with in the report –

    (i) summarise the range of opinion, and
    (ii) give reasons for his own opinion,

(6) contain a summary of the conclusions reached,

(7) contain a statement that the expert understands his duty to the court and has complied with that duty (rule 35.10(2)), and

(8) contain a statement setting out the substance of all material instructions (whether written or oral). The statement should summarise the facts and instructions given to the expert which are material to the opinions expressed in the report or upon which those opinions are based (rule 35.100).

1.3 An expert's report must be verified by a statement of truth as well as containing the statements required in paragraph 1.2 (7) and (8) above.

1.4 The form of the statement of truth is as follows:

'I believe that the facts 1 have stated in this report are true and that the opinions I have expressed are correct.'

1.5 Attention is drawn to rule 32.14 which sets out the consequences of verifying a document containing a false statement without an honest belief in its truth.

(For information about statements of truth see Part 22 and the practice direction which supplements it.)

1.6 In addition, an expert's report should comply with the requirements of any approved expert's protocol.

Information

2 Under Part 35.9 the court may direct a party with access to information which is not reasonably available to another party to serve on that other party a document which records the information. The document served must include sufficient details of all the facts, tests, experiments and assumptions which underlie any part of the information to enable the party on whom it is served to make, or to obtain, a proper interpretation of the information and an assessment of its significance.

Instructions

3 The instructions referred to in paragraph 1.2(8) will not be protected by privilege (see rule 35.10(4)). But cross-examination of the expert on the contents of his instructions will not be allowed unless the court permits it (or unless the party who gave the instructions consents to it). Before it gives permission the court must be satisfied that there are reasonable grounds to consider that the statement in the report of the substance of the instructions is inaccurate or incomplete. If the court is so satisfied, it will allow the crossexamination where it appears to be in the interests of justice to do so.

Questions to experts

4.1 Questions asked for the purpose of clarifying the expert's report (see rule 35.6) should be put, in writing, to the expert not later than 28 days after receipt of the expert's report (see paragraphs 1.2 to 1.5 above as to verification).

4.2 Where a party sends a written question or questions direct to an expert and the other party is represented by solicitors, a copy of the questions should, at the same time, be sent to those solicitors.

Single expert

5 Where the court has directed that the evidence on a particular issue is to be given by one expert only (rule 35.7) but there are a number of disciplines relevant to that issue, a leading expert in the dominant discipline should be identified as the single expert. He should prepare the general part of the report and be responsible for annexing or incorporating the contents of any reports from experts in other disciplines.

Assessors

6.1 An assessor may be appointed to assist the court under rule 35.15. Not less than 21 days before making any such appointment, the court will notify each party in writing of the name of the proposed assessor, of the matter in respect of which the assistance of the assessor will be sought and of the qualifications of the assessor to give that assistance.

6.2 Where any person has been proposed for appointment as an assessor, objection to him, either personally or in respect of his qualification, may be taken by any party.

6.3 Any such objection must be made in writing and filed with the court within 7 days of receipt of the notification referred to in paragraph 6.1 and will be taken into account by the court in deciding whether or not to make the appointment (section 63(5) of the County Courts Act 1984).

6.4 Copies of any report prepared by the assessor will be sent to each of the parties but the assessor will not give oral evidence or be open to cross-examination or questioning.

PART 36: OFFERS TO SETTLE AND PAYMENTS INTO COURT

Scope of this part

36.1(1) This Part contains rules about –
  (a) offers to settle and payments into court; and
  (b) the consequences where an offer to settle or payment into court is made in accordance with this Part.

(2) Nothing in this Part prevents a party making an offer to settle in whatever way he chooses, but if that offer is not made in accordance with this Part, it will only have the consequences specified in this Part if the court so orders.

(Part 36 applies to Part 20 claims by virtue of rule 20.3)

Part 36 offers and Part 36 payments – general provisions

36.2(1) An offer made in accordance with the requirements of this Part is called –
  (a) if made by way of a payment into court, 'a Part 36 payment;
  (b) otherwise 'a Part 36 offer'.

(Rule 36.3 sets out when an offer has to be made by way of a payment into court)

(2) The party who makes an offer is the 'offeror'.

(3) The party to whom an offer is made is the 'offeree'.

(4) A Part 36 offer or a Part 36 payment –
    (a) may be made at any time after proceedings have started; and
    (b) may be made in appeal proceedings.

(5) A Part 36 offer or a Part 36 payment shall not have the consequences set out in this Part while the claim is being dealt with on the small claims track unless the court orders otherwise.
(Part 26 deals with allocation to the small claims track)
(Rule 27.2 provides that Part 36 does not apply to small claims)

A defendant's offer to settle a money claim requires a Part 36 payment

36.3(1) Subject to rules 36.5(5) and 36.23, an offer by a defendant to settle a money claim will not have the consequences set out in this Part unless it is made by way of a Part 36 payment.

(2) A Part 36 payment may only be made after proceedings have started.
(Rule 36.5(5) permits a Part 36 offer to be made by reference to an interim payment)
(Rule 36.10 makes provision for an offer to settle a money claim before the commencement of proceedings)
(Rule 36.23 makes provision for where benefit is recoverable under the Social Security (Recovery of Benefit) Act 1997)

Defendant's offer to settle the whole of a claim which includes both a money claim and a non-money claim

36.4(1) This rule applies where a defendant to a claim which includes both a money claim and a non-money claim wishes –
    (a) to make an offer to settle the whole claim which will have the consequences set out in this Part; and
    (b) to make a money offer in respect of the money claim and a non-money offer in respect of the non-money claim.

(2) The defendant must –
    (a) make a Part 36 payment in relation to the money claim; and
    (b) make a Part 36 offer in relation to the non-money claim.

(3) The Part 36 payment notice must –
    (a) identify the document which sets out the terms of the Part 36 offer; and
    (b) state that if the claimant gives notice of acceptance of the Part 36 payment he will be treated as also accepting the Part 36 offer.
(Rule 36.6 makes provision for a Part 36 payment notice)

(4) If the claimant gives notice of acceptance of the Part 36 payment, he shall also be taken as giving notice of acceptance of the Part 36 offer in relation to the non-money claim.

Form and content of a Part 36 offer

36.5(1) A Part 36 offer must be in writing.

(2) A Part 36 offer may relate to the whole claim or to part of it or to any issue that arises in it.

(3) A Part 36 offer must –
   (a) state whether it relates to the whole of the claim or to part of it or to an issue that arises in it and if so to which part or issue;
   (b) state whether it takes into account any counterclaim; and
   (c) if it is expressed not to be inclusive of interest, give the details relating to interest set out in rule 36.22(2).

(4) A defendant may make a Part 36 offer limited to accepting liability up to a specified proportion.

(5) A Part 36 offer may be made by reference to an interim payment.
   (Part 25 contains provisions relating to interim payments)

(6) A Part 36 offer made not less than 21 days before the start of the trial must –
   (a) be expressed to remain open for acceptance for 21 days from the date it is made; and
   (b) provide that after 21 days the offeree may only accept it if –
      (i) the parties agree the liability for costs; or
      (ii) the court gives permission.

(7) A Part 36 offer made less than 21 days before the start of the trial must state that the offeree may only accept it if –
   (a) the parties agree the liability for costs; or
   (b) the court gives permission.
   (Rule 36.8 makes provision for when a Part 36 offer is treated as being made)

(8) If a Part 36 offer is withdrawn it will not have the consequences set out in this Part.

Notice of a Part 36 payment

36.6(1) A Part 36 payment may relate to the whole claim or part of it or to an issue that arises in it.

(2) A defendant who makes a Part 36 payment must file with the court a notice ('Part 36 payment notice') which –
   (a) states the amount of the payment;
   (b) states whether the payment relates to the whole claim or to part of it or to any issue that arises in it and if so to which part or issue;
   (c) states whether it takes into account any counterclaim;
   (d) if an interim payment has been made, states that the defendant has taken into account the interim payment; and
   (e) if it is expressed not to be inclusive of interest, gives the details relating to interest set out in rule 36.22(2).
   (Rule 25.6 makes provision for an interim payment)
   (Rule 36.4 provides for further information to be included where a defendant wishes to settle the whole of a claim which includes a money claim and a non-money claim)

(Rule 36.23 makes provision for extra information to be included in the payment notice in a case where benefit is recoverable under the Social Security (Recovery of Benefit) Act 1997)

(3) The court will serve the Part 36 payment notice on the offeree unless the offeror inf6rms the court, when the money is paid into court, that the offeror will serve the notice.

(4) Where the offeror serves the Part 36 payment notice he must file a certificate of service.

(Rule 6.10 specifies what must be contained in a certificate of service)

(5) A Part 36 payment may be withdrawn only with the permission of the court.

Offer to settle a claim for provisional damages

36.7(1) A defendant may make a Part 36 payment in respect of a claim which includes a claim for provisional damages.

(2) Where he does so, the Part 36 payment notice must specify whether or not the defendant is offering to agree to the making of an award of provisional damages.

(3) Where the defendant is offering to agree to the making of an award of provisional damages the payment notice must also state –
  (a) that the sum paid into court is in satisfaction of the claim for damages on the assumption that the injured person will not develop the disease or suffer the type of deterioration specified in the notice;
  (b) that the offer is subject to the condition that the claimant must make any claim for further damages within a limited period; and
  (c) what that period is.

(4) Where a Part 36 payment is –
  (a) made in accordance with paragraph (3); and
  (b) accepted within the relevant period in rule 36.11,
  the Part 36 payment will have the consequences set out in rule 36.13, unless the court orders otherwise.

(5) If the claimant accepts the Part 36 payment he must, within 7 days of doing so, apply to the court for an order for an award of provisional damages under rule 41.2.

(Rule 41.2 provides for an order for an award of provisional damages)

(6) The money in court may not be paid out until the court has disposed of the application made in accordance with paragraph (5).

Time when a Part 36 offer or a Part 36 payment is made and accepted

36.8(1) A Part 36 offer is made when received by the offeree.

(2) A Part 36 payment is made when written notice of the payment into court is served on the offeree.

(3) An improvement to a Part 36 offer will be effective when its details are received by the offeree.

(4) An increase in a Part 36 payment will be effective when notice of the increase is served on the offeree.

(5) A Part 36 offer or Part 36 payment is accepted when notice of its acceptance is received by the offeror.

Clarification of a Part 36 offer or a Part 36 payment notice

36.9(1) The offeree may, within 7 days of a Part 36 offer or payment being made, request the offeror to clarify the offer or payment notice.

(2) If the offeror does not give the clarification requested under paragraph (1) within 7 days of receiving the request, the offeree may, unless the trial has started, apply for an order that he does so.

(3) If the court makes an order under paragraph (2), it must specify the date when the Part 36 offer or Part 36 payment is to be treated as having been made.

Court to take into account offer to settle made before commencement of proceedings

36.10 (1) If a person makes an offer to settle before proceedings are begun which complies with the provisions of this rule, the court will take that offer into account when making any order as to costs.

(2) The offer must –
   (a) be expressed to be open for at least 21 days after the date it was made;
   (b) if made by a person who would be a defendant were proceedings commenced, include an offer to pay the costs of the offeree incurred up to the date 21 days after the date it was made; and
   (c) otherwise comply with this Part.

(3) If the offeror is a defendant to a money claim –
   (a) he must make a Part 36 payment within 14 days of service of the claim form; and
   (b) the amount of the payment must be not less than the sum offered before proceedings began.

(4) An offeree may not, after proceedings have begun, accept –
   (a) an offer made under paragraph (2); or
   (b) a Part 36 payment made under paragraph (3),
   without the permission of the court.

(5) An offer under this rule is made when it is received by the offeree.

Time for acceptance of a defendant's Part 36 offer or Part 36 payment

36.11 (1) A claimant may accept a Part 36 offer or a Part 36 payment made not less than 21 days before the start of the trial without needing the court's permission if he gives the defendant written notice of acceptance not later than 21 days after the offer or payment was made.

(Rule 36.13 sets out the costs consequences of accepting a defendant's offer or payment without needing the permission of the court)

(2) If –
   (a) a defendant's Part 36 offer or Part 36 payment is made less than 21 days before the start of the trial; or
   (b) the claimant does not accept it within the period specified in paragraph (1) –
      (i) if the parties agree the liability for costs, the claimant may accept the offer or payment without needing the permission of the court;

(ii) if the parties do not agree the liability for costs the claimant may only accept the offer or payment with the permission of the court.

(3) Where the permission of the court is needed under paragraph (2) the court will, if it gives permission, make an order as to costs.

Time for acceptance of a claimant's Part 36 offer

36.12 (1) A defendant may accept a Part 36 offer made not less than 21 days before the start of the trial without needing the court's permission if he gives the claimant written notice of acceptance not later than 21 days after the offer was made.

(Rule 36.14 sets out the costs consequences of accepting a claimant's offer without needing the permission of the court)

(2) If –

(a) a claimant's Part 36 offer is made less than 21 days before the start of the trial; or

(b) the defendant does not accept it within the period specified in paragraph (1) –

(i) if the parties agree the liability for costs, the defendant may accept the offer without needing the permission of the court;

(ii) if the parties do not agree the liability for costs the defendant may only accept the offer with the permission of the court.

(3) Where the permission of the court is needed under paragraph (2) the court will, if it gives permission, make an order as to costs.

Costs consequences of acceptance of a defendant's Part 36 offer or Part 36 payment

36.13 (1) Where a Part 36 offer or a Part 36 payment is accepted without needing the permission of the court the claimant will be entitled to his costs of the proceedings up to the date of serving notice of acceptance.

(2) Where –

(a) a Part 36 offer or a Part 36 payment relates to part only of the claim; and

(b) at the time of serving notice of acceptance the claimant abandons the balance of the claim,

the claimant will be entitled to his costs of the proceedings up to the date of serving notice of acceptance, unless the court orders otherwise.

(3) The claimant's costs include any costs attributable to the defendant's counterclaim if the Part 36 offer or the Part 36 payment notice states that it takes into account the counterclaim.

(4) Costs under this rule will be payable on the standard basis if not agreed.

Costs consequences of acceptance of a claimant's Part 36 offer

36.14   Where a claimant's Part 36 offer is accepted without needing the permission of the court the claimant will be entitled to his costs of the proceedings up to the date upon which the defendant serves notice of acceptance.

The effect of acceptance of a Part 36 offer or a Part 36 payment

36.15 (1) If a Part 36 offer or Part 36 payment relates to the whole claim and is accepted, the claim will be stayed.

(2) In the case of acceptance of a Part 36 offer which relates to the whole claim –
   (a) the stay will be upon the terms of the offer; and
   (b) either party may apply to enforce those terms without the need for a new claim.

(3) If a Part 36 offer or a Part 36 payment which relates to part only of the claim is accepted –
   (a) the claim will be stayed as to that part; and
   (b) unless the parties have agreed costs, the liability for costs shall be decided by the court.

(4) If the approval of the court is required before a settlement can be binding, any stay which would otherwise arise on the acceptance of a Part 36 offer or a Part 36 payment will take effect only when that approval has been given.

(5) Any stay arising under this rule will not affect the power of the court –
   (a) to enforce the terms of a Part 36 offer;
   (b) to deal with any question of costs (including interest on costs) relating to the proceedings;
   (c) to order payment out of court of any sum paid into court.

(6) Where –
   (a) a Part 36 offer has been accepted; and
   (b) a party alleges that –
      (i) the other party has not honoured the terms of the offer; and
      (ii) he is therefore entitled to a remedy for breach of contract,
   the party may claim the remedy by applying to the court without the need to start a new claim unless the court orders otherwise.

Payment out of a sum in court on the acceptance of a Part 36 payment

36.16 Where a Part 36 payment is accepted the claimant obtains payment out of the sum in court by making a request for payment in the practice form.

Acceptance of a Part 36 offer or a Part 36 payment made by one or more, but not all, defendants

36.17 (1) This rule applies where the claimant wishes to accept a Part 36 offer or a Part 36 payment made by one or more, but not all, of a number of defendants.

(2) If the defendants are sued jointly or in the alternative, the claimant may accept the offer or payment without needing the permission of the court in accordance with rule 36.11(1) if –
   (a) he discontinues his claim against those defendants who have not made the offer or payment; and
   (b) those defendants give written consent to the acceptance of the offer or payment.

(3) If the claimant alleges that the defendants have a several liability to him the claimant may –

(a) accept the offer or payment in accordance with rule 36.11(1); and

(b) continue with his claims against the other defendants if he is entitled to do so.

(4) In all other cases the claimant must apply to the court for –

(a) an order permitting a payment out to him of any sum in court; and

(b) such order as to costs as the court considers appropriate.

Other cases where a court order is required to enable acceptance of a Part 36 offer or a Part 36 payment

36.18 (1) Where a Part 36 offer or a Part 36 payment is made in proceedings to which rule 21.10 applies –

(a) the offer or payment may be accepted only with the permission of the court; and

(b) no payment out of any sum in court shall be made without a court order.

(Rule 21.10 deals with compromise etc. by or on behalf of a child or patient)

(2) Where the court gives a claimant permission to accept a Part 36 offer or payment after the trial has started –

(a) any money in court may be paid out only with a court order; and

(b) the court must, in the order, deal with the whole costs of the proceedings.

(3) Where a claimant accepts a Part 36 payment after a defence of tender before claim has been put forward by the defendant, the money in court may be paid out only after an order of the court.

(Rule 37.3 requires a defendant who wishes to rely on a defence of tender before claim to make a payment into court)

Restriction on disclosure of a Part 36 offer or a Part 36 payment

36.19 (1) A Part 36 offer will be treated as 'without prejudice except as to costs'.

(2) The fact that a Part 36 payment has been made shall not be communicated to the trial judge until all questions of liability and the amount of money to be awarded have been decided.

(3) Paragraph (2) does not apply –

(a) where the defence of tender before claim has been raised;

(b) where the proceedings have been stayed under rule 36.15 following acceptance of a Part 36 offer or Part 36 payment; or

(c) where –

(i) the issue of liability has been determined before any assessment of the money claimed; and

(ii) the fact that there has or has not been a Part 36 payment may be relevant to the question of the costs of the issue of liability.

Costs consequences where claimant fails to do better than a Part 36 offer or a Part 36 payment

36.20 (1) This rule applies where at trial a claimant –

(a) fails to better a Part 36 payment; or

(b) fails to obtain a judgment which is more advantageous than a defendant's Part 36 offer.

(2) Unless it considers it unjust to do so, the court will order the claimant to pay any costs incurred by the defendant after the latest date on which the payment or offer could have been accepted without needing the permission of the court.

(Rule 36.11 sets out the time for acceptance of a defendant's Part 36 offer or Part 36 payment)

Costs and other consequences where claimant does better than he proposed in his Part 36 offer

36.21 (1) This rule applies where at trial –
  (a) a defendant is held liable for more; or
  (b) the judgment against a defendant is more advantageous to the claimant,
    than the proposals contained in a claimant's Part 36 offer.

(2) The court may order interest on the whole or part of any sum of money (excluding interest) awarded to the claimant at a rate not exceeding 10% above base rate for some or all of the period starting with the latest date on which the defendant could have accepted the offer without needing the permission of the court.

(3) The court may also order that the claimant is entitled to –
  (a) his costs on the indemnity basis from the latest date when the defendant could have accepted the offer without needing the permission of the court; and
  (b) interest on those costs at a rate not exceeding 10% above base rate.

(4) Where this rule applies, the court will make the orders referred to in paragraphs (2) and (3) unless it considers it unjust to do so.

(Rule 36.12 sets out the latest date when the defendant could have accepted the offer)

(5) In considering whether it would be unjust to make the orders referred to in paragraphs (2) and (3) above, the court will take into account all the circumstances of the case including –
  (a) the terms of any Part 36 offer;
  (b) the stage in the proceedings when any Part 36 offer or Part 36 payment was made;
  (c) the information available to the parties at the time when the Part 36 offer or Part 36 payment was made; and
  (d) the conduct of the parties with regard to the giving or refusing to give information for the purposes of enabling the offer or payment into court to be made or evaluated.

(6) The power of the court under this rule is in addition to any other power it may have to award interest.

Interest

36.22 (1) Unless –
  (a) a claimant's Part 36 offer which offers to accept a sum of money; or
  (b) a Part 36 payment notice,
  indicates to the contrary, any such offer or payment will be treated as inclusive of all interest until the last date on which it could be accepted without needing the permission of the court.

(2)   Where a claimant's Part 36 offer or Part 36 payment notice is expressed not to be inclusive of interest, the offer or notice must state –
(a) whether interest is offered; and
(b) if so, the amount offered, the rate or rates offered and the period or periods for which it is offered.

Deduction of benefits

36.23(1) This rule applies where a payment to a claimant following acceptance of a Part 36 offer or Part 36 payment into court would be a compensation payment as defined in section 1 of the Social Security (Recovery of Benefits) Act 1997.

(2)   A defendant to a money claim may make an offer to settle the claim which will have the consequences set out in this Part, without making a Part 36 payment if –
(a) at the time he makes the offer he has applied for, but not received, a certificate of recoverable benefit; and
(b) he makes a Part 36 payment not more than 7 days after he receives the certificate.
(Section 1 of the 1997 Act defines 'recoverable benefit')

(3)   A Part 36 payment notice must state –
(a) the amount of gross compensation;
(b) the name and amount of any benefit by which that gross amount is reduced in accordance with section 8 and Schedule 2 to the 1997 Act; and
(c) that the sum paid in is the net amount after deduction of the amount of benefit.

(4)   For the purposes of rule 36.20, a claimant falls to better a Part 36 payment if he fails to obtain judgment for more than the gross sum specified in the Part 36 payment notice.

(5)   Where –
(a) a Part 36 payment has been made; and
(b) application is made for the money remaining in court to be paid out, the court may treat the money in court as being. reduced by a sum equivalent to any further recoverable benefits paid to the claimant since the date of payment into court and may direct payment out accordingly.

PRACTICE DIRECTION 36: OFFERS TO SETTLE AND PAYMENTS INTO COURT

This practice direction supplements CPR Part 36

Part 36 offers and Part 36 payments

1.1   A written offer to settle a claim[1] or part of a claim or any issue that arises in it made in accordance with the provisions of Part 36 is called:
(1)   if made by way of a payment into court, a Part 36 payment,[2] or

---

1   Includes Part 20 claims.
2   See rule 36.2(1)(a).

(2) if made otherwise, a Part 36 offer.[3]

1.2 A Part 36 offer or Part 36 payment has the costs and other consequences set out in rules 36.13, 36.14, 36.20 and 36.21.

1.3 An offer to settle which is not made in accordance with Part 36 will only have the consequences specified in that Part if the court so orders and will be given such weight on any issue as to costs as the court thinks appropriate.[4]

Parties and Part 36 offers

2.1 A Part 36 offer, subject to paragraph 3 below, may be made by any party.

2.2 The party making an offer is the 'offeror' and the party to whom it is made is the 'offeree'.

2.3 A Part 36 offer may consist of a proposal to settle for a specified sum or for some other remedy.

2.4 A Part 36 offer is made when received by the offeree.[5]

2.5 An improvement to a Part 36 offer is effective when its details are received by the offeree.[6]

Parties and Part 36 payments

3.1 An offer to settle for a specified sum made by a defendant[7] must, in order to comply with Part 36, be made by way of a Part 36 payment into court.[8]

3.2 A Part 36 payment is made when the Part 36 payment notice is served on the claimant.[9]

3.3 An increase to a Part 36 payment will be effective when notice of the increase is served on the claimant.[10]
(For service of the Part 36 payment notice see rule 36.60 and (4).)

3.4 A defendant who wishes to withdraw or reduce a Part 36 payment must obtain the court's permission to do so.

3.5 Permission may be obtained by making an application in accordance with Part 23 stating the reasons giving rise to the wish to withdraw or reduce the Part 36 payment.

Making a Part 36 payment

4.1 To make a Part 36 payment the defendant must file the following documents:

(1) where that court is a county court or a district registry –
   (a) the Part 36 payment notice, and
   (b) the payment, usually a cheque made payable to Her Majesty's Paymaster General, with the court, and

3   See rule 36.2(1)(b).
4   See rule 36.1(2).
5   See rule 36.8(1).
6   See rule 36.8(3).
7   Includes a respondent to a claim or issue.
8   See rule 36.3(1).
9   See rule 36.8(2).
10   See rule 36.8(4).

(2) where that court is the Royal Courts of Justice –
   (a) the Part 36 payment notice with the court, and
   (b) the payment, usually a cheque made payable to the Accountant General of the Supreme Court, and
   (c) a sealed copy of the Claim Form,
   (d) the Court Funds Office form 100 with the Court Funds Office.

Part 36 offers and Part 36 payments – general provisions

5.1 A Part 36 offer or a Part 36 payment notice must:
   (1) state that it is a Part 36 offer or that the payment into court is a Part 36 payment, and
   (2) be signed by the offeror or his legal representative.[13]

5.2 The contents of a Part 36 offer must also comply with the requirements of rule 36.5(3), (5) and (6).

5.3 The contents of a Part 36 payment notice must comply with rule 36.6(2) and, if rule 36.23 applies, with rule 36.23(3).

5.4 A Part 36 offer or Part 36 payment will be taken to include interest unless it is expressly stated in the offer or the payment notice that interest is not included, in which case the details set out in rule 36.22(2) must be given.

5.5 Where a Part 36 offer is made by a company or other corporation, a person holding a senior position in the company or corporation may sign the offer on the offeror's behalf, but must state the position he holds.

5.6 Each of the following persons is a person holding a senior position:
   (1) in respect of a registered company or corporation, a director, the treasurer, secretary, chief executive, manager or other officer of the company or corporation, and
   (2) in respect of a corporation which is not a registered company, in addition to those persons set out in (1), the mayor, chairman, president, town clerk or similar officer of the corporation.

Clarification of Part 36 offer or payment

6.1 An offeree may apply to the court for an order requiring the offeror to clarify the terms of a Part 36 offer or Part 36 payment notice (a clarification order) where the offeror has failed to comply within 7 days with a request for clarification.[14]

6.2 An application for a clarification order should be made in accordance with Part 23.

6.3 The application notice should state the respects in which the terms of the Part 36 offer or Part 36 payment notice, as the case may be, are said to need clarification.

Acceptance of a Part 36 offer or payment

7.1 The times for accepting a Part 36 offer or a Part 36 payment are set out in rules 36.11 and 36.12.

7.2 The general rule is that a Part 36 offer or Part 36 payment made more than

---

13 For the definition of legal representative see rule 2.3.
14 See rule 36.9(1) and (2).

21 days before the start of the trial may be accepted within 21 days after it was made without the permission of the court. The costs consequences set out in rules 36.13 and 36.14 will then come into effect.

7.3 A Part 36 offer or Part 36 payment made less than 21 days before the start of the trial cannot be accepted without the permission of the court unless the parties agree what the costs consequences of acceptance will be.

7.4 The permission of the court may be sought:

(1) before the start of the trial, by making an application in accordance with Part 23, and

(2) after the start of the trial, by making an application to the trial judge.

7.5 If the court gives permission it will make an order dealing with costs and may order that, in the circumstances, the costs consequences set out in rules 36.13 and 36.14 will apply.

7.6 Where a Part 36 offer or Part 36 payment is accepted in accordance with rule 36.11(1) or rule 36.12(1) the notice of acceptance must be sent to the offeror and filed with the court.

7.7 The notice of acceptance:

(1) must set out –

(a) the claim number, and

(b) the title of the proceedings,

(2) must identify the Part 36 offer or Part 36 payment notice to which it relates, and

(3) must be signed by the offeree or his legal representative (see paragraphs 6.5 and 6.6 above).

7.8 Where:

(1) the court's approval, or

(2) an order for payment of money out of court, or

(3) an order apportioning money in court –

(a) between the Fatal Accidents Act 1976 and the Law Reform (Miscellaneous Provisions) Act 1934, or

(b) between the persons entitled to it under the Fatal Accidents Act 1976,

is required for acceptance of a Part 36 offer or Part 36 payment, application for, the approval or the order should be made in accordance with Part 23.

7.9 The court will include in any order made under paragraph 8.8 above a direction for;

(1) the payment out of the money in court, and

(2) the payment of interest.

7.10 Unless the parties have agreed otherwise:

(1) interest accruing up to the date of acceptance will be paid to the offeror, and

(2) interest accruing as from the date of acceptance until payment out will be paid to the offeree.

7.11 A claimant may not accept a Part 36 payment which is part of a defendant's offer to settle the whole of a claim consisting of both a money and a non-money claim unless at the same time he accepts the offer to settle the whole of the claim. Therefore:

(1) if a claimant accepts a Part 36 payment which is part of a defendant's offer to settle the whole of the claim, or

(2) if a claimant accepts a Part 36 offer which is part of a defendant's offer to settle the whole of the claim,

the claimant will be deemed to have accepted the offer to settle the whole of the claim.[15]

(See paragraph 9 below for the method of obtaining money out of court.)

Payment out of court

8.1 To obtain money out of court following acceptance of a Part 36 payment, the claimant should file a request for payment with the court.[16]

8.2 The request for payment should contain the following details:

(1) where the party receiving the payment –

    (a) is legally represented –

        (i) the name, business address and reference of the legal representative, and

        (ii) the name of the bank and the sort code number, the title of the account and the account number where the payment is to be transmitted, and

(2) where the party is acting in person –

    (a) his name and address, and

    (b) his bank account details as in (ii) above.

8.3 Where the request for payment is made to the Royal Courts of Justice, the claimant should also complete Court Funds Office form 201 and file it in the Court Funds Office.

8.4 Subject to paragraph 9.5(1) and (2), if a party does not wish the payment to be transmitted into his bank account or if he does not have a bank account, he may send a written request to the Accountant-General for the payment to be made to him by cheque.

8.5 Where a party seeking payment out of court has provided the necessary information, the payment:

(1) where a party is legally represented, must be made to the legal representative,

(2) if the party is not legally represented but is, or has been, in receipt of legal aid in respect of the proceedings and a notice to that effect has been filed, should be made to the Legal Aid Board by direction of the court,

(3) where a person entitled to money in court dies without having made a will and the court is satisfied –

    (a) that no grant of administration of his estate has been made, and

    (b) that the assets of his estate, including the money in court, do not exceed in value the amount specified in any order in force under section 6 of the Administration of Estates (Small Payments) Act 1965,

may be ordered to be made to the person appearing to have the prior right

---

15 See rule 36.4.

16 In practice form N243.

to a grant of administration of the estate of the deceased, e.g. a widower, widow, child, father, mother, brother or sister of the deceased.

Foreign currency

9.1 Money may be paid into court in a foreign currency:
(1) where it is a Part 36 payment and the claim is in a foreign currency, or
(2) under a court order.

9.2 The court may direct that the money be placed in an interest bearing account in the currency of the claim or any other currency.

9.3 Where a Part 36 payment is made in a foreign currency and has not been accepted within 21 days, the defendant may apply for an order that the money be placed in an interest bearing account.

9.4 The application should be made in accordance with Part 23 and should state:
(1) that the payment has not been accepted in accordance with rule 36.11, and
(2) the type of currency on which interest is to accrue.

Compensation recovery

10.1 Where a defendant makes a Part 36 payment in respect of a claim for a sum or part of a sum:
(1) which fails under the heads of damage set out in column 1 of Schedule 2 of the Social Security (Recovery of Benefits) Act 1997 in respect of recoverable benefits received by the claimant as set out in column 2 of that Schedule, and
(2) where the defendant is liable to pay recoverable benefits to the Secretary of State,
the defendant should obtain from the Secretary of State a certificate of recoverable benefits and file the certificate with the Part 36 payment notice.

10.2 If a defendant wishes to offer to settle a claim where he has applied for but not yet received a certificate of recoverable benefits, he may, provided that he makes a Part 36 payment not more than 7 days after he has received the certificate, make a Part 36 offer which will have the costs and other consequences set out in rules 36.13 and 36.20.

10.3 The Part 36 payment notice should state in addition to the requirements set out in rule 36.6(2):
(1) the total amount represented by the Part 36 payment (the gross compensation),
(2) that the defendant has reduced this sum by £   , in accordance with section 8 of and Schedule 2 to the Social Security (Recovery of Benefits) Act 1997, which was calculated as follows:
Name of benefit   Amount
and
(3) that the amount paid in, being the sum of £ is the net amount after the deduction of the amount of benefit.

10.4 On acceptance of a Part 36 payment to which this paragraph relates, a claimant will receive the sum in court which will be net of the recoverable benefits.

10.5 In establishing at trial whether a claimant has bettered or obtained a judgment more advantageous than a Part 36 payment to which this paragraph relates, the court will base its decision on the gross sum specified in the Part 36 payment notice.

General

11.1 Where a party on whom a Part 36 offer, a Part 36 payment notice or a notice of acceptance is to be served is legally represented, the Part 36 offer, Part 36 payment notice and notice of acceptance must be served on the legal representative.

11.2 In a claim arising out of an accident involving a motor vehicle on a road or in a public place:

(1) where the damages claimed include a sum for hospital expenses, and

(2) the defendant or his insurer pays that sum to the hospital under section 157 of the Road Traffic Act 1988,

the defendant must give notice of that payment to the court and all the other parties to the proceedings.

11.3 Money paid into court:

(1) as a Part 36 payment which is not accepted by the claimant, or

(2) under a court order,

will be placed after 21 days in a basic account[17] (subject to paragraph 11.4 below) for interest to accrue.

11.4 Where money referred to in paragraph 11.3 above is paid in in respect of a child or patient it will be placed in a special investment account[18] for interest to accrue.

(A practice direction supplementing Part 21 contains information about the investment of money in court in respect of a child or patient.)

(Practice directions supplementing Part 40 contain information about adjustment of the judgment sum in respect of recoverable benefits, and about structured settlements.)

(A practice direction supplementing Part 41 contains information about provisional damages awards.)

---

17 See rule 26 of the Court Funds Office Rules 1987.
18 See rule 26 as above.

Legal Aid Board Housing Guidance

Advice & Assistance and Extension Guidance

1 ADVICE & ASSISTANCE AND EXTENSION GUIDANCE
1.1 Harassment/Wrongful Eviction

1.1.1 The initial two hour limit should normally be sufficient to take full instructions, to write to the landlord and/or the local authority, contact the tenancy relations officer and/or apply for legal aid. If an injunction is to be sought, an application for legal aid would need to be submitted on an emergency basis. It would therefore be unusual for extension applications to be made. Solicitors or applicants will normally be expected to contact the tenancy relations officer prior to applying for legal aid and the justification for not doing so must be set out in the application. If contact has been successful but the matter has not been resolved, solicitors should indicate this, and what steps, if any, have been taken by the tenancy relations officer, when applying for emergency legal aid.

1.1.2 However, an extension of **up to ten units (1 hour)** may be appropriate if negotiations with the landlord would appear likely to be successful in avoiding the need for court proceedings. If negotiations are ongoing, further extensions may be appropriate if the negotiations are likely to avoid court action and may secure the return of the tenant.

1.1.3 Civil legal aid and ABWOR are not available for proceedings under the **Protection from Eviction Act** in the magistrates' court and therefore, although individuals may take proceedings, most prosecutions are brought by the local authority. If the local authority is pursuing a prosecution, some advice and assistance on that aspect may still be given, but the initial limit should normally be sufficient.

1. 1.4 Advice and assistance may also be appropriate on civil proceedings where such action would achieve a worthwhile benefit in addition to that arising from the prosecution.

1.1.5 Even if an injunction is not to be sought in civil proceedings the initial limit should be sufficient for the solicitor to provide preliminary advice on liability and quantum and to complete an application for legal aid, if appropriate.

1.2 Disrepair

1.2.1 The initial two hour limit should normally be sufficient for the solicitor to take instructions, identify the issues and advise the client as to appropriate remedies. The instructions should include details of the property, the tenancy, full details of the disrepair, losses caused by the disrepair, any health problems suffered by the family, whether and how complaints or notification of the disrepair have been made to the landlord in the past. Advice should cover details of the possible courses of action, including:

• negotiations with the Environmental Health Department and/or with the landlord to ensure that the repairs are carried out,

• pursuing local arbitration/mediation arrangements where available or the Independent Housing Ombudsman or Local Government Ombudsman (as appropriate),

• possible legal proceedings, the remedies available as a result of those proceedings and quantum,

• steps to be taken to achieve the desired outcome, which should be identified and recorded on the file.

1.2.2   If the allegations of disrepair are of a trivial or insignificant nature further advice and assistance is unlikely to be justified, eg a cracked window pane, cracked tiling, or matters predominantly of a decorative nature. A tenant should normally be able to report minor disrepair to the landlord and pursue the matter without the assistance of a solicitor.

1.2.3   In the case of potential civil proceedings, the instructions obtained from the client should normally be sufficient to support an application for legal aid without the need for a report from a Surveyor/Environmental Health Officer. If a certificate is granted a report can be obtained at that stage. The initial limit should be sufficient for the solicitor to identify the extent of the disrepair, write to the landlord and apply for legal aid, Where, in exceptional circumstances, it is necessary to investigate the disrepair further an extension of **10 units (one hour)** may be appropriate. If, in exceptional circumstances, it is considered that a report is needed prior to an application for legal aid, this decision must be justified in the application for extension of the financial limit. Where there are sufficient grounds for pursuing both magistrates' court and civil remedies, any report already obtained in connection with the potential magistrates' court proceedings must be submitted with the application for legal aid.

1.2.4   If a civil legal aid certificate is unlikely to be granted, eg because the value of the claim is within the small claims limit, an extension of **10–20 units (one to two hours)** may be justified to advise on conducting the matter in person, depending on the value of the claim and having regard to the effect of the solicitor's charge on any damages recovered.

1.2.5   Where the condition of the premises is prejudicial to health so as to constitute a statutory nuisance, magistrates' court proceedings may be appropriate under the **Environmental Protection Act 1990**. Legal aid is not available, but advice and assistance may be provided where it is reasonable to do so. Such proceedings would be appropriate where the defects are only actionable in the magistrates' court (ie where the disrepair does not fall within **section 11 Landlord and Tenant Act 1985**, or any other relevant statutes, for the purpose of civil proceedings.) Where there is a mixture of defects which can give rise to either civil or magistrates' court proceedings, the decision as to which remedy to pursue will depend on the urgency of the situation (eg an urgent need to remedy a statutory nuisance which constitutes a real danger to the occupants), the value of any claim for damages and the ultimate benefit desired by the client (eg to see work undertaken rather than pursue a relatively modest claim for damages). A decision to pursue more than one remedy must be justified when claiming costs.

1.2.6　Except in cases of real urgency, extensions beyond the initial limit are unlikely to be granted in civil or magistrates' court cases unless the solicitor has already written to the landlord setting out the client's allegations of disrepair with a request for remedial repair and compensation and this has not been resolved within a reasonable period. A reasonable fee paying client would not embark upon costly litigation without first attempting to resolve matters by negotiation, even where previous complaints had been made.

1.2.7　The obtaining of an expert's report should not be regarded as an automatic first step in a potential disrepair case. The onus is on the solicitor to obtain full details from the client and assess the merits of taking further action in the light of all the information available, including any response received from the landlord. It is not sufficient to rely on information received from a referral agent. Once the necessary information has been obtained from the client, the solicitor should carry out an initial screening of the case to determine whether any further action is appropriate. The decision to instruct an expert must be one that is in the best interests of that client in those particular circumstances.

1.2.8　An extension of the financial limit would not normally be granted to instruct a surveyor or Environmental Health Officer to inspect the property and prepare a report unless the landlord had first been contacted by the solicitors, notified of the defects, requested to effect repairs and/or offer compensation within a reasonable period. This is the approach which a reasonable fee paying client would be likely to take. The time given and action demanded will depend on the urgency/severity of the particular case but in most cases would be a period of 2 to 4 weeks.

1.2.9　An extension for an expert's report may be appropriate either where the landlord has failed to respond, failed to inspect, failed to effect repairs or offer adequate compensation within the time given. If a surveyor is instructed the client's statement should be attached to the instructions. The name and qualifications of the expert to be instructed, a breakdown of the fee to be incurred and an indication of the nature of the disrepair must be provided in support of the application for extension together with details of the steps taken so far.

1.2.10　Where the client has a potential and worthwhile claim for damages, extensions of the financial limit are unlikely to be granted for the purpose of gathering further evidence, eg a surveyor's report, and an application for legal aid should be submitted.

1.2.11　In magistrates' court proceedings the client will be acting in person. Advice and assistance may cover the drafting of the statutory notice and information, obtaining a schedule of works necessary to abate the statutory nuisance and correspondence with the landlord. In some cases a medical report may also be required. Extensions of **20–40 units (two to four hours)** plus disbursements may be justified to assist in bringing the case to the point of trial.

1.2.12 If a solicitor is instructed by a private landlord for advice on the defence of proceedings for disrepair the initial limit should be sufficient to enable a solicitor to take full instructions, identify the issues, advise on prospects and submit an application for lega1 aid.

1.2.13 Before advising a client to commence any proceedings, the availability of alternative methods of resolving the matter should be considered. Such alternatives would include local arbitration/mediation arrangements or a referral to the Independent Housing Ombudsman/Local Government Ombudsman (as appropriate). A fee paying client would be likely to take advantage of such arrangements before incurring the costs of litigation. An explanation for not pursuing alternative remedies, where available, should be provided with any application for extension of the financial limit or claim for costs.

1.2.14 The work set out in paragraphs 1.2.1 to 1.2.3 above should be undertaken under a single application for advice and assistance. More than one application form should be signed only when reasonable grounds have been established for pursuing separate remedies **and** a definite and justifiable decision has been reached to pursue both remedies, eg a claim for damages in civil proceedings and statutory nuisance proceedings in the magistrates' court. It is only when such a decision has been taken that there can be said to be two genuinely separate matters. Two forms for advice and assistance are therefore not appropriate for the initial preliminary investigations.

1.2.15 Where solicitors submit more than one claim for payment for a single client (together or at separate times), the area office may call for the files of papers. The need for separate proceedings must always be justified by reference to the additional benefit to be gained for the client in relation to the costs incurred.

1.2.16 Where solicitors receive referrals of cases from a third party they must comply with Practice Rule 12.04 and the Solicitors' Introduction and Referral Code 1990, where applicable. In the case of such referrals solicitors must take care to satisfy themselves, by way of full and continuing instructions from the client, of the basis of the claim and the reasonableness of incurring costs and disbursements. Before advising a client to pursue any remedy the solicitor must have regard to the wishes and best interests of the client and the reasonableness of expending public funds in the particular circumstances of the case.

1.3 Possession cases

1.3.1 The initial two hour limit should normally be sufficient to take full instructions and to give advice on the type of tenancy, the rights and obligations involved, and any available defences and counterclaims. The solicitor may write to the landlord in an attempt to settle the matter, and/or submit an application for legal aid. The client may seek advice when notice of proceedings is received, in which case there may be greater opportunity for negotiation. However, if advice is not sought until proceedings are issued and there is an imminent hearing date, an application for civil legal aid will have to be made as a matter of urgency (provided that there is a defence to the landlord's application for a possession order). Where negotiation is ongoing, an extension of **5–10 units (30 minutes to one hour) may be justified.**

1.3.2   Advice may be sought on whether or not a proper notice has been served either to determine the tenancy or indicate proceedings will be issued. The initial limit should be sufficient to provide such advice.

1.3.3   Even if there is no defence to the possession proceedings, the solicitor may still be able to negotiate in relation to the terms of a possession order. The landlord may agree not to pursue arrears of rent, and/or to allow more time for the tenant to vacate the premises. The solicitor may even be able to negotiate terms under which the tenant is allowed to remain under a suspended possession order, provided that rent is paid regularly. An extension of **about 10 units (one hour)** may be justified to cover negotiations in these circumstances.

1.3.4   In some circumstances, there may be a defence to possession proceedings based on the landlord's failure to keep the premises in repair. The solicitor would need to take full instructions on the condition of the premises in order to establish the value of any counterclaim in addition to the defence of the proceedings. This can entail extra work. It may be that the amount of the damages that would be awarded for the disrepair would extinguish the landlord's claim for arrears of rent. The usual extensions in relation to disrepair may be appropriate.

1.3.5   If a landlord is taking accelerated possession proceedings to obtain possession of premises let on an assured shorthold tenancy, an application for civil legal aid will not be appropriate because there is no court hearing. The solicitor will have to go through the landlord's affidavit with the client. There are, however, several reasons why objections could be made to the accelerated procedure. For example, there may be a dispute as to whether or not the correct notice of shorthold tenancy was served on the tenant before the tenancy commenced. If there is a dispute, the solicitor will need to assist the client to prepare a detailed reply for the court. This reply would raise the relevant issues and provide evidence to persuade the court that an immediate order for possession should not be made, and that the matter should be listed for a hearing. An extension of **up to 5–10 units (30 minutes to one hour)** would normally be sufficient to make the application for legal aid.

1.3.6   If there is a defence to the possession proceedings based an incorrect notice, it would not be unusual for there to be other problems with the tenancy. There may be rent arrears and/or disrepair and/or welfare benefit problems. In cases where there is no defence, the solicitor may have to advise on homelessness. The amount of any extension which could be justified would always depend on the number of issues arising.

1.4   Homelessness

1.4.1   The initial two hour limit should normally be sufficient to take detailed instructions, identify the issues and advise the client as to any appropriate action. Those instructions should include details of whether the client is actually homeless or threatened with homelessness and the history of events leading to the client's current circumstances. Advice should also be given on whether or not the local housing authority has any duty towards the individual and what that duty is. Local Authorities are under an obligation either to provide accommodation for homeless individuals or, in cases where there is no duty to re-house, provide advice in obtaining accommodation. It would not be reasonable for the solicitor to provide advice on obtaining accommodation as the Local Authority has a statutory duty to provide it. If an application to the housing authority has been made but no decision yet reached, the solicitor may enter into correspondence with the housing authority to set out the client's case. An extension of **up to 10 units (one hour)** may be appropriate for this correspondence.

1.4.2   Further extensions may be justified if negotiations and investigations are ongoing because there is a long delay between the notification of homelessness /threatened homelessness to the housing authority and any decision.

1.4.3   Once the housing authority's decision has been made it will be communicated in writing. The housing authority has a duty under **section 184 Housing Act 1996** to give notice of its decision on its duty to the applicant, the reasons for it and to notify the applicant of the right to request a review of the decision or to seek assistance in obtaining accommodation. The solicitor will have to consider the reasons given and should obtain the housing authority's file (if not already obtained) to decide whether it would be appropriate to seek a review of the decision. A further extension of **20 units (two hours)** may be justified to obtain the file, review it and to advise and assist the client in deciding whether to request a review.

1.4.4   When the review is completed, if the decision remains that there is no duty, a further extension of **up to 10–20 units (one to two hours)** may be justified to consider and advise the client whether to exercise the right of appeal to a county court under **section 204 Housing Act 1996** and to submit an application for legal aid for that appeal.

1.4.5   If at any stage a decision favourable to the client is made a further extension of **5 units (30 minutes)** may be justified to enable the solicitor to advise the client as to the suitability of any accommodation offered if the client considers that the offer made is inadequate. The client may seek a review under **section 202 Housing Act 1996** and if so further extensions of **up to 20 units (two hours)** may be appropriate to pursue that review. Once that review is completed, the client may be advised whether to pursue an appeal to the County Court (see para 1.4.4 above for the appropriate extensions).

1.4.6   At each or any of the above stages a further extension of **5–10 units (30 minutes to one hour)** may be justified to enable the solicitor to consider whether temporary accommodation is needed/being provided/is suitable and to correspond with the housing authority about such provision. If suitable temporary accommodation is not being provided a further extension of **5–10 units (30 minutes to one hour)** may be justified to consider whether an application for judicial review should be made as a county court does not have power to grant interim relief ie to order the provision of temporary accommodation pending the outcome of any appeal.

Any extension should enable the solicitor to send a letter before action and in the absence of a satisfactory response, submit an application for legal aid.

1.5 Mortgage repossession

1.5.1 Claims by lenders against borrowers whose property is subject to a mortgage/legal charge

1.5.1.1 The initial two hour limit should normally be sufficient for instructions to be taken, relevant issues identified, and advice given as to the legal position, any defence, and relevant steps to be taken. This would include details of the property, the nature of the loan, instalments, capital and interest outstanding. Advice would be necessary as to the nature of any proceedings threatened or already issued, and the nature of any defence/counterclaim which could be mounted. A single form for advice and assistance would be appropriate in this context, and this should cover the limited amount of initial correspondence necessary. If additional correspondence is necessary where information is outstanding from the lender or negotiations are ongoing an extension of up to 10 units (one hour) may be justified.

1.5.2 The following issues may arise when the client seeks advice of this nature:

(a) Arrears

In many cases this is the only issue in dispute. It should be possible to write to the court to explain the borrower's position. An immediate possession order is unlikely to be granted in light of the decision in **Cheltenham & Gloucester Building Society v Norgan** as the Court can consider the remaining period of the mortgage as the reasonable period for repayment of arrears. If there is some dispute as to the level of arrears a modest extension of **up to 10 units (one hour)** may be appropriate.

(b) Linked relationship breakdown or other disputes/litigation

This may be a factor justifying more extensive advice and correspondence, although an extension of more than **ten units (one hour)** is unlikely to be justified unless an application for legal aid in relation to the possession proceedings is made in which case **another 5 units (30 minutes)** will be required. In most cases it should be possible to write to the Court to explain the position.

(c) Fraud

It is sometimes alleged by the assisted person that his/her signature has been fraudulently added to a document, usually by his/her co-habitant/spouse. An extension of **not more than 5 units (30 minutes)** would be appropriate to obtain a copy of the document, and to make the application for a legal aid certificate in this context. If the fraud is blatant, advisers would be expected to write to the lender pointing this out before any application for legal aid is made.

(d) Duress/Undue Influence

If it is claimed that signatures have been obtained under duress/pressure and/or that inadequate independent advice has been given advisers will need to have regard to the guidelines laid down in the case of **Royal Bank of Scotland v Etteridge** (which expands upon **Barclays Bank v O'Brien**). If the client has had the benefit of independent advice from a solicitor before entering into the transaction, the lender is in fact in a strong position. The client will have difficulty in establishing duress/undue influence in these circumstances. Where the client did not have advice from a solicitor limited correspondence may be necessary to establish whether any defence exists and an extension of **up to 10 units (one hour)** may be justified.

Advisers may find that a combination of two or more of the issues above may arise and, should this be the case, an extension of 10 to 20 units (one to two hours) might be justified prior to seeking a legal aid certificate.

(e) Arrears cases/Consumer Credit Act issues

Advice should usually be provided within the initial limit but an extension of **not more than 10–20 units (one to two hours)** may be necessary if the case is unusually complex and/or the borrower seeks to request time to pay and/or to reduce interest charges.

(f) Addition of Parties

Where an occupant is not a party to the secured loan agreement he/she may wish to apply to be added as a party to the proceedings. If the adviser considers that there is real benefit in so doing it should be possible to consider the issue and apply for legal aid within the initial two hour advice and assistance limit. An extension is unlikely to be necessary.

(g) Counterclaims

Advice and assistance may be appropriate for this purpose, eg as to a negligent survey. An extension of **up to 10 units (one hour)** may be appropriate.

(h) Advice to tenants of borrowers

Advice may be given as to the tenant's position in relation to the mortgage and possible action against the borrower, if evicted. The issues should usually be investigated and considered within the initial limit, to include any application for legal aid.

(i) Advice following issue of warrant for possession

If this is the first time the client has been seen, then full details will need to be obtained so that the adviser can consider if there is any possibility of judgement being set aside and/or an application can be made to set aside or suspend any warrant issued. If an application to set aside judgement can be made then an application to seek legal aid may be considered justified. An extension of **up to 10 units (one hour)** may be appropriate to go into sufficient detail to seek a legal aid certificate. If none of these factors apply and the only issue is the amount of arrears, advice should be given within the initial limit. If advised to make an application to the court to suspend the warrant an extension of up to one hour/ten units may be appropriate.

(j) Sale by building society/bank in possession

Advice may be sought by borrowers against whom possession has been ordered and whose property is to be sold. It is sometimes suggested that the lender is pressing ahead with a sale at an undervalue. It should be possible in most cases to establish the approximate value of the property without a formal valuation report (eg from an estate agent's valuation or client's estimate of the current market value) and to advise the borrowers of their rights. If the solicitor considers undervalue can be established then an extension may be justified to enter into negotiations with the lender on value/conduct of sale and/or to obtain a formal valuation.

(k) Costs

Should judgement be obtained by a lender the costs will be added to the debt due under the charge. Advice may be sought on the possibility of taxing the lender's solicitors costs under **section 70 Solicitors Act 1974**. An extension of **between 5–15 units (30 minutes to one and a half hours)** may be appropriate for this to enable the bill to be scrutinised.

1.6   Miscellaneous Issues

1.6.1   *Unlawful occupiers and trespassers*

1.6.1.1   The initial two hour limit would normally be sufficient for the solicitor to take instructions and advise, In many cases the adviser's role may be limited to no more than brief advice that the occupier/trespasser has no right to remain and limited correspondence. Advice might be necessary to establish whether a tenancy/licence has been determined, whether possessory title can be alleged, or whether there is an ongoing licence to occupy. Should there be a defence to proceedings which have already been issued then the initial two hour limit should be sufficient to include an application for legal aid.

1.6.2   *Travellers*

1.6.2.1   Advisers may be consulted by Gypsies/Romanies and other persons with a nomadic life-style including new travellers (sometimes referred to as new age travellers). Gypsies are a distinct ethnic group under the **Race Relations Act** and anti-discrimination legislation will apply to them.

1.6.2.2   It is frequently the case that advisers may provide advice and assistance or work under a legal aid certificate to one person, although it is likely that this may be of benefit to not only this person and his/her family, but other persons on the site, or in the same group. Where any application for legal aid is to be made solicitors should consider whether it is appropriate to suggest that the advice should be jointly funded with reference to regulation 32 of the Civil Legal Aid (General) Regulations 1989. It is likely that the individuals will have cases which are not identical, but are similar to others of the group.

1.6.2.3   The initial two hour limit is likely to be sufficient for detailed instructions to be taken, the relevant issues identified and advice given as to the legal position, and the appropriate response to any contact made by the owner of the land, the police or the local authority.

1.6.2.4   The following issues may arise when advisers are consulted by gypsies and other travellers:

(a) Sites

Advice may be required as to obtaining or keeping a pitch, the quality of services, and evictions. Poor sites may contravene a local authority's duty under the **Children Act 1989** to provide adequate conditions for children. Advisers may be asked to write to the Local Authority. If ongoing correspondence takes place an extension of **up to 20 units (two hours)** may be appropriate in this context. Where the poor quality of site is in dispute action can be taken under the **Environmental Protection Act 1990**. The initial two hour limit should normally be sufficient to take instructions, identify the issues, and advise the client. Legal aid is not available but advice and assistance may be provided where it is reasonable to do so and the extensions for disrepair apply.

(b) Harassment

Problems may arise as to issues of harassment and advice may be sought as to this. An extension to the initial two hour advice and assistance limit is unlikely to be justified.

(c) Eviction by the Local Authority from Unoccupied Sites or land forming Part of the Highway

Travellers may be subject to a local authority direction to leave land and remove all vehicles and property where they are on unoccupied sites/land forming part of the highway. Advice might be sought by travellers as to the steps which need to be carried out by the local authority before issuing the removal direction under **section 77 of the Criminal Justice and Public Order Act 1994** and/or in negotiations and correspondence with the authority in relation to its obligations under the **Children Act 1989** for education, housing, access to local health and welfare services, and relevant humanitarian considerations as set out in any relevant Department of the Environment circular. (Gypsy Sites and Unauthorised Camping (DOE circular 18/24) and DETR/Home Office Good Practice Guide 'Managing Unauthorised Camping' Oct 1998). Should ongoing correspondence take place an extension of **20 to 40 units (two to four hours)** might be appropriate.

(d) Eviction by the Local Authority from its Own Land

Travellers may be subject to Civil Procedure Rules, Schedule 2 CCR Order 24 Possession Proceedings from caravan sites or other council owned property which they occupy as trespassers. The relevant circular does not apply in this context as the council is exercising eviction powers rather than initiating removal directions. The initial two hour limit for advice and assistance should be sufficient to establish that this is the case and to consider appropriate remedies, including judicial review. If judicial review is considered an extension of **5–10 units (30 minutes to one hour)** may be justified which would include applying for legal aid where appropriate.

(e) Occupation by Travellers of Land Already Occupied

Where two or more travellers are on land which is occupied and the landlord has taken reasonable steps to ask them to leave, the police can become involved in the eviction. Advice and assistance might be appropriate in relation to the powers of the police which include removal and destruction of vehicles. If the traveller fails to comply with a direction by the senior officer to leave the site, a criminal offence might be committed punishable by imprisonment. An extension of **10 to 20 units (one to two hours)** may be appropriate to advise on the power of the police and to advise on occupation. Advice on any criminal charge(s) should be the subject of a separate green form or an application for a legal aid order.

1.6.3 *Mobile Homes*

1.6.3.1 The initial two hour limit would normally be sufficient for the solicitor to take detailed instructions, identify the issues and advise the client as to appropriate remedies. The initial limit should be sufficient to advise fully and include any application for legal aid, if appropriate.

1.6.3.2 Advice may be sought as to various matters including:

• Whether or not the site is protected under the Mobile Homes Act and the effects of this.

• The provision and interpretation of a written statement of rights under the Mobile Homes Act 1983.

• Utilities and the price at which fuel is re-sold to occupants.

• Breaches of site licence, eg by overcrowding.

• Harassment.

1.6.3.3 Matters of this nature can be the subject of litigation in the County Court. However, advice will need to cover details of the possibility of other courses of action, eg:

• Negotiation with the site owner

• Involvement of the Local Authority

• Involvement of the police

• Whether the site falls within the Independent Housing Ombudsman Scheme and a reference to the Ombudsman is appropriate.

Given that occupants of mobile homes will all have their own case, it is likely in most cases that legal advice should not be jointly funded.

1.6.3.4 Where individuals own their mobile home the initial two hour limit will normally be sufficient for detailed instructions to be taken, issues to be identified and advice given as to the legal position and as to appropriate remedies. Issues specific to clients in this position include:

• Failure to provide a written statement within three months of occupancy. If it is not forthcoming, advice may be appropriate as to the possibility of seeking a County Court order that the site owner provide a statement and the initial limit would be sufficient to include applying for a legal aid certificate.

• Termination of the agreement by the site owner for eg disrepair and/or other breach of condition. A surveyor's report may be needed and an extension of **up to 10 units (one hour)** plus the cost of the report may be justified.

• Change of the written statement and negotiations relating to this. An extension of up to **20 units (two hours)** may be appropriate, to include any application for legal aid for a reference to the County Court.

• The site owner may wish to move the mobile home to a new pitch and advice may be sought as to the terms of the agreement and the nature of the move. An extension of **up to 10 units (one hour)** may be appropriate for negotiations and any application for legal aid in the event of reference to the County Court.

• Unreasonable refusal of consent to a sale. Advice may be sought as to this and the possibility of seeking a County Court declaration. An extension of up to 5 units (30 minutes) may be appropriate to cover applying for legal aid in this context. Advice may be sought as to a change in the site rules or an increase in the pitch fee. There is a requirement that the owner of the site consult with the mobile home owner and in certain circumstances either party can seek a County Court declaration. An extension of **up to 20 units (two hours)** plus the cost of any report may be justified, to include any application for legal aid.

1.6.3.5 Where individuals rent their mobile home the initial two hour limit should be sufficient for instructions to be taken, issues to be identified and advice given. In many cases only brief advice will be appropriate as security of tenure is limited. Four weeks notice is all that is required although a court order is necessary. Advice would cover details of the legal position and any possible remedies including:

• Early termination of a fixed term agreement for breach eg for non-payment of rent. Advice may be sought as to whether there has been a breach.

• Increases of rent.

• Change to a new pitch.

Extensions beyond the initial limit are likely to be unusual. Where a legal aid certificate is sought then it should be possible to apply for legal aid within the two hour limit.

1.6.4 *Advice in relation to a lease/notice of assured shorthold tenancy*

1.6.4.1 The initial two hour limit should normally be sufficient for instructions to be taken, and advice given on the terms and conditions of the lease or tenancy agreement where correspondence needs to be entered into a further extension of **up to 5–10 units (30 minutes to one hour)** may be justified.

1.6.5 *Arrears of rent*

1.6.5.1 The initial two hour limit should normally be sufficient for the solicitor to take full instructions and advise as to possible defences and action to be taken. If proceedings have been issued in respect of a sum over £5,000 or for a lesser sum together with a claim for possession, and there is a defence, an application for civil legal aid would normally be made within the initial limit. The tenant may have a counterclaim in respect of the costs of repairs, or the amount of rent claimed may be incorrect.

1.6.5.2 If a tenant has been threatened with distress or property has been impounded, the solicitor will be able to advise about the process, including exempt and protected goods ie goods which cannot be taken. The solicitor may also be able to negotiate repayment of the arrears with the landlord in order to avoid the immediate removal of property.

1.6.6 *Service Charges*

1.6.6.1 The initial limit should normally be sufficient for instructions to be taken and advice to be given which will include an explanation of the remit/workings of the Leasehold Valuation Tribunal. If the case is complex or ongoing correspondence is necessary a further extension of **up to 10–20 units (one to two hours)** may be justified.

2   SUGGESTED TIMES FOR GREEN FORM EXTENSION REQUESTS

Type of Case	Reason	Reference	Time (unit = 6 mins)
Harassment	Negotiations to settle	1.1.2	10
Disrepair	Further investigation of the disrepair	1.2.3	10
	Cases where legal aid is unlikely to be granted, including small claims cases	1.2.4	10–20
	Magistrates' Court cases	1.2.11	20–40 plus expert's report and other disbursements
Possession	Negotiations to avoid proceedings	1.3.1	5–10
	Negotiation to agree terms of order	1.3.3	10
	Assist with accelerated possession proceedings	1.3.5	10
Homelessness	Correspondence pending decision	1.4.1	10
	Consideration of options following decision	1.4.3	20
	Consideration of right of appeal	1.4.4	10–20
	Consideration of suitability of offer of accommodation	1.4.5	5
Mortgage re-possession	Negotiations with lender	1.5.1.1	10
	Dispute on level of arrears	1.5.2(a)	10
	Linked disputes and application for legal aid	1.5.2(b)	10
	Fraud	1.5.2(c)	5
	Duress/undue influence	1.5.2(d)	10
	Arrears/Consumer Credit Act	1.5.2(e)	10–20
	Counter-claims	1.5.2(g)	10
	Set aside warrants	1.5.2(i)	10
	Application to suspend	1.5.2(i)	10
	Costs	1.5.2(k)	5–15
Miscellaneous issues	Sites	1.6.2.4(a)	20
	Disrepair of sites	1.6.2.4(a)	20–40
	Eviction by local authority	1.6.2.4(c)	20–40
	Judicial review	1.6.2.4(d)	5–10
	Police directions	1.6.2.4(e)	10–20
	Mobile homes – termination of agreement	1.6.3.4	10 plus expert's report
	Change of written statement	1.6.3.4	20
	Moving to new pitch	1.6.3.4	10
	Unreasonable refusal to sale	1.6.3.4	5
	Changes to rules/fees	1.6.3.4	20
	Lease/notice of assured shorthold tenancy	1.6.4.1	5–10
	Service Charges	1.6.6	10–20

Civil Legal Aid

1   GENERAL ISSUES

1.1   Alternative remedies for tenants of social landlords

1.1.1   Generally, unless a matter is urgent, it would not be reasonable to grant legal aid to take proceedings until the tenant has fully considered the use of any local arbitration or mediation arrangements and/or the pursuit of a complaint within the jurisdiction of the Ombudsman (Independent Housing Ombudsman or the Local Government Ombudsman, as appropriate).

Where solicitors are not familiar with the Ombudsman scheme it should be noted that both the Independent Housing Ombudsman and the Local Government Ombudsman publish information about their work and jurisdiction. Contact details are set out below:

Independent Housing Ombudsman   0171 836 3630

(This includes membership by social landlords and voluntary membership of private landlords, including some park home owners (for tenants of mobile homes))

Local Government Ombudsman

Website: http://www.open.govuk/lgo

Mr E Osmotherly (Greater London, Kent and East Sussex)   **0171 915 3210**

Mrs P Thomas (Birmingham, Cheshire, Derbyshire, Nottinghamshire, Lincolnshire and the North of England)   **01904 663200**

Mr J White (remainder of England)   **01203 695999**

Mr E R Moseley (Wales)   **01656 661325**

1.1.2   The Board does not seek to automatically refuse legal aid in every case where an Ombudsman or local mediation/arbitration scheme exists. The issue is whether, in applying the private client test, it is reasonable to grant legal aid before options other than legal proceedings have been explored with the client and/or pursued. Regard should be had to the specific concerns of the client and what s/he wishes to secure as this will be relevant to whether the Courts, arbitration/mediation, or an Ombudsman might be better able to deliver what the client wants. Solicitors should be aware of the jurisdiction of the relevant Ombudsman, the local mediation/arbitration schemes and be able to discuss the alternative avenues with their client when making the decision whether to apply for legal aid.

1.1.3   When applying for legal aid solicitors should indicate:

a) whether any local arbitration or mediation schemes are available;

b) why a local scheme and/or either of the Ombudsmen are not suitable for the individual case; and,

c) the particular circumstances that make litigation the most appropriate route.

Solicitors should be able to illustrate that they have considered the available options with the client, and to justify the decision to pursue litigation.

Alternative remedies should always be considered before initiating court based litigation. This is because if arbitration/mediation is available either locally through the Landlord, or under the auspices of an Ombudsman, a private client would be likely to exhaust those avenues before issuing proceedings.

1.1.4 There are limited circumstances in which a complaint to an Ombudsman could be an adjunct to litigation (eg in judicial review cases where the public law remedy cannot result in a damages award). If the client is pursuing both avenues, solicitors should indicate this in the application for legal aid.

1.1.5 If the tenancy agreement contains a compulsory arbitration clause, solicitors should explain whether arbitration took place, and if so its outcome. If arbitration was not pursued, solicitors should explain why the case was not suitable. Any correspondence with the landlord should be submitted with the application.

1.2 Cost benefit and housing cases

1.2.1 Cost benefit is unlikely to be the only relevant factor in the consideration of an application for a housing case, in that the importance to the client to peacefully occupy a home that is in a proper state of repair may be equally relevant. However, the applicant must be able to show that the benefit to be gained from the proposed proceedings justifies the potential costs.

1.2.2 In determining whether the reasonableness criteria are met, the Board will consider what the applicant is seeking to achieve, what other remedies are available, and what action a private fee paying client would take in similar circumstances. Solicitors will be expected to show that they have considered these issues when evaluating the merits of the case.

1.2.3 The key information needed to assess costs benefit is:

• the predicted amount of any damages if the proceedings are successful (A);

• the total estimated costs inclusive of disbursements and counsel fees but excluding VAT (C). Any estimate of costs should include costs incurred to date, and those which would be incurred if the matter proceeded. If reasonable prospects of settlement exist they should be taken into account when arriving at the figure, unless the application is to amend the scope of the certificate to allow the case to be taken to trial. In such cases the estimate must include final costs. The 'C' figure should consist of estimated profit costs (at legal aid rates, with enhancement where appropriate) and estimated disbursements including counsel's fees. VAT is to be excluded.

• the likely net amount of recoverable damages after application of the statutory charge (D) – this will be A plus any recoverable costs minus C;

• the probability of success (P).

1.2.4 Even if it is considered that representation is justified, legal aid should not normally be granted in cases involving only a monetary claim (and not any injunctive or other relief) unless the reasonableness criteria are satisfied as to cost benefit. They are likely to be satisfied where consideration of the **key information** (ie P, D and C) produces a result on the risk based assessment in the following ranges:

Prospects of success (P)	Net Damages compared to costs (D:C)
less than 50%	whatever the ratio the application is likely to be refused
50%–60%	D must be at least 2 times C
60%–80%	D must be of least 1.5 times C
more than 80%	D must be at least equal to C

1.2.5   If the rates in the matrix are not satisfied the solicitor will need to justify why, in the circumstances, it would be reasonable for legal aid to be granted/continued. This will include considerations, other than the damages, which make it reasonable to assume that a private client of moderate means would continue to fund the case.

1.2.6   In proceedings that are being defended against or brought by a private landlord consideration of the probability of success must also include an assessment of the prospects of successfully recovering any order for costs made in the proceedings.

2   HARASSMENT/WRONGFUL EVICTION

2.1   Harassment/Wrongful Eviction

2.1.1   Legal aid is likely to be granted to a tenant/occupier to take proceedings if he/she can show a breach of covenant for quiet enjoyment, trespass or unlawful eviction, interference with and trespass to goods or assault.

and

reasonable prospects of obtaining one or more of the following:

a) an order enabling the applicant to return to the property; and/or
b) recovery of any personal possessions; and/or
c) an award of damages; and/or
d) an injunction.

2.1.2   Legal aid is unlikely to be granted to take proceedings in circumstances where:

a) there has been no letter before action or other prior contact with the landlord/agent with a view to resolving matters without the need for proceedings (unless it is demonstrated in the application that the matter is so urgent and/or serious that this would not be appropriate or would have no effect); and/or

b) the conduct complained of is trivial or is not recent and unlikely to be repeated; and/or

c) if an order for return to the property is sought, the benefit to be obtained may be insufficient to justify legal aid where the nature and length of the tenancy are such that the order would exist for only a short period of time eg where the length of time left in an assured shorthold tenancy is less than a month; and/or

d) the basis of the estimated value of the claim is not set out in the application, including claims for aggravated and/or exemplary damages. In cases involving personal possessions the nature, age and current actual second-hand values of the items should be specified rather than the purchase prices or cost of replacement as new.

e) any order obtained could not be enforced within a reasonable time.

f) there are no reasonable prospects of recovering costs and the operation of the statutory charge would therefore extinguish any benefit likely to be obtained. Some details of the opponent's financial circumstances and ability to pay damages/costs must be provided.

2.1.3 Where the tenant or the local authority is taking action in the magistrates' court under the **Protection from Eviction Act 1977**, legal aid is unlikely to be granted unless the benefit of separate civil proceedings can be shown. Where the primary remedy sought is an injunction or return to the property, legal aid is unlikely to be granted unless the matter has first been reported to the tenancy relations officer. If that step has not been taken justification for not doing so must be specifically set out in the application. If contact was made solicitors should indicate, if known, what steps have been taken by the tenancy relations officer.

2.1.4 Legal aid is likely to be granted to a private landlord to defend proceedings where the tenant's allegations are answered in sufficient detail to show reasonable prospects of successfully defending the claim. A simple denial, without any further explanation, is unlikely to justify legal aid.

2.1.5 Legal aid is likely to be granted to pursue a counterclaim if reasonable grounds are shown for taking those proceedings, an order is likely to be made and, where a financial remedy is the main remedy sought, the cost/benefit criteria set out in para 1.2.4 is met and the tenant would be able to satisfy judgement within a reasonable time, eg on a counterclaim for arrears of rent.

2.2 Protection from Harassment Act 1997

Note: ABWOR is not available.

2.2.1 Legal aid may only be granted by a franchisee in the housing category where the proposed proceedings are between a landlord and tenant. Proceedings between tenants and neighbours do not fall within the housing franchise category.

2.2.2 Legal aid is only likely to be granted to take proceedings if:

a) a warning letter has first been sent (or the circumstances are such that this would not be appropriate – the reasons must be made clear in the application);

b) the police have been notified and have nonetheless failed to provide adequate assistance having regard to their powers under the Act (or the circumstances are such that going to the police first would not be appropriate – the reasons must be made clear in the application) and a fee paying client of moderate means would in all the circumstances be advised to apply to the court for an order; and

c) reasonable grounds to take the proceedings to establish liability and/or causation can be shown; and

d) a fee paying client of moderate means would be advised to take the proceedings in all the circumstances of the case; and

e) where an injunction is sought, there has been conduct sufficient to constitute harassment/apprehended harassment within the last two to three weeks or, if earlier, on the particular facts there is a likelihood of repetition.

2.2.3   Legal aid is unlikely to be granted to take proceedings if:
a)   on the facts the conduct complained of is trivial or not likely to be repeated; and/or
b)   the other party is under an existing obligation not to molest, for example is subject to bail conditions, or is remanded in custody or is the subject of a restraining order in criminal proceedings under the Act (unless on the facts the existing obligation is likely to end imminently); and/or
c)   in the circumstances of the case other steps would be more appropriate eg referral to the tenancy relations officer, proceedings in the magistrates' court under the **Protection from Eviction Act 1977** or a complaint to the Housing Ombudsman (where there is a scheme in existence covering matters of that type); and/or
d)   any order is likely to be unenforceable due to the mental incapacity or minority of the defendant, or in a claim for damages there is no evidence of the opponent's ability to satisfy judgement within a reasonable period.

2.2.4   Legal aid is likely to be granted to defend proceedings if:
a)   there are any very serious allegations which are denied wholly or substantially; and/or
b)   there is a question of inability to defend (eg because of mental incapacity or minority); and
in all cases
c)   the defendant has answered any allegations in sufficient detail to show a prima facie defence. A simple denial, without any further explanation, is unlikely to justify legal aid.

2.2.5   Legal aid is unlikely to be granted to defend proceedings if the matter could reasonably be dealt with by way of an undertaking for which representation is not considered necessary.

2.2.6   Legal aid is unlikely to be granted for enforcement proceedings unless the matter has first been reported to the police who have nonetheless failed to provide adequate assistance having regard to their powers under the Act.

3   DISREPAIR
3.1   Legal aid is likely to be granted:

3.1.1   Legal aid is likely to be granted to the tenant to take proceedings under **section 11 Landlord and Tenant Act 1985** and/or other relevant statutes and/or in negligence where the landlord has been given notice of the relevant defects and has not taken action to remedy them within a reasonable time.

3.1.2   Applications by the tenant may include a claim for **personal injury** where this is incidental to proceedings within the housing category. Separate applications for legal aid for personal injury claims should be submitted by all individuals other than the tenant who are to be parties in the proceedings eg children of the tenant. However, where claims relate solely to personal injuries suffered by a person who is not a tenant, they will fall within the personal injury category rather than the housing category.

3.1.3 Legal aid applications from private landlords to defend/counterclaim are, in practice, very rare. However, legal aid is likely to be granted where the landlord can establish reasonable grounds to defend the proceedings and the value of the claim/benefit to be gained by contesting the proceedings justifies the costs likely to be incurred by satisfying the cost/benefit criteria set out in para 1.2.4.

3.2 Legal aid is unlikely to be granted:

3.2.1 Legal aid is unlikely to be granted in circumstances where:

a) the value of any claim for damages falls within the small claims limit, unless the allocation by the court has been or is likely to be changed or the circumstances are exceptional;

b) an alternative remedy is available which would achieve largely the same benefit and which could reasonably be pursued in the circumstances eg statutory nuisance proceedings in the magistrates' court which would result in essential repairs being undertaken or the use of local arbitration/mediation arrangements or reference to a Housing Ombudsman. An explanation for not using such alternatives must be given in the application form;

c) the main purpose of the proceedings is to obtain damages and the cost/benefit criteria set out in para.1.2.4 have not been met.

3.3 Legal aid is likely to be refused:

3.3.1 Legal aid is likely to be refused because of lack of information if the following details are not supplied with the application for legal aid:

a) an adequate statement of case setting out the allegations of disrepair in detail;

b) the date(s) when the landlord was put on notice and the method by which this was done;

c) an indication of whether there have been any previous proceedings eg in the magistrates' court and, if so, details of the outcome and copies of any expert(s) report(s) already obtained in connection with the issues of disrepair;

d) details of the availability of local arbitration/mediation arrangements or inappropriateness of a referral to an Ombudsman scheme;

e) an explanation where there have been previous proceedings, to justify further action;

f) an estimate of the value of the claim, with reference to the severity of the disrepair, the small claims limit and relevant case law;

g) copies of any relevant correspondence with the landlord/agents; and

h) details of the opponent's financial circumstances and ability to pay (in all cases where compensation and/or costs will be claimed). This is particularly important in the case of private landlords.

3.4 Miscellaneous

3.4.1 Solicitors must provide a report to the Area Office if the client moves from the property in question. Notification of a new address is not sufficient for this purpose. The report should set out the effect of the move on quantum or on any other remedy being sought in the proceedings.

4 POSSESSION CASES
4.1 Landlords: generally

4.1.1 Legal aid is likely to be granted to a private landlord to take possession proceedings:
   a) where the type of tenancy is specified, eg, where the tenant is a protected tenancy under the **Rent Act 1977**; and
   b) the landlord has specified the cases/grounds set out in the Schedule of the Act upon which he/she is relying; and
   c) the case will not be dealt with under the accelerated possession procedure within the county court.

4.1.2 It would not be reasonable to grant legal aid unless the landlord has firstly determined the tenancy or served and sent a letter before action to the tenant.

4.1.3 When applying for legal aid, private landlords should indicate whether the tenant has sufficient means to satisfy any monetary claim made within the proceedings.

4.2 Possession: generally

4.2.1 Legal aid is unlikely to be granted if the only issue to be placed before the court is whether an immediate possession order would be inappropriate. Consideration needs to be given as to whether this is only a short term remedy for the applicant and whether a private client would incur such costs.

4.2.2 Legal aid is unlikely to be available to defend proceedings solely to establish that one or more of the technical defences are available where it would be reasonable to approach the landlord to seek a compromise. A private client would be unlikely to incur the costs involved in defending the proceedings without making representations to the landlord about the procedural defects. It is recognised, however, that in some cases it would be tactically advantageous to the individual client for the defects not to be drawn to the landlord's attention thus allowing the tenancy to continue longer. This tactical advantage would need to be considered as against the time saved/costs to be incurred/what the private client would do. Solicitors should, when applying for legal aid, indicate whether steps have been taken to persuade the landlord either to withdraw the proceedings or to remedy the technical breaches. If no approach has been made the solicitors should identify which considerations influenced the decision not to do so and why the costs of continuing the proceeding would be justified.

4.2.3 The technical defences referred to are set out below:
   a) where the notice is defective and the court is unlikely to exercise a discretion;
   b) the notice is not in the prescribed form or in a form substantially to the same effect;
   c) the tenant's name has been inserted incorrectly;

    d)   the ground set out in the notice does not match with that pleaded in the particulars of claim or where the particulars of claim do not set out the ground relied on;

    e)   the notice does not give sufficient details or particulars;

    f)   the material dates are omitted or incorrectly stated;

    g)   the validity of the notice has lapsed;

    h)   the notice has not been served correctly;

    i)   the pleadings are defective; or

    j)   possession proceedings have been improperly brought.

4.3 Substantive Defences

4.3.1 Legal aid is likely to be granted where there is a substantive defence to a possession action. This will include defences which turn on the reasonableness of a possession order being made, even if the ground for possession has been made out by the Plaintiff. Whilst set-off can be a complete defence where the counter-claim is an amount equal or greater than the sum claimed by the Plaintiff, it is not a substantive defence when it is the only defence relied on.

4.4 Suspended possession orders

4.3.1 Legal aid is unlikely to be granted where the probable order would be a suspended possession order, eg, where rent arrears are not in dispute, reasonableness is not being asserted as a defence, and the only issue is the terms on which a suspended order will be made.

4.5 Anti-social injunctions

4.5.1 Legal aid is unlikely to be granted to defend an application either where the conduct is admitted or the evidence against the tenant is overwhelming. It would not be reasonable for legal aid to be granted where undertakings are likely to be accepted by the court.

4.5.2 Legal aid is likely to be granted to defend the proceedings if the alleged conduct is disputed and/or it is likely that possession proceedings may subsequently be sought (under **Schedule 2 grounds 14 or 14A of the Housing Act 1988** as amended by the **Housing Act 1996**) and a substantive defence including the issue of reasonableness would be raised by the tenant.

4.6 Possession for anti-social behaviour

4.6.1 Legal aid is unlikely to be granted where the conduct is admitted or the proceedings have been issued as a result of breached undertakings. If the client is vulnerable or has community care needs (which led to the breach) reasonableness may be in issue and legal aid may, exceptionally, be granted.

4.6.2 Legal aid is likely to be granted if the alleged conduct is disputed and a substantive defence including the issue of reasonableness can be raised by the tenant.

4.7 Introductory tenancies

4.7.1 Legal aid is unlikely to be granted if a solicitor is instructed after the service of the preliminary notice but before the expiry of the 14 day period. It would not be reasonable to grant legal aid if the tenant has not yet instigated the internal review procedure.

4.7.2   Legal aid is unlikely to be granted unless the tenant reasonable prospects of establishing any of the following:

    a)   the tenancy was not 'introductory' at the date the proceedings were issued;

    b)   the Section 128 notice is defective or was not served;

    c)   the proceedings have been commenced prematurely.

4.7.3   A tenant wishing to challenge the decision to give preliminary notice, the decision on review, or the procedure/handling of the review may do so by way of judicial review. Solicitors will be expected to justify the decision to pursue judicial review rather than the alternative of making a complaint to an Ombudsman.

4.8   Suitable Alternative Accommodation

4.8.1   Legal aid is unlikely to be granted to defend a discretionary ground for possession where a local authority certificate is available (confirming that it will provide suitable alternative accommodation) unless the accommodation can clearly be shown to be unsuitable or not available within a reasonable period of time and/or reasonableness is in issue.

4.8.2   Where a discretionary ground is relied on the tenant should make enquires of the local authority as to whether it will provide such a certificate. A private client faced with such proceedings would be likely to do so before taking a decision to defend or continue defending the proceedings. Whilst the certificate does not provide details of the address or size of the suitable alternative accommodation solicitors should consider whether or not the accommodation is suitable in accordance with the **Schedule 2 Part III, paras 2 to 6 of the Housing Act 1988.**

4.8.3   If the landlord has offered suitable alternative accommodation, solicitors will be expected to report to the area office on the court's likely view as to the suitability of that accommodation.

4.8.4   If the local authority subsequently makes a certificate available solicitors will be expected to report to the area office on the merits of the case.

4.9   Rent Arrears

4.9.1   Legal aid is unlikely to be granted to a tenant where rent arrears are the only issue and the arrears are not in dispute unless a substantive defence can be established on the basis of reasonableness. It would not usually be reasonable to grant legal aid to defend unless a significant issue of fact or law has been raised.

4.9.2   Legal aid is likely to be granted to a tenant if it can be shown that there are no arrears of rent and/or the tenant has a valid counterclaim for a sum exceeding the alleged arrears (eg damages for breach of quiet enjoyment or for disrepair) or where the issue of reasonableness is asserted.

4.9.3   It should be noted that where the delay in payment has been generated by delay/failure of a local authority, either to determine or to make housing benefit payments, that delay/failure is not a valid defence to the proceedings. Such delay/failure may, however, go to the issue of reasonableness where a reasonableness defence is being asserted. If not, the tenant may be able to seek an adjournment to clarify the housing benefit position and, either await a determination or use the local authority's complaint system to generate a decision.

4.9.4 Legal aid is likely to be granted to a private landlord if he/she can show that the tenant is in arrears of rent and has sufficient means to satisfy any judgement which may be made against him/her.

4.10 Service Charges

4.10.1 As **section 81 Housing Act 1996** places a restriction on re-entry/forfeiture whilst service charges are in dispute, legal aid is unlikely to be granted where service charge arrears are the only issue in dispute as it is unlikely that an immediate order for possession would be made. As the jurisdiction of the Leasehold Valuation Tribunal (LVT) has been extended to determine service charge issues, there is an alternative no cost venue. County court proceedings may be referred to the LVT by an application to the court by either party. Legal aid will normally be refused where the LVT provides an effective way of pursuing/defending the claim. There are cases where a reference to the LVT is not appropriate, ie where a determination needs to be made whether the freeholder is entitled to claim for the item of work under the lease (as distinct from the reasonableness of the cost of that item).

4.11 Accelerated Possession Procedure

4.11.1 Legal aid is unlikely to be granted in cases that fall within the accelerated possession procedure under Civil Procedure Rules, Schedule 2 CCR Order 49 Rules 6 and 6A, unless, following consideration of the papers, the matter is listed by the court for an oral hearing.

4.11.2 Where the following issues arise:
a) a dispute as to the nature of the tenancy;
b) defence to the claim for possession;
c) it is argued that the case does not come within the accelerated procedure; or
d) there is some defect in the application

solicitors may assist tenants to make representations to the court either by assisting the tenant to complete the Form N11A or by preparing an affidavit. Legal aid is unlikely to be granted to cover the solicitor's assistance with the client's representations.

4.11.3 The decision as to whether or not to hold an oral hearing is one taken by the court on the papers. Until there is a decision that the matter should be listed for an oral hearing it would not be reasonable to grant full representation. One the matter has been listed for an oral hearing legal aid may be applied for in the usual way.

4.12 Warrants to suspend possession/execution

4.12.1 A solicitor would not normally be employed in proceedings relating only to rent arrears or for an application to suspend a warrant of possession or execution as these applications generally do not raise any significant issues of fact or law. Legal aid is unlikely to be granted unless a significant issue of fact or law can be shown. **Examples** of cases which involve complex issues of law may be where a non party is trying to stop the eviction, or where it is asserted that the landlord has waived the breach by subsequent acceptance of rent and/or other conduct.

5   HOMELESSNESS
5.1   Appeal to a County Court

5.1.1   A right of appeal to a county court exists from an unfavourable decision of a local housing authority in relation to either the eligibility for assistance, what duty, if any, is owed, referral to another local authority, suitability of accommodation and the reviews of those decisions, where available. Any appeal from a decision of a county court is to the Court of Appeal.

5.1.2   Legal aid is likely to be granted to an applicant who is dissatisfied with a decision by the local housing authority where a point of law can be shown. The appeal is on 'any point of law arising from the decision, or as the case may be, the original decision'. A point of law arising from the original decision will arise if there is no decision on the review or if the error of law was repeated in the review or not rectified by the review. What will be in issue on an appeal on a point of law is likely to be largely the same as any grounds for judicial review.

5.1.3   Legal aid is unlikely to be granted where:
   a) the 21 days time limit for appeal has expired or
   b) what is in issue is not a point of law but rather a difference of opinion or judgement between the housing authority and the applicant on the facts of the case.

5.2   Judicial Review

5.2.1   In view of the provision of the appeal procedure referred to above the majority of cases will fall to be dealt with in a county court. However, judicial review remains an available remedy in appropriate circumstances.

5.2.2   Legal aid is likely to be granted where the application stands a reasonable prospect of success ie the decision or failure to act can be shown to be unlawful, perverse or procedurally improper and where eg:
   a) the housing authority unreasonably refused to extend the time (under section 202) to apply for a review;
   b) two housing authorities are at odds eg as to local connection;
   c) the housing authority refuse to exercise the power to provide/continue to provide accommodation;
   d) the housing authority simply fails to make a decision so the applicant cannot request a review eg refuses to accept an application for accommodation;
   e) the applicant seeks to challenge their allocation assessment or the legality of the housing authority's allocation scheme;
   f) the suitability of interim accommodation secured under section 188 is to be challenged;
   g) the applicant seeks to challenge an unlawful policy;
   h) the applicant is outside the 21 day period for an appeal where there is

good reason for the delay (no power exists to permit the time stipulated in **section 204(2)** to be extended).

5.2.3   Applications for legal aid will not be granted:
   a)   until the applicant has exhausted all available remedies
   b)   the housing authority has been notified of the proposed litigation and given a reasonable opportunity to respond. A letter before action should always be sent (**R v Horsham District Council ex parte Wenman**).

6   MORTGAGE REPOSSESSION
6.1   Possible defence
6.1.1   Legal aid is likely to be granted to the borrower to defend proceedings brought by the lender where there are issues of fact and/or law for consideration by the court. This is likely to be the case when one or more of the following issues arise:
   a)   allegations of fraud;
   b)   allegations of duress/undue influence (see below);
   c)   where there are linked or (imminent) concurrent proceedings involving the borrower's spouse/co-habitee/trustee in bankruptcy;
   d)   where it might be appropriate for a party to be joined;
   e)   cases where there are counterclaims.

6.2   No substantive defence
6.2.1   Legal aid is unlikely to be granted in circumstances where:
   a)   There is no substantive defence to the claim which relates to arrears only (given the
   operation of the Administration of Justice Act and the case of **Cheltenham & Gloucester Building Society v Norgan** in most cases the issues are straightforward).
   b)   Judgement has been entered and the adviser has been consulted as to setting aside a warrant of possession in an arrears only case.
   c)   The borrower has been advised by a solicitor in a duress/undue influence case - see the guidelines in **Royal Bank of Scotland v Etteridge**.
   d)   There is no substantive defence but there is a procedural irregularity. In these circumstances, a worthwhile outcome will have to be shown as a realistic possibility. A private client would be unlikely to incur the costs involved in defending the proceedings if the only aim is to establish that a technical defence of some sort is available and no approach has been made to the plaintiffs to resolve the matter.

6.3   Appeals
6.3.1   A legal aid certificate to pursue an appeal may be justified if the discretion of the District Judge has been exercised unreasonably, or the District Judge has misdirected himself in law and there is real advantage to be derived in pursuing an appeal. Legal aid is not likely to be granted if there has been lengthy delay before consideration of an appeal and/or there is limited benefit to be derived from pursuing the appeal. A legal aid certificate to resist an appeal by an unsuccessful plaintiff lender is likely to be granted unless there is no significant benefit to be derived from defending such an

appeal. Legal aid to pursue an appeal to the Court of Appeal will only be justified when there appears to be real benefit to be derived by the borrower as well as reasonable grounds for an appeal. A certificate limited only to counsel's opinion would be likely to be granted initially, whether or not leave has been granted.

6.4   Litigation about the sale price and timing of the sale

6.4.1   A legal aid certificate for an action or counterclaim in this context is likely to be granted if there is, or is likely to be, favourable evidence obtained by a valuer's report or other evidence and the quantum justifies legal aid. Legal aid is less likely to be granted if there is a mortgage income guarantee scheme in operation as this clearly makes timing less crucial (although value may remain an issue).

6.5   Costs

6.5.1   A legal aid certificate can be sought to cover attending a taxation of the lender's solicitor's costs under **section 70 Solicitors' Act 1974**. Legal aid is likely to be granted only in exceptional circumstances where the costs, and the reduction likely to be achieved, are considerable (£3,000 or more). Legal aid is not likely to be granted where the likely reduction is small and/or the prospects of obtaining a worthwhile reduction are slim. It is not reasonable for legal aid to be granted where the taxing officer's role is inquisitional and is to decide what sums are fair and reasonable, so separate legal representation is usually not necessary.

7   MISCELLANEOUS ISSUES

7.1   Unlawful occupiers

7.1.1   Legal aid is likely to be granted to defend proceedings where there are issues of law and/or fact which can be brought before the court and there is a substantive defence, eg:

• The client asserts that a tenancy or licence exists which has not been validly determined.

• There is an intermediate undetermined tenancy or licence.

• There is a procedural irregularity. (Note that in all cases a worthwhile outcome will have to be shown as a realistic possibility. A private client would be unlikely to incur the costs involved in defending the proceedings if the only aim is to establish that a technical defence of some sort is available and no approach has been made to the plaintiffs to resolve the matter.)

• It is alleged that the occupier has acquired possessory title (twelve years' adverse possession).

• The client asserts that he has been given a licence to remain by the Local Authority. A legal aid certificate may be justified if such a licence has secure status and if there are real benefits to be obtained by asserting this defence.

NB: In the event of legal aid being granted a limitation to the initial summary hearing is likely to be imposed - it is at that point that the court will decide whether there is a triable issue.

7.1.2   Legal aid is unlikely to be granted in circumstances where occupiers are:
- Persons who have entered the premises as trespassers (and their status has not changed) and an interim possession order under the **Criminal Justice and Public Order Act 1994** is sought.
- Persons occupying hostels.
- Persons sharing accommodation with the landlord or the landlord's family.
- Persons staying on in holiday lets when the holiday lease has expired.
- Persons living rent-free.

7.2   Mobile Homes

7.2.1   Under the Mobile Homes Act 1983 either party may apply to the County Court for a declaration as to various matters eg utilities, changing the pitch, refusal of agreement to a sale, etc. Possession proceedings may be brought by site owners.

7.2.2   A legal aid certificate is likely to be granted to an occupant of a mobile home where negotiation has been unsuccessful and/or the involvement of other agencies has not resolved the dispute. Some cases may involve several site occupants. Whilst all occupants of mobile homes will have their own particular circumstances and each eligible owner/renter of a mobile home should apply for legal aid advisers should consider the possibility of generic issues being funded jointly.

7.2.3   Legal aid is unlikely to be granted circumstances where:
- The applicant is a person renting a mobile home and the only issue is that of non-payment of rent and there is no defence to proceedings.
- The advantage to be obtained by seeking a declaration in the County Court is limited in scope and a fee-paying client would not be advised to issue proceedings.
- An alternative remedy in the form of referral of an issue to the Local Authority is available. An explanation for not using such an alternative must be given in the application form.

7.2.4   Legal aid is likely to be refused because of lack of information if the following details are not supplied with the application for legal aid:
  a) an adequate statement of case setting out the issues clearly;
  b) a copy of the agreement if an agreement has been provided;
  c) copies of any correspondence with the site owner;
  d) details of the breach of the agreement.

7.3   Travellers

7.3.1   A civil legal aid certificate may be justified either for judicial review proceedings in relation to a local authority's decisions/facilities or where proceedings have been issued under the Mobile Homes Act against travellers. Civil legal aid/ABWOR is not available for any criminal/civil proceedings under the Criminal Justice and Public Order Act 1994 before the magistrates' court.

7.3.2   Solicitors will need to consider and advise as to the extent to which others are concerned jointly with or having the same interest as the applicant and should therefore defray costs under regulation 32 of the Civil Legal Aid (General) Regulations 1989. The Board must consider the applicability of Regulation 32, although in many instances the applicant's case may not be the same but similar to that of others.

Contracting for advice and assistance is due to be introduced on 1 January 2000. After this date the guidance may be subject to change. The Funding Code relating to the merits test for civil legal aid is due to come into force on 1 April 2000. This will supersede the guidance relating to civil legal aid contained in the Housing Guidance.

For further information regarding changes, readers should contact the Legal Aid Board, 85 Gray's Inn Road, London WC1X 8AA (tel: 0171 813 1000)

Control of condensation in buildings

BS 5250: 1989 (extracts)

SECTION TWO: THE NATURE OF CONDENSATION

3 Behaviour of water vapour in air

At a given temperature air is capable of containing a limited amount of water as invisible vapour; the warmer the air the more water vapour it can contain. If moisture-laden air comes into contact with a cold surface, either inside the building or an interface within the building fabric, condensation will occur at the temperature at which the air becomes saturated (dewpoint).

Water vapour in the air exerts a pressure, the vapour pressure, and so air containing a large mass of water vapour has a higher vapour pressure than drier air. This pressure will cause vapour to diffuse from high to low pressure areas. The term usually used to describe whether air is dry or water laden is relative humidity (r.h.).

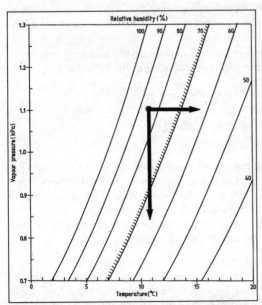

Figure 1 shows the inter-relationship of these factors and is called a psychrometric chart. The vapour pressure is plotted on the vertical axis with the temperature on the horizontal axis. The curved lines show the percentage relative humidity resulting from the combination of temperature and vapour pressure. Percentage relative humidity is a good indicator of the risk of condensation, mould growth and degradation of absorbent materials. Where the air remains around or above 70% r.h. for lengthy periods, there is

Figure 1. Relationship between air temperature, vapour pressure (moisture content) and relative humidity

a high risk of condensation and mould growth on some part of the external fabric. The arrows on the chart indicate that the risk can be reduced by increasing the temperature, by decreasing the vapour pressure or by a combination of these two factors.

NOTE The inter-relationship of moisture content and temperature is given in greater detail in appendix A [of BS 5260].

4   Causes of condensation

4.1   *General*

Two categories of condensation should be distinguished:

(a) surface condensation; and

(b) interstitial condensation.

The former occurs on visible surfaces within the building whilst the latter occurs within or between the layers of the building envelope.

Most materials will absorb water vapour from the environment: some, subjected to high humidity, can absorb moisture sufficiently to cause damage even though no actual condensation has taken place. In considering the risk of condensation, consideration should therefore also be given to the actual levels of humidity to which materials will be exposed.

Sources of water vapour will include atmospheric moisture, construction water, the occupants and their activities (see tables 1, 2 and 3).

4.2   *Causes of surface condensation*

Surface condensation will occur on surfaces which are at or below the dewpoint of the air immediately adjacent to them eg, internal surface of external elements of a building and cold pipes and cisterns within a building.

The two parameters which control this effect are the temperature of the surface and the vapour pressure of the air.

The temperature of the surface will depend on the following factors:

(a) the type(s), amount, time and rate of heating of the building;

(b) the ventilation rate;

(c) the thermal properties of the element and its surface finish;

(d) the external temperature.

The vapour pressure of the air is determined by:

(1) the water vapour production;

(2) the ventilation rate;

(3) the moisture content of the replacement 'fresh' air;

(4) the ability of the building fabric and contents to absorb or desorb water vapour (sponge effect). This will reduce or increase the vapour pressure depending on whether the building is cooling or heating.

Anything which warms surfaces or reduces the vapour pressure of the air will reduce the effect of problems due to surface condensation.

4.3   *Causes of interstitial condensation*

4.3.1   **General**   The interior of buildings in winter will usually be warmer and the air contain more moisture than outside, so heat and water vapour will try to migrate out through the structure, both by air leakage and by diffusion.

For air leakage, rates of flow will depend on wind and stack pressures and on the dimensions of openings, joints and cracks. Unless these gaps are sealed, it has been found that the dominant internal/external transport mechanism of water vapour is by mass movement of air.

For diffusion, rates of flow will vary depending on the interior/exterior conditions and the thermal and vapour resistance properties of each part of the structure. This process alone is able to transport sufficient water vapour through the structure to cause interstitial condensation.

Interstitial condensation occurs within the fabric of a building when the temperature of some part of the structure equals the dewpoint. At this temperature the air is saturated; thus further vapour passing through the structure will condense rather than increase the vapour pressure.

Such condensation is more likely to occur on the surfaces of materials within a structure, particularly on the warm side of relatively vapour resistant layers, but it is possible to have condensation occurring within the material when the dewpoint and the structural temperatures coincide throughout the material.

It is possible to have interstitial condensation on more than one surface in a structure due to moisture evaporating from one surface and recondensing on a colder one.

4.3.2 **Reverse condensation**   The phenomenon of reverse condensation or summer condensation is most frequently observed when the sun shines on damp walls. It is caused by the moisture in the wall being vapourized by the heating effect of the sun; the resulting pressure difference drives the water vapour towards the inside of the building. If a vapour control layer is included in the construction, interstitial condensation may occur on the outside face where it may run down to affect vulnerable materials.

This is most likely to be observed in the thermal improvement of solid walls by the use of internal insulation systems. Although the severity of the problem is not known it is more common in thin masonry walls, walls of an absorbent nature or on walls which remain saturated because of their exposure. The moisture content of such walls and the consequent risk of reverse condensation may be reduced by a weatherproof treatment or system. Weatherproofing should be applied to the outer surface of the wall and should be of low vapour resistance or be vented.

Reverse condensation should not be confused with the problems of interstitial condensation that can occur in building elements where the environmental conditions on both sides of that element differ from those normally encountered (for example in cold stores where the temperature conditions on both sides of the element are the reverse of those normally encountered in buildings).

5   The effects of condensation and high humidity

5.1   *General*

Condensation can reveal itself in a number of ways, the most common being the presence of condensate, mould growth, decay of timber, and corrosion of metals.

5.2 *Condensate*

Condensation may be treated as nuisance condensation, provided that the condensate can be adequately dealt with by drainage or by mopping it up before it collects and runs to vulnerable parts. For example, such nuisance condensation often occurs on single glazed windows in bathrooms and kitchens.

5.3 *Mould growth*

Mould growth is often associated with surface condensation and damp houses can provide good conditions for its development (see MANT Report, in the list of publications referred to).

Mould spores exist in large numbers in the atmosphere and to germinate need a nutrient, oxygen, a suitable temperature and moisture. Sources of nutrition are widespread in buildings and the internal environment provides a suitable temperature for growth. As oxygen is also always present, mould growth is principally dependent upon the moisture conditions at surfaces and the length of time these conditions persist. Studies have shown that moulds do not necessarily require the presence of water. As a guide, if the average relative humidity within a room stays about 70% for a long period of time the localized relative humidity at external wall surfaces will be higher and is likely to support the germination and growth of moulds.

5.4 *Dampness*

Condensation or dampness can occur on or in furniture and furnishings if they are situated in unheated spaces or in parts of rooms sheltered from heating systems. Typical cases are unheated bedrooms, cupboards or wardrobes placed against external walls, and roof spaces.

Interstitial condensation can cause dampness of components in a structure, but this may be inconsequential. An example is condensation on the outer leaf of a masonry cavity wall, where the amount of condensate may be small compared to the effect of wetting by rain.

5.5 *Degradation of materials*

Sustained condensation may cause decay of timber or corrosion of metal coverings and/or components and so should be termed harmful. Hygroscopic materials should not be used in locations where a high relative humidity is maintained as they may degrade even though no condensate is deposited upon them. Persistent timber moisture contents in excess of 20% (by mass) may lead to decay. Over a winter season, absorbent and hygroscopic materials are likely to accumulate moisture; during the summer this will tend to evaporate. The rate of this evaporation is difficult to calculate, but it should be borne in mind when assessing whether condensation is harmful.

In addition to mould growth and deterioration of fittings or components, condensation can cause dimensional changes, reduction of thermal resistance, migration of salts, liberation of chemicals or electrical failure.

SECTION THREE: DESIGN TO CONTROL CONDENSATION
8 Design principles

8.1 *General*

8.1.1 The fundamental principle of designing to minimize condensation is to
maintain a balance of the three factors
shown in figure 3 in order to achieve
either low vapour pressure and/or
high structural temperature.

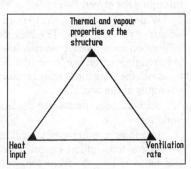

Figure 3. Balance of factors

8.1.2 **Controlling surface condensation** To
minimize surface condensation it is
necessary to do one or more of the
following:
(a) obtain low vapour pressures by
ventilating, or reducing moisture
input in the building;
(b) obtain high surface temperatures by providing more insulation and/or
increasing the heat input.

8.1.3 **Controlling interstitial condensation** To minimize interstitial condensation it
is necessary to do one or more of the following:
(a) obtain low vapour pressures by ventilating, or reducing moisture input in
the building;
(b) use materials of high vapour resistance near to the inner, warm side of
the construction;
(c) use materials of low vapour resistance, or provide ventilated cavities, near
to the outer, colder side of the construction;
(d) obtain higher internal temperatures by increasing the heat input and/or
providing more insulation;
(e) use materials of low thermal resistance near to the inner side of the
construction;
(f) use materials of high thermal resistance near to the outer side of the
construction.

Note that any one particular procedure taken in isolation may not necessarily
minimize the risk of condensation.

8.2 *Occupant activity and heating and ventilating regime*

In considering the effect of occupant requirements and activity on building
plan and structure and on heating and ventilation requirements, designers
should be aware that:
(a) occupants and some domestic appliances generate moisture;
(b) rising fuel costs can introduce a reluctance to provide adequate heating
for buildings or alter the type and pattern of heating;
(c) patterns of use of buildings have changed and can change eg. there has
been an increase in intermittent heating of dwellings due to alterations
in working patterns.

8.3 *Building configuration*

In a heated building, air will rise and leak from the building via the roof space
and through gaps and ventilators, carrying moisture with it; this is the so-

called 'stack effect'. Replacement colder drier air will be pulled in at low level through gaps or ventilators.

Wind will tend to push fresh air in from one side of a building and stale air out of the other side. The balance of these two effects will be the natural infiltration movement: generally it is in at low level on the windward side and out at high level on the leeward side. At high level, windward and low level, leeward, the direction will be found to alter depending on the relative strengths of the two effects.

Such air movements are the main cause of moisture movement within buildings.

In addition, water vapour will tend to spread from areas of high vapour pressure to those of low vapour pressure (irrespective of the relative humidity and temperature), ie, from areas of high moisture content to areas of low moisture content.

Thus in the absence of other constraints, moisture producing areas should be located with regard to these flows so that air and moisture tend to flow directly out of the building rather than spreading within it, especially to unheated areas.

If it is intended to use mechanical air movers in some form, the above is of less importance. Fans will almost certainly alter the direction of natural flows (but only of course whilst they are running).

8.4 *Construction*

There are many forms of construction available for walls, floors, glazing and roofs and often the choice will be made on grounds other than for condensation control, eg structural requirements or client preferences. However, the following principles should be considered.

It is important to match the thermal response of the internal layers with the proposed heating and activity regime. High mass elements will warm and cool slowly (slow thermal response) and they are therefore more suitable for buildings which are heated for long periods. Low mass elements will warm and cool quickly (fast thermal response) and are particularly suitable for infrequent heating.

The more a part of the structure is insulated, the warmer will be the internal surface for the same room heat input and hence there will be less of a surface condensation risk. Conversely, layers to the outside of any extra insulation will be colder, and therefore more prone to interstitial condensation. If that condensation is judged to be harmful, then steps need to be taken to limit the amount of moisture reaching the colder elements by using vapour control layers or inner layers of relatively high vapour resistance or by having some ventilated airspace between the insulation and the outer elements.

Thermal bridging should be minimized and decisions made on how much nuisance condensation is to be tolerated, balanced by the cost of reducing it. For example, consideration should be given to nuisance condensation on cold water pipes, cisterns and to areas around window and door openings.

8.5   *Heating and ventilation*

8.5.1   **Heating systems**   Heating will normally be tailored to personal comfort in the building, taking the cost into consideration. However, in addition, for condensation control, it should match the combined effects of occupancy pattern, building mass and insulation, the period it is intended to heat the building, and any ventilation system, natural or induced. The principles are explained by reference to extreme conditions.

If the heating maintains comfort levels in the whole building at all times, condensation problems will be minimized, but costs will be high. If the heating is infrequent and only in one room, that room may suffer condensation because the structure will remain cold, and moisture resulting from the sponge effect will add to moisture being produced by the occupants; other rooms will also remain cold and moisture will migrate to them causing severe condensation problems. These infrequent heating effects will be exacerbated if the structure has a high thermal mass and if the heating is purely convective. A whole range of conditions exist between these extremes.

8.5.2   **Ventilation**   If stale air is extracted from each room and replaced by external air (and loss in temperature compensated for by heating), condensation risk is again minimized, but costs are high. At the other extreme, if minimal ventilation exists and the air movement is from the moisture-producing areas into the rest of the building, problems are likely.

The ideal ventilation system would extract air from the moisture producing areas to outside and replace it with fresh air flowing in via the other rooms. This would reduce the amount of moisture at source, prevent its spread and ventilate the whole building with fresh air.

Adequate ventilation for condensation control exceeds the minimum rate of fresh air change necessary for health and comfort and should normally be between 0.5 and 1.5 air changes per hour for the whole building (see table 4 in appendix B [of BS 5260] and BS 5925).

8.6   *Heating and ventilating costs*

Control of condensation is always carried out at some cost and having designed the building with its heating and ventilating system the construction and running costs can be determined. If these are not acceptable some alteration to the heating and ventilating system will be required, possibly in conjunction with improvements to the building fabric. Where achieving these acceptable running costs involves compromise, this may result in increased condensation risks.

NOTE 1   An assessment of heating costs can be obtained by reference to a suitable computer program such as BREDEM, or by reference to BS 8211: Part 1 or the Department of Energy Notes 'Cutting Home Energy Costs' (see publications referred to).

NOTE 2   The designer should agree with the client the heating programme required to produce the minimum amount of heating necessary to minimize condensation. The building owners should then decide whether or not to retain sufficient control of the heating system to ensure that this heating is provided. Where this obligation is transferred to users, they should be provided with simple operating instructions. To avoid misunderstandings in landlord/tenant situations the obligations of each party should be defined in the leasing agreement.

8.7 *Risk assessment*

At this stage it is advisable to make full checks on the likelihood of surface and interstitial condensation and determine if these would be harmful. The calculation procedures are given in appendix C and appendix D. Saturation vapour pressures are given in table 5 and thermal and vapour properties are given in tables 6, 7 and 8 in appendix B. If the checks are considered satisfactory, then construction can proceed as far as condensation control is concerned; if not, it means that the design will have to be altered by following through the above procedure again. Vapour resistances and permeances of materials can be expressed in many varied and unusual units; conversion factors to change some of the more commonly occurring ones into the units used in this standard are given in appendix E and table 12.

9   Application of design principles

9.1 *General*

Basic principles for condensation control have been outlined in clause 8. The following clauses provide more detailed guidance on building according to those principles and are set out for ease of reference. It is essential that designers read the general information on the particular element before referring to the specific examples (eg, read 9.3.1 before 9.3.2).

SECTION FOUR: EXISTING BUILDINGS

10   Diagnosis and remedial work

10.1 *General*

It should be determined what precautions to prevent condensation have been included in the building and these should be retained, adapted or improved.

Where a building is to be upgraded the new design should, as far as possible, follow the guidance set out in section three.

If the building is merely to be repaired, then a diagnosis of its existing condensation problems must be made and remedial action taken along the lines described below.

In either case, it will be necessary for an investigation to be carried out to identify all other sources of dampness in the existing structure and for these to be eliminated before dealing with condensation problems.

10.2 *Diagnosis of dampness*

NOTE It is not possible to device an infallible system for differentiating between condensation and other sources of dampness. A building element may be damp for a number of reasons, for example, because of rising damp, condensation, water penetration, or presence of hygroscopic salts. The following guidance should be of assistance in an investigation.

10.2.1 **History** Enquiries should be made into the recent history of the building to determine whether it has been left unoccupied for any length of time or whether it has been open to the weather or flooded.

If the building has remained unoccupied for come time, it is not possible to determine every area in which condensation problems related to occupancy have previously occurred. Potential areas of risk will have to be discovered by an examination of the structure taking into account the proposed use of the building. The risk of interstitial condensation within the structure may need to be assessed using the methods set out in appendix D.

Areas showing the effects of condensation such as mould growth and staining, are more easily identified where a building has recently been occupied. If the inspection takes place during cold weather while the premises are in occupation or soon after they are vacated, damp patches may be evident.

The opportunity should be taken to obtain as much relevant information as possible from the occupants. For example the following factors may need to be considered.

(a) The number and ages of occupants.
(b) The occupancy pattern.
(c) The heating pattern.
(d) Family economics: how much do they spend on heating?
(e) Types of domestic appliances which are likely to generate water vapour such as cookers, washing machines, driers and free-standing room heating equipment.
(f) Whether the system for washing clothes is one which will generate a lot of moisture within the dwelling.
(g) The weather and seasonal dependency of the phenomena.
(h) Ventilation: what means of mechanical ventilation are installed and are they used?
(i) Whether or not the family open the windows and when.
(j) The extent and position of insulation.
(k) Internal temperatures and humidities.
(l) Comparison with adjacent or similar properties.

This information should be considered in the light of the principles outlined in 8.1 to assist in an assessment of the building.

10.2.2 **Causes of dampness** The causes of any dampness other than that resulting from condensation should first be determined.

The following is a suggested check list.

(a) Roof leaks, eg, valleys, flashings around parapets and chimneys.
(b) Defects in the rainwater drainage system.
(c) Defects in wastepipes.
(d) Leaks in the plumbing system.
(e) Penetration around door and window openings.
(f) Defects in damp proof courses and membranes.
(g) Area of wall surface affected by hygroscopic salts.
(h) Water transmitted by projecting elements, ie. parapets, balconies, porches, etc.

10.2.3 **Recognition of surface condensation** Surface condensation occurs where the temperature falls below the dewpoint temperature of the adjacent air and may result in mould growth. This is likely to be found in the following locations.

(a) Corners of rooms, especially external corners.
(b) Lintels, reveals and sills.
(c) Behind furniture placed against external walls.
(d) Within built-in furniture on external walls.

(e) Floor/external wall junctions especially those containing ring beams.

(f) On the internal surface of north facing walls.

10.2.4 **Recognition of hygroscopic effects** Certain salts will absorb moisture from the atmosphere to such an extent that, if they are present in brickwork, damp patches will appear in plaster covering the bricks every time the weather becomes sufficiently humid and will fade away when dry weather returns.

The affected areas may relate to a single brick and such areas often show a well defined edge. Typical locations to be affected are chimney breasts, brickwork previously affected by rising damp or damp penetration through the wall from adjoining structures.

10.2.5 **Recognition of rising damp** Water travelling through a wall containing soluble salts, will dissolve and carry them with it. As the water evaporates at or just below the surface of the wall, these salts crystallize out (efflorescence). When this occurs at the surface, the crystals will form a fragile feathery 'growth' usually white in colour and often forming 'tide' marks. When it occurs below the surface, for example behind a paint film or plaster, the crystals will grow and may disrupt the paint film or force the plaster off the wall.

The presence of efflorescence is an indication that water has arrived at the surface from within the wall and not as condensate from the atmosphere. Conversely however, the absence of efflorescence is not proof that the dampness is caused by condensation.

If, for example, because of the presence of a thermal bridge, or because of variations in air temperature or humidity at different points in a room, water condenses on a non-absorbent surface, it will form droplets. Rising damp does not appear in this form.

10.2.6 **Measurement of dampness** Accurate measurements of moisture contents of brick or mortar cannot be obtained by the use of electrical moisture meters because the presence of salts increases the electrical conductance of the water, giving a falsely high reading. Gravimetric methods carried out on samples taken from the fabric give the most reliable results, while the use of a chemical absorption type meter will give a result in a short space of time which is almost as reliable.

One of the most reliable ways of differentiating between dampness due to condensate and that due to rising damp is to compare the moisture contents of samples of masonry, or preferably mortar, from within the depth of the wall and near the inner surface of the wall. Samples from within the wall will not be damp if surface condensation is the sole cause.

10.2.7 **Condensation on thermal bridges within the roof-spaces** In many cases wet patches on ceilings close to the wall may be due to condensate running down from within the roof space. This phenomenon occurs more often in warm deck flat roofs where the perimeter wall is for example thermally bridged by the lintel of a window which extends into the roof space.

10.3 *Damage caused by dampness*

10.3.1 **Damage to structure** The most likely forms of damage to structure are decay in timber or cellulose products, corrosion of metals or excessive moisture movement of materials. Dampness may cause distortion and in some cases serious weakening of sheet or thin slab materials, eg in roof decks or ceilings. Moisture trapped beneath impermeable roof finishes may, in hot weather, cause vapour pressure sufficient to cause damage to the roof finish.

Where inspection reveals damage, appropriate replacement, repair or preservative treatment should be carried out.

Any precautions against future condensation should ensure that further structural damage will be prevented. It is essential therefore that remedial treatment should be directed to overcoming harmful interstitial condensation as well as surface condensation. Freedom from the latter does not necessarily ensure that the former does not occur.

10.3.2 **Damage to finishes** Damage to decorations occurs mainly from surface condensation, but occasionally may be caused by interstitial condensation moisture for example, roof condensate dripping on to ceilings, or wall condensate drying inward and damaging surface finishes.

Mould growth on room surfaces, particularly in room corners, first appears as spots or small patches which may spread to form a furry layer usually grey-green, black or brown in colour. On paint it may show as pink or purple.

Soft distempers are liable to flake if repeatedly wetted and dried, whilst emulsion paints are more likely to remain undamaged. Moisture on the exposed surface tends to reduce the gloss of some impervious paints but otherwise does not cause damage. If moisture penetrates behind impervious paint films blistering of the paint may occur. In extreme cases the plaster may break down and/or loose its adhesion.

Repeated or prolonged absorption of condensate may cause distortion of sheet materials, eg plasterboard or fibreboard. Water absorbed from a surface may reach and break down an adhesive by which a surface finish is fixed. This may occur on floors or walls, but is more likely to be harmful in the case of ceilings when the effect of gravity adds to the risk of displacement of adhesive fixed tiles.

10.4 *Remedial works*

10.4.1 **Action to control condensation** It is essential that the action taken to achieve a technically and economically balanced system, planned to cope with the intended use of the building, is comprehensive. The design process should involve consideration of provision for heating and ventilating, as well as insulation.

10.4.2 **Heating** All surface condensation problems can, in principle, be solved by the application of heat to raise temperatures above the dewpoint and to evaporate existing dampness, coupled with adequate levels of ventilation.

A common cause of harmful condensation in existing buildings is lack of adequate heating. If the existing system is inadequate, a heating system should be installed with an output ample for the task required of it, designed in accordance with guidance given in 9.8.

Heating and insulation should always be considered together since there is often scope for a saving in capital cost as well as in running cost.

10.4.3 **Ventilation** It should be recognized that some energy will have to be expended on the removal of water vapour if condensation is to be controlled.

It is essential that adequate ventilation is provided to maintain the dewpoint temperature of the air below the inside surface temperature of the building envelope at all times. Provision of mechanical ventilation to kitchens and bathrooms is recommended and any replacement windows fitted in other rooms should include separate ventilators. Condensate drainage should be provided when single glazing is used.

10.4.4 **Insulation** It is important to note that little change in condensation risk, if any, will result from improvements in thermal insulation, however extensive, unless a satisfactory balance of heating and ventilation is achieved.

Sufficient insulation should be added to the fabric of the building in the best practical positions calculated to enable an equilibrium temperature condition to be achieved under the worst anticipated conditions, whereby the risks of either surface or interstitial condensation are reduced to a minimum.

10.5 *Mould growth*

10.5.1 **General** Mould growth is often associated with surface condensation and damp houses can provide good conditions for its development. Mould spores exist in large numbers in the atmosphere and to germinate need a nutrient, oxygen, a suitable temperature and moisture. Sources of nutrition are widespread in buildings and the internal environment provides a suitable temperature for growth. As oxygen is also always present, mould growth is principally dependent upon the moisture conditions at surfaces and the length of time these conditions persist. Studies have shown that moulds do not necessarily require the presence of water. As a guide, if the average relative humidity within a room stays above 70% for a long period of time the localized relative humidity at external wall surfaces will be higher and is likely to support the germination and growth of moulds.

10.5.2 **Treatment** Although the symptoms of mould growth are fairly easily dealt with by either washing with a household bleach diluted 1:4 followed by clean water or the use of a proprietory toxic wash, it is better to remove the cause of the mould growth, ie the moisture. Also available are proprietory anti-fungal paints and wallpaper pastes which can be used in areas where condensation occurs regularly. (See BRE Digest 139.)

11 Particular aspects

11.1 *Initial period at commencement of re-use*

It is important to remember that if the building has been unoccupied for a number of years in a state of disrepair a great deal of water may be present in the fabric and one or even two years may elapse before it has all dried out.

During this period, moisture may continue to appear on the walls, some of it as a result of evaporation from the fabric and some of it as condensation forming on the surfaces of parts of the envelope which, due to water absorbed within them, offer little thermal resistance. It is essential to recognize the danger of entrapping stored water behind new work such as dry lining to wells.

11.2 *Thermal insulating materials*

The insulation values of open cell or fibrous materials will be adversely affected if wetted. Remedial work should include drying out materials which are to be re-used to an optimum dryness. Precautions should be taken to prevent wetting of all new materials introduced into the structure.

The provision of protection against mechanical damage to insulating materials should be considered. (See 'Cavity insulation of masonry walls – dampness risks and how to minimize them', 'All about loft, tank and pipe insulation', 'Cutting home energy costs', 'Keep your home free from mould and damp'. For availability of these publications, see publications referred to.)

11.3 *Furniture*

Consideration should be given to removing built-in furniture from an outside wall, to allow heat to reach the wall from the room; otherwise water vapour would penetrate to these areas and condense, resulting in the growth of mould, not only on the well but also on the contents of the furniture.

11.4 *Larders and unheated stores*

Particular attention should be paid to the ventilation of larders, unheated storage spaces and enclosed porches. Water vapour migrates to these areas from adjacent heated spaces where the vapour pressure is higher. Consideration should be given to the heating and insulation of such storage spaces.

11.5 *Redecoration*

The materials used for decoration during this period should be capable of allowing moisture to evaporate through them without incurring damage. Neither wallpaper nor impervious paints should be used till the structure has achieved a near equilibrium condition with the prevailing internal conditions. Occupants should be warned that the drying out period will be protracted and be advised not to commence the decoration of walls until an equilibrium condition is attained.

11.6 *Heating*

Special problems in existing buildings arise because building owners may not provide the heating for their buildings, but devolve heating and its costs to tenants. In rented property it may benefit the owner to make a provision for background heating, some of the cost of which may be included in rent, so as to ensure that the building is not damaged by the accumulation of condensation.

11.7 *Ventilation*

In existing buildings special problems often arise because higher levels of comfort expectations, combined with rising costs of heating, have led to a reduction of unwanted air movements which have become apparent as draughts, for example by:
(a) removal of fireplaces;
(b) draught proofing as a cost effective method of energy saving.
Fortuitous means of natural ventilation have often, therefore, been eliminated.

While the removal of moisture at source by mechanical extraction, for example in kitchens, bathrooms and general moisture generating areas, is an obvious remedy, it needs to be remembered that the air extracted has to be replaced by incoming air, which in turn has to be heated.

In dealing with ventilation rates and methods in existing buildings, all the technical and economic considerations and methods of assessments given previously, should be employed.

Damp housing, mould growth, and symptomatic health state

Stephen D Platt, Claudia J Martin, Sonja M Hunt,
Chris W Lewis

British Medical Journal 24 June 1989

Abstract

Objective – To examine the relation between damp and mould growth and symptomatic ill health.

Design – Cross-sectional study of random sample of households containing children; separate and independent assessments of housing conditions (by surveyor) and health (structured interview by trained researcher).

Setting – Subjects' homes (in selected areas of public housing in Glasgow, Edinburgh, and London).

Subjects – Adult respondents (94% women) and 1169 children living in 597 households.

End points – Specific health symptoms and general evaluation of health among respondents and children over two weeks before interview; and score on general health questionnaire (only respondents).

Measurements and main results – Damp was found in 184 (30.8%) dwellings and actual mould growth in 274 (45.9%). Adult respondents living in damp and mouldy dwellings were likely to report more symptoms overall, including nausea and vomiting, blocked nose, breathlessness, backache, fainting, and bad nerves, than respondents in dry dwellings. Children living in damp and mouldy dwellings had a greater prevalence of respiratory symptoms (wheeze, sore throat, runny nose) and headaches and fever compared with those living in dry dwellings. The mean number of symptoms was higher in damp and mouldy houses and positively associated with increasing severity of dampness and mould (dose response relation). All these differences persisted after controlling for possible confounding factors such as household income, cigarette smoking, unemployment, and overcrowding. Other possible sources of bias that might invalidate the assumption of a causal link between housing conditions and ill health – namely, investigator bias, respondent bias, and selection bias – were also considered and ruled out.

Conclusion – Damp and mouldy living conditions have an adverse effect on symptomatic health, particularly among children.

Introduction

Showing a direct relation between damp housing and ill health is by no means straightforward. Firstly, those living in the worst housing conditions are likely to be experiencing other forms of adversity, such as low income and unemployment. Secondly, personal behaviour may also play a part in the

341

causation of ill health. An equally important methodological concern is the process of the data collection itself. If information about health and housing conditions is elicited in the same interview respondents may exaggerate the prevalence of problems, leading to a spurious association between the two phenomena. Moreover, the researchers themselves may influence reporting.

In 1986 we carried out a preliminary study in Edinburgh, which attempted to overcome these methodological difficulties by using a double blind research design.[1] Children living in damp houses, particularly where there was also mould growth, were reported to have higher rates of respiratory and gastrointestinal symptoms, aches and pains, and fever than children in dry dwellings. These differences could not be attributed to smoking or differences between damp and dry households regarding unemployment, income, overcrowding, or duration of tenancy. The numbers of households that included a child was not large enough (n=101), however, to permit a full analysis of the role of other possible confounding variables. Accordingly, we carried out a larger scale, more detailed investigation.

Subjects and methods

The study was conducted in three major cities: Edinburgh, Glasgow, and London. Within each city discrete geographical areas of public housing were identified in which (a) families with young children predominated; (b) the prevalence of damp housing was thought to be in the range of 25–50% of total dwellings; (c) socioeconomic state was likely to be fairly homogeneous; and (d) types of housing and structures of buildings, including any renovations, could be clearly specified. Two sites were chosen in Edinburgh, two in Glasgow, and one in London. Tenants' groups were contacted and their cooperation elicited. Lists of addresses at the chosen sites were obtained from the relevant housing departments. The intention was to achieve a sample of 500 eligible households in Edinburgh and in Glasgow and 200 in London. A random sample of addresses was drawn according to the total number of dwellings in the area.

Only those households with at least one child aged under 16 were eligible for inclusion in the study. As official statistics on the exact location of families with young children were not available the sample was identified in two ways: (a) at the time of the main health interview (see below) the interviewers identified suitable families by contacting each dwelling on the list; and (b) in two of the sites members of the tenants' association identified addresses on the list containing families who met the study criteria.

Two surveyors carried out an assessment of dampness (severity and type) and mould (severity and location) and details of the structure of the dwelling. Using an air sampler (Surface Air Systems) they extracted air samples from rooms and, where visible mould growth was present, a sample from each affected room was collected. A microbiologist estimated spore counts from the air samples and identified the fungi from air and walls when possible.

We devised and pretested two survey forms. The form for the house conditions survey contained items on type of building, location, number of rooms, dampness, mould, ventilation, insulation, and renovations. The health survey was a revised version of that used by Martin et al.[1] In the course of a structured interview the respondent (whenever possible the female householder) answered detailed questions about her own and her children's health during the past two weeks; smoking by all adults and children; type of heating, washing, and drying facilities; presence of pets; economic activity and occupation of all adults in the household; household income; and housing conditions and facilities.

The study was carried out during February–April 1988. Once the health interview had been completed the surveyors were instructed to visit the dwelling. The petri dishes containing air and wall mould samples were taken each day to the University of Strathclyde, where they were refrigerated and cultured. Air spore counts were calculated and fungi identified when possible. The surveyors and the microbiologist were blind to each other's findings and also to the findings of the health survey team.

We used four categorical independent variables relating to housing conditions. Households that received a house conditions survey were classified into three groups: those where there was no objective evidence of dampness or mould growth (dry), those with only damp, and those with mould (whether or not dampness was also present). The overall dampness in the household was calculated by averaging the score for each bedroom, sitting room, and kitchen on a four point scale of severity (0=none; 3=severe). Households in which the average dampness score exceeded zero (no dampness whatsoever) were divided into three approximately equal sized groups labelled mild (score ranging between 0.01 and 0.52), moderate (0.53 to 1.05), and severe (≥1.06). A similar procedure was adopted to divide households into four groups differing in average severity of mould (none, mild (0.01 to 0.45), moderate (0.46 to 0.77), and severe (≥0.78)).

The spore concentration per m^3 air was measured in the kitchen, living room, and bedrooms of households in Edinburgh and Glasgow visited by the surveyors. On the basis of preliminary work in Edinburgh (B Flanagan and C A Hunter, unpublished data) and elsewhere[2-4] we devised a five point scale (coded 1 to 5): low (≤100 viable spores/m^3 air), medium (101–300), high (301–1000), very high (1001–5000), and extremely high (>5000). The household spore concentration was the mean score on the scale per available room. A new variable was created by dividing this mean score into three groups: low (scoring 1), medium (1.01 to 2.00), and high (>2).

To ensure that the relation between housing conditions and ill health was not invalidated by covariation with other variables several possible confounding factors were also examined, particularly cigarette smoking in the household (no/yes), respondents' cigarette smoking (no/yes), net household income (above median (£80)/below median), overcrowding (less than/more than 1.5 people per room), employment in the household (somebody employed/nobody employed), and employment state of the respondent (employed/unemployed, no paid employment).

The respondent was asked to report on the presence of 16 specific symptoms seen in the past two weeks in any child (aged 0–15) living in the household. We devised two summary symptom scores relating to children: the unadjusted score being the total number of symptoms among all children in the household and the adjusted score being the total of symptoms divided by the number of children – that is, the mean number of symptoms per child. Another summary dependent variable for children was the mean score on health evaluation derived from the respondent's general evaluation of each child on a scale of 1 (excellent) to 5 (very poor). The respondent was also asked to report whether she had suffered from any of 17 specific symp-toms over the past fortnight. A summary symptom score was merely the sum of individual symptoms. In addition, the respondent was asked to rate her general health on the same five point scale used for children and to complete the 30 item general health questionnaire[5] (range 0–30), here used as a general indicator of psychological distress. Finally, we inquired about medical treatment for symptoms and the presence of a recurrent or longstanding illness among both respondents and children.

Univariate analyses of the relation between each independent variable and dependent variables were carried out with χ^2 tests (categorical variables) or one way analysis of variance (metric variables). Subsequently, multivariate analyses were performed to examine the association between housing conditions and ill health after controlling for possible confounding factors. When the response variable was binary/categorical we used logistic linear regression analysis;[6] for metric response variables we used analysis of covariance.[7] The extent of any dose-response relation between severity of dampness, mould growth, and air spore concentration and health was assessed by means of tau c (categorical variables) and the Pearson correlation coefficient (metric variables). Identical results were obtained with respect to metric variables transformed to base 10 logarithms. Only original values are reported below.

On the basis of previous work we expected to find a distinct effect of adverse housing conditions on respiratory and gastrointestinal symptoms in children and on emotional distress in adults. Evidence of a dose response relation was considered to be particularly relevant in assessing the likelihood of a causal impact of dampness and mould on symptomatic health.

For the purposes of this report the results from Edinburgh, Glasgow, and London have been combined. (Although the prevalence of damp and mould varied in each city, there were no pronounced differences in the association between housing conditions and symptomatic health state between cities.)

Results

Rates of response
Of 1220 households with children eligible for inclusion in the study, a health interview was secured in 891 (73.0%); 156 (12.8%) respondents refused to be interviewed, and 173 (14.2%) could not be contacted. Surveyors completed their investigations of housing conditions in 597 households, constituting 48.9% of eligible households and 67.0% of those who had the health interview. A comparison between surveyed (n=597) and non-surveyed (n=294) households showed no differences in sociodemographic characteristics, such as gender, marital state, household size (including number of children), social class, and overcrowding, or regarding disposable income, cigarette smoking, length of time at current address, presence of pets, or self-reported damp or mould. The only significant difference concerned

employment: 131 (22%) respondents in surveyed households were employed compared with 100 (34%) respondents in non-surveyed households (χ^2=12.54, df=1, p<0.001); corresponding figures for any adult in employment were 257 (43%) and 156 (53%), respectively (χ^2=7.55, df= 1, p<0.01).

All subsequent analyses were based on the 597 households, containing 1169 children, that received both a housing survey and a health interview.

Comparison of three housing conditions groups

Out of the 597 households, only 184 (30.8%) were free from damp or mould (dry). In 139 (23.3%) households surveyors found evidence of damp and in 274 (45.9%, of which all but nine were also damp) actual mould growth was visible. The three housing conditions groups (dry, only damp, mouldy) were compared for descriptive purposes on a number of background (sociodemographic and other) variables. (It was, of course, recognised that a variable could act as a confounder even if it did not differentiate significantly between groups.) Only one significant difference emerged: respondents living in dry households had been living an average of 5.9 (SD 4.9) years at the address compared with 4.8 (4.1) years among respondents in damp houses and 6.4 (5.5) years among respondents in mouldy houses (F=4.35, df=2,584, p<0.02); only the difference between damp and mouldy houses was significant (Scheffe test, p<0.05). Housing groups did not differ in number of children (mean (SD) 2.0 (1.0)), total number of household members (3.8 (1.2)), respondent's gender (559 (93.6%) women), respondent's marital state (384 (64.3%) married), net household income (293 (49.0%) under £80 per week), respondent's smoking (415, (69.5%)), any smoker in household (476 (79.7%)), respondent employed (136 (22.8%)), any household member employed (259 (43.4%)), overcrowding (109 (18.3%)), presence of pets (269 (45.1%)), tenure of last house (465 (77.9%) council dwelling), reasons for moving from last dwelling (90 (15.0%) because of dampness; 247 (41.4%) because of other problems with the house; 26 (4.3%) for health reasons), and use of Calor gas heating (81 (13.5%)). Respondents in mouldy households, however, reported more problems apart from the damp (especially noise, poor repair, and cold) than respondents in damp or dry households. (Mean (SD) problems 2.7 (1.5), 2.5 (1.6), and 2.2 (1.6), respectively; F=5.0, df=2,594, p<0.01). In particular, the prevalence of cold as a problem was reported in 222 (81%), 100 (72%), and 114 (62%) households, respectively; x^2=20.4, df=2, p<0.001).

Housing conditions and respondent's health

Table I shows the relation between prevalence of symptoms in the respondent and housing conditions. Significant differences between groups were found regarding bad nerves, aching joints, nausea and vomiting, backache, blocked nose, fainting spells, constipation, and breathlessness. The lowest proportion reporting symptoms was found in dry households; with only one exception (fainting spells) the highest proportion was found in mouldy households. Although housing conditions were unrelated to the presence of any particular symptom, there was a significant variation in the total number of symptoms and in the respondent's evaluation of her health. In particular, those living in mouldy houses scored significantly higher than those living in dry conditions (Scheffe test, p<0.05). The general health questionnaire score was not related to housing conditions (table I).

Preliminary univariate analyses had shown that only two of the possible confounding variables (respondent's economic position and cigarette smoking) were significantly associated with the presence or absence of individual symptoms. We therefore undertook a series of logistic regression analyses in which the dependent variables were the eight symptoms previously shown to be significantly associated with housing conditions. After controlling for the respondent's economic position and cigarette

Table I: Respondent's health during past two weeks by housing conditions. Figures are numbers (percentages) unless stated otherwise

Symptom	Housing conditions			Significance		
	No damp or mould (n=184)	Damp only (n=139)	Mould (n=274)	χ^2	Degrees of freedom	p value
Tiredness	76(41.3)	69(50.0)	141(51.5)	4.84	2	0.089
High blood pressure	9(4.9)	7(5.1)	22(8.0)	2.33	2	0.312
Persistent cough	30(16.3)	27(19.4)	64(23.4)	3.47	2	0.177
Bad nerves	35(19.0)	31(22.3)	80(29.2)	6.62	2	0.036
Wheezing	19(10.3)	17(12.2)	37(13.6)	1.07	2	0.587
Aching joints	28(15.2)	23(16.5)	65(23.7)	6.05	2	0.049
Skin problems	26(14.1)	23(16.5)	43(15.7)	0.39	2	0.825
Persistent headaches	49(26.6)	43(30.9)	75(27.4)	0.82	2	0.664
Nausea-vomiting	7(3.8)	9(6.5)	27(9.9)	6.17	2	0.046
Backache	41(22.3)	48(34.5)	81(29.6)	6.13	2	0.047
Blocked nose	25(13.6)	19(12.9)	58(21.2)	6.53	2	0.038
Palpitations	8(4.3)	9(6.5)	22(8.0)	2.44	2	0.295
Fainting spells	3(1.6)	12(8.6)	17(6.2)	8.37	2	0.015
Diarrhoea	5(2.7)	9(6.5)	19(6.9)	4.06	2	0.131
Constipation	11(6.0)	8(5.8)	33(12.0)	7.08	2	0.029
Breathlessness	19(10.3)	24(17.3)	51(18.6)	6.01	2	0.049
Feeling depressed	51(27.7)	47(33.8)	104(38.0)	5.15	2	0.076
Any symptom	144(78.3)	113(81.3)	217(79.2)	0.46	2	0.795
Mean (SD) No of symptoms	2.40(2.37)	3.05(3.01)	3-43(3.25)	F=6.67	2,594	0.001
Mean (SD) health evaluation score	2.41(0.93)	2.49(0.99)	2.66(0.97)	F=4.09	2,594	0.017
Mean (SD) general health questionnaire score	5.74(7.12)	6.87(7.78)	7.20(8.35)	F= 1.92	2,583	0.148

smoking these differences remained significant for all eight dependent symptom variables (problem free households always having the lowest proportion of respondents positive for symptoms).

The relation between housing conditions on the one hand and the total number of symptoms, health evaluation score, and general health questionnaire score on the other was further examined by means of analyses of covariance. After we controlled for length of time at address, other housing problems (or cold alone), respondent's economic position, respondent's cigarette smoking, and household income housing conditions remained significantly associated with the total number of symptoms (6 ranging between 0.10 and 0.14, p<0.05 to <0.005), with those living in mouldy households reporting most and those in dry households fewest symptoms. Housing conditions were not significantly associated with health evaluation score after we controlled for other possible confounding variables, and the

Table II: Respondent's health during past two weeks. Dose-response relation with damp, mould, and air spore count. Figures are tau c values (p values) unless stated otherwise

Symptom	Dampness (Max n=597)	Mould growth (Max n=589)	Air spore count (Max n=485)
Tiredness	0.09(0.028)	0.06(0.076)	−0.02(0.341)
High blood pressure	0.04(0.024)	0.04(0.027)	0.05(0.017)
Persistent cough	0.09(0.010)	0.04(0.110)	0.06(0.062)
Bad nerves	0.07(0.036)	0.09 (0.008)	0.08(0.031)
Wheezing	0.05(0.047)	0.03(0.125)	0.01(0.413)
Aching joints	0.05(0.080)	0.07(0.022)	0.06(0.083)
Skin problems	0.03(0.209)	0.00(0.474)	0.06(0.063)
Persistent headaches	0.04(0.150)	−0.02(0.279)	−0.11(0.006)
Nausea-vomiting	0.04(0.044)	0.05(0.015)	0.02(0.230)
Backache	0.04(0.167)	0.02(0.332)	0.11(0.009)
Blocked nose	0.11(0.001)	0.08(0.005)	0.00(0.451)
Palpitations	0.03(0.096)	0.03(0.051)	0.08(0.001)
Fainting spells	0.05(0.013)	0.01(0.381)	−0.01(0.289)
Diarrhoea	0.02(0.146)	0.02(0.109)	−0.01(0.413)
Constipation	0.02(0.271)	0.04(0.054)	0.01(0.414)
Breathlessness	0.09(0.003)	0.05(0.057)	0.08(0.019)
Feeling depressed	0.06(0.081)	0.08(0.026)	0.06(0.107)
Any symptom	0.02(0.319)	−0.02(0.299)	0.00(0.482)
No of symptoms	r=0. 14 (0.001)	r=0.09(0.014)	r=0.08(0.039)
Health evaluation score	r=0.07 (0.047)	r=0.10(0.008)	r=0.05(0.115)
General health questionnaire	r=0.06(0.082)	r=0.06(0.086)	r=0.01(0.414)

relation with the general health questionnaire score remained non-significant.

We examined the dose-response relation between the respondents' symptoms and increasing severity of dampness, mould growth, and air spore concentration. Table II summarises the findings of these analyses. There was a significant tendency for increasing severity of dampness to be associated with a greater prevalence of the following symptoms: tiredness, high blood pressure, persistent cough, bad nerves, wheezing, nausea and vomiting, blocked nose, fainting spells, and breathlessness. The greater the extent of mould growth the higher the proportion of respondents reporting high blood pressure, bad nerves, aching joints, nausea and vomiting, blocked nose, and feeling depressed. Finally, the concentration of the air spores was positively associated with high blood pressure, bad nerves, backache, palpitations, and breathlessness and negatively associated with persistent headaches. Overall, the total number of symptoms tended to increase with higher degrees of dampness and mould and air spore concentration, while the health evaluation score was related only to severity of dampness and mould growth. No dose-response effect on the general health questionnaire score was evident.

Respondents living in the three different housing conditions were compared regarding action taken during the past two weeks to deal with symptoms and presence of recurrent and long-standing illness. No significant differences were found.

Housing conditions and children's health

Table III shows the prevalence of symptoms among children in the household by housing conditions. Significant differences were found regarding wheezing, sore throat, persistent headache, fever and high temperature, persistent cough, and runny nose. The highest proportion reporting these symptoms was always found in mouldy households; with only one exception (sore throat) the lowest proportion with symptoms was found in the dry households. Not only was there a significant difference in the proportion with any symptom (147 (79.9%) in dry households, 119 (85.6%) in damp houses, 248 (90.5%) in mouldy houses) but the mean number of symptoms (overall and per child) also differed significantly and in the same direction. The mean child health evaluation score was not significantly different between groups (table III).

In our preliminary univariate analyses we had noted that three of the possible confounding variables (overcrowding, any cigarette smoker, nobody employed) were significantly associated with presence or absence of individual symptoms. Another set of logistic regression analyses was therefore undertaken in which the dependent variables were the six symptoms previously shown to be significantly associated with housing conditions. After controlling for these three confounding variables differences remained significant for wheezing, sore throat, persistent headache, fever and high temperature, runny nose, and for any symptom. Only the main effect of housing conditions on cough was no longer significant.

Table III: Children's health during past two weeks by housing conditions. Figures are number (percentages) unless stated otherwise

Symptom*	Housing conditions			Significance		
	No damp or mould (n=184)	Damp only (n=139)	Mould (n=274)	χ^2	Degrees of freedom	p value
Bodily aches-pains	23(12.5)	30(21.6)	43(15.7)	4.90	2	0.086
Diarrhoea	34(18.5)	30(21.6)	50(18.2)	0.73	2	0.694
Wheezing	30(16.3)	26(18.7)	74(27.0)	8.41	2	0.015
Vomiting	22(12.0)	25(18.0)	52(19.0)	4.18	2	-0.124
Sore throat	56(36.4)	34(24.5)	116(42.3)	14.99	2	<0.001
Irritability	23(12.5).	28(20.1)	56(20.4)	5.32	2	0.070
Tiredness	25(13.6)	28(20.1)	48(17.5)	2.55	2	0.279
Persistent headaches	23(12.5)	19(13.7)	58(21.2)	7.16	2	0.028
Earache	27(14.7)	15(10.8)	47(17.2)	2.95	2	0.228
Fever-high temperature	21(11.4)	25(18.0)	67(24.5)	12.30	2	0.002
Feeling depressed-unhappy	20(10.9)	25(18.0)	42(15.3)	3.45	2	0.178
Temper tantrums	37(20.1)	37(26.6)	74(27.0)	3.13	2	0.209
Bedwetting	41(22.3)	29(20.9)	64(23.4)	0.33	2	0.846
Poor appetite	31(16.8)	37(26.6)	68(24.8)	5.49	2	0.064
Persistent cough	57(31.0)	52(37.4)	117(42.7)	6.45	2	0.040
Runny nose	72(39.1)	56(40.3)	139(50.7)	7.43	2	0.024
Any symptom	147(79.9)	119(85.6)	248(90.5)	10.41	2	0.006
Mean (SD) No of symptoms	3.73(3.95)	4.39(4.63)	5.44(5.19)	F=7.56	2,594	<0.001
Mean (SD) No of symptoms per child	2.04(1.98)	2.46(2.36)	2.86(2.43)	F=7.23	2,594	<0.001
Mean (SD) health evaluation score	2.24(0.89)	2.30(0.91)	2.41(0.94)	F= 1.98	2,592	0.140

*Symptom present in any child living in household.

The relation between housing conditions on the one hand and mean number of symptoms and mean health evaluation score on the other was further examined in a series of analyses of covariance. As before, we took into account differences in the length of time at address and other housing problems (or cold alone). We also added a control for the number of children in the household and the adult's general health questionnaire score (included because although it did not differ significantly with housing conditions, it was correlated highly with both the mean number of symptoms in children (r=0.30, p<0.001) and mean child evaluation score (r=0.35, p<0.001)). Finally, we partialled out the effects of cigarette smoking in the household, unemployment, low income, and overcrowding. There was still a significant effect of housing conditions on the mean number of symptoms (6 ranging between 0.10 and 0.13, p<0.02 to <0.005). Children living in mouldy households were reported to have the highest number of symptoms and those living in dry households the fewest. Mean child evaluation score remained unrelated to housing conditions.

Table IV shows the dose-response relation between children's symptoms and increasing severity of dampness, mould growth, and air spore concentration. The more serious the dampness the greater the prevalence of bodily aches and pains, wheezing, vomiting, sore throat, irritability, tiredness, persistent headache, fever and high temperature, feeling depressed and unhappy, poor appetite, persistent cough, and runny nose. Dampness was also associated overall with the presence of any symptom. The more severe the mould growth the greater the likelihood of wheezing, sore throat, irritability, persistent headache, fever and high temperature, and runny nose. Mould growth was also associated with the presence of any symptom. The greater the air spore concentration the greater the prevalence of wheezing, irritability, and fever and high temperature.

Overall, the mean number of symptoms tended to increase with greater severity of dampness, mould growth, and air spore concentration, whereas the mean number of symptoms per child and the mean child health evaluation score were related only to greater doses of dampness and mould growth. The mean number of symptoms per child and the mean child health evaluation score were unrelated to the extent of air spore concentration.

The three groups of housing conditions were compared regarding the action taken to deal with children's symptoms during the past two weeks and presence of recurrent and longstanding illness. Children in mouldy households were more likely to have been given medicines (51.8%) than children in damp (43.2%) or problem free households (36.4%) (χ^2=10.82, df=2, p<0.005). Other differences did not reach significance.

Discussion

Before offering an account of the role of damp and mould in the aetiology of symptoms it is necessary to consider four types of bias that may invalidate the assumption of a causal link between housing conditions and ill health – namely, investigator bias, respondent bias, selection bias, and omitted variable bias.

Investigator bias may be dismissed as housing conditions and the health of household members were independently assessed by two different groups of researchers, neither of which included the principal investigators. In addition, questionnaires were coded and data prepared by workers who were not familiar with the objectives of the study.

Some previous investigations of the housing-health relation, particularly those carried out by tenants' groups, have been criticised on the grounds that people living in damp and mouldy houses will be inclined to exaggerate the

Table IV: Children's health during past two weeks. Dose-response relation with damp, mould, and air spore count. Figures are tau c values (p values) unless stated otherwise

Symptom	Dampness (Max n=597)	Mould growth (Max n=589)	Air spore count (Max n=485)
Bodily aches-pains	0.08(0.006)	−0.01(0.383)	-0.01(0.384)
Diarrhoea	0.02(0.291)	−0.01(0.386)	0.01(0.361)
Wheezing	0.10(0005)	0.09(0.005)-	0.07(0.044)
Vomiting	0.06(0.029)	0.04(0.106)	0.03(0.238)
Sore throat	0.09(0.020)	0.14(<0.001)	0.03(0.264)
Irritability	0.10(0.004)	0.06(0.040)	0.07(0.033)
Tiredness	0.06(0.043)	0.01(0.365)	0.01(0.351)
Persistent headaches	0.12(<0.001)	0.09(0.002)	0.00(0.456)
Earache	−0.01(0.349)	0.03(0.170)	−0.04(0.130)
Fever-temperature	0.12(<0.00 1)	0.10(0.002)	0.06(0.046)
Feeling depressed-unhappy	0.08(0.007)	0.02 (0.237)	−0.02(0.294)
Temper tantrums	0.04(0.159)	0.06(0.069)	0.01(0.399)
Bedwetting	0.02(0.313)	0.00(0.460)	−0.01(0.437)
Poor appetite	0.08(0.015)	0.03 (0.200)	0.02(0.336).
Persistent cough	0.11(0.006)	0.06(0.068)	0.05(0.139)
Runny nose	0.08(0.033)	0.09(0.023)	0.06(0.123)
Any symptom	0.08(0.005	0.07(0.011)	0.00(0.492)
Mean No of symptoms	r=0.17(0.001)	r=0.14(0.001)	r=0.11(0.010)
Mean No of symptoms per child	r=0.13(0.001)	r=0.12(0.002)	r=0.05(0.161)
Mean health evaluation score	r=0.08(0.025)	r=0.07(0.044)	r=0.06(0.107)

extent of their own and their children's health problems. A recent study suggested that the observed association between mould and respiratory symptoms may be accounted for by parental awareness of mould in the home.[8] Our reliance on informants' reports about the health of themselves and their children was deliberate. We were unconvinced about the reliability and appropriateness of diagnostic data derived from official records, especially those of general practitioners. We thought that it was valid to assess health state by means of self reported symptoms while at the same time recognising that the likelihood of respondent bias was thereby increased. This problem was minimised, however, by the use of inde-pendent, expert assessments of housing conditions. Although subjective (self reported) and objective (expert) evaluations of the presence of damp and mould were significantly and positively associated (k=0.26, p<0.001), there was disagreement about damp and mould state in 183 (30.7%) of the dwellings. Furthermore, respondents could not have been aware of the air spore concentration in the building. (The association between self reported damp mould and spore count, although significant, was not high: $r=0.14$, $p<0.001$.) Nevertheless, symptoms in both children and respondents were related to this measure. We also included the general health questionnaire score as a covariate when examining the effect of housing conditions among children as respondents with greater levels of psychological distress tended to report more ill health. The mean number of symptoms remained significantly higher in damp and mouldy dwellings than in dry dwellings. Thus though the overall number of symptoms may have been higher than would be obtained by an independent observer, there is no reason to believe that such a bias affected the main findings.

Another possible source of error is that of selection bias. People who already suffer from ill health may tend to live in damp or mouldy dwellings: symptoms may exist before, rather than be a consequence of, living in poor housing conditions. This could happen, for example, where the least desirable dwellings were allocated to those most in need who, by virtue of low income, social circumstances, or medical history, were more likely to report ill health. Although housing departments may not always act impartially in the selection of tenants to households, there is no evidence to suggest that they systematically allocate families in poorer health to damp and mouldy households. In this study families in damp and mouldy dwellings were not more likely to have come from previously poor con-ditions or to have moved for health reasons or to have lived a shorter period of time in the dwelling than families in dry houses. In addition, many of the children in all three housing groups were born in the household in which they were currently living. Thus selection bias is highly unlikely to account for the findings.

Omitted variable bias can arise when variables that are correlated with the major independent variable (in this case housing conditions) and have a significant (possibly causal) relation with the dependent (outcome) variable (such as symptom score) are excluded from the analysis. Whereas several factors were significantly associated. with health state, only cold was also associated with housing conditions. Cold stress may have made some contribution to the experience of symptoms: a damp house is usually a cold house. Unfortunately, we were unable to assess the temperature of dwellings. We did, however, gather information on perceived coldness of the dwelling and this variable was included in the covariance analysis.

In summary, adult respondents living in damp and mouldy dwellings were more likely to report nausea, vomiting, constipation, blocked nose, breathlessness, backache, aching joints, fainting, and bad nerves than respondents living in dry dwellings. These differences remained after controlling for the respondent's economic position and cigarette smoking. In a more extensive covariance analysis respondents living in mouldy dwellings were found to have the highest number of symptoms even after taking account of possible confounding factors such as length of time at address, other housing problems, household income, economic position, and cigarette smoking. This analysis, however, showed that the respondent's sub-jective evaluation of health and psychological distress were both unrelated to housing conditions. Increasing doses of dampness and mould were especially linked to nausea, blocked nose, breathlessness, high blood pressure, and bad nerves and to a greater number of symptoms and a poorer health evaluation score.

For children, living in damp and mouldy dwellings was associated with a greater prevalence of wheeze, sore throat, runny nose, cough, headaches, and fever compared with those living in dry dwellings. With the exception of cough these differences were unaffected by the introduction of controls for smoking in the household, employment, and overcrowding. Additional possible confounding variables were added in an analysis of covariance, which still showed a significant effect of housing conditions on the mean number of symptoms among children in the household. A dose-response relation was particularly noted with respect to wheeze, sore throat, runny nose, irritability, persistent headache, and fever and high temperature. Increasing severity of dampness and mould and any symptom, the mean number of symptoms (overall and per child), and the mean child health evaluation score were also associated.

Several studies have suggested that some varieties of fungal spores are allergenic and give rise to respiratory conditions. Burr et al identified *Penicillium notatum*, *Cladosporium herbarum*, and *Aspergillus* species in the homes of asthmatic patients and found that the moulds gave positive skin test reactions for allergy.[9] Fungal spores are also believed to affect the respiratory tract by producing tissue lesions, by forming saprophytic colonies on mucus plugs, and by causing inflammation and irritation of nasal and bronchial passages and the alveoli.[3 10 11]

An investigation by May et al found symptoms of fever, muscular pain, chest tightness, cough, and headache to be directly caused by organic toxic dust and suggested that this 'pulmonary mycotoxicosis' may represent a systemic reaction to inhaled fungal toxins.[12] Although their study was concerned with acute episodes after exposure to massive doses of organic dust, possibly similar, though less severe, symptoms occur as a chronic response to prolonged exposure to low concentrations of fungal toxins.

Analysis of the moulds collected from the dwellings in our study is still proceeding and a supplementary report on the relation of specific moulds to symptoms will be prepared. Single dwellings in the study were found to be harbouring over 15 species of mould and probably some of these would give rise to allergenic or toxic reactions, or both.

Emotional symptoms in children such as irritability and unhappiness are probably linked to physical symptoms and indicate that the mental health of children is also at risk. Some of the adults' symptoms are difficult to explain by reference to mould, though aching joints and nausea could both be reactions to fungal toxins. Reports of 'bad nerves' are not surprising where living areas are unpleasant, children are sick, and family life may be fraught. Backache and constipation are puzzling phenomena and may be indirect consequences of conditions in the home. Breathlessness and blocked nose may be more closely related to low temperature. Increased blood pressure and hypoxia have been observed as reactions to cold stress.[13]

We have attempted at all stages of this study, which is probably the largest of its kind ever undertaken, to refute the null hypothesis – namely, that there is no relation between housing conditions and health state. To that end, we adopted double-blind interviewing procedures, included a wide array of possible confounding factors, and used multivariate statistical techniques. Having eliminated (as far as possible) alternative explanations for our findings, we concluded that damp and mouldy dwellings have direct deleterious effects on the physical and psychological wellbeing of adults and children. Our confidence in this conclusion is enhanced in more positive fashion by two observations: firstly, the similarity of these findings with those reported in our earlier study,[1] especially concerning children's respiratory symptoms; and, secondly, the strong relation between increasing doses of adverse housing conditions (dampness, mould growth, and air spore concentration) and symptoms of ill health, which is unlikely to be the result of respondent bias.

A considerable body of evidence now exists that supports the contention that dampness and mould is an important public health issue, not solely for its immediate impact but also for the longterm implications. Poor housing conditions in childhood, for example, are associated with higher rates of admission to hospital and higher morbidity and mortality in adult life.[14 15] Hopefully, planners, policy makers, and medical practitioners will now plan concerted joint action to eradicate this unacceptable and needless health risk.

Medical Research Council, Unit for Epidemiological Studies in Psychiatry, Royal Edinburgh Hospital, Edinburgh EH10 5HF, Stephen D Platt, PhD, research sociologist

Research Unit in Health and Behavioural Change, University of Edinburgh, Edinburgh EH1 2QZ, Claudia J Martin, PhD, research fellow; Sonja M Hunt, PhD, senior research fellow

Division of Applied Microbiology, Department of Bioscience and Biotechnology, University of Strathclyde, Glasgow G1 1XQ, Chris W Lewis, PhD, research fellow

Correspondence to: Dr Platt

This study was supported by grants from Glasgow and Edinburgh district councils and the London Research Centre. Many associations and people have contributed to this research. In particular, we acknowledge advice and practical assistance from the Community Health Resource Unit, Glasgow; Easthall Residents' Association; Royston, Molendinar community councils, and the Technical Services Agency, Glasgow.

1 Martin CJ, Platt SD, Hunt, SM. Housing conditions and ill health. *Br Med J* 1987;**294**:1125–7.

2 Institute of Environmental Health Officers. *Mould fungal spores – their effects on health and the control, prevention and treatment of mould growth in dwellings.* London: IEHO, 1985.

3 Gravesen S. Fungi as a cause of allergic disease. *Allergy* 1979;**34**:135–54.

4 Larsen LS. A three year survey of microfungi in the air of Copenhagen 1977–1979. *Allergy* 1981; **36**:15–22.

5 Goldberg; DP. *The detection of psychiatric illness by questionnaire.* London: Oxford University Press, 1972.

6 Baker RJ, Nelder JA. *The GLIM system manual. Release 3.* Oxford: Numerical Algorithms Group, 1978.

7   SPSS. *SPSS-X user's guide.* New York: McGraw-Hill, 1983.

8   Stracham DP. Damp housing and childhood asthma: validation of reporting of symptoms. *Br Med J* 1998;**297**:1123–6.

9   Burr ML, Mullins J, Merret TG, Scott NC. Indoor moulds and asthma. *J Res Soc Health* 1988;**3**:99–101.

10   Hosen H. Moulds in allergy. *Journal of Asthma Research* 1978;**15**:151–6.

11   Maunsed K. Sensitisation risk from inhalation of fungal spores. *J Larygol Otol* 1954;**68**:765–75

12   May JJ, Stallones L, Darrow D, Print DS. Organic dust toxicity (pulmonary mycotoxicosis) associated with silo unloading. *Thorax* 1986;**41**:919–23.

13   Lloyd E. Cold stress and ischaemic heart disease. *Radical Community Medicine* 1987;**30**:9–11.

14   Folmer-Anderson T. Persistence of social and health problems in the welfare state: a Danish cohort experience from 1949 to 1979. *Soc Sci Med* 1984;**18**:555–60.

15   Britten N, Davies JMC, Colley JRT. Early respiratory experience and subsequent cough and peak expiratory flow rate in 36 year old men and women. *Br Med J* 1987;**294**:1317–20.

(Accepted 29 April 1989)

Client questionnaire

Date of statement:

Property address:

Telephone no:

Client's name and date of birth:

Partner's name and date of birth:

Children's names and dates of birth:

Names and dates of birth of other occupants, with description of relationship (eg, partner's grandfather):

Landlord's name and address:

Date tenancy commenced:

Duration of tenancy:

Names of tenants:

Type of tenancy:

Written or oral tenancy agreement:

Express terms relating to repair:

Description of the principal defects (present and past)
(repeat for each defect)

Defect:

Complaints:

Damage/discomfort caused by defect:

Date of repair:

Post repair problems:

Summary of special damages claimed:

Summary of general damages and estimate of value:

Likely cost of outstanding works:

Details of any personal injury with details of GP/hospital:

Potential claims by other occupiers:

Precedents

This appendix contains precedent documentation for a routine disrepair case in which the tenant:

1) brings an action for damages in the county court (see chapter 4);

2) complains to a magistrate under HA 1985 s606 (see chapter 7); and

3) brings proceedings under EPA s82 (see chapter 6).

It is assumed that, before launching the proceedings, the tenant's advisers have (as appropriate):

a) taken a detailed statement of facts from the client (see appendix K);

b) instructed an independent EHO/surveyor to inspect and report;

c) sought medical reports and evidence;

d) had the premises professionally photographed;

e) set the client gathering receipts etc for items of special damage; and

f) sent a 'letter before action' to the landlords.

Anna Tennant lives with her three-year-old son in a two-bedroom council flat on the fourth (top) floor of a council block. She has been the tenant for three years. Throughout the tenancy the premises have been damp. There are damp patches on the ceilings of the small bedroom and kitchen and rainwater penetration around the windows. There are numerous other defects. Her rent is £35 per week and is covered by housing benefit.

She has complained frequently to the council's estate officer, reported the defects at the neighbourhood housing office and called in the council's Environmental Health Officer. She has also seen her councillor. With only limited (and largely 'botched') repair work having been undertaken, and her son in declining health, she has turned to the Rainbow Community Law Centre. Its letter addressed to the Director of Housing has received no reply. Its letter to the Legal Department has received only an acknowledgement.

1   THE CIVIL ACTION

1A   Particulars of claim (could be adapted for use as a counterclaim)

PARTICULARS OF CLAIM

In the Anytown County Court   Case No: 99/7273

BETWEEN

ANNA TENNANT   Claimant

and

ANYTOWN DISTRICT COUNCIL   Defendant

PARTICULARS OF CLAIM

1   In or about January 1996 the Claimant was granted a secure tenancy of 17 Tower House, Moors Estate, Anytown ('the premises') by the Defendant. The premises consist of a two-bedroom flat and have at all material times been occupied by the Claimant and her son Jeremy who was born on 3 December 1995.

2   It is an express term of the tenancy that the Defendant will keep in repair the structural parts of the premises.

3   Further and in the alternative, it is an implied term of the said tenancy that the Defendant will keep in repair the structure and exterior of the dwelling and keep in repair and proper working order the installations therein for the supply of water, gas and electricity and for sanitation, space heating and heating water.

4   Yet further and in the alternative, it is an express term of the tenancy that the Defendant will keep in repair the common parts of the building containing the premises.

5   Yet further and in the further alternative, it is an implied term of the said tenancy that the Defendant shall not derogate from its grant and more particularly that it shall ensure that the parts retained in its possession and control remain reasonably safe and do not cause damage to the Claimant or the premises.

6   The Defendant has throughout the period of the tenancy been in breach of the terms duties and obligations aforementioned.

Particulars

i)   Some two months after the commencement of the tenancy a damp patch (approximately 2 feet in diameter) formed on the ceiling in the small bedroom. It is intermittently wet and dry and has discoloured the ceiling paper. Plaster in the area is cracked and since December 1997 rainwater has dripped from the cracks in periods of heavy rain.

ii) In March 1998 a patch similar to that described above developed on the kitchen ceiling. The area is covered during winter months with black mould which the Claimant is forced to clear regularly with a disinfectant wipe.

iii) From the outset of the tenancy there has been a half-inch gap above the window frame of the main window in the living room.

iv) In or about April 1997 a crack developed around the window frame of the window in the main bedroom. The plaster around the said window is loose and crumbling.

v) The inner sills to both the aforementioned windows are rotted by reason of the accumulation of water upon them.

vi) From the outset of the tenancy the sole gas fire provided in the living room at the premises has operated only to approximately two-thirds capacity even when switched full on.

vii) The wallplaster to the external kitchen wall immediately below the window is cracked and since in or about November 1997 has crumbled and flaked upon contact.

viii) The parapet wall to the walkway balcony immediately opposite the front door of the premises has throughout the tenancy had three of its upper row of bricks missing.

ix) The window glazing to the common stairwell providing access to the premises has been broken on two occasions. In 1997 the Defendant replaced the same after a delay of eight months. In 1998, after the glass was again broken, the Defendant replaced the same after six months.

x) In or about September 1998 a patch of damp began to develop on the wall of the premises immediately above the front door as a result of overflows from the roof guttering above.

xi) From the outset of the tenancy, the pull-cord switch to the bathroom ceiling light has operated intermittently and the electrical socket provided in the hallway of the premises emits a spark when used.

7 The matters complained of in paragraph 6 above are known to the Defendant.

Particulars

i) On occasions too numerous to particularise (but no less frequently than six times each year throughout the tenancy) the Claimant has reported the defects by telephone and in person to the Defendant at its Neighbourhood Housing Office.

ii) On occasions too numerous to particularise Estate Officers, workmen and other persons employed by the Defendant have visited the premises for the purpose of inspection.

iii) Without prejudice to the generality of the foregoing the Claimant has been visited at the premises by two successive Estate Officers (Ms Jenkinson and Mr Peters) in or about April 1996 and June 1997 respectively and both were shown the defects in the premises at the dates of their visits.

iv) In or about July 1998 an Environmental Health Officer in the employ of the Defendant visited the premises and inspected the state thereof.

v) In or about September 1998 the Claimant reported the aforementioned defects to one Desmond Haines who is a councillor of the Defendant authority.

8   By reason of the aforementioned breaches of terms, obligations and duties the Claimant has suffered loss, damage, injury, distress and inconvenience.

Particulars

i) For the duration of the tenancy the premises have been damp and unsightly and each winter have carried a pervading smell of dampness.

ii) Decorations, carpets and soft furnishings provided at the premises by the Claimant have been ruined by dampness and/or mould growth.

iii) The Claimant has expended additional monies on heating the premises as a result of the dampness of the premises.

iv) Clothing kept in the premises by the Claimant and her son has to be repeatedly washed and/or replaced as a result of permeation by damp odour and the effect of mould.

v) For the duration of the tenancy, the Claimant has suffered from repeated colds and influenza.

vi) For six weeks in the winter of 1997/98 the Claimant was forced by conditions in the premises to leave and stay with her own mother. She paid her mother £20 weekly for expenses during that stay.

vii) For the duration of the tenancy the Claimant has suffered stress as a result both of the defects particularised above and the dangerous state of the premises. Further stress has resulted from the failure of remedial work carried out by the Defendant in or about May 1997 and the failure of the Defendant to respond to complaints thereafter.

viii) From the winter of 1996/97 and during each successive winter the premises have been infested with insects most particularly in the kitchen area which has caused additional stress and inconvenience to the Claimant and caused her to incur additional expenditure through the cost of eating out.

9   The Claimant claims interest pursuant to the provisions of section 69 of the County Courts Act 1984 at the rate of 15% or such other rate as the court may think fit.

AND THE CLAIMANT CLAIMS

1   An order for specific performance to remedy the defects set out at paragraph 6 above.

2   Damages exceeding £5,000 but not exceeding £15,000.

3   Interest at the rate of 15%.

    Costs.

Dated this 26th day of April 1999

I believe that the facts stated in these Particulars of Claim are true.

Anna Tennant

> *Rainbow Community Law Centre*
> *Rainbow High Street*
> *Anytown*
> *Solicitors for the Claimant*

To: The District Judge and the Defendant

1B   **Application for an interim injunction**

In the Anytown County Court   Case No: 99/7273

BETWEEN

ANNA TENNANT   Claimant

and

ANYTOWN DISTRICT COUNCIL   Defendant

APPLICATION NOTICE

TAKE NOTICE that the Claimant intends to apply to a Judge of the Court sitting at the Court Offices, Court Street, Anytown on the 12th day of April 1999 at 10.30 o'clock in the forenoon for an order by way of interlocutory injunction in the following terms:

1   That on or before Monday 10th May 1999 the Defendant does:

   a) repair the roof immediately above the premises let to the Claimant to prevent the ingress of rainwater

   b) seal the gaps and cracks around the windows to the main bedroom and main living room of the premises

   c) overhaul and repair or replace the fixed gas fire in the main living room of the premises

   d) clear, clean and repair the roof guttering immediately above the front door of the premises.

2   That the Defendant does pay the costs of and incidental to this application in any event.

AND TAKE NOTICE that the grounds of the Claimant's application are set out in her evidence served herewith.

Dated this 8th day of April 1999

Rainbow Community Law Centre
Rainbow High Street
Anytown
Solicitors for the Claimant

To: The District Judge and the Defendant

1C   **Draft order**

In the Anytown County Court   Case No: 99/7273

BETWEEN

ANNA TENNANT   Claimant

and

ANYTOWN DISTRICT COUNCIL   Defendant

ORDER

Before His Honour Judge Right sitting at Anytown on Monday the 12th day of April 1999

UPON HEARING the solicitor for the Claimant and the Defendant and

UPON READING the Claimant's evidence dated the 8th day of April 1999

AND UPON the Claimant undertaking by her solicitor to abide by any order that this Court may make for the payment of damages in case this Court shall hereafter find that the Defendant has sustained any loss or damage by reason of this Order

IT IS ORDERED THAT on or before Monday 10th May 1999 the Defendant does:

a) repair the roof immediately above the premises let to the Claimant to prevent the ingress of rainwater

b) seal the gaps and cracks around the windows to the main bedroom and main living room of the premises

c) overhaul and repair or replace the fixed gas fire in the main living room of the premises

d) clear, clean and repair the guttering to the roof of the premises immediately above the front door.

IT IS FURTHER ORDERED that the Defendant should pay the costs of and incidental to this hearing in any event.

DATED this 12th day of April 1999

To the Mayor and Burgesses of the Anytown District Council, Council Offices, Anytown.

TAKE NOTICE that unless you obey the directions contained in this order you will be guilty of contempt of court and will be liable to be committed to prison.

Judge Right

2   COMPLAINT UNDER HA 1985 s606

2A   Complaint to the magistrate

IN THE ANYTOWN MAGISTRATES' COURT

To: Thomas Hardy being a Justice of the Peace for the Anytownshire County area.

The complainant one Anna Tennant complains that the property occupied by her at 17 Tower House, Moors Estate, Anytown being a dwelling-house within the area of the Anytown District Council is unfit for human habitation having regard to the matters set out in Housing Act 1985 section 604 as amended.

The complainant applies to you as Justice of the Peace for the area that you do cause complaint to be made to the said District Council in writing as provided by Housing Act 1985 section 606(2) requiring them to carry out an inspection of the said premises and to make a report stating the facts of the case and to make a finding as to whether, in the opinion of that council, the dwelling is unfit for human habitation.

Dated this 13th day of April 1999

Rainbow Community Law Centre
Rainbow High Street
Anytown
Solicitors for the Claimant

2B   Draft complaint by magistrate

IN THE ANYTOWN MAGISTRATES' COURT

To: The Proper Officer of the Anytown District Council
Council Offices
Anytown

I, Thomas Hardy being an appointed JUSTICE OF THE PEACE for the area of Anytownshire County, do hereby make complaint to you in the terms of section 606(2) Housing Act 1985 that the premises at 17 Tower House, Moors Estate, within the area of your Council are unfit for human habitation and that I call for an inspection and report to be made in the terms of that provision.

Dated this 14th day of April 1999

Signed
Thomas Hardy JP

---

3   EPA PROCEEDINGS

3A   Initial information

IN THE ANYTOWN MAGISTRATES' COURT

Dated this 14th day of February 1999

Defendant: The Anytown District Council

Address: Council Offices, Anytown

Alleged offence: That on this 14th day of February 1999 a statutory nuisance as defined by section 79(1)(a) Environmental Protection Act 1990 exists at 17 Tower House, Moors Estate, Anytown and continues to exist and that the nuisance (particulars of which are given in the attached statement) is the responsibility of the Anytown District Council and in so far as it results from structural defects is its responsibility as owner.

The Information of: Anna Tennant who being a person aggrieved for the purposes of section 82 of the said Act complains that the defendant is responsible for the said nuisance, has given the required notice to bring these proceedings and asks that the accused be summoned to answer this information.

Address: Solicitor
Rainbow Community Law Centre
Rainbow High Street
Anytown

Taken before me this 14th day of February 1999

Justice of the Peace/Clerk to the Justices

3B   Further information laid in magistrates' court

IN THE ANYTOWN MAGISTRATES' COURT

Dated this 14th day of April 1999

Accused: The Anytown District Council

Address: Council Offices, Anytown

Alleged Offence: That contrary to section 82(8) of the Environmental Protection Act 1990 you have without reasonable excuse failed to comply with an order made by this court on 10th March 1999 requiring you to abate a statutory nuisance at 17 Tower House, Moors Estate, Anytown.

The Information of: Anna Tennant who being a person aggrieved for the purposes of section 82(1) of the said Act alleges that the accused committed the alleged offence and applies that the accused by summons do answer this information.

Address: Solicitor
Rainbow Community Law Centre
Rainbow High Street
Anytown

Taken before me this 14th day of April 1999

Justice of the Peace/Clerk to the Justices

3C   Draft summons

IN THE ANYTOWN MAGISTRATES' COURT

To the accused: The Mayor and Burgesses of the Anytown District Council

Of: Council Offices, Anytown

You are hereby summoned to appear on 8th May 1999 at 10.00 am before the Magistrates' Court at Court House, Rainbow Street, Anytown to answer the information (of which particulars are given in the attached schedule).

Alleged Offence: that you have without reasonable excuse failed to comply with an order made under s82(2) Environmental Protection Act 1990 by this court on 10th March 1999 requiring you to abate a statutory nuisance at 17 Tower House, Moors Estate, Anytown as defined by section 79(1)(a) of the said Act.

The Prosecutor is: Solicitor, Rainbow Community Law Centre, Rainbow High Street, Anytown.

Dated this 14th day of April 1999

Justice of the Peace/Clerk to the Justices

Index

LAG Legal Action Group

Supporting the work of housing law professionals working in the legal aid and advice sectors

Legal Action magazine

The only monthly magazine published specifically for legal aid practitioners and the advice sector. Every issue features 'Recent developments in housing law' by acknowledged experts Jan Luba and Nic Madge – keeping you right up to date with law and practice in this area.

1998/99 annual subscription: £73
Concessionary rates available for students and trainees – call the LAG office for details

Books

LAG's catalogue includes a range of housing titles:

Homelessness and Allocations (5th edition)
Andrew Arden QC and Caroline Hunter
1997   0 905099 60 5   £32

Defending Possession Proceedings (4th edition)
Jan Luba, Nic Madge and Derek McConnell
1997   0 905099 79 6   £37

Quiet Enjoyment (5th edition)
David Carter and Andrew Dymond
June 1998   0 905099 85 0   £20

Housing Law Casebook (2nd edition)
Nic Madge
October 1998   0 905099 86 9   £35

Housing Law Statutes
David Dixon (editor)
Autumn 1999   0 905099 87 7   £35

Community Care Law Reports

The only law reports devoted entirely to community care issues. Compiled by an expert team and published quarterly, each issue contains:

- editorial review
- community care law update
- law reports
- cumulative index
- full tables

Training

LAG's training programme includes courses for housing practitioners and advisers.

Conferences

LAG runs major conferences to examine issues at the cutting-edge of legal services policy and to inform practitioners of their implications.

Membership

LAG campaigns for equal access to justice through improvements in the law and the administration of justice. If you support our aims, join us!

For further information about any of Legal Action Group's activities please contact:

**Legal Action Group
242 Pentonville Road
London
N1 9UN
DX 130400 London (Pentonville Road)
Telephone: 0171 833 2931
Fax: 0171 837 6094
e-mail: lag@lag.org.uk**